A HISTORY OF
German Literature

A
History
of
German
Literature

By ERNST ROSE

NEW YORK UNIVERSITY PRESS

1960

THE TEXT of this history of German literature is partly based on the author's earlier work *Geschichte der deutschen Literatur auf kulturgeschichtlicher Grundlage* (New York: Prentice-Hall, Inc., 1936). The publisher's generous permission to use this earlier work in many details is gratefully acknowledged.

Preface

THIS BOOK *has been planned as a readable history of German literature for students of European culture and educated Americans in general. Specialists are able to use the many excellent handbooks and detailed surveys in German. If one tried to find names, dates, and titles with the help of this book, one would probably be disappointed, for it is not meant as a substitute for a dictionary. I have consistently omitted facts which would only be a burden to the general reader and would mar the presentation of the essentials. What these essentials are is often debatable. In the last chapters I have therefore tended to be more lenient in my exclusions.*

In part the present survey has been based upon my previous German survey, Geschichte der deutschen Literatur auf kulturgeschichtlicher Grundlage (New York: Prentice-Hall, Inc., 1936), which was conceived as a college textbook. In the twenty-four years that have passed between the writing of the two surveys, the author has learned a great deal and has corrected some of his basic assumptions. Many chapters have been completely rewritten—for example, those on Goethe, on Hölderlin, on Heine; other chapters contain entirely new passages, such as those dealing with Rilke or Thomas Mann or Kafka. Even chapters that have remained comparatively intact have been rephrased for the general

Preface

reader. Numerous revisions in detail are to be taken for granted. And finally the general emphasis of the story has changed. The original German version aimed at being something like a cultural survey seen through the medium of literature. The new English version has attempted to develop the story of German literature as a theme in itself through the consistent employment of aesthetic criteria. General cultural history has been used as a background rather than a basis. A comparison of the chapter headings of the two versions will make the shift in emphasis quite apparent.

In the preparation of this new survey the author has made judicious use of the work produced by many distinguished predecessors and colleagues. Even to barely mention them all would require an extensive bibliography. The specialist will know, in any case, what I have learned from Böckmann, from Lange, from Schwietering, etc. I freely acknowledge that not all the thoughts contained in this book are my own. And I also freely acknowledge the many helpful hints and corrections I have received from readings and discussions of my manuscript by critical friends and colleagues: the late Dr. Erich Berger of Queens College; Dr. Dorothea Berger, Dr. Edgar Lohner, Dr. Charlotte Pekary, and Mrs. Pauline Roth of New York University; Mrs. Marjorie Wilde, a graduate of Dalhousie University. I am also indebted to Mr. Guenther Gerlitzki of New York University for valuable help in reading page proof and making the index. If the final version of the text has become more concise and lucid, I owe it to these devoted friends, and I assure every one of them of my heartfelt gratitude. Those errors in fact and slips in style that may have remained the author himself has to answer for, and the plan and execution of the whole has, of course, been his own undivided responsibility. It has been a pleasant task, and he hopes to have succeeded at least in part. His final thanks go to his wife who for many years has put up with good grace with a rather preoccupied and sometimes uncommunicative husband.

E. R.

Contents

[xi

Contents

Contents

Introduction

ERMAN literature is the linguistic and written expression of German culture. It is written mostly, though not exclusively, in the German language, either in standard German or in one of the historical and regional German dialects.

The people of German culture have not always been people of German nationality. During most periods of German history, the boundaries of the German nation have been ill-defined and its coherence has been weak. It has often expressed itself in a multiplicity of political organizations. Until about 1250, Belgium and the Netherlands still moved within the orbit of German culture; since then they have developed independently. In the centuries from the end of the Middle Ages to the end of the Second World War, a rich German literature flourished in Prussia and the Baltic countries, in Pomerania and Silesia, as well as the northern and northwestern parts of Czechoslovakia; now the German inhabitants of these regions have been expelled and their homesteads have been claimed by Russia, Poland, and Czechoslovakia. At the present time, people of German culture live in at least six states: the German Federal Republic, the German Democratic Republic (a Russian satellite state), Austria, northeastern Switzerland, Luxemburg, and northeastern France (i.e., Alsace-Lorraine).

Biologically speaking the people of German culture are a largely homogeneous group, although one might point to minor physiognomic differences between North Germans and South Germans, and also be-

Introduction

tween East Germans and West Germans. But the German group as a whole does not represent a distinct race, nor is it essentially different from the French and British groups to the west, the Scandinavian groups to the north, and the Slavic groups to the east. Most of the existing differences call for a linguistic or historical rather than a racial explanation. In fact, any exclusively racial interpretation of human culture isolates man from his environment and thereby speaks of man as an abstraction; concrete man can only be understood together with his environment.

In German culture, too, environmental factors have played a decisive role. Geographically, Germany is a region without strong or clearly defined boundaries. Its boundaries have shifted more than once, and have always invited other European influences. This fact accounts for the rich affinity between German literature and the other literatures of the continent. But it also explains why the assertion of specifically German attitudes has so often been necessary and has so often been made with painful aggressiveness and bureaucratic pedantry.

Climatically, Germany—and especially its northern part—is less sunny than Italy and France; heavy rains, and, in winter, snow and ice are common occurrences. The Germans have therefore developed into a sheltered nation, with the concomitant accents on home life and on family life, on homely virtues and on individuality, personal religion and inwardness. But the withdrawal from inhospitable nature has also led to a withdrawal from the market place, to a lack of civic-mindedness, and to a disposition to accept governmental changes and decisions as just another unexplainable elemental force. The great diversity of German culture, the frequency of subjective and peculiar philosophies, the slowness of the German reaction to general and international trends all in part yield to a climatic explanation.

Together with geography and climate one must also consider the third environmental factor, the factor of history. Man not only lives in a certain landscape under certain weather conditions, but he also lives in a certain time, and only by adding the historical dimension to the spatial can we understand man's life in its fullness. Our present treatment of German literature aims at interpreting German culture through its direct literary expression, as it has developed and changed in time.

Literature can give expression to a common culture only when that culture exists and after it has been formed. Without a common culture there is no common public, and without a common public any literary

Introduction

work must remain a merely personal or local expression. But even where a common culture exists, not every one of its literary expressions can have equal artistic value. Literature in the sense of belles lettres presupposes that its authors possess a certain originality and that their work reflects the spirit of the time truly and impressively, not by an appeal to our logical and reasoning powers but to our imagination. Products of undoubted originality and creative imagination therefore deserve the first place in a history of poetic literature, and only they will be found to be really representative.

Such representative literature for the first time occurs in Germany in the twelfth century. There were, to be sure, interesting personalities and works of local importance on the German scene even before that time. But German culture had not yet formed, and we can therefore treat these works only as historical documents, as early and partial expressions of a culture that was still in the making.

CHAPTER ONE

The Threefold Origin
of German Culture

The Germanic Inheritance

GERMAN literature grew up as a part of the literature of the late Roman Empire, and subsequently formed a part of the European literature developing from it. It has tried to be independent only in the last two centuries, like other national literatures in the Western orbit.

Before the contact with the late Roman Empire the Germans were just as illiterate as the other Germanic tribes. All Germanic peoples originally lived in northern Europe. Several centuries before the Christian era they had abandoned the nomadic way of life and had settled on small farms, sometimes cleared from the forest. They had learned to build houses of mud reinforced by wickerwork, and had taken to weaving, pottery making, and bronze foundry. They baked bread and drank mead. They kept draft animals and augmented their agrarian diet with dairy products. For the procurement of raw materials such as metals, and the acquisition of luxury items, some trade had sprung up; indeed, the first information we possess about the old Teutons was jotted down by Roman and Greek traders. Practical agricultural and defensive needs had also led to the rudiments of village and tribal organization. The implements of war on land and sea were considerably developed; but the Germanic warriors preferred to fight singly or in small parties, and the discipline of larger armies was little known. Beyond the tribal stage the Germanic people were only loosely connected.

The Teutonic religion also was no longer primitive by the time its believers entered history. Originally the Germanic tribes had believed in all sorts of ghosts and demons. At the time of the migrations the Germanic tribal gods had largely become superhuman personifications of powerful forces of nature; they were actually less concrete than they may appear in modern popularizations. The important ideas expressed by the often-realistic images and myths were basic interpretations of the beginning and meaning of life, about death and the end of the world.

As to poetry, there existed some incantations and short mythological stanzas, and some poetic proverbs and facts or rules rhythmically arranged for memorization. There were harvest songs and spring songs, recited by the village community. But this poetry did not belong to the realm of conscious artistic creation and was not written down. In fact, an alphabet was totally lacking, and when finally some Germanic letters were devised and put into the form of the so-called Runic alphabet, it presented the first instance of Italian influence on the tribes of the north.

About two centuries before the dawn of the Christian era the Germanic tribes began to grow restless. Climatic changes and poor harvests put arable land at a premium, and more and more Germanic tribes began to send out their best warriors on forays for food or on campaigns of conquest. Roman policy succeeded for some time in damming up or deflecting the rising tide. In fact, the German territory south of the Danube and west of the Rhine was under Roman rule for three to four centuries, and was joined together by a strong Roman line of fortifications called *limes*. But in the end even the firmest boundary walls were broken, and the Germanic flood engulfed the very heart of the Empire. The Romans of the imperial era had been bled white by continuous wars of conquest and defense, and their homogeneity had been diluted by new citizens of differing customs from all the Roman provinces. So the Germanic warriors appeared more vigorous and were able to defeat the Romans, especially after they had adopted their military techniques. Germanic warriors then founded new states on formerly Roman territory, and some of these states continued to preserve their character until the eighth century A.D.

Then the crest of the tide passed, and from the ruins of many of the new Germanic states slowly rose the Romance national states of western and southern Europe; the Anglo-Saxons gradually became English; the tribes that had remained behind in central Europe developed into Germans. Even these German tribes had often changed their locations. Slavic tribes had advanced to the Elbe and Saale rivers, and it took the colonizing energies of the whole Middle Ages to return great chunks of formerly Germanic territory to the Germans.

When the last wave of migrations passed by, and the sea-roving Vikings founded new states of conquest in northern France, in England, and in southern Italy, Germany was already consolidating its national realm between the Meuse and the Elbe.

The Germanic migrations represented one of the most energetic upsurgings in history, and led to a surprising advance of civilization. But it was Roman civilization that advanced into the north, and the military conquerors became the culturally defeated. It is hardly justifiable to describe the conquerors of the Roman Empire as hordes of northern barbarians. The Roman Tacitus in his *Germania* of about A.D. 98 has given us a far different impression which on the whole has been confirmed by modern scholarship. It is surprising how little of unquestionably pagan character has come down to us from Germanic times, and how difficult it is to single out clearly Germanic features in the German cultural heritage up to the end of the Middle Ages. Until about 1000 or 1100, it is best to describe German culture as a variation of late Roman culture, and German literature as a variation of late Roman literature.

This is also partly true for most examples that have come down to us of old Germanic poetry. Genuine artistic forms transcending the primitive phase of poetry came into being only through contact with the Romans, and were created at the courts of the Gothic kings around A.D. 500. From there they spread, together with their Gothic elements, through the rest of the Germanic territory. The songs of the migration period percolated even to the north. The songs of the *Edda* may provide the most adequate general idea of the old Germanic poetry, although these songs were only written down in the thirteenth century. The forms of the Old High German *Hildebrandslied*, and especially of the Anglo-Saxon epic *Beowulf* already represent higher developments that are no longer characteristic of all Germanic tribes.

The care of tradition and development of finer forms were left to gifted individuals. All Germanic tribes in the migration period respected the institution of the scop, the warrior of noble birth who at festival gatherings recited short hymns in praise of the gods and heroes. His audience was composed of the richest and ablest leaders and kings forming the Germanic courts. Naturally, the scops were also popular with the rank and file of the people. But the scops did not adopt the new art of writing, and left the transcription of documents and of literature to Roman scribes and to the priests; artistic literature in these early times rarely became written literature.

The oldest remnants of specifically German poetry have been preserved and discovered by accident. Other and perhaps more valuable poems may have been lost, and what has come down to us can only serve as an illustration. The earliest extant documents of German poetry are the so-called *Merseburg Incantations* of the sixth century which were written down much later. One of the incantations was used to free prisoners of war who had fallen into the hands of the enemy. The other incantation was used in bonesetting. The names of the gods mentioned in the incantations are one of the few details we know of truly German mythology. For the rich sources of Scandinavian mythology throw only an oblique light on old German religion. In fact, its almost complete obliteration is convincing proof of the overwhelming impact of Christianity on the German tribes coming into contact with it.

The most important of the known documents is the *Hildebrandslied* ("The Lay of Hildebrand"). It was written down between 810 and 820 by monks who seem to have superimposed their own latter-day image of God when they copied the poem; their text contains no clear trace of the old pagan religion.

The poem takes us back some centuries into the time of the Germanic migrations when the Ostrogoths had to yield before the Asiatic Huns, and later conquered Italy under their king Theodoric. We hear that Hiltibrant followed his lord Theodoric, leaving behind his wife and son. Riding home to his family years later, he is met by a young warrior of whom he asks his name. The warrior happens to be Hiltibrant's son Hadubrant who has himself meanwhile become a full-grown fighter. Hiltibrant joyfully offers Hadubrant a gift. But Hadubrant doubts his father's identity. He takes him for an old Hun who wants to deceive him by friendliness; Hiltibrant must be dead long since.

Hadubrant's old father is heartbroken:

> "*welaga nû, waltant got,   wêwurt skihit.*
> *ih wallôta sumaro enti wintro   sehstic ur lante,*
> *dâr man mih eo scerita   in sceotantero folc:*

The Threefold Origin of German Culture

sô man mir at burc ênîgeru   banun ni gifasta,
nû scal mih suâsat chind   suertu hauwan
bretôn mit sînu billiu,   eddo ih imo ti banin werdan."

*

"Woe now, mighty God, misfortune strikes anew.
Sixty summers and winters I wandered in strange lands
Where I always ranked in the spear-shooters' troop.
Yet by the walls of no fortress did anyone fell me.
Now my own son's sword is set to slay me,
His blade will kill me, or I will murder him."

Yet Hiltibrant complains only for a moment. Then he grimly accepts the unavoidable challenge. And the battle begins. . . .

The Old German manuscript is a fragment, and thus we do not hear the result of the fight. From an Old Norse source we may surmise that the lay ended with Hadubrant's death. For Hiltibrant was the more experienced fighter, and any other end would have contradicted the personal experience of the warriors of the migrations.

The *Hildebrandslied* is not devoid of realism. Yet one must admire the stubborn fight of its characters for their ideals. Hiltibrant must keep his honor unstained. When his offer of hospitality is rejected, he can only retaliate with the sword. He is obliged to defend the honor of his arms, and thus he experiences the deepest sorrow: his tragic fate is to slay his own son.

When a scop recited the *Hildebrandslied* to his fellow warriors, he described the actual world in which they lived. For oral recitation the lay had to be short. Only the essential parts of the action could be given. Long-winded explanations had to be avoided. All these demands are satisfied by the style of the lay. It is also well adapted for memorization by its metrical form, the long line with its four accents, strengthened and embellished by partial alliteration. The outer form of the *Hildebrandslied* is as little arbitrary as its treatment of the narrated events; it is a unified work of art which can give one a good idea of the Old Germanic heroic poems. But no other example has come down to us.

The language of the *Hildebrandslied* and of the *Merseburg Incantations* is Old High German. By this term we do not mean a unified German speech, for this did not exist in any form in the period before 1100. Old High German is rather the common term for a number of dialects which show pronounced differences. They still have full vowels even in unaccentuated syllables, and a rich and diversified inflection, both factors characteristic of languages little developed. The original dialect of the *Hildebrandslied* was Bavarian.

The Coming of Christianity

THE Germanic tribes took over from the Romans many implements of material civilization. They learned from the older culture how to build with stones, they became acquainted with Roman weapons and tools, they took over horticulture and viniculture, fine cooking and the raising of fishes in ponds. The Romans also taught the Teutons their calendar and their script, the organization of their army, and their system of taxation. All these details are still evident to us in the many Latin loan words in the German vocabulary, which would be very poor indeed if it were restricted to words of purely Germanic origin. Such common German words as *Mauer* (wall), *Ziegel* (tile), *Mantel* (coat), *Münze* (coin), *Zwiebel* (onion), *Keller* (cellar), *Wein* (wine), *Koch* (cook), *Butter* (butter), *Weiher* (fishpond), *Kalender* (calendar), *Tinte* (ink), *Schule* (school) have come down from the Latin.

But not only techniques and tools were borrowed. There was also the field of ideas. Roman culture was a universal culture, and in principle claimed to have subjected the whole of mankind. Society was organized within the Roman Empire, and the emperor was the ruler of the world. When Roman rule was overthrown, the most powerful of all the Germanic states succeeded the Empire, and its king put himself in the place of the old Roman emperor. This king was Charlemagne, the ruler of the Franks, who in 800 was crowned emperor. Thus the medieval Holy Roman Empire was born, which became a definite reality only under the dynasty succeeding the Carolingians, and which then played such an important part in German history. Its ruler was called *Kaiser*, a German spelling of the Latin word *Caesar*.

The new Empire being termed "Holy" points to another significant idea that the Germanic tribes took over from the Romans. When they overran the old Roman Empire, they became acquainted with Chris-

[9

tianity which in 323 had been declared its official religion. The invaders adopted it quite easily and without major struggles. Their own pagan mythology had already become somewhat obfuscated, and in foreswearing their gods the pupils of the Christian missionaries did not feel that they gave up anything essential. The old myths only lingered on in fairy tales and provincial customs which often merged with the much older primitive demonism. Outcroppings of that demonism occurred from time to time in the witch hunts of the sixteenth and seventeenth centuries, in the religious fanaticism of the Reformation period, in the atrocious anti-Semitism of the Nazis. But the mainstream of German culture moved free from it.

The elements in Christianity that attracted the Teutonic leaders were its high ethical ideals and the deep symbolism of its customs. Even before the coming of Christianity, life for the Old Teutons had begun to assume a transcendental meaning. To be sure, the warrior's life after death was pictured as a simple continuation of life on this earth. But according to the Teutonic myths about the end of the world, even that life would not last forever. And although the Germanic rites appealed outwardly to eye and ear, their symbolism was anything but simple and direct. If it had been otherwise, the Germanic tribes would have been more hesitant to accept Christianity.

Of course, Christianity is not synonymous with asceticism or complete rejection of the world, and the Teuton warriors did not become oriental hermits. They did not understand each facet of Christianity equally well. No Teuton shared the cultural pessimism of late antiquity which to a large degree had contributed to the spread of Christianity. It was also hard for them to get accustomed to the idea of a transcendental world actually better and more perfect than this world. Externally the Teutons became converted to Christianity rather quickly, but a complete fusion of the Teutonic and Christian spirit was another matter, and it took centuries even to approach it.

Those Teutonic tribes which accepted Christianity first got acquainted with its older, Arian form. The bishop Arius had rejected the dogma of the Holy Trinity, which his opponent, the bishop Athanasius, had upheld. The oldest Germanic archbishop, the Visigoth Ulfilas, was an Arian Christian; he was consecrated as a missionary bishop in 341. He translated the Bible into Visigothic language, and his translation is one of the oldest Teutonic manuscripts still extant. It also assumed importance for other Teutonic tribes, and the Visigothic language for a while served as a common language of worship. The

Visigothic Bible is therefore the most important document of Teutonic Christianity.

In 496, almost one and a half centuries later, Clovis, the king of the Franks, was baptized in the Athanasian creed. His conversion started a new chapter of Christian missions. But one must not assume that all his subjects at once became Christians. The Franks on the right shore of the Rhine remained heathens up to 750. Germany proper became the object of individual Irish and Scottish missions in the sixth and seventh centuries. Columbanus and Gallus were the most important of these missionaries. Finally the Anglo-Saxon Bonifatius (d. 754) founded a national German Church. The last of the German tribes to become converted were the Saxons at the Lower Elbe river. They offered active resistance to the new creed, and Emperor Charlemagne (768–814) had to fight them for thirty years before they were ready to be converted.

The language of the Christian Church was the Latin of late antiquity, and its theological literature was as yet untranslated. Instructing the Germans in Christianity therefore involved two approaches: to instruct them in Latin, and to present them with translations which they could appreciate. Both tasks were soon taken up by the Christian monks and missionaries. Benedictine monasteries such as those of Fulda, Reichenau, Corvey, and St. Gallen (founded in 720) became centers of the new studies. Here Latin glossaries with Old High German translations were assembled; interlinear translations and students' summaries of apologetic writings were worked out; and young Germans were instructed in the Church language. In this way many new words and ideas found their way into German culture, and the syntax and style of the Church authors became a model for imitation. The new Christian literature could not take over many of the old heathen traditions and on the whole had to lean on the Latin predecessors. The learned cleric therefore took over the role of the old scop who no longer enjoyed any standing. Emperor Charlemagne and his successors had no choice but to foster classical learning if they wanted to foster Christianity. In part they naturally also fostered writings in German.

The German works written in the monasteries often were mere translations from the Latin, and even where they were original they by no means constituted a national literature. What has come down to us are individual documents which can only be understood in connection with the general endeavor to Christianize the Germans.

It appears probable that Ludwig the Pious, the successor of Charlemagne, gave the original impetus to Bible poetry in the Old Saxon language. Old Saxon was a Low German dialect and was spoken by the same Saxons whom Charlemagne had converted by the use of force. They must soon have grown into the new creed, for about 830 an Old Saxon poet wrote a forceful version of the New Testament which has come down to us by the name of *Heliand*, i.e., *Heiland* ("Savior").

The Savior is indeed the center of the Old Saxon epic which presents an independent Germanic conception of the old oriental tradition. The Jewish itinerant teacher has become a Germanic prince or duke of the migration period. The disciples of Christ are pictured as retainers, following their prince from castle to castle; the Old Saxon poet does not yet know real towns. He has also made other changes in conformity with the experience of his readers. After his temptation Jesus does not go into the wilderness or desert, but into the forest.

Still, the poet of the *Heliand* could not and did not want to transform the essential parts of the Gospel. He gives a prominent place to the Sermon on the Mount. He treats it as an unexplainable mystery that the great Prince of Peace knowingly allows Judas to betray Him. And he does not understand why Jesus prohibits Saint Peter from fighting his captors with the sword. To a simple German such self-denial was difficult to grasp. Even the *Heliand* poet understands it only by considering that such actions led the Lord to immeasurable power—power over heaven, and power to judge the quick and the dead on Judgment Day. The disciples too will be rewarded by power in the Beyond. One gains the clear impression that Old Germanic ideas of life after death still in part inspired the poet.

The style of his epic was unquestionably Germanic. He used long lines with three to four alliterations. But these lines were no longer sung or recited. The *Heliand* was the first German book epic, and its predecessors were not German but Anglo-Saxon. After the *Heliand* alliterative verse disappears. Only in the nineteenth century is it revived again. In other respects, also, the *Heliand* has formed no tradition.

The other important literary documents of the Carolingian period were written in High German dialects. In connection with their missionary work, the monks wrote prayers (e.g., the *Wessobrunn Prayer*, 800) and pilgrims' hymns in popular language, and they told spiritual truths in poetic form. For example, *Muspilli* ("World Destruction") is a prophetic poem about the end of the world.

Another Old High German poetic document is the gospel harmony of the monk Otfrid from the Alsatian monastery of Weissenburg. His epic was completed about 870 and was dedicated to Ludwig the German, the grandson of Charlemagne and the first king of Germany proper. Otfrid's epic is sometimes called *Krist*, to distinguish it from the *Heliand*. It is less powerful than its Old Saxon counterpart and must rather be called a sermon than an epic. On the whole this sermon follows well-known models, but some lyrical parts excel by their fine images.

However, Otfrid's importance does not derive from these few lyrical gems, but from his metrical innovations. His epic is the first German document using rhyme. Nowadays, popular German poetry is unthinkable without rhyme. But originally rhyme was a late Latin development and had often been used in church hymns. Now Otfrid introduced it into the literature in the popular language. He kept the rhythm of the old alliterative verse and therein showed commendable stylistic tact. He set a good model for following poets.

A poem using the new form is the *Ludwigslied* ("Song of Ludwig") which celebrates a victory of the western Franks over the Normans. This worldly song was also written by a cleric. Its existence indicates that the old heroic songs were still known at this time. But they were not written down, and can be proven only indirectly. They were handed on by oral tradition, and naturally their contents and forms gradually changed. Their original alliterative form must have disappeared in late Carolingian times.

German Poetry in the Latin Language

IT WOULD have been strange indeed if, in the universal process of Romanization, poetic literature had been omitted, and if literature in the popular language had been allowed to continue without major changes. In the Carolingian period the few people able to read for their education took to the Latin originals, and what works there were translated were mostly works of an apologetic or doctrinal Christian content. Original works composed in Latin mostly dealt with practical or historical facts, like Einhard's famous life of Charlemagne, the *Vita Caroli Magni*. In the age of the Saxon emperors (919–1024) the German pupils of Roman culture became more independent and endeavored to imitate Latin poetic literature. They also chose for their subjects native German themes. Noble ladies and princesses often took a leading part in these creative efforts.

The new movement can be discerned not only in poetry. The scientific prose of the tenth century also often elicits our interest. For instance, around the year 1000, there lived the St. Gallen monk Notker III. Labeo ("the Thick-Lipped") who consciously tried to combine characteristics of Latin and of German style into a prose of peculiar charm. At the same time we find the first attempts to overcome the simple imitation of late Roman basilica style and to create a new form of architecture. After 1100 this so-called Romanesque architecture will reach its full fruition.

Naturally, the Latin tradition was primarily upheld by the people who had mastered the Latin language, i.e., the clergy and their disciples, the clerics (*clerici*). Popular poetry was spread by different agents. The classical Roman Empire had had its *mimi* and *joculatores*, wandering actors and jesters traveling from place to place. From the eighth century such people also appeared in Germany. They entertained villagers and city people with trained monkeys and bears, they performed acrobatics and dance routines, they played for village dances, and they spread the latest news in a period yet devoid of printed papers. In course of time the Latin actors became German *Spielleute*, fiddlers or strolling players who had a primarily musical function. Any major poetic contribution from these uneducated itinerant performers (*fahrende Leute*) cannot be expected. They often changed their "hits" in order to please their public, and taste was rather coarse and vulgar.

Not that the lower clerics always displayed a superior culture! To be sure, they were somewhat better educated, but their morals were not always of the best. A Cambridge manuscript, the so-called *Carmina Cantabrigiensia* (Cambridge Songs) has preserved for us a Latin anthology of pieces of various origin, Latin as well as German. Most of the fables and stories written down by these clerics seem to emanate from western Germany. One of the songs praises the emperor Otto III (d. 1002). Another song delights in telling rather tall stories. A third one is about a woman who bore a child during her husband's absence and asserted that its father was the snow. The oldest of these Latin songs are musical texts without definite rhythm or stanzas. Such texts were first introduced into the liturgy of the St. Gallen monastery about A.D. 900 by the monk Notker I. Balbulus ("the Stammerer"); their place was after the gradual and they were therefore called "sequences." The rhymed Latin texts of the collection represent a later phase of literature.

The same mixture of German and Latin traits can also be discerned in other clerical endeavors. It was monks who copied the *Hildebrandslied* and the *Merseburg Incantations*. It was monks who added their own grotesque exaggerations and blood-curdling details to inherited German materials, in accordance with the prevailing taste of the century; none of these versions still exists, but we can find their traces in the Middle High German *Nibelungenlied*.

In exceptional cases, a German legend found its way into congenial Latin. For instance, a student of the St. Gallen monastery school turned the Walther legend into Latin verses in the tenth century. The student's name was Ekkehard, a name that occurs in the St. Gallen roster several times; this one was called Ekkehard I, and died in 973. In his youth he set the German legend, about 935, in Latin hexameters. He had Vergil's *Aeneid* as a model before him, and he also knew other Latin writers, some of them rather well. But the complexion of his *Waltharius* remained German and still betrayed the heroic attitude of the Germanic migrations. The style of lost songs current during Ekkehard's period can still be guessed from it.

The beginning of the Walther epic leads us back into the middle of the fifth century when the Huns under Attila had reached the summit of their power. All the Germanic kings have been forced to leave hostages with Attila. In the case of Gibich, the king of the Franks, it is Hagen who has become a hostage. With the Burgundians, it is the king's daughter, Hiltgund. The Aquitanians have left the king's son, Walther.

When Gibich dies, his son Gunther ascends the throne and breaks the alliance with Attila, whereupon Hagen takes flight. Hiltgund has become Walther's betrothed during their years of captivity, and the two royal heirs also decide to escape. They make the Huns drunk and steal away under cover of night. They roam through pathless woods and over wild mountains, and they live on fish and birds. After forty days, Walther and Hiltgund reach the Middle Rhine in the neighborhood of Worms. The king of the Franks hears about the treasure which Walther has brought along from the treasure house of Attila, and decides to take it. Under Gunther's leadership, twelve Frankish heroes, including Hagen, pursue Walther and finally meet him in a narrow pass in the Vosges forest. The tired warrior is resting in the lap of his beloved

[15

when he is called upon to fight the Frankish attackers. The narrow pass only permits attack singly, and thus Walther can kill one of his opponents after the other, until Hagen and Gunther are the only ones left. The two now decide to let Walther come into the open. They fall upon him when he leaves his cave in the morning, as Hiltgund waits in the forest. For seven long hours the fight remains undecided. Then Walther hews off a piece of Gunther's thigh, Hagen cuts off Walther's right hand, and Walther stabs Hagen in his right eye and hacks off a piece of his jaw. Now the three can no longer continue the fight. Hiltgund comes riding up and dresses their wounds. She serves the heroes wine, and Hagen and Walther renew their friendship. Then they all ride home, Hagen and Gunther to Worms, Walther and Hiltgund to Aquitania.

Ekkehard used a German story, probably consisting of a fairly short song that could be memorized by a traveling singer. The warriors' taste of the period is demonstrated by the long, detailed description of Walther's bloody fights with the Frankish heroes. A note of coarse humor is introduced by the grotesque exaggerations at the end of the Latin epic. But Ekkehard also introduces finer traits into his song. He describes Walther's relation to Hiltgund in warm, intimate colors. When her betrothed, after forty nights in harness, for the first time puts his shield and his helmet aside, Hiltgund watches his sleep with loving care. And Walther himself is equally considerate. After the hot fight in which he has killed eleven Frankish heroes, he rests only half the night and then insists on taking over the watch so that Hiltgund can sleep. Ekkehard knew how to humanize the ideal figures of the popular tradition. In spite of its Latin dress, he has created a genuine German narrative.

About a hundred years later, somebody corrected the style of the Walther epic and purified its Latin in the classic manner, but this was a somewhat schoolmasterly procedure. Ekkehard himself employed the thoroughly alive Middle Latin of his time, and like his contemporaries thought nothing of using idiomatic expressions and phrases that were peculiarly medieval.

The same can be said of the style of *Ruodlieb*, a piece of poetry written by a traveling cleric from a Bavarian monastery. The intermixture of Latin and German phrases here is so strong that it has led some scholars to the assumption that the poem represents a first draft which never became known beyond the walls of the monastery. *Ruodlieb* can perhaps best be described as a kind of novel containing fantastic elements from heroic legend and fairy tale as well as realistic descriptions of festivities and village happenings. Stories similar to this "novel," which was written after 1050, occur in German literature only much later.

Another poem composed in a monastery is of equal interest to us, the so-called *Ecbasis cujusdam captivi per tropologiam* ("The Parable of the Flight of a Prisoner"). This first allegorical animal fable was written down after 930 and has become the ancestor of a whole genre. Aesop's fable of the sick lion cured by the fox has here been inserted into the other fable of the calf that runs away from its shepherd. The calf symbolizes the author who in this poem ruefully confesses his transgressions against his spiritual superior.

Dramatic writings in Latin were attempted about 965 by the gifted nun Hrotsvith of the convent of Gandersheim. She attempted to counterbalance the pagan plays of Terence by skits with more pious themes. She cannot have envisaged actual performances, but her dialogues betray the mind of a mature observer of life.

Hrotsvith's dramatic attempts remained without followers. Medieval German drama originated from the short Latin dialogues which were used for the embellishment of the Easter and Christmas services, and were sung by young clerics. These dialogues were introduced into the St. Gallen monastery by the monk Tutilo, and became known as *tropi*. An awareness of the Latin and Christian derivations of German medieval drama should be sufficient warning against a narrowly nationalistic interpretation of the literature of these centuries.

German Poetry Written
by Clerics

THE fusion of Germanic, Christian, and Roman elements that grew into German culture became ever stronger with the centuries. Ties developed between the Latin theology of the monasteries and the faith and simple life of the people, and ties developed between the

[17

traditional classical and patristic literature and the stories and motifs of native Germanic origin.

In the beginning, many Germans adopted the teachings of the Church only externally; in the time of the Saxon emperors, bishops often rode as generals, and many priests were married and had children. But in course of time the Germans were also influenced by the inner spirit of the Church. In the tenth and eleventh centuries the Benedictine monasteries became centers of spiritual revival. The new movement started in the Burgundian monastery of Cluny, and from its beginnings was strongly influenced by ideas that had evolved in Germany. The abbots schooled in Cluniac ideas demanded from their monks a strict and literal observance of the three Benedictine vows of poverty, chastity, and obedience, and insisted on their complete aloofness from all worldly pleasures. Naturally, a similar asceticism could not be expected from laymen; but they were expected to take the commandments of Christ seriously, and to lead a life becoming to a good Christian.

A special influence was exercised by the new movement upon the external organization of the Church. The Cluniacs demanded its absolute independence from all worldly infringements. This lead to a head-on clash with the policies of the Holy Roman emperors; these since Otto I had undisputedly ruled the German Church. For the emperors needed the bishops as administrative officials, and therefore also needed a controlling power over them. Naturally the emperors did not want to give up their right of investing the bishops; but the popes brought to power by the Cluniac reform movement were denying them this right. So the scene was set for the bitter fight over investiture (*Investiturstreit*). Emperors and popes were joined in battle during the whole knightly period, and the fortunes of war were now with the popes, then with the emperors. But actually the fight was decided under the Frankish emperors, especially during the unhappy reign of Henry IV (1056–1106). In the interest of orderly administration the German emperors had to champion an outdated external interpretation of a bishop's office, and in the unequal battle against a new and deeper conception of Christianity their old idea could in no way prevail.

In the eleventh century Christian doctrine was also strengthened by a new systematization and a new rationalistic interpretation. Scholastic theology firmly corroborated the dogmas of the Church and found its first leading representatives, e.g., the great Abelard (1079–1142).

At the same time the religious feelings of the masses found an outlet in the mystical endeavor of reconquering the Holy Land from the infidels. The Year of Our Lord 1096 saw the beginning of the First Crusade.

Mystics as well as ascetics were convinced of the power of evil. The zealots interpreted life as a continuous temptation which man could only overcome by abjuring the world and turning his eyes toward Heaven and the life hereafter. More lenient priests, though not less serious, stressed the values of a good, Christian everyday life as a proper preparation for eternity. Modern interpretations tend to overlook the fact that under the Frankish emperors the old Roman legalistic conception of God as a stern judge gradually gave way to a greater accentuation of God's love for the sinner and of God's desire as Creator to bestow blessings upon man in His image. Thus the Christian enjoyment of a sober workaday life and of harmless worldly joys was not always looked upon askance. Of the seriousness and the stress upon a good moral life during the Cluniac period there cannot be any question. But we should not overstress its asceticism and its unworldliness. Numerous spiritual poems of the eleventh century testify to the fact that laymen as well as priests and monks during this age began to understand Christianity more deeply. None of them looked upon life as the ultimate of all values. But by no means all were mortifying the flesh and completely turning away from the world. The language used by these poems was mostly the language of the people.

About 1100 the Old High German dialects became Middle High German dialects. There did not yet arise a common German speech. To be sure, the tendencies of linguistic development were the same in all the dialects. The vowels of the endings and the unaccentuated syllables became weaker, and the richness of the Old High German inflection was lost and became simplified. But the demarcation lines between the dialects continued, and one cannot yet speak of anything resembling a common German language.

As an example of the spiritual poetry of the eleventh century one can quote the powerful hymn of the Bamberg deacon Ezzo, which is usually called *Ezzolied* ("Ezzo's Hymn"). It expresses the whole doctrine of man's salvation in beautiful images and metaphors. Ezzo was a layman, like Brother Henry who lived in the Austrian monastery of Melk and about 1160 wrote his poem *Von des tôdes gehügde* ("Remembrance of Death"). Brother Henry warns against the dangers of the world which threaten us daily.

Yet not all spiritual poems of the period are as powerful and as elevated as these. We also have rhymed sermons and other didactic poems which sometimes must have bored the poets' contemporaries. In their endeavor to bring the Gospel message home to the layman, some of the poets tried to write down to a more worldly taste. Among these poems there are some based on interesting Biblical stories such as that of the three youths in the fiery furnace, or the story of Judith. There are treatments of the whole history of Creation or of the exodus of the children of Israel from Egypt. There is also to be found one treatment of the life of Christ, and there is an increasing number of Marianic hymns. The average taste of the worldly public seems to have been satisfied by the legends of the saints with their many adventures and their many miracles. Miracles, to be sure, could also appeal to the mystically inclined.

The *Annolied* ("Song of Saint Anno") may serve as an example of an elaborate treatment of a legend. It was written soon after the death of the bishop Anno of Cologne (d. 1075), the tutor of Henry IV. The song does not confine itself to his life and to the praise of the saint, but also brings in an abundance of historical detail. We hear of the creation of the world, of the five eras of the world, of the birth of Christ and the spread of Christianity, of famous cities and battles, and finally of Anno himself and the miracles that occurred at his grave. It is a veritable compendium of Christian and Latin lore. But it is a very short compendium. All the themes are somewhat hastily indicated and are not developed in detail. The clerical author has inspected his Latin sources only superficially. The rhythm and rhyme of his poem also do not point to particularly careful workmanship. The clerics continuously had the efforts of strolling players (*Spielleute*) in their ears, and their bad example was adversely affecting popular taste and literary style. The author of the Song of Saint Anno wanted to replace the old heroic epics by more spiritual work. But in his battle scenes he hardly showed better taste than the "fiddlers" he despised. His delight in battles and the shedding of blood surely cannot be called spiritual. The joy of the world crept into his work, the same joy that had already pervaded the *Walther* epic and the *Ruodlieb*.

Of the newly rising class of noble knights asceticism could not be expected, and lords belonging to it immediately favored a more worldly attitude. They read French rhymed novels with enthusiasm, and handed them on for translation to clerics who had often received their training in France. French culture, which had derived from the Latin mother culture, was slowly superseding it in literary and social importance, and the direct influence of classical culture became somewhat restricted.

About 1130 a Trier priest by the name of Lambrecht rewrote a French

German Poetry Written by Clerics

epic which related the story of Alexander the Great in the ornate fashion of a baroque novel. Forty years later Duke Henry the Lion of Bavaria commissioned the priest Konrad to translate the old French *Chanson de Roland* ("Lay of Roland"). Konrad found it suited his purpose to describe Roland as a defender of Christianity against the heathens; the enthusiasm of the crusaders directed his pen. But the style of Konrad's work still shows the primitive exaggerations of the eleventh century. The same can be said of the mighty *Kaiserchronik* ("Chronicle of the Emperors") that was finished before 1150. It treats the history of the Roman and German emperors down to Emperor Konrad II (1138–1152), and intersperses its tale with all kinds of arresting legends, stories, and fairy tales.

The clergy also attempted to write more imaginative narrative poems. One of them describes the adventurous journey of *Herzog Ernst* ("Duke Ernest") into the fabulous Orient. Others adapted the old songs of Dietrich von Bern and of the Nibelungs, as we can indirectly conclude from later sources. After 1160 some knights may have taken part in such poetic endeavors.

A somewhat independent piece of literature is represented by the song of *König Rother* ("King Rother"). Here a cleric has treated the Langobardic story of King Authari in the form of a heroic poem that replaces the Langobards by Normans. The Bavarian lord of this cleric must have felt friendly toward the Normans.

Rother, the hero of the poem, wishes to court the daughter of King Constantine of Constantinople. But Rother's messengers are thrown into prison, and their king is forced to set out on a campaign. Arriving at Constantinople, Rother keeps his real name secret. Constantine is impressed by the stranger's army and receives him with all honors. Now Rother can meet Constantine's daughter and can free his messengers. Finally he abducts his bride-to-be during Constantine's absence. But her father cunningly brings his daughter back to Constantinople, and Rother has to undertake a second campaign. This time he has a rival whom he finally defeats in a mighty battle. Now Constantine can do nothing less than consent to his daughter's and Rother's marriage.

The author has treated of Rother's campaign twice, and thus has repeated the same motif. This shows how such songs agreed with the taste of the public. Many other details corroborate that impression. The song tells of a giant who throws a lion against a wall so that all his bones are broken. There are humorous elements and fairy-tale traits. Nevertheless, *King Rother* on the whole is a well-told story and at least avoids

[21

The Threefold Origin of German Culture

the very worst exaggerations. It served as a model for other similar stories, and influenced the literature of the period a good deal.

King Rother was written down about 1150, and two years later Frederic I ("Barbarossa") succeeded to the German throne. His reign saw the most splendid period of German knighthood. The elements of German culture had finally fused, and a unified spirit could find expression in distinct literary forms. That these forms were international, and that the spirit moving Germany was also moving the rest of Western Christianity, must of course be taken for granted.

A greater interest in worldly affairs marks the end of the early Middle High German period. This can even be said of a part of literature that otherwise seems to be closely connected with the Church, namely the spiritual drama. We have called attention to the originally modest conversations between priest and choir at the Easter and Christmas festivals, the so-called *tropi*. Now these *tropi* became more elaborate, and developed into Easter and Christmas plays of a somewhat worldly character. Finally they had to leave the church buildings, and were performed in the nearby market place. From the eleventh and twelfth centuries come the oldest reports of performances and the oldest examples of longer spiritual dramas. These oldest plays still used the Latin language, and thus still showed some direct connection with their ritual origins.

We have to reckon with such plays during the whole Middle High German period, although these plays do not belong to the narrower sphere of the new, courtly literature. And yet, many of them might have been revised in the new spirit, as is proved by the Tegernsee *Ludus de Antichristo* ("Play of the Antichrist"), about 1160. This was a spiritual drama on a political background supplied by contemporary history. The author clearly took the part of the emperor whom he portrayed as the protector of Christianity.

CHAPTER TWO

The Symbolic Style of the Middle Ages

The World of the Knight

DURING the Middle Ages, great armies were unable to take part in such far-flung campaigns as the Crusades or the Roman expeditions of the German kings. The necessary provisions could neither be taken along nor be gathered on the way. The logistics of the time required small but strong military units with the largest possible radius of action. Such exigencies led to the formation of small mobile companies of well-armed knights. The individual knight in his heavy armor on a strong charger possessed a tactical value comparable to that of the modern tank.

Before the knightly period, armies had consisted of all the freeborn men available. Now the armies were armies of specialists, and specialists had to be adequately paid. In a time when money hardly existed, they had to be paid in other valuables. Thus the kings invested them with real estate and gave them special privileges. The knights originally were best armed because they could either afford good weapons or else were courageous enough to take them away from their enemies. Now they also became feudal lords possessing large tracts of land.

Since these German knights had special duties as well as special privileges, they soon developed a class feeling. In France and England this feeling had arisen earlier, and when German knights during the Crusades met their equals from Western Europe, their class feeling

[23

increased measurably. In addition they took over many Western customs. At common festivals the knights were brought even closer together, for instance at the splendid Mainz festival of the dubbing (*Ritterschlag*) of the sons of the Emperor Barbarossa in 1184. During the time of the Hohenstaufen emperors the knights represented a clearly circumscribed type. The typical knight lived on his own territory in his castle, and left the tilling of the soil to his tenants. The lord and his retainers were often away from home on some campaign. If they did not fight for the king or the Empire, they fought for the enlargement of the lord's own power. Some periods, of course, were more peaceful than others; but even then the knights had plenty of exercise on hunting expeditions or through competitive tournaments.

The whole life of the knight was so ordered as to increase his strength and courage. The young page was educated according to fixed rules. Then he became a squire and had to prove himself worthy of knighthood. Dubbing was a solemn occasion; now nobody could strike the knight without retribution, and the young man came into possession of all his proper weapons. Naturally he looked down upon the rustics and townspeople whose arms were not equal to his and whose courage in battle was less.

In the Hohenstaufen period, the knights replaced the clerics as the leading figures in literary culture, and founded a style that adequately expressed the medieval view of the world. It was the first real style of German literature. Before its ascendancy there were individual literary efforts, but there was no generally accepted body of symbols and motifs, and there was no stylistic ideal to which the various works of art could conform. All of this changed in the twelfth century when German lyric and epic poetry was consciously subjected to the demands of a style. Latin poetry which was written by the clerics and theological students was not affected by this ideal, and the same can be said for the religious dramas of the period, which were not conceived as literature but rather as adjuncts to religious worship. But all unquestionably worldly literature followed the new style which had its correspondences in the other fine arts. The musical style of the period also expressed similar principles. In fact, the lyric poems of the knights were songs, and therefore equally partook of the new poetical and the new musical style.

The new literary style was not exclusively German. Its origins were definitely French; its antecedents were Latin, with some admixture of Arabic and Celtic elements. And the style itself was common to all Western Europe; where national differences existed, they should not be

The World of the Knight

unduly stressed. Man was considered primarily as an heir apparent to Heaven; his life on this earth was a preparation for the world beyond or a prefiguration of it. Man was created in God's image, and if he lived according to God's intentions, he would grow into his rightful transcendental heritage. If he acted perversely and succumbed to the temptations of his baser instincts, he would become the fair prey of the Devil. Yet if he watched but a little, he could not be mistaken about the will of God. For that will was expressed in a meaningful way throughout His creation. No detail of nature and no act of life had a meaning in itself; they were all *bezeichenlich*, all symbols full of meaning. Self-sufficient realism in the modern sense was just as absent as self-sufficient activity. The style of the knightly age must therefore be called formalistic or symbolic.

All men had to live according to God's will. But there were variations and grades in the ways by which they expressed it. Children and servants obviously had a more subsidiary role in the scheme of things, and peasants also did not serve God directly. One possible manner of serving God was the manner of the clerics and the saints, and various literary productions of the twelfth and thirteenth centuries described the ideal life by such examples. But for most of the knights a symbol closer to reality had to be found, and there evolved the image of the ideal knight of the world, the gallant member of King Arthur's *Table Ronde*. He was an adventurer, but an adventurer in pursuit of high ideals; he did not succumb to the world, but controlled and ruled it. In doing so, the knight displayed the special virtues of *mâze* (wise self-control), *staete* (steadfast loyalty), and *milte* (liberal generosity); in addition, he was charitable to children and orphans, and chivalrous and considerate toward women. All this was included in the term *hovelich* (cf. modern *höflich*, polite) or courtly; for at the courts these new virtues were cultivated first.

Thoroughly Christian as this courtly ideal was, it was hardly compatible with monkish asceticism. Nevertheless the attempt to combine perfect knighthood with perfect monkhood was made by the knightly orders. The most important of them was the Teutonic Order which was founded in 1190. From the year 1230 it was engaged in conquering Prussia and slowly colonizing the heathen country.

Knightly literature prevailed between 1150 and 1300, and reached its summit shortly before and after 1200. It was not restricted to a few monasteries and convents like the previous literature but spread over the whole German-speaking territory. The literary center of gravity at first lay in the west and the south of the Empire. Later, around 1200, it moved toward the northeast. Especially did the court of the Landgrave of Thuringia become an important cultural center.

One indication of the stylistic unity of knightly literature was the character of its language. All knightly poets avoided at least the coarsest forms of dialect, and thus established a language convention that is sometimes erroneously noted as the forerunner of a standardized national language. But a stylistic ideal is not a political one. The new "unified Middle High German" disappeared with the style itself.

Minnesong

THE new courtly philosophy achieved a vigorous expression primarily in two fields of literature: in lyric poetry, and in epic poetry.

The new style can most easily be recognized in the lyric poetry of the knights, the so-called Minnesong. One must not interpret Minnesong as a continuation of the primitive love lyric. On the contrary, its essence represents a profound contrast. The songs that preceded Minnesong expressed general feelings characteristic not simply of one distinct individual, and they expressed them rather artlessly. Such popular songs were sung in celebration of spring, when the people danced around the village linden tree. The songs were in praise of the burgeoning of the flowers, the singing of the birds, the victory of spring over winter; and they always used the same formulas. Occasionally one could find stanzas full of a warm feeling of love, e.g.:

Dû bist mîn, ich bin dîn:	*Thou art mine, I am thine,*
des solt dû gewis sîn.	*Of that thou shalt be certain.*
dû bist beslozzen	*Enclosed thou art*
in mînem herzen:	*Within my heart.*
verlorn ist das sluzzelîn:	*Lost thereof is now the key,*
dû muost och immer darinne sîn.	*And thou within must ever be.*

Such stanzas must not be confused with the later folk song which originated under conditions which can hardly any longer be called primitive.

Minnesong

We also have a rich tradition of rhymed riddles and blessings, and they too can be considered as constituents of popular literature. Closely related are the so-called *Sprüche*, didactic poems usually written by lower knights after the second half of the twelfth century, and containing all kinds of rules for proper behavior.

All these poems somehow helped prepare for Minnesong, and their style can still be discovered in the lyrics of Walther von der Vogelweide. Yet they did not represent a particularly high form of poetry.

The only really artistic poetry existing before Minnesong, and also paralleling it, was written not in German but in Latin. During the eleventh and twelfth centuries a peculiar Latin poetry flourished at the colleges and universities of Western Europe; Germany proper founded its first university in 1348. The authors of these poems were usually students who did not achieve the status of well-endowed clerics. They were called vagrant scholars or goliards. The best of their lyrics can be found in a collection called *Carmina Burana* after the monastery of Benediktbeuren where the manuscript was preserved. Its most excellent poems were written by a German calling himself Archipoeta who served the chancellor of the Emperor Frederic Barbarossa (1152–1190). This so-called "arch-poet" wrote the famous goliard's confession later translated by Bürger, a poet of the eighteenth century. It starts with the stanza:

meum est propositum	*In the tavern yet to die*
in taberna mori,	*Is my proposition,*
ubi vina proxima	*Where my mouth will never dry*
morientis ori:	*In the imbibition.*
tunc cantabunt laetius	*Happier the angels' chant*
angelorum chori:	*Will be in addition:*
deus sit propitius	*May God to this toper grant*
isti potatori.	*Of his sins remission.*

Other songs are just as free in praising the joys of love and in ridiculing the Church and its well-paid clergy. In general the contents of goliardic lyrics are as worldly as possible and sometimes almost pagan. Their supreme goal is to enjoy life, a goal foreign to the spirit of the new Minnesong.

The symbolic interpretation of the world characteristic of the Middle Ages was not only held in theory, but pervaded the entire life. As a matter of course it was also applied to the relations between the sexes. Marriage was a holy sacrament considered inviolable. But it was not

[27

the only field in which the two sexes met, and the characteristic achievement of knightly culture was a spiritualization of other social relations. This was achieved through the concept of *minne*, a term which can only loosely be translated by "love." The knight usually showed *minne* toward a married lady of higher rank for whom he proved his admiration and devotion in countless ways: by gracious behavior, by defending his lady's colors in jousts, by sending her chivalrous presents, by praising her in songs. And she would return his favors by greeting him with radiant smiles, by designating him as her champion, by bestowing upon him the prizes won in knightly competition. The scale of favors was only limited by good taste and by Christian morals. Erotic emotions certainly played their secret part, and occasionally *minne* developed into a flirtatious game. But anything even approaching an affair would have been punished by the lady's irate husband swiftly and mercilessly. It is best to translate *minne* as ideal devotion or veneration, and to think of it as a suspended feeling of longing and pining, of temporary hope and passing despair. Many minnesongs are merely songs of conventional homage and polite admiration, and even the more expressive ones must not be misinterpreted as personal confessions in the modern sense. Most exponents of Minnesong wrote to display their chivalrous refinement and to show their mastery of a literary form.

The chivalrous lyric first developed in southern France around 1100, in Provence, the old Roman *provincia* which had never lost its antique feeling for form. Some influences can be traced to the neighboring Arabs who were still the rulers of large parts of Spain; but Arabic culture in turn also went back to antiquity in many respects. The Provençal poets called themselves *trobadors* or inventors. Their lyrics flourished about 1150, and from the beginnings had a fixed relation to music. They had an obligatory accompaniment by the fiddle or the lute; the word lute itself is Arabic. Naturally, music made special demands upon the form of the stanzas. The original tune was usually simple; it was repeated once and was then replaced by a new somewhat fuller tune, so that the stanza consisted of three parts. The German mastersingers later called these parts the two *Stollen* and the *Abgesang*. The new idea of spiritual veneration was described in the customary terms of feudalism, and the professed "love"—in the manner of late antiquity —always appeared as an illness. The new emotions of the troubadours had little in common with primitive, undivided feelings. They could only be felt by men belonging to a higher social class, who had finer and at the same time weaker sensibilities. At their best, *trobador* lyrics were more than a mere social game.

The art of the troubadours early reached northern France and finally came to the German Rhineland. It is easy to overestimate its influence on German Minnesong. For German Minnesong did not borrow everything from the French. It merely took over what it could use, and even that it changed and developed in its own distinct fashion.

The Austrian poet von Kürenberg (if that was his real name) can be called the first German minnesinger. He wrote his songs in the middle of the twelfth century, still using the ancient form of rhymed long lines, the so-called Nibelungen stanza. He sang of knightly love, but not yet of *minne* in the later sense. It was the unmarried lady who desired the knight to come to her. The knight had not yet become the pursuer of the married noblewoman whose love was unattainable to him.

A contemporary of the lord von Kürenberg was the baron Dietmar von Aist. This other Austrian had a similar background, and he was already acquainted with Provençal forms.

Still more a man of the new period was Heinrich von Veldeke, a knight from the Lower Rhine. He began a long line of minnesingers who followed the new trend in sometimes a more slavish, sometimes a more independent manner. With all of them the male was represented as the active partner in the relationship. It was he who was longing for the favors of his lady, and the lady was entirely at liberty to grant or refuse them.

The first of the really great minnesingers was the Alsatian Reinmar von Hagenau (from about 1160 to 1210) who also brought the new Provençal forms to Austria. His poems demonstrate that *minne* had little in common with our idea of passion. His attitude was the distant and therefore somewhat sad admiration for beauty. A tinge of sublime asceticism colored his poems. Reinmar presupposed that the adored lady was unapproachable, and he was satisfied when she permitted him to serve her. He was nobly and unselfishly devoted to her regardless of any possible favors. This devotion was expressed in objective reflections, and in immaculate rhymes and stanzas. He did not permit himself in the least to depart from tradition. To do so would have been equal to a social error.

Of more appeal to modern readers are the poems of the Thuringian Heinrich von Morungen (about 1200). He had thoroughly studied the love poems of Ovid. He also was deeply inspired by Provençal poetry, and took over its forms. Yet he still preserved his independence of feeling and vision. The passionate longing for his adored lady absorbed and almost consumed him. He envisioned her entering his room through the wall, like the Holy Queen of Heaven, and himself soaring upward with her:

> In sô hôe swebender wunne
> sô gestuont mîn herze an fröiden nie.
> ich var, alse ich fliegen kunne
> mit gedanken iemer umbe sie,
> sît daz mich ir trôst enpfie,
> der mir durch die sêle mîn
> mitten in daz herze gie.

*

> In such high raptures of joy
> My heart was never before.
> My thoughts soar back evermore
> To her, as though I could fly,
> Since she gave her trust unto me
> And pierced my soul to its core.

But such attention on the part of his lady was rare, and Morungen would wish that he was dead, or he dreamed that he would continue to serve her in the Beyond. Sensuous and spiritual emotions were strangely mixed and were expressed in the most colorful images, the most musical words, and the most lively rhythms. Morungen's visual imagery was unique in its daring and vigor. His contemporaries barely understood him, and instead preferred Reinmar.

Next to Reinmar and Heinrich von Morungen, the two great romancers Hartmann von Aue and Wolfram von Eschenbach should be mentioned for their courtly lyrics. To be sure, Hartmann's lyric gifts were not very pronounced. But Wolfram wrote splendid aubades (dawn songs) in which the break of dawn forces the knight to depart from the castle of his lady. One of Wolfram's songs, probably the last he wrote, ends in the reflection that it is only the lover who has to leave in the morning; the husband can stay. As Wolfram grew older he realized that the exclusiveness of the *minne* emotion could only find proper expression in marriage. He felt that the Provençal situation of the ever-frustrated knight was somewhat artificial and undignified. As a mature man he no longer wrote in this foreign fashion. His independent personality collided with the convention.

He was not the only German poet tending in that direction. Sir Walther von der Vogelweide, the greatest lyric poet of the courtly period, finally extended the convention. We do not know where Walther von der Vogelweide was born, and we can only guess at his birth date (between 1160 and 1170). No doubt Austria was the country where he felt at home. The poor scion of noble parentage, he learned the elements of his art in Vienna at the court of Duke Frederic von Babenberg. It was Reinmar von Hagenau who taught him *singen unde sagen,* i.e., to satisfy courtly demands in the text as well as in the accompanying music. The years of Walther's youth were happy and carefree, and the poet was forever looking back to them. As a man he had no place of his own to which he could retire in winter. He became a vagrant by necessity as well as inclination, and he was forever on the move. We find him at the hospitable court of Landgrave Hermann of Thuringia in Eisenach, we find him at the castle of the Margrave of Meissen. Part of his roaming was prompted by political developments. In the beginning Walther was a strong Hohenstaufen (Ghibelline) partisan, upholding the cause of Philipp von Schwaben. When the newly elected king was murdered in 1208, Walther espoused the cause of his Guelph opponent Otto IV. But when the new Ghibelline pretender Frederic II had become old enough, Walter again changed sides and made the Hohenstaufen cause his own once more. The young emperor soon recognized the value of Walther's propagandist service, and presented him with a fief before he was crowned by the Roman pope in 1220. Walther heartily rejoiced at this fulfillment of his long-felt wish for economic security and retirement in old age, and naturally continued to speak for the interests of the new emperor. He urged his fellow knights to take part in Frederic's crusade of 1228, and perhaps joined the imperial army himself. He probably died in 1230, shortly after his return from the Holy Land, and was buried in the New Cathedral at Würzburg.

As a poet Walther far surpassed the material as well as the formal conventions represented by Reinmar. He early asserted his independence and personally challenged the older poet. Yet he never rejected the tradition completely, and in general only built on it and enlarged its possibilities. He began with songs expressing the traditional veneration for high-born ladies. In one of his early songs he praised German ladies in preference to all others:

The Symbolic Style of the Middle Ages

Ich hân lande vil gesehen
unde nam der besten gerne war:
Übel müeze mir geschehen
kunde ich ie mîn herze bringen dar
Das im wol gevallen
wolde fremeder site.
nu waz hulfe mich, ob ich unrehte strîte?
tiuschiu zuht gât vor in allen. . . .

Tiusche man sint wol gezogen,
rechte als engel sint diu wîp getân . . .
Tugend und reine minne,
swer die suochen will,
der sol komen in unser lant:
da ist wunne vil.
lange müeze ich leben dar inne!

*

I have seen so many countries
And was happy visiting the best:
May misfortune rather overtake me
Than my heart should ever acquiesce
In enjoying
Foreign customs.
What availed it if I fought unfairly?
German virtue supersedes them clearly. . . .

German men are well behaved,
And the women almost look like angels . . .
Virtue and chaste minne—
He who for them is searching,
Let him come into our country:
It has many delights.
May I live there for long years!

But this poem should never be called a nationalistic poem in the modern sense. It was merely another expression of the same joy Walther always felt when at the beginning of spring his thoughts turned to charming ladies:

Sô die bluomen ûz dem grase dringent,
same si lachen gegen der spilden sunnen,

Minnesong

in einem meien an dem morgen fruo,
Und diu kleinen vogellîn wol singent
in ir besten wîse die si kunnen,
waz wunne mac sich da genôzen zuo?
Es ist wol halp ein himelrîche
Suln wir sprechen waz sich deme gelîche,
sô sage ich waz mir dicke baz
in mînen ougen hât getân, und taete ouch noch,
  gesaehe ich daz.

Swâ ein edeliu frouwe schoene reine,
wol gekleidet unde wol gebunden,
durch kurzewîle zuo vil liuten gât,
Hovelîchen hôhgemuot, niht eine,
umbe sehende ein wenic under stunden,
alsam der sunne gegen den sternen stât—
Der meie bringe uns al sîn wunder,
Was ist dâ sô wunneclîches under,
als ir vil minneclîcher lîp?
wir lâzen alle bluomen stân und kapfen
  an das werde wîp.

*

When the flowers from the grass are springing,
As if they would greet the sun with laughter
On an early morning in the month of May,
And so prettily the birds are singing
In the best way they are after,
Could a greater joy be thought than they?
It is almost half the joy of heaven!
Should my tongue what this resembles say,
I would speak of something that with pleasure
Has impressed my eyes in even greater measure.

When a noble lady pure and pretty,
In rich robes adorned and splendid headgear,
Graces with her presence an assembly,
Gay and courteous like to her companions—
Glancing at the circle now and then,
As the sun outshines each constellation—
Let the month of May his wonders bear!
Can his niceties at all compare

The Symbolic Style of the Middle Ages

With this loveliest collation?
All the flowers are fast forgotten
In the lady's admiration.

From this traditional expression Walther soon found his way to more personal feelings. In the song for which he is best remembered, Walther let a girl with whom he was really in love proclaim her feelings. She was a simple girl of the people and not a lady of noble birth. But her wholesome purity was more inspiring than the social status of the conventional objects of admiration. Walther gave free reign to his imagination and wrote a poem expressing a strong wholesome emotion, at once sensuous and spiritual:

Under der linden	*Under the linden*
an der heide,	*On the heath*
dâ unser zweier bette was,	*Where we two enjoyed our rest,*
Da muget ir vinden	*There you'll find*
schône beide	*All sweetly bruised*
gebrochen bluomen unde gras.	*Grass and flowers that we pressed.*
Vor dem walde in einem tal,	*Before the forest in a vale*
tandaradei,	*—Tandaradye—*
schône sanc diu nahtegal.	*Sweetly sang the nightingale.*

Here the language of the heart was heard again, and it was not the only poem of Walther's which renewed the simplicity of pre-courtly love lyrics. The mature Walther did not restrict himself to one theme, as Reinmar had done, and he surpassed the older poet by this versatility. He also did not restrict himself to the one medium of the *Lied*, but took over the epigrammatic form of the *Spruch* from the traveling poets, and employed it in the expression of general philosophical and political speculations. Walther the poet of love was but the other half of Walther the deep and serious thinker. He was one of the few poets embracing the entire culture of the age, its sensuous as well as its speculative sides. Walther had a clear conception of the *Civitas Dei*, the City of God, and lamented the sad condition of the Holy Roman Empire which was rent by discord:

untriuwe ist in der sâze,
gewalt vert ûf der strâze;
fride unde reht sint sêre wunt.

*

Minnesong

Treason sits in the saddle,
Violence roams all the roads;
Peace and justice both show wounds.

And this condition would last as long as people strove for worldly goods and worldly honors without proper regard for God's commandments:

> *ja leider desn mac niht gesîn,*
> *daz guot und werltlich êre*
> *und gotes hulde mêre*
> *zesamene in ein herze komen.*
>
> *
>
> *Alas, it seems it cannot be*
> *That worldly goods and honors*
> *Together with God's holy grace*
> *Can mingle in one human heart.*

or:

> *swer âne vorhte, herre got,*
> *will sprechen dîniu zehen gebot,*
> *und brichet diu, daz ist niht rehtiu minne.*
>
> *
>
> *Who without fear, oh Lord our God,*
> *Your ten commandments can recite*
> *and break them, does not love you truly.*

Yet most of the poet's countrymen could not visualize the Holy Roman Empire as a whole. It was easy for foreign powers to foment civil war. Walther chastised the Roman pope in sharp words as a wolf in sheep's clothing, and has therefore been taken by some critics as a predecessor of Luther. Such critics, however, overlook the exclusively political and national motivation of Walther's deprecations. He never harbored doubt about the dogmas of the Holy Church, and as was expected of good Christians, took part in a Crusade. He certainly did not want to abolish the papacy but to exhort the pope to live up to Christian ideals and to abstain from interfering in German politics.

Walther's misgivings about knightly culture were not unfounded. He was permitted to experience it at its height, but as an old man he saw it go down and lose its luster:

> *Ouwê war sint verswunden alliu mîniu jâr?*
> *ist mir mîn leben getroumet, oder ist es wâr?*
> *daz ich ie wânde daz iht waere, was das iht?*
> *dar nâch hân ich geslâfen und enweiz es niht.*

*

> *Woe to me that the past has claimed all my years.*
> *I wonder whether all my life has been a dream or real.*
> *What I deemed to have existed, was it ever there?*
> *Oh, perhaps I was asleep; I no longer know.*

Walther complained about the ever-increasing decline of courtly culture. Great lords were reduced to poverty, and fine ladies began to wear peasant dress. And the Holy Roman Empire entered a period of crisis. Frederic II was the last great emperor of the Hohenstaufen dynasty, but he was more interested in his Italian than his German domains. His successors did not even bother with German affairs, and slowly there began the "dreadful time without emperors" (*die kaiserlose, die schreckliche Zeit,* to quote Schiller). It ended only when the electoral princes could again agree on a German king. He was Rudolf von Habsburg (1273–1291), elected because the princes believed that he would not be able to show a too powerful hand. Yet to everybody's surprise he vigorously combated the lawless conditions that had come to prevail. He broke the power of many an arrogant Junker who had become robber or highwayman. But he could stop the general debasement of aristocratic behavior only temporarily.

It was a sign of changing times when the Austrian knight-poet Neidhart von Reuental (*ca.* 1190–1250) tried to achieve comical effects by conferring *minne* customs upon his relations with peasant girls. His object was not exactly to ridicule them, but to show their inappropriateness in lower social surroundings. However, he betrayed a sportive predilection for peasant life that was at variance with high knightly ideals and surpassed anything that Walther von der Vogelweide had ever indicated. Neidhart enjoyed entertaining his audience with coarse peasant tales and rough peasant melodies. He did not mind flirting with village beauties and arousing the jealousy and anger of jilted village swains.

Neidhart followed popular custom when he started his so-called "summer songs" with nature descriptions; usually he lets us see his village maidens dancing under the linden trees. He also wrote "winter songs" where he used peasant parlors and village taverns as his locales. Certainly he employed courtly meter and used the entire stylistic apparatus of traditional Minnesong. But his good-natured clowning detracted from the seriousness of the ideals.

Other poets from the beginning of the thirteenth century show the deterioration of customs even more pronouncedly, although their poems still profess to uphold the old ideals. The figure of Tannhäuser is symbolic of a loose and dissolute life. This knightly poet spent all he owned on drunken revelry, and ended as a poor vagrant.

With the passing of time the great representatives of Minnesong became legendary figures. The poetic narrative of a *Sängerkrieg auf der Wartburg* ("Singing Contest at Wartburg Castle") described a contest between Walther von der Vogelweide, Wolfram von Eschenbach, and Heinrich von Ofterdingen, a poet who is also mentioned in other literary documents. The life and art of these old masters tended to assume an unreal character, and when latecomers still tried to uphold the tradition, they appeared misplaced in a time which grew coarser and coarser. The patrician Konrad of Würzburg with all his stylistic gifts became little more than a lyrical craftsman, and Master Johannes Hadlaub but continued a tradition. This Zürich citizen of the end of the thirteenth century no longer represented the knightly class, but belonged to the rising city civilization of the German southwest. His poetry did not reflect his actual surroundings, but was fashioned by literary models. Hadlaub was a collector of literary treasures, and probably had a hand in assembling the great manuscript collection of minnesongs. In his own poems he meticulously followed a pattern and avoided the appearance of originality.

Other poets tried bridging the widening gap between literature and reality by explaining and teaching the ideals of chivalry. About 1216 there appeared *Der Winsbeke*, a didactic poem in which a knight of that name instructs his son in all the proper customs. Didacticism in general now became a fashionable pastime. A Swabian vagrant poet by the name of Freidank collected rhymed proverbs under the title *Bescheidenheit* ("Sagacity"); he still satisfied the traditional demands of pure rhymes and rhythms. But he was followed by *Der Renner* ("The Roughrider") of Hugo von Trimberg, a Bamberg schoolmaster who tried to foist a dead-letter morality upon his contemporaries. They read him a great deal, but he was hardly a deep educational influence.

Knightly Romances

THE courtly attitude was also strongly expressed in epic poetry. The number of knightly romances continued to grow from the middle of the twelfth century.

Modern readers think of a long prose tale when they speak of a novel, but novels can also be written in verse. Essentially a novel is not characterized by its external form but by its peculiar setting of an apparently individual problem. To concur with Goethe, a novel is a subjective epic (*eine subjektive Epopöe*), and its theme is the struggle of an individual with the world; the setting for this struggle is objective, social or historical. Homer's *Odyssey* should be called a novel, and like it, the novels of courtly society were written in verse. Couplets of verses with four accents each were the conventional form.

These novels were different from the great national epics, e.g., the *Nibelungenlied*. They were not based on a national tradition. For their sources they mostly had French verse tales treating materials of various origins. Some themes were French, others Latin, English, or Celtic. On the whole, French literature represented the common European tradition, taking it over to a large extent from late Latin antiquity and incorporating in its Romance language form such native Western materials as seemed compatible with its Christian and classical tenor. Naturally, the individual poets including the German ones exercised their own gifts of combination, and at times used their personal experiences for the free decoration of these stories. Yet they never invented their stories entirely. They placed little stress on originality, and a poet introducing his own inventions appeared to them suspicious; he was criticized as a *vindaere wilder maere* ("a man of wild imagination"). The poets tried to excel by their style rather than their materials.

The true romances of knighthood begin where this new style appears first. To be sure, we have some treatments of courtly materials as early as 1170. Yet these first representatives of the type hardly differ from their immediate predecessors, the *Lay of Alexander* of the priest Lambrecht, the *Lay of Roland* of the priest Konrad, the *King Rother* and similar rhymed tales of adventure. These first romances abound in external events, although from the beginnings there is an attempt to interpret these events symbolically. Roland to Konrad is not the historic general but a model Christian fighter against the heathens, and Alexander to Lambrecht has become a representative of divine rule. Yet the new picture is not altogether clear.

The new type is found only with Heinrich von Veldeke, a knight from the Lower Rhine. He no longer intends to startle his audience by novel adventures, but concentrates on their proper relation. He knows the new style and he knows the new experience of *minne* which he also treated in minnesongs. Thus he is the first representative of the age of chivalry. His principal work is called *Eneit* (1184–1190) and is based on a French version of Vergil's *Aeneid*. But the German as well as the French author is less interested in the warlike exploits of his hero than in Aeneas' amorous adventures with Dido and later Lavinia. To be sure, the description of *minne* here is rather superficial. Nevertheless Heinrich von Veldeke's *Eneit* is the first romance of knighthood. The author pays much attention to form. With infinite care and regularity he adds couplet to couplet; they all have four accents, and they have pure rhymes. He writes in Old Limburg dialect, but avoids vulgar and local expressions. All these reforms were taken over by Heinrich von Veldeke's successors and became a milestone in German stylistic development.

To be sure, the author of *Eneit* was completely understood only by a small group of masters. Most romances of knighthood still succumbed to the lure of adventure, and though we have a large number of them their intrinsic value is often small. The majority of knightly romances provide important sources for the history of civilization, but mark no poetic achievements.

The first truly great author of knightly romances was Hartmann von Aue who lived between 1170 and 1215. He was a liegeman of the Swabian barons von Aue, but a liegeman possessing an unusual amount of education. He grew up in a monastery school, and we also know that he took part in a Crusade.

Hartmann's philosophical view is the view of gradualistic theology which during his time was developed by the great teachers of the medieval Church, and later assumed its classical form in the *Summa Theologiae* of St. Thomas Aquinas (1268–1273). According to this theology there are various ways to Heaven; although the ascetic way to sainthood is the best, it is not open to everybody, and ordinary human beings too can lead a pious Christian life. Thus Hartmann von Aue does not contradict himself when in a tale he praises asceticism and in lyric poems the sweetness of *minne*. Asceticism may be the only solution to life's problems for Pope Gregorius, the hero of Hartmann's narrative of this name, and spiritual courtship or *minne* is the way in which a knight may show his piety. The choice between various ways of life is a personal one, but is not a choice between heaven and hell.

In our time, Thomas Mann's novel *The Holy Sinner* has revived the narrative *Gregorius*, but actually only Hartmann's verse story of *Der Arme Heinrich* ("Henry the Hapless") is still generally known. This short work has for its theme a family legend of the barons von Aue. In the beginning the knight Henry is portrayed as a good knight in the sense of the world, handsome and courageous, rich and liberal. Yet his life lacks the proper perspective, he is not humble enough to realize that life is but a fief from God that has to be faithfully administered as a preparation for Heaven, and has only symbolical value. Therefore God afflicts him with leprosy to bring him to his senses. But, like Job, Henry believes himself unjustly punished, and is even willing to accept the blood of another human being for his personal salvation. A pure virgin, the daughter of a loyal farmer, travels with him to Salerno where a surgeon might work a wondrous cure with her blood. However, when Henry witnesses the preparations for the operation, he experiences a change of heart and rejects the virgin's sacrifice: he knowingly and unconditionally resigns himself to the will of God. Now that Henry's affliction has served its purpose, God can take it from him. Completely cured in mind and body, Henry returns to Swabia, and in humble gratitude he marries the virgin (in a time of still unsettled social stratification the marriage of a knight to a freeman's daughter presented no problem). Henry and his wife can now live an earthly life of harmonious moderation in the service of God:

> nach süezem lanclîbe   After a life long and joyful
> do bezazen si gelîche   They acquired likewise
> das êwige rîche.   The joys of Heaven.

Hartmann's story is told in a simple, straightforward style, and a modern reader is only startled by the tender age of the young girl and by the detailed theological reasoning that is put into her mouth. But the number of her years is symbolical and stands for purity and innocence, and the theological disquisition is a somewhat primitive device to point out that in her self-effacing way the girl has the right attitude toward life, which Henry has not yet achieved. If one does not expect realism from such a tale, Hartmann's *Der Arme Heinrich* can serve as an excellent introduction to medieval style.

In his own age Hartmann was read primarily for his Arthurian romances. These knightly tales did not attempt to portray life realistically, but to establish an ideal, and this aim could best be reached by moving the world of poetry measurably away from everyday reality. This was made possible by the utopian fairy-tale world of the Arthurian legends. These legends originally came from Britain and were brought by the Bretons to France. Hartmann von Aue's immediate sources were the versions of Chrestien de Troyes (d. 1175), the greatest Old French romancer. The German poet wrote his *Erec* about 1191 and completed his *Iwein* about 1203. Neither are translations, but rather free treatments of the French versions. Hartmann's primary purpose was to achieve clarity. In the contemplative parts he often indulged in digressions and elaborations.

Both romances center about the great problem of courtly society: how a knight can avoid succumbing to leisure (*sich verliegen*); in other words, how can he remain a courageous knight practiced in war, and yet follow the commands of his lady who admonishes him to enjoy the finer things of life? Erec almost forgets his knightly vocation in following the call of *minne*, and Iwein almost forgets his lady in his search for adventure. Both achieve a balance between *minne* and knightly honor only after prolonged struggle. Neither the knight absorbed in adventure nor the knight lost in *minne* correspond wholly to the ideal of chivalrous society, even if they outwardly qualify to belong to the Round Table of King Arthur. Only a balance between their views represents the right attitude toward the world, and to achieve this *mâze* (moderation) was the object of Hartmann.

The most impressive artistic image of the ideals of German chivalry was drawn by Wolfram von Eschenbach in his *Parzival*. Wolfram's personality entirely recedes behind his work, as do the personalities of most authors mentioned here. We know that he was a Franconian knight living after 1170. He probably was a vassal of the counts von Wertheim and was not too well off. He was not a member of the old aristocracy, and took his name from the village where he was born. He did not have any formal schooling but certainly was not as uneducated as he would make us believe. Like Walther von der Vogelweide, Wolfram often changed his abode. One of the courts he visited was the court of the Landgrave of Thuringia where he started his *Parzival*. Wolfram was happily married and enjoyed having children. He must have died after 1217. Thus he experienced the flowering of German knighthood under Frederic I ("Barbarossa") and during the first years of Frederic II's reign.

The material for his *Parzival* was found by Wolfram in an uncompleted romance of Chrestien de Troyes which was written about 1180. The story probably was derived from Breton fairy tales. For its continuation Wolfram got many ideas from a certain Kyot (probably Guillaume from Tudèle in Navarre) which, however, he used rather independently. His *Parzival* is a unified work of literature, and cannot be called a mere imitation or translation.

The content of the novel is as follows. The boy Parzival (his name means Pierce-the-Valley) grows up in the loneliness of the forest. His father Gachmuret has been killed in a battle in the distant Orient. His mother Herzeloyde is afraid that Parzival might have a similar fate, and therefore keeps the boy from the knowledge of arms. Yet accidentally Parzival meets some knights and thereafter nothing can keep him at home any longer. His mother puts fool's clothes on him in order to keep him from mischief, but he proves himself a man anyhow, and old Gurnemanz teaches him knightly customs.

Parzival now roams the countryside and finally comes to the castle of Munsalväsche ("Mount of Salvation") where a company of knights lives in the service of the Grail. The Grail is a mysterious stone brought down to earth by angels who have entrusted it to the Grail king for safekeeping. The present king of the Grail is Amfortas, but he is bedridden on account of a wound. Parzival sees the Grail brought in in solemn procession, and takes part in the common meal of the *Templeisen*, the Templar Knights of the Grail; the Grail provides their daily food and drink. A bleeding lance is also carried past, at the sight of which loud moaning and complaining is heard. Parzival would like very much to ask for the meaning of all that he sees; but in deference to good social conduct he keeps silent, as he does not want to appear forward.

Next morning the castle of the Grail is vacated; riding away, Parzival must tend to his own horse. He goes to King Arthur who has already heard of his deeds and wants to accept him into the renowned company of the Round Table where all are equal and nobody can sit at the head of the table. Yet just when Parzival's acceptance is being celebrated, Lady Kundrie arrives as the messenger of the Grail, and states that the new knight is unworthy of joining Arthur's company. For Parzival has not inquired after the meaning of Amfortas' suffering. Thereupon Parzival curses God for not treating him charitably, and rides away.

During the following cantos of *Parzival* we almost lose sight of our hero. We only hear at intervals that he roams the world in his quest for adventure. His place is taken over by Gawan, the most famous knight of the Round Table and the acme of purely worldly knighthood. Gawan defeats all his opponents, as does Parzival; but the latter remains true to his wife Kondwiramur, while Gawan becomes involved in various love affairs.

Finally Parzival experiences his hour of remorse. On a Good Friday he arrives at the hermitage of the knight Trevrizent, his uncle, who charges him with his transgressions. Parzival again turns to God, and realizes that he has not given proper testimony to the pity in his heart. In this highly symbolical world his behavior toward Amfortas betrayed a hidden obtuseness and callousness that culminated in his denial of God's charity. From this deep and grievous sin the errant knight cannot be saved immediately. He has to be patient until Heaven in its mercy relents and calls him back into the community of the Grail. He is again accepted by the Round Table. He also meets his half-brother Feirefis whom his father Gachmuret left behind in the Orient.

Again Lady Kundrie arrives and recalls our hero to the castle of the Holy Grail; the stone has revealed the will of God by a magic inscription. Parzival rides to Munsalväsche with his brother Feirefis and his wife Kondwiramur, and also the sons to whom she has given birth in the meantime. Parzival saves Amfortas by his symbolical and compassionate inquiry after his suffering, and then himself accedes to the kingdom of the Grail. Feirefis embraces Christianity and returns to the Orient. One son of Parzival is endowed with his father's worldly possessions. The other son, Loherangrin, is initiated into the service of the Grail. And Feirefis will convert the rest of the world, which Wolfram visualizes as completely Christian in the end.

Like all the authors of knightly romances, Wolfram in his *Parzival* portrays an ideal. Yet his ideal encompasses the highest. For Parzival is not merely a worldly knight, but also a Christian knight. The king of the Grail not only displays all the worldly virtues, but also stands in the service of God, to which one can only be called by an act of special grace. A condition of God's call is that the future king show the proper understanding of earthly life. Up to his conversion by Trevrizent, Parzival has lived it naïvely for its own sake, and has assumed that worldly behavior based on established conventions is adequate. Then he becomes aware that life is but a symbol and that behavior serves to bring out the true meaning of the world. Only by such behavior can Parzival achieve human perfection, and it is this inner perfection at which Wolfram aims in preference to the worldly prowess exemplified by Gawan. This Utopia is meant for more than one class.

The Symbolic Style of the Middle Ages

Wolfram's conception of life has also determined the form of his romance. A symbolical interpretation of life cannot be demonstrated in the abstract, but has to be visualized by appropriate images. Wolfram's images are concrete and adroitly juxtaposed. The background of the romance is formed by conditions existing in real life. Even the *Templeisen* had their parallel in the religious orders of knights which were constituted in the same period. Seldom are we disturbed by too great a diversity of action; the numerous adventures of Gawan, which are told in abundant detail, form an important worldly counterpart to Parzival's higher sphere of knighthood.

A poet largely becomes great by his use of language, and it is in this respect that Wolfram is quite different from his contemporaries. His style is unique. Just as life is never explainable in terms of its surface meaning, Wolfram's language is full of hidden implications which go beyond mere ornamentation and rhetoric. Wolfram gave free reign to his imagination, and his bold allusions and assumptions disturbed his contemporaries. His similes and metaphors go to the limits of the language, and some critics have termed him dark or even devoid of artistic taste. In an age of conventionality he dared to be original even in his use of words.

We previously met Wolfram as a minnesinger. As an epic poet he wrote not only his *Parzival* but also employed other themes. Yet he never surpassed his *Parzival*. The love story of *Schianatulander and Sigune*, which he treated independently, grew out of his occupation with the *Parzival* theme. To an entirely different field belongs his *Willehalm* which he wrote between 1215 and 1218. It is a German version of the French *Bataille d'Aliscanz* ("Battle of Aliscanz") and was never completed. Its style is especially "dark" and mysterious, and in part perhaps tries to emulate Provençal models.

With Wolfram's successors the same style became turgid and precious. They continued and enlarged the Parzival story with all kinds of learned additions, and assembled every possible sort of adventure without rhyme or reason.

Wolfram, the protagonist of the significant and the meaningful, had as a contemporary Gottfried von Strassburg, a great seeker for clarity. While Wolfram at times becomes awkward by his indirectness, Gottfried sometimes achieves but an elegant virtuosity. They are opposites also in their philosophies. Wolfram is deeply moved by transcendental problems, while Gottfried as an Alsatian is more open to the world. It is still not the world of everyday realism but a world of symbolical actions, and Gottfried's general disposition betrays the same psychic tension as the epics of Wolfram, although this tension is expressed by different means.

Gottfried von Strassburg was no knight and may have been a learned cleric. As his model he chose Bligger von Steinach's collection of verse stories which unfortunately is no longer extant.

About 1210 Gottfried gave a new Middle High German form to the Celtic story of *Tristan* which before him had been treated by Eilhart von Oberge. Gottfried's model was the Norman version of the *trouvère* (Northern French for *trobador*) Thomas. Both Thomas' as well as Gottfried's versions evoke the reader's interest more through their style than through their material. For the story of Tristan and Isolde by their time was no longer new, and originally had caught the courtly poets' attention primarily because it was fraught with meaning.

The problem finding expression here was the problem of earthly love, a love overwhelming Tristan and Isolde quite against their intentions and against the conventions of courtly morality. Tristan conducts Isolde across the sea as the intended bride of his uncle and lord Marke. By mistake the two drink a love potion prepared for the betrothed couple, and they are now inextricably entangled in a fatal passion. The magic potion serves as Gottfried's symbol for the fatality of this passion and also for its existential innocence. Measured by the rules of social convention, it is a crime against Marke's prerogatives both as bridegroom and lord. Worse, it becomes a sin against the sacrament of holy matrimony. For Tristan and Isolde continue their illicit relationship after Isolde's marriage to Marke, and plunge from forbidden emotions into acts of adultery. If ever this adultery were unmistakably observed or proved, Marke, according to the medieval code, would have no other choice but challenging Tristan to a mortal duel or brutally killing him outright. But Marke never discovers him with Isolde, and proof is never adduced, although the reader is clearly aware of the facts.

This indicates that on the worldly plane a solution for Gottfried's problem cannot be found, and indeed we have to look for an answer that belongs to the sphere of religion. Tristan's and Isolde's life in adultery is a symbol for the primary stark fact of Christian existence that life is always life in sin, and therefore liable to extinction. Tristan is a true child of sorrow. His father died before his birth and his mother died in childbed. He grew up as an orphan, and as a homeless wanderer he lives his precarious life. Catastrophe is sometimes avoided only by a hair's breadth. His is a life without legitimate fulfillment, a life in the shadow of death. Yet it is still a life worthy to be lived by a noble soul, and Tristan never falters in his devotion to Isolde. He invents ever new stratagems to circumvent Marke's suspicions in order to be with her. He accepts temporary banishment and the challenge of humiliation, of sickness and privation. Isolde, on her part, undergoes some of the same trials. Life is a duty to be undertaken unflinchingly. It is also a gift to be enjoyed to the utmost. In their most exalted moments Tristan and Isolde experience a supreme bliss made even sweeter by the constant threat of death. But an unequivocal answer as to the value of such a life is never given; it remains an unending challenge and tension. One might call it significant that Gottfried's romance was not completed; the poet died before he could finish his work. Even so, he made his meaning clear and wrote one of the lasting and most poetic expressions of the courtly mood.

Gottfried's images are clearer and also livelier than those of Wolfram. He was the first to go deeply into a psychological description of love and to fathom its complexity. On the other hand, the flight of his imagination rarely soared into the transcendental, and his basic Christian attitude was implied rather than expressed; modern criticism has sometimes mistaken him for a forerunner of Humanism which most assuredly he was not. The strong, pure air of courtly ideals still permeates his work. Life is still symbolical, and if material concerns as such enter Gottfried's world, they do so in hidden ways. But the number and importance of realistic factors is increasing. Gottfried often gives of his best in nature descriptions. He also anticipated a future period by certain stylistic devices, e.g., his detailed allegories which later became the fashion.

After Gottfried and Wolfram the courtly style changes and deteriorates in many ways. The learned Rudolf von Ems can no longer be called a courtly poet in the original sense. He wrote between 1220 and 1254. In his romance *Barlaam und Josaphat* he treated a Buddhistic legend that had spread to Greece and thence in Christian garb to the rest of Europe. Here the world is interpreted as a world of mere appearances. Equally one-sided is the spiritual attitude of his *Weltchronik* ("World Chronicle") which retells stories from the Old Testament in elaborate detail. But the poet cannot consistently pursue one attitude. In the tale *Der gute Gerhard* ("Good Gerhard") the simple kindness of a merchant is held up as a moral example. The hero is taken from real life and is no longer a knight. To be sure, Rudolf von Ems in his *Alexander* romance and in other knightly tales still seems to display a conservative courtly attitude. But in view of his other works he no longer convinces, except that at least the poet knows the courtly ideal from his own experience.

Konrad of Würzburg, who died at Basel in 1287, no longer writes from personal experience, but is merely inspired by the literature of the courtly period. For Konrad belongs to the middle classes. We have already met him among the minnesingers. He is little more than a clever virtuoso who for his own ends knows how to use the forms created by others. He is best in his short tales and legends, in those small forms of writing which are so characteristic of the new bourgeois period. Some of these tales are allegories conforming to the new standards of taste. As an example we refer to the poem *Der Welt Lohn* ("The World's Wages") in which Dame World visits a knight who up to then has loyally served her. She turns around and displays her back, which is crawling with festering toads and ugly snakes. The horrified knight swears off the service of Dame World and enters upon a Crusade.

Another poet exemplifying the decline of the knightly period is the Styrian minnesinger Ulrich von Lichtenstein. This strange character led an outward life of calculated sobriety and manly activity. But he described it as a queer romance in his *Frauendienst* ("Chivalrous Courtship") 1255. Reality and poetry no longer match, and the world of courtly society is falling apart. It is characteristic of such times of disintegration that people often become egocentric, and Ulrich von Lichtenstein is no exception to the rule. He clearly puts his personality into the limelight.

Yet in spite of all that has been said, Konrad of Würzburg and Ulrich von Lichtenstein still represent the courtly tradition. Other poets of the thirteenth century are already dissolving it. They use the old epics and romances as quarries, and put together new works out of the fragments they have broken loose. Many of these later works can no longer be called integrated romances. They rather impress one as collections of tales and anecdotes. This is in line with the great popularity, now beginning, of the short tale.

The Renewal of Germanic Traditions

THE courtly romances introduced great masses of foreign material into German literature, and established a knightly ideal that in many ways contrasted with the customary conceptions of Germanic times. These conceptions lived on in a great number of indigenous stories, the existence of which can be traced back through direct sources and through many allusions and indirect testimonies. Naturally, these stories were now reinterpreted in the style of courtly literature, and thus arose the great medieval epics, the *Nibelungenlied*, the epics of the Dietrich cycle, the *Kudrunlied*, and others. Sometimes the tradition was powerful enough to resist the new poets' intentions and to assert its original primitive character; even the great epics contain occasional chapters that mar the artistic unity and can be understood only on the basis of existing or assumed older versions. Sometimes the new poet forced his modern will upon the old materials, and the original meaning of the stories was distorted or destroyed. But generally the interplay of old and new forces resulted in an interesting and unique group of literary monuments that must be set aside from the knightly romances employing foreign materials.

Literary works of the type of the *Nibelungenlied* are best called national epics. They use national materials in the same sense as the French *Chanson de Roland*, the Spanish romances of the Cid, the epics of Homer and of Vergil. And just like these, they do not always treat of the exploits of an individual hero but rather describe the heroic deeds of a whole group. These deeds go back to the formative period of the national past and represent the manner in which that past lives on in the memory of the various nations. As the German nation originated in the period of the Germanic migrations, the German national epics treated material from that ancient period. But they also kept the old tradition alive by repeatedly reshaping it in conformity with the aspirations of later and different centuries. Like most epics, the German epics occasionally picked up other elements, e.g., fairy-tale elements of a preliterate nature representing ancient religious superstitions and imaginative complexes.

We must not expect from such literary movements polished stylistic perfection, although their authors bravely worked at their task. And, of course, we have to think of the authors as individual poets, although their names usually have not come down to us. It is an unsubstantiated romantic theory to assume that the nation as a body invented epics. Still, the individual poets based their stories on national traditions and contributed to them.

The most important German epic is the *Nibelungenlied* ("The Lay of the Nibelungs") which in Middle High German was called *Der Nibelunge Nôt* ("The Nibelungs' Misfortune"). It was composed between 1200 and 1210 by an unknown Austrian cleric of fairly high gifts. He independently combined two older forms of the legend, one a Brunhild legend from the end of the twelfth century, and the other an Austrian epic about the downfall of the Burgundians from the sixties of the twelfth century. Both older epics are no longer extant, and we can therefore make only general statements about them. The poet was well read and knew a great number of French romances, some of which have left their traces in his work; he also knew the standard Latin authors, the popular myths, and the German literature of his time.

The epic about the Burgundians was based on historic tradition. In A.D. 437 the Mongolian Huns attacked and annihilated the Germanic tribe of the Burgundians, which had probably settled in the central Rhine region. The best-known leader of the Huns was Attila; the Burgundian prince in Latin was called Gundicarius. These meager facts were augmented by other historic events which impressed contemporaries and their successors, and were presented in song. The songs wandered to Scandinavia where they assumed the form known to us through the *Edda*. In Austria the same short songs developed into an epic which then became the second half of the *Nibelungenlied*.

Its first half originally was an independent story which was combined with the Burgundian legend, because it happened to contain the same names. The hero of the story was of fairy-tale derivation; no historical prototype has been discovered, but fairy-tale elements abound in the story, although an attempt has been made to play them down. Siegfried himself is the mythical hero *par excellence*. He is of mysterious origin, he forever seeks adventure, he fights with dragons and monsters, like Achilles he can only be killed if one knows his one vulnerable spot. Another fairy-tale figure is Brunhild, a virgin of superhuman powers

[49

with the proverbial cruelty of all the fairy queens' and kings' daughters for which heroes have ever contended. Her unsuccessful suitors are killed, and exceptional cunning and an almost magic energy are needed to subdue her. But after her submission she becomes harmless and docile. Between the fifth and sixth centuries a Frankish lay apparently treated the legend of Siegfried. This legend found its way to Scandinavia, where it also found its way into the *Edda*. In Germany the lay was revised at the end of the twelfth century and finally became the first half of the *Nibelungenlied*.

The long period of gestation of the *Nibelungenlied* led to a number of awkward slips and contradictions. Geiselher remains a youth throughout the epic. Siegfried's son as well as Brunhild simply disappear before the second half of the story. And so on. Yet on the whole these faults disturb us but little. The unknown Austrian poet has been most successful in combining the Siegfried legend and the Burgundian epic into a unified work of poetry. He has not merely effected a superficial combination of the two tales, but has mutually balanced their weight and has imbued them with the same high spirit. His additions have brought the two parts to about equal length.

His merit also pertains to the form. The epic acquired a uniform stanza and a neat verse form. The stanza is called the *Nibelungenstanza* and goes back to the old Germanic long line, which we met in the *Hildebrandslied*. It has combined four such lines into one single stanza. Each verse of this stanza is divided by a caesura into two unequal halves. The first half has four accents, the second three. Each two verses form a rhymed couplet. The last half of every second couplet has four instead of three accents, and thus rounds out the stanza as a whole. This form was rather exacting and could not always be filled with poetic images and with fresh, unhackneyed rhymes. The language of the epic is thus characterized by a certain rigidity in the choice of words and rhymes, by repetitions and formulas, by stereotype comparisons. However, it would be wrong to call it unpoetic or monotonous, as its very severity contributes to the somber atmosphere of the story. The same effect is attained by an antiquated vocabulary, by time-honored stylistic devices taken over from Latin rhetorics, and by a general stress upon the typical. The *Nibelungenlied* might be called the poetic equivalent of Romanesque statuary.

The unknown Austrian was more than a clever compiler of existing material. Only a gifted poet could provide such a fine description of the customs and the inner life of the characters. Only a gifted poet could avoid the stylistic crudeness of his models. As a result of his work, we now enjoy the *Nibelungenlied* as a unified poetic whole. Still, the story is composed of two different parts. The first part could bear the title "Siegfried's Death," the second one "Kriemhild's Revenge."

Kriemhild, the beautiful daughter of the Burgundian king, grows up at the same time as noble Siegfried, the son of the king of the Netherlands. When Siegfried has become of age, he hears of Kriemhild's beauty and desires to make her his bride. He travels to Worms, the Burgundian capital, and is received very courteously. He helps the Burgundians in their wars and soon becomes indispensable to King Gunther, Kriemhild's brother. At the victory celebration Kriemhild shows Siegfried her special favor by descending to address him.

News of the beautiful royal princess Brunhild then reaches Gunther's court. The king decides to woo her, and Siegfried agrees to accompany him in the guise of a vassal which, of course, he is not. They reach the Isenstein ("Iron Castle") island where Brunhild rules. She accepts Gunther as her betrothed on condition that he defeat her in three games. But the three games presuppose superhuman strength, and Gunther would lose all three if the invisible Siegfried did not help him from beneath the protection of a magic cloak. Gunther owes his success to Siegfried, and shows his gratitude by betrothing his sister to his friend. But Brunhild has met Siegfried as Gunther's vassal and therefore believes the hero's marriage to her sister-in-law to be a misalliance. She keeps Gunther away from the bridal bed during their wedding night. Gunther in his desperation turns to Siegfried who again uses his magic cloak and invisibly tames Brunhild. Afterward Siegfried entrusts his secret to Kriemhild with whom he soon leaves for home.

Several years pass before Gunther yields to Brunhild's repeated requests to invite the so-called vassal to Worms. Brunhild attempts to treat Kriemhild as her inferior, whereupon Kriemhild feels insulted and publicly calls Brunhild Siegfried's mistress. Brunhild is insulted even more deeply and decides to get her revenge. She calls upon Gunther's vassal Hagen von Tronje who promises to kill Siegfried, and she persuades Gunther to give his assent. Hagen approaches Kriemhild in the guise of a friend, and induces her to make known to him her husband's vulnerable spot. For Siegfried once killed a dragon and has made himself invulnerable by bathing in the dragon's blood; yet a linden leaf fell between his shoulder blades, causing one spot not to become protected by the horny cover, and it is that spot that Hagen asks Kriemhild to point out to him. He completes his malicious design by inducing Siegfried to race him to a lonely fountain in the forest and by robbing him of his arms while he bends down to drink. Finally Hagen throws his javelin at the marked spot on Siegfried's shoulder and thus murders the hero.

When Kriemhild hears about Hagen's deed, she immediately longs for revenge. But she cannot yet achieve her design and spends years in mourning. Hagen is afraid of her and takes away her magical dowry in case she might use it to win friends. This dowry he throws into the Rhine. Siegfried had stolen it from the dwarfs Niblung and Schilbung, and from them it had taken the name of the Nibelungen Treasure. In the subsequent parts of the epic the name Nibelungen is applied to Gunther and Hagen with all their followers. In all probability the name originally applied only to Hagen's clan. The poet invented the dwarf story in order to explain the name and its connection with Siegfried.

At the request of her mother, Ute, Kriemhild does not return to the Netherlands and stays in Worms, mourning and biding her time. Then Etzel, the king of the Huns, sends Rüdiger von Bechlaren to her as his messenger. Etzel's first wife has died, and Rüdiger is supposed to ask Kriemhild to become Etzel's second wife. Kriemhild does not accept the proposal right away, and only gives her assent when Rüdiger swears an oath of allegiance; she suddenly realizes that she will now be able to revenge Siegfried's death.

Kriemhild is crowned queen of the Huns, but not for a moment does she give up her thoughts of revenge. When some time has passed, she invites her relatives to Etzel's court. Hagen sees through Kriemhild's designs, yet his masters decide to accept the invitation anyway. But upon Hagen's advice they go well armed.

The nearer the Burgundians (or Nibelungs as they are now called) approach the land of the Huns, the more indications they meet of their final fate. Yet determinedly they press on. At Bechlaren, Margrave Rüdiger receives them very cordially and betrothes his daughter to Gunther's brother Geiselher. It is the last festival for the Nibelungs, for Kriemhild enters upon her revenge immediately after her relatives' arrival in Etzel's castle. A few hours pass in waiting. Then, during a feast, the battle breaks out. Etzel and Kriemhild leave the hall under the protection of Dietrich von Bern, and the furious slaying continues. Finally the Huns set fire to the hall, and the heat of the conflagration becomes so unbearable that the heroes are forced to drink the blood of the dead in order to quench their thirst.

Only six hundred Nibelungs remain. More and more warriors take up the fight with them. Even Rüdiger must take part in the battle, although it is directed against his prospective in-laws; but he is not allowed to break the oath to his queen. Gunther's brother Gernot and Rüdiger kill each other. Then Dietrich von Bern commissions Hildebrand and the Amelungs to claim Rüdiger's corpse, and this leads to a fight between the Nibelungs and the Amelungs. When the chaos dies down, only Gunther and Hagen are left on the side of the Nibelungs and only Hildebrand on that of the Amelungs.

Dietrich von Bern is furious and himself takes up arms. He subdues Gunther and Hagen, makes them his prisoners, then hands them over to Kriemhild, who asks Hagen about the Nibelung Treasure. Hagen answers that he will not surrender it as long as Gunther is alive. Kriemhild has Gunther beheaded, but still Hagen refuses to reveal his secret. Then Kriemhild cuts off Hagen's head with her own hands. Hildebrand cannot bear to see a hero killed by a woman. He slays Kriemhild, and that is the end of the story.

Our bald recapitulation of the *Nibelungenlied* may not have given an idea of its greatness. The epic reflects the heroic spirit of the Germanic migrations, although in Christian and courtly disguise. The lodestar of the principal characters is personal loyalty, loyalty of the wife to the husband, of the vassal to the lord, of the friend to the friend. They do not follow any impersonal principle; once these heroes have given their word, they blindly keep it under all circumstances and cannot be deterred by anything from executing their plans. To be sure, this unwavering personal loyalty is primitive. These heroes do not tolerate any insult, and fight at the least provocation. They know only Yes or No, and are unaware of any subtle transitions between consent and refusal. In a more sophisticated era Siegfried would have refrained from supporting Gunther during his wedding night in such a dubious way; nay, Gunther would not have asked him for help. In a more discerning age Hagen would have refrained from such a brutal betrayal; perhaps he would have fulfilled his feudal obligations toward Brunhild by means of an open duel. In more civilized times Kriemhild would have slaked her thirst for revenge less immoderately, and would not have destroyed a whole army including all her relatives.

The heroes of the *Nibelungenlied* are strong individuals who consistently follow their decisions and despise compromise and hesitation. The Burgundians do not turn home again when the warnings multiply. They keep their promises and take up the challenge with grim determination. Their supreme law is faithfulness to themselves.

To be sure, this faithful consistency runs against ever-changing reality. The conflict is insoluble and therefore truly tragic. The tragic mood of the *Nibelungenlied* is unmistakable. It does not give us a wishful picture of an ideal life as we find it in the romance of *Parzival*. It depicts the real world where the ideal and the real fight an eternal battle. From the first to the last stanzas of the epic the conviction is repeatedly expressed that love at last ends in suffering. Siegfried expects to gain Kriemhild by helping Gunther against Brunhild; in reality he prepares for his death. Kriemhild hopes to protect Siegfried by revealing his one vulnerable spot to Hagen; in reality she makes possible the execution of her enemy's designs. The Burgundians keep their promise to visit Etzel; in reality they move to their destruction. The world of the *Nibelungenlied* is a world of continuous conflict between hero and reality, conflict without solution and conflict for its own sake.

Of course, the *Nibelungenlied* contains numerous Christian details, since it was composed at the beginning of the thirteenth century. But the basic thought is not Christian. These heroes do not expect that the riddles of the present world will be solved in the great Beyond or that an eternal reward in Heaven will repay the faithful knight for his loyalty; here the world has no symbolic meaning, and life and battle are ends in themselves. Magic forces play quite an important role.

Similar things can be said about the epic's relation to courtly society. The heroes fulfill its demands externally but do not understand its spirit. Brunhild is an arrogant hoyden, Kriemhild becomes an avenging fury, and both would be impossible as objects of veneration for a minnesinger. Finer erotic emotions are more often implied than expressed. This strangely contrasts with the richness of the military vocabulary and the cruel detail of the battle scenes. The ruthless Hagen is an exemplary hero of the old order totally different from Rüdiger, who embodies the spirit of courtly society.

Even in its own century the *Nibelungenlied* represented an old-fashioned attitude. Yet many knights of the thirteenth century must have shared or appreciated it. The popularity of the story is attested by the many attempts to give form to the material and by the many manuscripts that have come down to us, of which the St. Gallen manuscript is the best. Even after the completion of the Middle High German epic we meet with new versions of the Nibelungen material in Scandinavia and in Germany, and it was a long time before the legend was relegated to the limbo where it remained until the eighteenth century.

Besides the *Nibelungenlied*, Middle High German literature also comprises other epics the material of which goes back to the time of the

The Renewal of Germanic Traditions

Germanic migrations. But none of the other epics can compare with the *Nibelungenlied* in regard to poetic form, and most of them are of value only as sources of German folklore.

At the end of the twelfth century Theodoric the Great, the founder of the Ostrogoth kingdom, became the central figure of an epic which we no longer possess. His name in the epic was Dietrich von Bern, the name also given to him in the *Nibelungenlied*. His legend likewise wandered to the Germanic north where in the thirteenth century we find the *Thidrekssaga*. In Germany itself we later find a number of smaller epics based on this legend, epics such as *Dietrichs Flucht* ("Dietrich's Flight"), *Die Rabenschlacht* ("The Battle of Ravenna"), *Der Rosengarten* ("The Rose Garden"), *König Laurin* ("King Laurin"). As works of poetry they represent a level no higher than the pre-courtly romances of adventure in the manner of *König Rother*.

No High German versions have come down to us of the legends of Wieland, the master smith, and of Ermanarich, the last king of the Goths. Still, they continued as part of the national tradition like the legend of Walther the Strong. We did meet it in the Latin *Waltharilied*, and we find it again in Middle High German fragments which were part of a longer epic.

The legend of Wolfdietrich leads us back to the beginnings of the kingdom of the Franks. With it was soon combined the Low German Ornid legend which contained many fairy-tale elements. A summarizing epic has not come down to us, but we possess several versions of the two separate parts. This material continued to appeal to popular taste and finally became a part of the later *Heldenbuch* ("Book of Heroes").

The *Nibelungenlied* must largely be interpreted as a monument to Germanic attitudes predating the thirteenth century. Its younger and less successful literary rival, the *Kudrunlied*, must be characterized as an interesting attempt to rework some of the old materials in the new Christian spirit of the thirteenth century.

The *Kudrunlied* is written in a stanza obviously derived from the *Nibelungenlied* stanza, and also in other respects was influenced by the older epic. But it went new and independent ways in its interpretation of traditional east and north German stories. It has come down to us in only one version, a very modern copy written shortly after 1500 at the command of the romantic Emperor Maximilian. From this main source and a few minor allusions we can reconstruct the Bavarian-Austrian *Kudrunlied* of about 1240.

It centers around a noble woman who through long years has to suffer a cruel fate, but bears it with Christian fortitude and conquers it by charity. In order to make Kudrun better understood, the unknown author first tells the story of two preceding generations. The first part of the epic contains the story of Kudrun's grandfather Hagen, an almost superhuman hero of the olden times, primitive enough to be called *der wilde Hagene*. The second part relates the abduction of his fair daughter Hilde by Hetel, the king of the Hegelingen. He is pursued by his unwilling father-in-law Hagen and attacked by him on the island of Wülpensand. No doubt in the original version of the story father and son-in-law were both killed in a tragic conflict of two men equally mindful of their personal honor. In the later version Hilde interferes and establishes peace between her husband and her father.

The third part of the *Kudrunlied* contains the main story. Hilde's daughter Kudrun is wooed by three heroes and becomes betrothed to the bravest of them, Herwig of Seeland. But one of the others, Hartmut of Normandy, abducts the bride-to-be and successfully retains her against Hetel and Herwig. For many years Kudrun is kept prisoner in Normandy, and steadfastly refuses to become Hartmut's wife. Hartmut's cruel mother, Gerlind, subjects Kudrun to all kinds of humiliations in order to bend her will; but the noble princess does not yield. Finally, a new generation of fighters has grown up among the Hegelingen. They attack Hartmut's castle and free their princess. Gerlind is justly punished for her cruelty by an ignoble death. But Hartmut, who has never abused his power, is saved by Kudrun from a similar fate, and on all sides war is replaced by peace and harmony.

The story ends in no less than four marriages, in two of which friend and foe are united. A third one takes place between Kudrun's most intimate friend and an old Moorish suitor of hers, the noble heathen knight Siegfried von Mohrland; this express acknowledgment of the noble hero of another race and another creed underscores the Christian and courtly attitude of this remarkable medieval epic. We found similar ideas with Wolfram von Eschenbach and Walther von der Vogelweide. Like them, our author clearly sees this as an ideal. He approaches a fairy-tale atmosphere by a cursory treatment of geographical and chronological relations. On the other hand, he again tried to connect the story with reality by bringing in some representatives of the old, hard-fighting, and even ill-mannered type of hero; the ideas of *minne* were foreign to him. He was aware that the Christian way of life was hard and had to be attempted again and again. Perhaps he already saw it threatened by a decline in knightly chivalry.

The Renewal of Germanic Traditions

The *Kudrun* epic appeals to an urban taste by its many romantic episodes culled from fairy tales and travel stories, and by its happy ending reminding us of sentimental middle-class novels; it does not possess the tragic depth of the *Nibelungenlied*. About ten years after its completion Frederic II died, and his death presaged the decline of the mighty Hohenstaufen empire and the culture it had engendered.

The traditions of the Germanic migrations, however, were treated of down to the sixteenth century. Then they disappeared from worth-while literature, to be slowly rediscovered in the eighteenth century. In nineteenth-century romanticism they experienced an astonishing poetic revival.

CHAPTER THREE

The Parodistic and Hyberbolic Style of the Waning Middle Ages

The Waning Middle Ages

THE end of the Hohenstaufen dynasty foreshadowed the end of knighthood. In order to hold the pope in check, the Hohenstaufen emperors had consistently strengthened their Italian domains. During the time of the Interregnum, these dependencies were lost, and when Rudolf von Habsburg acceded to the throne in 1273 the strengthening of domestic power became the foremost concern of German politics. Strong expeditionary forces for the Italian dependencies were no longer needed. In 1270 the crusades also came to an end. During their time religious orders of knights had been founded, and these were now lacking a satisfactory task. The most vigorous of the religious orders, the Order of the Teutonic Knights, substituted a crusade against the heathens in East Prussia, and in 1230 began its colonization after a carefully prepared plan. This meant a political reorientation in more ways than one. The order became actively interested in domestic German policies, as it could not accomplish its task without the help of German burghers and peasants. Yet the change was a beneficial one. The worldly compeers of the Teutonic Knights in many cases could not find a worth-while task at all, and wasted their strength in petty quarrels. Armies of heavily armed knights gradually became obsolescent, and the easily movable infantry increased in importance over the years. Firearms were known from the middle of the fourteenth century.

Economic changes were also working against the landed nobility. Partly by reason of the crusades, oriental trade had been developed, and the south German cities were increasing in importance. In the German north, maritime trade was flourishing and favored the establishment of ruling trade centers. Trade stimulated manufacture, and the cities were growing. The Italian cities had developed a very useful system of money trading, and this system spread across the Alps and replaced the old methods of bartering. All this, however, robbed the landed aristocracy of some of its importance. Many knights struck back and started private wars against the rising cities. They tried to uphold their economic standing by arbitrarily levied tolls and taxes, and bitterly fought the trading caravans that had to cross their territories. Yet in doing so the knights gave up their noble ideals and became little better than highwaymen. A cynical rhymester of the thirteenth century saw fit to express knightly reasoning in the often-quoted lines:

> Rauben und Sengen,   Robbing and burning
>   das ist kein' Schand,   leads not to shame.
> Das tun die Besten   'Tis done by lords
>   von dem Land.   of honor and fame.

Nevertheless, knightly depredations could not stop the rising tide. The middle classes prospered, and the influence of the cities became ever more pronounced. Strong regional forces were set in motion, and the power of the emperors decreased continuously; they never recovered the status they had enjoyed before the Interregnum. One very important reason was the economic one. The emperors depended upon the financial good will of the new municipal powers, and that could often be bought only by the granting of special charters and privileges. Wherever favorable geographical conditions were supported by political developments, powerful cities arose which were strongly fortified by walls and gates, and were inhabited by townsmen willing to fight for their livelihood. To be sure, the very largest of these cities seldom held more than 30,000 inhabitants; yet even cities with only 10,000 inhabitants often were self-conscious and civic-minded. Almost overnight the privileges of many of these cities increased and broadened. For a time their powerful leagues conditioned German and occasionally European politics. The Hanseatic League in the north and the Swabian League in the south were not easy to cope with for territorial as well as foreign rulers. Cities such as Nuremberg and Augsburg, Strasbourg and Cologne, Magdeburg, Lübeck and Danzig prospered far into the sixteenth century.

In a similar way the Swiss territories became more independent. From the end of the thirteenth century they asserted their rights against Habsburg encroachments, and no longer followed imperial policies unconditionally. Although Swiss independence was first recognized by the Westphalian Peace Treaty of 1648, its foundations were laid at the end of the Middle Ages. Swiss civilization very early showed a special character, and its connection with general German civilization became sometimes tenuous; but it was never broken.

On the western border of the Empire the Netherlands also began to develop their own culture. The process started in the thirteenth century, but for a long time led to no political consequences. In fact, the Netherlands would continue as part of the Holy Roman Empire until 1648; for by definition this was an international order of states. After 1250 it is not always easy to draw a clear dividing line between German and Dutch culture, and some leading figures such as Erasmus of Rotterdam belong to both cultures. The disintegration of the Holy Roman Empire and its culture took a very long time.

The new cultural impetus of the waning Middle Ages was provided by the townspeople. But they were slow in developing any special class consciousness. From the beginnings they were primarily interested in their workaday tasks. Their commerce was continually threatened by wars and highway raids, and their profits had to offset the necessities of life harvested in the neighboring countryside. Famine and high prices often jeopardized their very existence. Fire could easily consume entire quarters of a city. And when there were plagues, they raged with a vengeance in the thickly populated and poorly laid-out cities of the Middle Ages. Often during the thirteenth and fourteenth centuries we hear of the "Black Death," the fearful bubonic plague.

Life under such circumstances was a continuous hazard. It had to be handled roughly and grasped with tight fists. No wonder that many townsmen became worldly and sensuous, that they fought feverishly for their due share in the city's common business and majesty. The lower classes of the cities scoffed at mere privileges of birth and murmured against the patricians who enriched themselves at the expense of their neighbors. In the fourteenth century battles arose between the poorer tradesmen and the few influential families. The usual outcome was a certain democratization of city government, and a certain vulgarization of speech, manners, and dress. The knightly ideal of courtesy was hardly known to these rising tradesmen.

At the same time the uncertainties of life were so great that one's thoughts could not long be deflected from the risks of death and of judgment in the Hereafter. Questions as to the value of life and the proper way to Heaven continued to occupy the minds of most city people. The period of lusty sensuality and of rude vulgarity was also a period of deep religious searching. Large crowds flocked to the sermons of itinerant preachers, and on every road groups of pilgrims could be seen doing penance or accumulating merits against religious rainy days. Despite all social change, German civilization continued as a Christian civilization.

The cathedral rather than the market square with its proud city hall was the center around which German city life revolved. Germany's great Gothic church buildings were begun in the thirteenth and fourteenth centuries. The Gothic style had originated in France as a fitting expression of a deeply spiritual conception of God. The better Christianity was understood, the less satisfactory appeared the image of God as a stern judge and a heavenly ruler whose earthly counterparts were the emperor and the pope. The God of Christianity was more properly described as loving Father and radiant Spirit. The Romanesque house of God resembled a courthouse or a royal hall, and by about 1150 it no longer seemed adequate to French architects. In St. Denis and Paris (Notre-Dame), in Reims and Amiens it was replaced by cathedrals emphasizing the spiritual nature of God. Slowly the new style was spreading over Europe. In Germany its victory was assured about 1250. Here, as in the rest of Europe, Gothic style underwent certain changes; the French cathedrals never gave such disproportional emphasis to the steeple as is found in some German churches. But on the whole, the features common to French and German Gothic buildings do not allow us to set them too far apart. Most German exaggerations derive from the deep disturbance of the period. The German Gothic cathedrals in many cases are monuments to escape from reality, to fear of the world, and to fervent longing for Heaven. These lofty giants of stone towered over the modest human dwellings at their feet in the same sense as thoughts of the Hereafter dominated the souls of the people who built them. The silhouettes of Cologne, of Freiburg, of

The Parodistic and Hyperbolic Style

Strasbourg, of Lübeck, with their huge church structures, have asserted the townsmen's spirit to this very day. In these Gothic churches all the vertical lines are emphasized as if everything were reaching for Heaven. The heavy stone masses of Romanesque architecture have been dissolved into ornamental carvings and latticework, the weighty walls have been broken by tall, colorful glass windows. Sculptures and paintings expressing the same spirit are everywhere, and at hours of worship, Latin choir hymns echoed through the Gothic spaces and surged to the heavens.

Compared with the fine arts of the period, its literature did not culminate in monuments of the same lasting value. It was short of eminent names and great works, but it reflected the inner contradictions of the age just as truly.

In the twelfth century the ideals of courtly poetry had appeared at least attainable, and were believed in by the great number of knights. Now these values had become questionable. The contrast between the knights of poetry and the knights of real life was often marked, and the contrast between knightly idealism and middle-class materialism was certainly profound. Courtly poetry for a long time was still effective as a model and an inspiration. Yet it could not simply be continued or slavishly imitated. One could either take its remoteness from real life for granted and thus interpret it in a romantic way; one could uphold it as a mirror to a depraved age and interpret it in a satiric vein; or one could feel it waxing pale before the onrush of coarse but vigorous reality, and interpret it realistically. All these attitudes were adopted, and in all three ways the tradition changed. Seen from the point of view of the knights, the middle classes were simply debasing the forms of courtly poetry by taking them over. The new poets did not possess the aristocratic feeling for style and moderation. Their verses grew out of bounds, their language became vulgar and favored dialect expressions. The composition of new epics became disjointed and grotesque; accumulations of undigested and unrelated material annoyingly interrupted the progress of the narration. At the end of the age, metrical forms showed a tendency to disappear altogether. They were often replaced by German prose which now gradually became more voluminous and important.

In some aspects certainly the new literature was markedly realistic and materialistic. The comic plays performed by townsmen were full of coarseness and sexuality. Even their religious plays were interspersed with slapstick humor and with cruel torture scenes. And an unabashed worldliness occasionally expressed itself in verses such as the following:

The Waning Middle Ages

Gott geb' ihm ein verdorben	*May God spoil*
Jahr	*his whole yearly crop*
Der mich macht zu einer	*For him who made*
Nunnen	*me take the vows*
Und mir den schwarzen	*And gave me the black*
Mantel gab,	*robe to wear*
Den weissen Rock darunten!	*Over white skirt and blouse.*

However, this was not the only emotion of the period. For in spite of all the inroads of materialism and realism, the traditional ideals were by no means given up. The adaptation of knightly modes of thinking by the rising middle classes was a sincere and serious process. Like the knights, the middle classes also wanted to lead a Christian life. Christian virtues were emphasized again and again in middle-class literature, and problems of everyday morality occupied many of the best minds. This was the time of the great religious plays and of popular church hymns, this was the time of the German mystics who in their prose writings took up the cudgels against the older scholastic philosophers. In these, one often finds a preoccupation with meaning and sense to the exclusion of aesthetic considerations. Religious and theological change seems to predominate, and the form of literature therefore can no longer be harmonious or uniform. Its very essence demanded a different style. Thus originated the style of parody and hyperbole.

As in all times of profound change, the language of the people was changing too. The German dialects began to take on the New High German color, and this has therefore been termed the period of Early New High German. In place of the Middle High German long vowels *î, û, iu* (in *wîn, hûs, liute*) we find the New High German diphthongs *ei, au, eu* (*Wein, Haus, Leute*), and the stem syllables are prolonged. In the beginning, literature was exclusively dialectal. But toward the end of the period, tendencies toward a common written language began to appear, and there developed a certain unifying trend which was to be consummated through the efforts of Martin Luther.

Ideal and Reality

IT WAS natural for the rising middle classes to take over the literature of the nobility. Yet it was also natural for them to select from this literature what they liked best, and to adapt the courtly stories to the changed conditions of the time. The townspeople had little understanding for the high ideals presented in the best courtly epics. They could only appreciate the more primitive adventures of an earlier literary period. Thus the genuine courtly literature was bypassed in favor of more ancient stories centering around heroes of an earlier type. Their rough-and-ready swordsmen were more similar to the actual knights of the fourteenth and fifteenth centuries. The adventures of *Herzog Ernst* ("Duke Ernest") were written up again, and the legends about Charlemagne and his burly warriors were retold for the delight of knightly and middle-class readers. They also liked the Arthurian stories for their entertainment value, and as when other courtly material found new versions, the accent was put on the plot and discussions of moral behavior were played down. Colorful episodes were added to many courtly epics, and condensed versions presented the main events for easier reading.

Treatments of indigenous material achieved great popularity for similar reasons. Few of the traditional stories had been presented in courtly versions as had the *Nibelungenlied*, although those that had were diligently copied for the benefit of knightly and middle-class readers alike. But the more primitive stories were also rediscovered and found worthy of being retold. The story of Hildebrand's homecoming was revived and transformed in a grotesque manner. Where the ancient *Hildebrandslied* of Germanic times had a tragic ending, its thirteenth-century counterpart showed Hildebrand giving a sound beating to his brazen offspring and bringing the young man home to the maternal nest. Similarly, the stories of Siegfried's youth which had found little favor with the poet of the *Nibelungenlied* were now taken up again, and were told in the *Lied vom Hürnen Seyfrid* ("Lay of the Horny-skinned Seyfrid"). Siegfried here was distorted into a legendary superman. Perhaps even readers of the fourteenth century found his exploits comical.

64]

Ideal and Reality

Hyperbole also characterized many of the stories told about the Christian saints, and the number of such stories increased in the second half of the thirteenth century. Legends about the Virgin Mary became ever more current.

About 1300 the great *Passional* was composed, a work of no less than 100,000 verses of superior craftsmanship. It treated stories from the New Testament and legends of the Christian saints. A similar work, perhaps written by the same author, was the *Väterbuch* ("The Book of the Church Fathers") which related the life of hermits at the beginning of the Christian era. Some of the later treatments of religious legends were written for the entertainment of the masses who relished the miraculous.

The age was also characterized by its numerous chronicles. Rhymed chronicles were favored by the knights of the Teutonic Order who were still upholding the old virtues, and whose literary taste was more conservative. Prose chronicles in German appeared in greater number toward the end of the period. Naturally the masses of the people were unable to read either prose or verse chronicles. But they were informed of current events by short songs. Such songs have come down to us from these centuries in considerable numbers. An especially realistic flavor characterizes the Swiss songs which tell of the fight of the Swiss people against their Habsburg masters and the desire of the Swiss to achieve independence.

Not all the writers of the period allowed themselves to be swept along by the desire for greater realism and for better entertainment. The best minds preserved a feeling for the high ideals of the past and continued to look at earthly life as a poor substitute for the heavenly joys that came after the world. They could not help contrasting reality with the purity of the ideal and treating it satirically. An early example of such satirical treatment was the story *Meier Helmbrecht* ("Peasant Helmbrecht") by the itinerant poet Wernher der Gartenaere (the Gardener); it was written between 1270 and 1282. The Helmbrecht of the story is the son of a liegeman farmer who vaults beyond his social station and achieves brief glory as a robber knight. The background of this story is the wild time of the Interregnum. Wernher has treated his story in a lively style full of condescending humor.

Another early satire was directed against sly and thievish priests, and was written by a vagrant poet called *"Stricker"* ("Ropemaker"). In his *Pfaff Amis* ("Amis the Priest") he combined twelve amusing tales in every one of which the clerical rogue got the better of the gullible laymen. Some of these stories were used again in a book about the priest from Kalenberg (*Der Pfarrer von Kalenberg*).

The most characteristic of all the mock-heroic treatments and social satires was Heinrich Wittenweiler's *Ring* which was written before 1453. The form of his story represents a complete breakdown of stylistic conventions; it mixes didactic sermonizing with fluent story-telling, and fairy-tale exploits with events from real life, so that it is hard to find it a literary classification. Yet when one looks at the contents, one must give Wittenweiler credit for his ambition to let his contemporaries see their reflection in a satirical mirror. In the manner of *Meier Helmbrecht*, we become acquainted with uneducated peasants whose highest ambition is the imitation of knightly behavior. Their so-called tourneys are described with satirical exaggeration; a knitted muzzle must serve as a helmet, and an old tub as an escutcheon. Then follows the love episode between the hero, Bertschi Triefnas ("Bertschi Nosedrip") and the peasant girl Metzli Rürenzump ("Metzli Trollop"). Of course, their *minne* is a coarsely sexual affair, followed by a wedding feast which consists for the most part of excessive eating and drinking, and culminates in a fight. The villagers of Bertschi's native Lappenhausen ("Ragham") clash with the people of Nissingen ("Lousytown") who have been invited. Neither party can win alone, and thus they summon auxiliaries; even figures from the fairy tales and the knightly romances take part in the bloodcurdling battle. In the end Lappenhausen is destroyed, and Bertschi flees to become a hermit.

In spite of its realistic detail the *Ring* turns out to be a hyperbolic allegory. In the fortunes of Bertschi and Bertschi's village Heinrich Wittenweiler shows us the ways of the world and reminds us of the only fitting preparation for Heaven, the renunciation of worldly pleasures. He frequently pauses to sermonize about the values of married life, about proper behavior, about the doctrines of the Christian religion. The *Ring* is more than a satire on peasant vulgarity. It is a serious call for reform and a plea for Christian life addressed to foolish contemporaries.

Similar attempts to uphold Christian ideals in a worldly society were made by the didactic poets of the fourteenth century who found a very appreciative public. Hadamar von Laber wrote *Die Jagd* ("The Chase," about 1340), a strange allegorical piece comparing love to a chase. More general was the theme of *Des Teufels Netz* ("The Devil's Net," between 1415 and 1418) where all social classes were taken to account for their sins. There were also collections of proverbs in prose and in rhyme. And there were descriptive enumerations of all kinds of useful knowledge where the rhyme was little more than a help for memorization. Such *Priamels* ("Preambles") were especially written by Nuremberg poets like Hans Rosenplüt ("Rosebud") and Hans Folz. Their mentality was narrowly practical and crudely earthy. Hans Folz specialized in vulgarities and improprieties which a modern sophisticate would find distasteful; his contemporaries raised no particular objection.

A special niche was occupied by the animal fable. It derived from ancient Greek and oriental models, but in Germany it found an interesting development. In tenth-century literature we come across the *Ecbasis captivi* in which clerics are described in animal guise. In later centuries also there was no lack of animal narratives. About 1350 Ulrich Boner's *Edelstein* ("The Jewel") was a popular collection. And in 1498 there came the Low German animal story *Reynke de Vos* ("Reynard the Fox"), the culmination of a long tradition represented by earlier French and German examples. Animal stories had always been popular in Lower Germany, and now the definitive story was composed by an unknown author residing at Lübeck. *Reynke de Vos* was no mere repetition or superficial adaptation. The author added moralizations of his own (so-called *Glossen*) at the end of each chapter, which were written in prose and thus contrasted with the rest of the epic which had been put into verse. These moral remarks betray a keen and independent mind, but find little favor with modern readers. Instead we admire the character types of his story, which combine a wonderful mixture of human and animal traits; and we are fascinated by the narrative events themselves. Reynard is a shrewd and ruthless diplomat and politician who partly circumvents, partly liquidates his opponents, and climbs the political ladder until he becomes the favored prime minister of King Noble, the lion. If the epic had been written in another language but Low German, it would have achieved earlier fame. It remained for Goethe to discover its greatness and to save it for international recognition through his version in High German hexameters (1794). Goethe aptly called *Reynke de Vos* an "unholy Bible of the world" where the greatest rewards are not always reserved for the worthy but often go to the cheat and the callous brute.

Also at the end of the period belongs another famous parody of late medieval life which depicts life as a paradise for simpletons. This was *Das Narrenschiff* ("The Ship of Fools," 1494). It was written by the Strasbourg citizen Sebastian Brant, and appraised the world in thoroughly sceptical terms. Brant was a learned writer who was acquainted with the new Italian Humanism, but he did not side with the moderns of his time who to him appeared to take life too lightly. He was hardly amused by the foolish behavior of his contemporaries but looked upon it with a jaundiced eye. He knew he could not change them, but he also knew that they needed to be told the plain, unadorned truth. Thus he lambasted the various species of contemporary fools each with a sermon in rhymed couplets. The first sermon of his book he addressed to pedantic scholars who thought that they could learn about life from books. In the following sermons Brant satirized all other contemporary faults whether they were of a spiritual or a material nature, and whether they emanated from physical causes or moral depravity. He held up the mirror to the intemperate eating and drinking habits of his time. He excoriated lazy monks for their cupidity, and newfangled philosophers for their heresy. He praised the old-fashioned virtues of temperance and continence, simplicity and industry. And he ardently supported the efforts of the German emperors to uphold the Christian glory of the Roman Empire. Brant wanted all contemporary foolishness to be put to rout. His idea was to pack all fools into the hold of a big ship and to give them the bum's rush to the land of "Narragonia." But the idea was not well executed, and almost floundered when Brant merely added one rhymed sermon to another.

However, this did not seriously hamper the popularity of the book, which was reprinted many times by authorized as well as pirate presses, and was translated into many languages. Brant was not the only writer of his time to whom life appeared as a madhouse overrun by all kinds of lunatics. His book created a tradition, and was much taken up and imitated more or less successfully. The most artistic among Brant's imitators was the outspoken Franciscan friar Thomas Murner (1475–1537).

Finally, let us take a look at the lyric poetry of the fourteenth and fifteenth centuries. During this period the songs of the courtly period were diligently collected and imitated by the burghers. But the courtly style was no longer alive. The division between ideal and reality became greater and greater. Even knightly poets such as Hugo von Montfort and Oswald von Wolkenstein (d. 1445) paid only lip service to the high aspirations of traditional Minnesong. In Oswald's poetry appeared an emphasis on personal and sensual experience, and also upon learned knowledge which in former periods one would have sought in vain. Neither of these knightly poets had mastered the courtly forms.

Middle-class poets who imitated the traditional manner often stressed didactic and moral elements, thus testifying indirectly to the breakdown of the conventions. Or they slavishly repeated the themes and forms of the older poetry, following narrow rules and patterns which they had derived from its study. These models were later taken over by the *Meistersinger* or "mastersingers," the poetic guilds which developed from the church choirs of the prospering cities. Clerics interested in embellishing the church services trained singers from the middle classes in hymn singing, and also introduced them to the literary style and musical forms of courtly poetry, although naturally the content of the hymns was exclusively theological.

Gradually thereafter the choral societies loosened their connection with the churches, and developed independently into so-called "schools." About 1300 the first of these schools arose in the city of Mainz, and the poets Heinrich of Meissen, called Frauenlob ("Glorifier of Our Lady," d. 1318) and Barthel Regenbogen belonged to it; they anticipated the style of the later mastersingers in their boasting of book knowledge, their tedious moralizing, and their preoccupation with intricate verse arrangements. Subsequent schools were established at Worms, Augsburg, Strasbourg, Nuremberg, Ulm, and other South German cities. Later schools developed in Eastern Germany, but Northern Germany did not take part in the movement.

The membership of these schools was primarily recruited from the tradespeople. They upheld and continued the courtly tradition, but strangely standardized it. From 1350 to 1480 only the *Töne* (i.e. rhyme schemes and melodies) of twelve so-called ancient masters of the Middle High German period were imitated. In the fifteenth century the tradition was codified into the rigid rules of the *Tabulatur* ("Code"). All the verses were meant to be sung, and the poets did not conceive of them as rhythmic in their own right; the syllables were counted. The strict observation of the rules was watched by special *Merker* or critics who were always present at the *Singschulen* ("church contests") as the public performances in the churches were called. Private gatherings of the singers took place in taverns and were called *Zechsingen* ("drinking recitals"); here, greater allowance was made for deviations and for levity, in language as well as theme. The townsmen had little education, and considered obscenities and coarse language as not particularly immoral. However, in spite of all their concessions to public taste the schools of the mastersingers were rather esoteric societies about whom even their social equals knew little. In later years, the mastersinger schools prohibited the publication of their jealously guarded literary treasures.

A rigidly enforced system of pedantic rules was not suited to the development of original poetry, but one should not underestimate the importance of the mastersingers. Under unfavorable conditions they upheld a great tradition and laid the groundwork for the better education of the rising middle classes. Although these classes excelled in literature only much later, they were, in their limited way, interested in cultural affairs. The generally favorable picture presented by Wagner's opera *Die Meistersinger von Nürnberg* agrees with the verdict of history.

Another derivative from the courtly tradition is represented by the so-called folk songs of the time. Romantic scholarship was wont to describe them as anonymous songs produced by a mysterious popular or national "soul." Yet we are now aware that they were composed by individuals even though their names remained largely unknown. To be sure, these individuals were of average character and of little originality or inventiveness; otherwise their productions would never have found favor among the masses. In the course of adoption by the public at large, these folk songs often lost their last trace of originality and underwent a continuous process of simplification and standardization.

The folk songs of the fourteenth and fifteenth centuries took over the tradition of courtly lyrics; their simpler forms, their situations, and even the personalities of certain minnesingers appear again and again. Of course, people selected the songs they could most easily understand and most easily sing. The typical folk song is concrete in its details, a few words sufficing to state the situation, which is always typical and general.

> *Dort hoch auf jenem Berge*
> *da geht ein Mühlenrad,*
> *das mahlet nichts denn Liebe*
> *die Nacht bis an den Tag.*
>
> *Die Mühle ist zerbrochen,*
> *die Liebe hat ein End;*

so gesegen dich Gott, meins Feinslieb,
jetzt fahr ich ins Elend.

*

High upon yonder mountain
A millwheel goes around,
By which from night till morning
True love is ever ground.

The wheelhouse now is broken,
Our love has reached its end;
God bless you, my fine sweetheart,
I go to another land.

Many folk songs are love songs. We also have songs about robber knights and highwaymen, about legendary heroes and about courtly poets who became legendary figures, e.g., Tannhäuser. Then we have gay feasting and drinking songs, in which the massive sensuousness of the period has found unmistakable expression:

Steck an die schweinen Braten,
dazu die Hühner jung;
darauf mag uns geraten
ein frischer, freier Trunk.

ruck her, du schönes Weib!
du erfreust mirs Herz im Leib,
wohl in dem Rosengarten
dem Schlemmer sein Zeit vertreih!

*

Let's put the dainty chicken,
The pork roast on the spit,
And then bring in cool liquids
And let us drink a bit.

Move up, my pretty lass!
Under roses in the grass
Gladden the heart in my body,
The feast time with me pass!

[71

Such simple outbursts of primitive lustfulness reveal the realistic tendencies of the age. Its religious yearnings were expressed in a different form. Spiritual songs too were governed by the example of Minnesong. Some of them sprang up spontaneously, while others, the so-called *Kontrafakturen*, arose as labored imitations of worldly songs. The following *Kontrafaktur* is an example:

Es kommt ein Schiff, geladen
bis an seinn höchsten Bord;
es trägt Gotts Sohn voll Gnaden,
des Vaters ewigs Wort.

Das Schiff geht still im Triebe,
es trägt ein teure Last;
der Segel ist die Liebe,
der heilge Geist der Mast.

*

There comes a ship well laden
Up to its highest board;
God's son and grace it carries,
The Bible's precious hoard.

The ship is calmly sailing,
It bears a noble host:
Love in the sails is blowing,
The mast is the Holy Ghost.

The Religious Plays

IT WOULD be taking a one-sided view to dismiss the entire literature of the rising middle classes as imitation or secondhand. Somehow the new classes were developing new forms of their own, and they cultivated vast fields of literature which in the courtly period had found but scant representation and had not been influenced by the prevailing style.

The Religious Plays

It was in the fourteenth and fifteenth centuries that the religious plays reached their fullest development. The early plays had originated as a part of the church service on high holidays and were of course written in Latin, the official language of the service. Now the plays were translated into German or were already conceived in German, thus being made understandable to a larger audience. The Germanization of these plays also meant a general disassociation from the church. Another literary genre became free of immediate priestly supervision.

As early as the thirteenth century we find Latin plays interspersed with German scenes, and occasionally a complete German drama. Now the plays, gradually growing independent of the Church, became great shows for the edification of the urban masses. The public life of the age entered the religious plays in a broad stream. In the Easter plays the conversation of the sentinels at Christ's tomb, the devil scenes, the "shopping trip" of Mary and Magdalene to the market, the apostles' race to the Holy Grave, were extended into small realistic "comedies." The Nativity plays were utilized for intimate descriptions of the Holy Family. And finally the whole life of Christ was unfolded in elaborate Passion plays which often required two or three days for their performance.

The market place where the plays were staged represented the medieval universe, and therefore was divided into the three areas of Heaven, Earth, and Hell. In addition it had to represent the symbolical character of all worldly events, and thus needed action that went on nearly simultaneously in the three areas. There was no action on Earth that did not correspond to an action in Heaven or Hell and did not lead to consequences in Heaven or Hell. And since worldly history was but a symbol of the transcendental history of salvation, both geographical relationships and the chronological sequence were replaced by the transcendental sequence and the symbolical meaning. One can see this principle most clearly at work in the so-called prefigurations where historical events are used as allegories for transcendental truths, e.g., when Moses' erection of a brazen serpent is represented as an allegory of Christ's crucifixion, or when Jonah's salvation from the whale is used to symbolize the Resurrection. Psychological causation was less important than transcendental relationship.

In becoming more secular, the plays changed their inner structure. While they were in Latin, they still followed a clear plan according to the place they had in the divine service. Now the number of scenes became more or less arbitrary. Everything must be translated into action for the benefit of the masses who liked shows and lacked reading ability. Every small detail was carefully worked out in circumstantial speeches. Weeks in advance, the whole town was preoccupied with the performance of the plays. The performance itself took place in the market square and moved around on it like a pageant. Sometimes between three hundred and four hundred persons were involved in such a play. Before and after the plays there were religious services, so that nobody should forget their religious significance.

However, significance and meaning were brought out in such a way as to appeal to the taste of the masses. They wanted to experience the frightfulness of hellish punishment through vivid representations. They wanted to weep with St. Mary when she mourned for her son. So the dramatic style became hyperbolic. It was partly through these plays that the German masses took personal possession of the Christian dogma which up to that time had been accessible only to the upper strata of society. In spite of all their crude realistic details, these plays acquainted the people with the spiritual philosophy of the age; although summary and no longer uniform and consistent, they still reflected the Christian view of the world.

Significant developments beyond the Passion plays likewise foreshadowed the gradual secularization of the medieval drama. Some plays treated subjects which bore no immediate relation to Christ's act of redemption. About 1300 a play was performed about the ten wise and the ten foolish virgins of the New Testament (cf. St. Matthew, 25, 7–13). Then came a legendary play about Theophilus who sold himself to the devil and then became converted. There also was a play about an arrogant female who managed to become pope until her deception was found out. To us moderns the plots of such plays sometimes appear more dramatic than those of the spiritual plays proper. Perhaps this can be explained by the fact that in each of these cases we are dealing with works by individual authors, although their names we do not know. The elaborate Passion plays were usually written by several collaborators who often copied each other unscrupulously. This is why dramatic unity, as contrasted with theological unity, is seldom found in these plays.

To be sure, the contemporary audiences had no sense of real tragedy. The wailing of the souls tortured by the devil appeared either comical or deterrent, but nobody pitied the victims of Hell. Even Christ's own Passion was not interpreted in a tragic light; for it was only through the misery suffered by Him that the joyous possibility of salvation came about.

Besides the religious drama the age was also acquainted with secular plays. Most of them were comedies of a primitive type which can only be understood in relation to their pagan origins. Old fertility rites and magic that the Church had not succeeded in suppressing were re-enacted during Shrovetide as a sort of last fling before the arrival of Lent. Yet the original meaning of the rites was no longer clear, and frank obscenity and filth became the order of the day. In some cases the vulgarity defied description, and the municipal councils of those by no means squeamish times had repeated reason for interference.

In Nuremberg these plays originally consisted of masquerades and small pageants; one mummer after the other recited and repeated his standing jokes. Gradually some action evolved. Hans Rosenplüt and Hans Folz constructed many such plays. Rosenplüt could also deal with political subjects, but obscene subjects delighted his audiences most. Hans Folz was less adroit as a playwright, though he knew how to draw folk scenes realistically and humorously. He also wrote violent scenes against the Jews whom his contemporaries so often persecuted with barbaric brutality.

Occasionally heroic legends and Arthurian tales were put into dramatic form, and popular narratives with a merry ending can also be found among these secular plays. Some of them became didactic and tried to enlighten the audiences on controversial subjects. Court scenes, too, were frequent. Few such plays besides those from Nuremberg have come down to us. After 1430 we hear of some Lübeck plays, although no example has been preserved. It is to be assumed that these mundane entertainments enjoyed a far greater vogue than the extant examples allow us to realize.

The Development of German Prose

THE restless, contradictory mind of the period was reflected not only in the changed forms of courtly literature and the German versions of the old liturgical dramas. It also began to create a new form of literature which was livelier and corresponded more to the realistic aspirations of the rising middle classes.

From the end of the courtly period the number of German prose works gradually increased and began to assume importance. To be sure, the great body of learned and professional literature still employed Latin, and it was impossible for a theologian or a philosopher, a physician or an advocate to dispense with classical education. But more and more German laws were codified, and German historians slowly began to give up the embellishment of rhyme. About 1300 we find the first translation of a French prose romance.

Naturally, the main share of German prose writing fell to the clerics, for they were the class best trained for writing. Even on modern readers the prose sermons of Berthold von Regensburg can make a strong impression. This Franciscan itinerant priest was a powerful advocate of penitence in an age given to worldly amusements following the example of courtly society. He addressed himself to an audience that felt strongly attracted by the world of reality, but was still troubled by its conscience and fervently longed for life in the Hereafter.

During the fourteenth and fifteenth centuries the realm of prose was extended to more subjects. Works on travel came to be written, and scientific writings made their appearance in the vernacular. German historical works, German legal pamphlets, and German sermons multiplied. Last but not least, the number of German prose romances increased by leaps and bounds. They were translated from foreign originals or were newly created by the discontinuance of old romances in rhymed form. Here too, subjects reflecting more primitive conditions were favored; they suited the raw taste of the time better than the chivalrous novels of the Arthurian cycle. This taste was not restricted to the middle classes. Courtly circles also could no longer resist the trend toward prose. Highborn ladies were the first writers who endeavored to translate and revise the prose romances which in France had existed since the thirteenth century.

Not only did the prose writings increase in number, they also improved in style. Their rhythms became smoother, and their syntax more adroit. This was especially noticeable in the prose of the German mystics who were important representatives of this age. It was their writings that, next to the religious plays, achieved Christianization of the broad masses who clamored for higher education after the end of the thirteenth century. The Latin writings of the scholastics were unable to give to the masses what they wanted. These learned men had summarized the theological doctrines of the Church in the second half of the thirteenth century. They had been introduced to Aristotelian philosophy by Arabian thinkers, and under this influence had erected imposing dogmatic structures. After some philosophical struggles the German Dominican Albertus Magnus and his great Italian disciple St. Thomas Aquinas (1225?–1274) had put the intellectual school of scholasticism into power. Faith was interpreted as an act of reasoning. Yet not all human beings were able to apply reason in the same degree, and thus simple untutored faith was not valued very highly.

The scholastics were not well equipped for the everyday tasks of the ministry, and their theological doctrines meant little for the laymen who were pondering the salvation of their souls. Scholasticism therefore found a complement in mysticism. In contrast to the scholastic divines with their theoretical interests the mystic thinkers were anxious to find a practical guide to salvation. They were concerned with the meaning of faith, and found it in pure contemplation. The word "mysticism" is derived from the Greek verb μύω (*myo*, I close my eyes) and denotes a contemplative union of the soul with God. This union could not be achieved by intellectual means, and was described as a kind of spiritual love in analogy to earthly love. The doctrines of theology became unessential; personal feeling or personal activity was what counted. The mystic movement of the age can be interpreted as a spiritual counterpart of its sensualism in material life.

Mystic thought satisfied the laymen, and the writings of the mystic thinkers found a wide public. They were no longer written in the language of the Church, and they did not require pastoral interpretation. Mysticism therefore became a lay movement, and helped to increase the efficacy of the popular religious dramas. Mysticism also did not stress church attendance but emphasized the importance of daily Christian living; it therefore exercised great influence over the workaday world of the period, and made the individual believer less dependent on the Church.

Mystic thought had of course always been present in Christianity. But during the centuries of missionary work and ecclesiastical organization it had been obscured by political and legalistic ideas. The spiritual core of Christianity had to be rediscovered again and again. Hugh of Saint Victor, the son of a Saxon count, described contemplation as the essence of piety. He as well as his great French disciple Bernard of Clairvaux (d. 1153) was partly influenced by Neoplatonic thought. St. Bernard early cultivated a religious eroticism concentrated on an ideal

[77

image of Jesus. His ideas found a ready response in German mystic writings of the twelfth century. The soul's relation to God was conceived as a spiritual courtship, a *Gottesminne*, and the Song of Songs was interpreted as a description of this courtship. In the thirteenth and fourteenth centuries mystic thought was especially fostered by circles of pious ladies, which originated in the Netherlands; these ladies called themselves Beguines. They did not take the traditional vows of religious orders, but were satisfied with a pious life as lay people. They sought an emotional approach to Christian truth, and channeled their desire into a direct, personal union with God. The nun Mechthild of Magdeburg (d. about 1282) gave one of the earliest accounts of such *Gottesminne*. In lofty Low German prose she spoke of the "flowing light of the Godhead." In emotional rhythms she confessed her blissful experiences: "I am seeing it with the eyes of my soul and am hearing it with the ears of my eternal spirit." At times she broke into rhyme.

From such groping beginnings arose the mystic speculations of the fourteenth century. They mostly originated with Dominican monks. The best known of them was Master Eckhart (d. 1327), a German contemporary of Dante. He was born in Thuringia and spent the most influential years of his preacher's life in the Rhineland. After Eckhart's death, part of his teachings was condemned as heretical, and admittedly he was influenced by Neo-Platonic and Jewish speculations. Nevertheless Master Eckhart had no intention of breaking with the Church or of disagreeing with its doctrines. But his thought did not center around the Church and around the importance of sacerdotal mediation. He wanted to help the individual soul in finding its own, direct way to God. Such intentions naturally fostered a more critical attitude toward the Church on the part of the laymen, and helped to lay the groundwork of the coming Reformation.

For Master Eckhart all life and growth begins and ends with God; all of His creation is suspended in Him. But individual beings tend to forget this connection and attempt to develop independently, thus alienating themselves from God. Pious submersion in God's reality can overcome this alienation. Master Eckhart lived a severely ascetic life and believed that man could further his salvation by applying his will power. The believer bent in the right direction would look behind the veil of appearances and return to God; he would also stand high above ecclesiastical laws and beliefs. Thus an independence from the institutions of the Church was stressed that could easily be taken for heresy, and Master Eckhart displeased his superiors even further by the success of

The Development of German Prose

his sermons. He had the ability to clothe his new and difficult thoughts in highly imaginative prose, and many of his expressions have stayed alive and still speak to us directly. Friedrich Nietzsche, who otherwise was a philosopher of the opposite persuasion, in his youth could not help being impressed by sentences such as: "The fleetest animal that carries man unto perfection is suffering."

The disciples of Master Eckhart did not withdraw from the world to such a radical degree. They rather stressed different aspects of mysticism, although their thoughts were seldom new. The South German Dominican Heinrich Seuse (d. 1366) was originally a patrician by the name of Heinrich von Berg. He especially developed the emotional side of mysticism. All his meditating and dreaming centered around God's wisdom which he would woo like a lover. He would suffer Christ's Passion by tormenting and crucifying himself. He would swoon in blissful vision. Yet Seuse also knew about the world which he observed with sharp perspection. As literature, his writings occupy a high rank. Seuse's autobiography was written down by a nun. It presented the first record of a personal life in the modern sense, which was as yet unknown to the Middle Ages.

Johannes Tauler (d. 1361), a Strasbourg Dominican, was another great mystic. He clearly visualized the dangers inherent in Seuse's enthusiasm, so he sought his way to God within this world and thereby appealed most to the contradictory soul of his period. According to him, man did not need a special method in order to reach God: "You must not ask for great, sublime tricks; be simple-minded, immerse yourself in your innermost soul, and get acquainted with your own self." A life full of plain work and fulfillment of one's daily duties is more pleasing to God than the raptures of emotion: "There is nowhere the smallest bit of work or the tiniest trick of artistry that does not derive from God and is not a wondrous mercy." Churchly methods of devotion are not necessary: "I tell you that I have seen the holiest of men, whom I ever saw inwardly and outwardly, who in all his days had never heard more than five sermons."

Tauler preached for laymen, and soon mystic thought spread through the masses. The forms employed by the mystic writers were always the same: the epistle, the tale, and especially the aphorism. Since their prose originated from religious passion, it was truly spirited and possessed of a strong rhythm.

Gradually the mystic movement grew. Regular conventicles of "Friends of God" formed everywhere, and in 1348 the Dutch mystic

The Parodistic and Hyperbolic Style

Geert de Grote founded the Brothers of the Common Life; soon their organization could be found all over northern and central Germany. If mysticism had not tilled the soil, the seed of reformation would never have sprouted.

Tauler became the most modern of mystics by refraining from transcendental speculations and instead emphasizing Christian practices. In this respect he was inclined toward the anti-metaphysical doctrines of his contemporary William of Occam. This British scholastic for the first time took the world wholly seriously, and resolutely rejected the transcendentalism of his age. One could even discern in these centuries the beginnings of a mathematical and scientific attitude.

Mysticism proper also shared in the contradictions of the period, although in a somewhat veiled manner. It is significant that the most important philosophical representative of the age, Nicolaus Cusanus (1401–1464), defined God dialectically as the *coincidentia oppositorum*, the synthesis of the contrasts of existence. In his personal life the bishop from Kues on the Moselle was an ecclesiastical partisan of the pope; and yet he taught with unmistakable clarity that *all* the faithful shared in God's mercy, and that mystic union with God was accessible to everybody. Through such thought Cusanus approached the spirit of a new period, the period of the Reformation.

CHAPTER FOUR

The Parabolic and Didactic Style of the Reformation Period

Humanism

EVEN in the fourteenth and fifteenth centuries spiritual concerns determined most thought and action. To be sure, mundane concerns daily grew in importance. Still, it was reserved to Humanism to concentrate all attention on the senses and the practical life of the day. This attempt at first succeeded only for a limited time; for over a century the Reformation, with its preponderantly spiritual interests, successfully contended with Humanism. Yet the onrush of the new philosophy could no longer be stopped, and in the Enlightenment of the eighteenth century, the old Humanistic thought finally triumphed. Its first effect was limited, but its lasting significance can hardly be overrated.

German Humanism had its beginnings in Bohemia and adjacent regions in the second half of the fourteenth century. Western Germany at this time was preoccupied with the mystic movement or still continued the courtly tradition. But in Bohemia the Germans once more admired southern forms.

Humanism had started as an Italian national movement. After the fall of the Hohenstaufen dynasty, independent city-states arose, especially in northern Italy, such as Milan, Venice, Genoa, and Florence. Their urban society developed new forms and engendered an attitude which was outspokenly worldly. We see it for the first time in Boccaccio's (d. 1375) *Decameron*. At the same time the poet Petrarch (d. 1374) found in the man of classical antiquity the ideal for which all his contemporaries were striving. They wanted a new humanity and were therefore called Humanists. They tried to live up to the ideals of the old Romans of whom they believed themselves to be the rightful heirs and successors; classical times should be reborn, and the Italian movement therefore designated itself as *Rinascimento*, while the French used the term *Renaissance*. In early Italian Humanism the national element was very strong; Cola di Rienzo tried to revive the old Roman state, and in 1354 died for his pains. The early Humanists did not intend to imitate the ancient models slavishly; their attitude was independent.

Rienzo could not accomplish his aims without confederates, and in looking for them he visited the German Emperor Charles IV (1347–1378), who resided in Prague. For the same reason Petrarch addressed himself to the emperor, and thus connections arose between the German court and the Italian movement. They were welcomed as a matter of course, as Charles himself no longer had a medieval outlook. He was interested in practical problems, and busied himself in building an organized administration for the Empire. In 1348 he founded the University of Prague, which was supposed to train his officials; it was the first German university.

The Latin correspondence which the emperor received from Italy made a deep impression upon Charles' chancellor Johann of Neumarkt, the Bishop of Olmütz. Johann therefore compiled a handbook for his chancellery based on these models, and naturally the practices of the imperial chancellery soon influenced other German chancelleries. Johann of Neumarkt also tried to use the new style in German translations of Latin works. His aspiration seems to have been to unite German prose and Italian style.

Johann of Neumarkt found followers, and about 1400 a German work originated which must be called a monument to his efforts; Johann of Tepl's *Ackermann aus Böhmen* ("The Plowman from Bohemia"). In the form of a Humanistic disputation, the plowman and Death hold a debate, yet neither side wins; God leaves to Death only the body of man, but takes the soul into His eternal life. Sentences in this book are rich in striking images. Its subject was traditional, but Johann's treatment somehow overcame the medieval terror of death.

Then in 1415 the Czech reformer Jan Huss was burned at the stake by the Council of Constance. The Hussite rebellion began, and put an end to these promising beginnings of German Humanism. Later Humanists had to start all over again. But for them too the Italian Humanists were influential models; only they now were Humanists of the fifteenth century. In Italy, the first period might be characterized as naturalistic. It was followed by a reaction during which the classical form assumed greater meaning. The result was a close, almost slavish imitation of the classical models. The Italian Humanists of the fifteenth century attempted to purify the language of dialectical admixtures, and to make it more similar to historical Latin. This Italian model was now taken up by the German Humanists of the fifteenth century; they were independent only in minor respects.

In order to see German Humanism in its proper perspective, one must also keep in mind the German fine arts of the time, especially the art of painting. After the early transcendental style of Gothic painting, a naturalistic school was developed in the Low Countries by the brothers Hubert and Jan van Eyck, who in 1432 completed the altarpiece at Ghent. It represented a more splendid achievement than most previous Italian painting. Then, however, came Leonardo da Vinci (d. 1519), the Italian master of anatomic naturalism who by his unique example inspired the Germans Albrecht Dürer (d. 1528) and Hans Holbein the Younger (d. 1541). Both the artists worked in city surroundings conducive to artistic efforts. Dürer's home town, Nuremberg, acquired its fame not only through his religious paintings and his popular woodcuts and etchings, but also by the delicate carvings of Veit Stoss, the iron castings of Peter Vischer, and the stone sculptures of Adam Krafft. Together with them Dürer and Holbein represented German Renaissance art at its best. But German Renaissance literature never reached a similar level. True, there were many imitations and adaptations of Italian and Neo-Latin models. For the most part, however, these were superficial and never reached the German masses. They formed but one aspect of their age.

German Humanist literature originated in southern Germany. About 1450 the Nuremberg municipal clerk Nikolaus von Wyle began to translate exemplary works of Italian Humanists; yet he transliterated rather than translated the originals, and thus had little influence on German style. More independent translations and adaptations of Italian models were worked out by the Ulm physician Heinrich Steinhöwel and the Eichstätt and Bamberg canon Albrecht von Eyb. These pioneers of German Humanism emanated from urban society.

Soon there began a whole flow of Humanistic writings which lasted from about 1500 to 1521. It expressed an entirely new conception of life, the conception of *humanitas* derived from Cicero and Plato. Man as a whole was given consideration, including his body which in the Middle Ages had often been despised. Of course, the new Humanists did not reject religion outright; on the contrary, most of them showed a strong and original religious awareness. Still, they no longer accepted the Church as the ultimate wisdom; their attitude toward it was objective, critical, or avowedly uninterested. While in the Middle Ages the Church had dictated even imperial politics, it no longer could bridle these new independent spirits. Above all, science divorced itself from the Church and would no longer be equated with scholasticism which had confined itself to philosophical and theological problems. Scholarship now aimed to serve practical life, and the new philologists, historians, and scientists were busy laying the foundations for modern knowledge.

The most important issue for the Humanists was not the individual fact which could be isolated and memorized. The important issue was a renewal of man's whole life, and the German Humanists emphasized this even more than the average Italian Humanist. Man should follow the great examples of classical antiquity; the whole nation should be saturated with these ideas which were first realized by the people at the top. Classical ideals were not viewed with a sense of contemporary inferiority. One learned from the old authors as equals. This period witnessed the first editions of Latin sources of German history, and initiated a German national consciousness and pride.

The ideal figure incorporating all the new ideas was the so-called *poéta*. He was at once a scholar, a creative artist, and an educator. He interpreted the classical poets, and instructed his students in a neat and lucid Latin style. The Latin of the Middle Ages was ridiculed as "kitchen Latin" or "monk's Latin" and was put under prohibition; little was it realized that it had developed historically and was a living language whose demise left a gap in the fabric of European culture. The new *poéta* wrote his Latin works in the elegant language of Cicero and Seneca, which, unbeknownst to him, was long since dead. He delivered them to the printers who practiced the new art of typography invented by the Mainz patrician Johannes Gutenberg about 1445. The works of the *poéta* were illustrated by renowned artists, and were bought by leading citizens who could appreciate them. The *poéta* even Latinized or Grecized his family name, and thereby lifted himself above the mere commoner. A German Fischer became a Latin "Piscator," a Habermann an "Avenarius," a Schmidt a "Faber," a Neumann a Greek "Neander," and a Schwarzerd a Greek "Melanchthon." The Humanists displayed pride in their fictitious classical ancestors, and considered themselves the equals of princes and noblemen.

South German centers such as Basel, Heidelberg, Strasbourg, and Rhenish cities such as Mainz and the cities of the Lower Rhine listened first to the itinerant missionaries of the new movement. In Cologne they encountered the first organized opposition of the old scholastics. A baptized Jew had demanded that all Hebrew books without exception should be burned, and the great philologist Reuchlin opposed this theological intolerance. A battle arose between the two schools of thought and lasted for years. From 1515–1517 there appeared the so-called *Epistolae obscurorum virorum*, the "Epistles of Obscure People," a term which designated the opponents of Reuchlin as petty and insignificant, and also as shady and confused. The scholastics were ridiculed as stupid charlatans, and lampooned as hypocritical skirt-chasers. When the beleaguered party read these *Epistolae*, its fury knew no bounds. For the Humanists had made them ridiculous by means of their witty finesse, and had defeated them in the battle for the minds of the students.

Humanistic ideas were also taken up in Swabia and Bavaria, in the German east and the German north. In Nuremberg they were promoted by Wilibald Pirckheimer, in Ingolstadt and Vienna by Konrad Celtis. And in the distant northeast the Frauenburg canon Nicolaus Copernicus (d. 1543) laid the foundations of modern astronomy. Soon it was taken for granted that every university had its Humanistic scholars, just as it had its professors of traditional theology. And this arrangement became obligatory for the many new institutions which were founded during this time. The University of Heidelberg, founded in 1386, was the oldest one in Germany proper.

Humanism caused science as well as literature to soar toward new heights. And cases where the same man represented both fields were by no means rare. Erasmus of Rotterdam was perhaps the foremost Humanist of the age; a native Dutchman, he was actually an international figure connected during his long and fruitful life with various European universities, his most extended stay being at Basel. He edited the Greek text of the New Testament from the oldest manuscripts, and derived from it the conception of an urbane and tolerant Christianity. Luther's translation of the Gospels would have been impossible without the foundations laid by Erasmus. As a writer, Erasmus excelled in his *Encomium Moriae* (1509), his "Praise of Folly." In this he produced an amiable, witty satire on intellectual laziness such as can be found in all social strata, and again and again has prevented the human mind from reaching its fullest development.

What Erasmus did for the New Testament, Johannes Reuchlin did for the Old by publishing his Hebrew grammar in 1506. Reuchlin's name stood for fearless independent scholarship and for healthy philological criticism.

Other Humanists were model teachers rather than philosophers or philologists; or they proclaimed the new ideas by their personal example rather than by theoretical lectures. The aforementioned Wilibald Pirckheimer belongs to this group, together with the Augsburg diplomat Conrad Peutinger and the Alsatian Jakob Wimpfeling. The most interesting of this group was Theophrastus Bombastus von Hohenheim (1493–1541), known as Paracelsus, a philosopher and scientist of astonishing originality. He was the first to question the wisdom of the medieval medicine incorporated in Latin books, which had not changed in centuries; he insisted on an experimental approach and on personal observation. As a philosopher Paracelsus was a Neo-Platonist who erected a structure of deep mystical speculation on the enigma of life.

The literary efforts of the Humanists resulted in a rich harvest of Latin writings. It would be rash to relegate all of them as simple imitations of Roman and medieval authors, as occasional poetry without specific merit, or as school poetry written for an assignment. For even the average Humanistic production upheld an ideal deeply imbedded in the fabric of European culture—furthermore, an ideal needing renewed confirmation in an age of formlessness and mediocrity. And quite a few of the Humanist poets were exceptional and even great. Naturally the barrier of the Latin language prevented their poetry from making an immediate impression upon the increasing numbers of inquisitive laymen; but in this respect their poetry did not differ from the philosophical works of St. Thomas Aquinas or the historic writings of the medieval chroniclers. It was a long time before similar efforts were made in the vernacular.

Humanistic prose emphasized lucidity and elegance, finesse and wit. Among its practitioners was the Tübingen professor Heinrich Bebel whose *Facetiae* (1509–1512) depicted the rural conditions of his native region. There were the many silver-tongued orators who delighted in delivering a *declamatio*, as an ornamental speech was called. There was the dashing cavalier Ulrich von Hutten (1488–1523) with his dialogues written in the lively manner of Lucian. Hutten was one of the few

noblemen among the Humanists, and he continued the fight of Walther
von der Vogelweide against papal impositions; the example of antiquity
inspired him in his fight for German greatness. The inner logic of his
position finally led him to the employment of the native language. In
1521 some of Hutten's most effective dialogues were redone in German
and combined into his *Gesprächbüchlein* ("Book of Dialogues"). This
work of Hutten's might have bridged the gap between the Humanists
and the religious reformers, and might have made the latter aware of
related trends in the academic camp. But Hutten's attempts succeeded
just as little as the similar endeavors of others.

Humanistic lyric poetry was of greater merit. It could start from a
rich and proud Latin tradition which called for stylistic aptitude; contemporary Italian models were merely adding to it. Fortunately, a
mastery of this tradition was by no means rare, and in a number of cases
expressed itself with original brilliance. The general level of Neo-Latin
poetry was higher than that of contemporary German poetry. No form
of lyric expression was neglected. One finds odes and elegies, eclogues
and epigrams in addition to occasional poems of all kinds. A variety
of rhythms and meters was dexterously employed. Soon it became customary to address friends and patrons in poetic form, to commemorate
weddings, baptisms and other festivities with poems, and to write funeral
plaints and eulogies for the deceased. The custom continued both in
Latin and in German down to the eighteenth century.

Quite unusual sentiments were expressed by some of the erotic poets
among the Humanists. The German love poems of the time still followed the conventions of knightly Minnesong or expressed sober
thoughts about the joys and advantages of marriage. But the Neo-Latin
poets spoke of love in a fuller sense and were not afraid of enjoying its
sensuousness. The most daring of these was the Dutchman Jan Everaerts
(d. 1536), who wrote under the Latinized name of Joannes Secundus.
In Germany proper Konrad Celtis (d. 1508) boldly wrote *Amores*
("Amorous Poems") in praise of voluptuousness. Petrus Lotichius Secundus (d. 1560) wrote erotic elegies that melted the reader's heart.
He also displayed an awareness of nature rarely to be found in German
poetry of the time. Other Neo-Latin poets expressed the same feeling
for nature in descriptive poems commemorating journeys or visits to
great cities. Poems of this character were quite numerous and often
had a didactic purpose. The same can be said of the historical poems of
the time, and, of course, also of its numerous satires and epigrams. Likewise the religious poetry of the Neo-Latin poets makes a rather im-

personal impression and must be interpreted as poetry applied to pedagogic ends. The only exception was provided by the Marian poems of
the astronomer Copernicus who betrayed a personal depth of feeling.

Some of the more ambitious Humanists also tried to cultivate the
field of epic poetry, and to emulate or even surpass their master Vergil.
But these poets were not the most gifted of the group. Epic poetry no
longer spoke to the moderns, and in the seventeenth century became
rare.

There was only one field in which Humanistic endeavors were of
immediate and direct influence. This field was the drama. Modern
drama with but few exceptions has been derived from the drama of the
Humanists, and not from the religious drama of the Middle Ages.
Terence and Plautus, Aristophanes and Seneca were rediscovered or
revalued by the Humanists, and set up as poetic and technical models.
The Humanists no longer dealt with the well-known scenes of the Bible,
but portrayed new and different themes of all sorts. At first they merely
gave academic recitals employing the unfamiliar classical form, but
soon they wrote real Latin dramas brimming with life. Reuchlin and
Celtis were among the first to master the new form. Nicodemus Frisch-
lin used it at the end of the sixteenth century, and still displayed a fine
feeling for aesthetic values, but he already lived in a different age. The
Reformation for a long time had claimed all the inventive energies of
the period, and it had soon degenerated into a new form of scholasticism.
The later Protestant theologians were by then almost surpassing the old
schoolmen in the exercise of intolerance and spiritual narrowness. And
their avowed aim was a revival of Christian values as against the mundane philosophy and sensuality of the Humanists. Humanism was
threatened by a new wave of ecclesiasticism, and only a few philosophic
minds visualized the possibility of its continued existence. Such a mind
was Philippus Melanchthon (1497–1560) who is usually mentioned as
a mere disciple and collaborator of Martin Luther. Yet he was essentially
a Humanist who tried hard to introduce some of his new knowledge into
the Protestant Church. For him there existed no absolute contradiction
between theology and science, dogma and ethics. Only a few of the
younger theologians agreed with him, and they were bitterly persecuted
by the rising Lutheran orthodoxy.

Middle-class Literature

A<small>LTHOUGH</small> the new ideas of Humanism appealed to German academic and artistic circles, their influence on the ordinary townspeople was small. For the Humanists wrote in Latin, and the townspeople had no learned knowledge. Their own literary efforts were therefore not affected by Humanism, and still followed the courtly tradition. Yet they were also embodying new social and moral concepts. From a purely aesthetic point of view, German literature of the late fifteenth and sixteenth centuries is not particularly original. For the student of European culture it presents a novel and interesting development.

Even the poets of the upper classes began to display a different attitude toward poetic tradition. After all, the *Nibelungenlied* and Wolfram von Eschenbach's *Parzival* had been written three centuries ago, and could no longer be enjoyed in the original language. The old texts were still being copied, but the copyists did not always understand them and often modernized the spelling to their own satisfaction. Some of the manuscripts were adapted more thoroughly, and were then also published in print; in 1480 there appeared the all-inclusive collection of the *Heldenbuch* ("Book of Heroes"). Only a few poets felt inclined to add new rhymed epics to the old ones, and when they did, they wrote in an entirely different spirit.

The Emperor Maximilian I (1459–1519) displayed a romantic predilection for the heroic times of the past, and had one of his secretaries write a new copy of the best of the old epics. He also employed the old forms in his *Teuerdank* (1517), an epic finally completed with the help of his chaplain and his private secretary. The content of the story was no longer taken from the reservoir of courtly themes. Instead Maximilian described an episode from his own life, his wooing of Maria von Burgund, and thereby evinced the essential modernity of his character and attitude. The object of this chivalrous poet was no longer the description of an ideal hero, but the realization of the old ideals in his own private life.

This more realistic attitude was favorable to a continuation of the didactic genre; here the point of view changed from negative criticism to a positive concern for a better personal life. The successors to *Reynke*

[89

The Parabolic and Didactic Style

de Vos and to Brant's *Narrenschiff* sought to instruct rather than to ridicule. The Franciscan friar Thomas Murner (1475–1536) who like Brant himself was an Alsatian, produced a *Narrenbeschwörung* ("Incantation of Fools"), a *Schelmenzunft* ("Guild of Rascals"), and other such works. In print, all of them were decorated by woodcuts, and employed the technique of the *Narrenschiff* by singling out various types of foolish behavior and foolish characters, and assembling them under some common heading. In contrast to Brant, Murner was seriously interested in educating his fools. As an upright man he took his Franciscan vows to heart, and even dared to criticize his complacent brethren for their lack of Christian zeal. As an able preacher Murner addressed the people in their own popular language, and did not refrain from slang and colloquialisms. He considered it his calling to educate indifferent laymen as well as clerics; in his insistence on a thoroughly moral life he was a Catholic counterpart to that very Martin Luther whose most rigorous opponent he became in his later life.

A similar concern for private morality can be found in the many animal fables which continued to delight the citizens of the sixteenth century. They were shorter than the epic of *Reynke de Vos*, and therefore lent themselves to easier publication and memorization; some poets of this popular genre were quite talented. Evidently the townspeople preferred such interesting tidbits of homely advice to tedious tales of past times. The rhymed chronicles were in this century receding into the background.

Lyrical poetry proper is nearly absent in German literature of the sixteenth century. The best of the so-called folk songs of this time are its narrative ballads. Among them the much older Low German ballad of the *Twee Künningeskinner* ("The Two Royal Children") has acquired deserved fame; it transposes the Greek story of Hero and Leander into a German popular medium without any false sentimentality. Like other folk songs it uses the courtly formulas, simplifying them in a tasteful manner.

One might perhaps call some songs of the flourishing schools of the mastersingers lyrical. Yet they certainly were not lyrical in the modern sense, as they were closely restricted to traditional forms and contents. A fresh breath of wind seemed to loosen this tradition when, about 1500, the Worms barber and surgeon Hans Folz started an innovation in the Nuremberg school. This poet, whom in earlier chapters we mentioned as a representative of tradition, now pleaded the admissibility of new melodies. Soon the real masters had to prove their distinction by inventing new melodies of their own. They gave them characteristic names to distinguish them from other melodies; some of these names were strange, e.g. *geblümte Regenbogenweise, neue Veilchenweise, schreckliche Donnerweise, kurze Affenweise* ("the Melody of the Flowery Rainbow," "the New Violet Melody," "the Horrible Thunder Melody," "the Short Monkey Melody"). Yet no grandiose name could compensate for the poverty of invention; basically all the verses and stanzas followed the same pattern. Still, Hans Folz's example encouraged the singers to treat many new themes, and prepared the way for his famous fellow townsman Hans Sachs.

Of course, this Hans Sachs (1494–1576) could not be taken seriously by his Humanist contemporaries; and, of course, he had his obvious limitations. Nevertheless the poetic shoemaker from Nuremberg was a venerable figure who represented his age in almost every field of literary endeavor. As a person he was not particularly remarkable, and his life could hardly be called interesting. He spent the greatest part of it in his native city of Nuremberg, the only exception being the European journey of five years which was required of every journeyman; it served to complete not only one's professional, but also one's general education. When Hans Sachs returned, his ways were set and he experienced no further development; the problems of life he solved quickly in a matter-of-fact way, without too much pondering. While his thoughts were not superficial, they certainly lacked philosophic depth, and presented an unproblematical average. Hans Sachs literally counted his poems like his shoes, and at the end of every year accounted for them in a quaint balance sheet. But with all this pedantry he was industrious and meant well. He never achieved perfection, but he provided sound and charming poetic fare for his fellow townsmen, and undoubtedly contributed to their moral edification and betterment. He clearly wanted to teach a lesson, and meant to improve personal as well as public morality.

Hans Sachs's didactic strain predominates in the sixteen volumes of *Meisterlieder* he wrote for church performance. Here he treated religious themes in a conventional and pedestrian style. He was better in his rhymed narratives which exemplified common-sense moral principles in a friendly and humorous manner. Some of the stories employed were old, others were newly invented. Sachs's style is not of an even caliber. There are forced rhymes, and there are verses with clumsy, awkward rhythm. Some of his lines sound unconsciously comical. Yet on the whole Sachs's manner is fresh and unhackneyed. He has a lively and healthy imagination which has assured his popular appeal to this very

The Parabolic and Didactic Style

day. In 1523 he hailed Martin Luther in joyous verses as *Die witten-
bergisch Nachtigall* ("The Wittenberg Nightingale"):

> *Wohlauf, es nahent gen den Tag!*
> *Ich hör' singen im grünen Hag*
> *Ein wunderschöne Nachtigall.*

*

> *Greetings, the sun is rising!*
> *In the green forest I hear singing*
> *A beauteous nightingale.*

This is not the only rhyme by which the Nuremberg shoemaker is
remembered. Goethe later celebrated "Hans Sachs's poetic mission" in
one of his poems (*Hans Sachsens poetische Sendung*) and even followed his style in rhymed parables like *Legende vom Hufeisen* ("Legend of the Horseshoe") and in parts of his *Faust*.

Hans Sachs was an equally prolific writer of dramas and comedies.
Serious dramas which ended with the death of the hero he designated
as *Tragedia*, in keeping with Humanistic terminology. The other dramas
he called *Comedia*; but they were rarely comedies in our sense of the
word. As subject matter he employed material from various sources,
but he preferred Biblical themes such as the wedding at Cana or the
judgment of Solomon. The style of the serious plays on the whole followed the tradition established by the religious plays of the previous
centuries. These were continued in the fifteenth and sixteenth centuries;
in the Catholic regions of Germany they even preserved their character
down to the seventeenth century. But they were less characteristic of
the period than the morality plays in the manner of *Everyman*. The
actors in these moralities represented abstract ideas and emphasized the
moral aspects of everyday life. The human beings appearing in the plays
were not individuals, but types.

Hans Sachs likewise followed tradition in his Shrovetide plays. Yet
he was more circumspect than his predecessors Rosenplüt and Folz, although he too could be coarse and earthy. In *Das Kälberbrüten* ("The
Hatching of Calves") a peasant sits like a hen on an old cheese because
he believes he can thus hatch a calf, but he only hatches maggots and
of course becomes an object of ridicule. Still, such scenes were not obscene, and Hans Sachs never indulged in filth. His satire is usually
directed against the peasants who are described as boorish simpletons,

or against married women who are quarrelsome or faithless. He always ends with moral observations, and the last rhyme is always a rhyme on the author's name. Contrasted with Sachs's moral sensibilities, his aesthetic ones were poor. He was not aware that form and content should have an intrinsic relationship.

This prolific poet sometimes treated the same material first in rhymed narrative and then as a Shrovetide play. Strictly speaking, most of his Shrovetide plays were rhymed narratives in dialogue, and his serious dramas were in no way influenced by the new dramatic concepts of the Humanists. However, Hans Sachs could present characters in a rough and immediate manner, and could develop plots briefly and straightforwardly. His Nuremberg contemporaries enjoyed the Shrovetide plays immensely, and even sophisticated students of the twentieth century can chuckle over some of them.

The prose literature of the sixteenth century was rich and varied. Not only were the old genres continued, but new ones were added. Significantly, much of the new literature served practical and instructional ends. Political tracts were published, as also were popularized treatments of legal questions. A flood of geographical works started with the discovery of America in 1492; some of them were fiction and still aped the awkward fables of *Herzog Ernst* vintage. Favorite literary fare was also provided by the astrological *Prognostiken* and *Praktiken* ("Prognostical and Practical Almanacs") which served the many people who believed in the influence of the stars upon human life and activity. And, of course, one should not forget the theological sermons and treatises. The most gifted preacher of the time was Geiler von Kaisersberg (d. 1510), who in a clear and witty style emphasized the need for Christian charity in the vicissitudes of life. He made his points by means of all kinds of parables and illuminating stories. Later his disciple Johannes Pauli collected these preacher's stories (*Predigtmärlein*) in his anthology *Schimpf und Ernst* ("Wit and Solemnity").

Equally popular were the many chapbooks which in German are called *Volksbücher*. Of course, they were not written "by" the people, but for them, and the people in these centuries meant the townsmen. The earliest authors of chapbooks were ladies of the nobility. They were soon joined by schoolmasters and members of the upper *bourgoisie*. Almost any type of material could be treated in a *Volksbuch*. We find tales from the old knightly romances and popular parables, we find translations from French and Latin. Legends and saints' biographies were written up, artistic stories of Italian Humanists were popularized.

Industrious writers were kept busy supplying the trade, and the books achieved sales even though they were not yet cheap. Readers in the beginning were still found among the noble classes; in the sixteenth century they were primarily townsmen, and in the seventeenth and eighteenth centuries they became people of even lower rank, as long as they could read. Thus the chapbooks were an important medium of popular education, and shaped the mind of the German masses far into the nineteenth century.

The Low German chapbook of *Till Eulenspiegel* was perhaps the most influential of them all. It was composed about 1500, and soon found its way into High German literature. Its hero was a Brunswick peasant boy of the fourteenth century whose practical jokes became the subject of popular anecdotes. Soon he was also connected with other stories of a similar character, which had originally been told about Pfaff Amis, Pfarrer vom Kalenberg, and others. Finally some writer collected all this Eulenspiegel material and arranged it in a roughly biographical manner. In these stories it is always the smart country boy who leads the townspeople by the nose. However, one must not assume that these stories were read by the uneducated peasants of the century. They were written for the townspeople who liked to laugh at the shortcomings of the various trades.

The connecting link between the individual stories combined in the book of *Eulenspiegel* is but slight; one could arbitrarily omit some and add others without changing the essential character of the book. The same can be said of many chapbooks; they are story collections rather than well-constructed tales with a unifying theme. The people of the age were interested in strange happenings and unusual adventures, in problems created by a startling array of accidents, and their preferred literary form was therefore the novella. They had little understanding of the psychological novel with its slowly evolving plot and its detailed presentation of personalities.

Occasionally a chapbook did achieve a more cohesive form. An example of this is the Carolingian story of *Die vier Haimonskinder* ("The Four Children of Haimon"), printed in 1535. Here the homely virtue of loyalty was glorified, just as other chapbooks extolled industry and simplicity. The main characters in the story of *Fortunatus* (1509) achieved or lost happiness in accordance with the prudent or imprudent use they made of magical devices for becoming rich. This particular story was the first to break loose from the waning world of chivalry, and to attempt to describe the very real concerns of the business world. It stirred the townsmen as few other works of literature, and gave them a new sense of dignity and respectability. Wisdom was no longer the prerogative of the ecclesiastics, and could be achieved by due attention to daily commerce and conduct.

Such interest in personal virtues also led to a certain interest in individual experiences. The Emperor Maximilian I not only used an episode from his personal life in his *Teuerdank*, but also attempted to write an autobiography which he entitled *Weisskunig* ("The White King"). He used the form of the chivalrous novel for rendering an account of all he had done, and the book thus showed a strange mixture of traditional and contemporary features. Maximilian's death in 1519 prevented his autobiography from being completed. Yet even if it had been completed, few contemporaries would have read it. For in 1517, two years before the emperor's death, the German Reformation had started—an upheaval which for the next forty years occupied the minds of the German people. Literary and poetic activity came to a standstill.

The Reformation

THE Church as an actual institution is merely the external organization of the invisible community of believers united by their faith in Christ. It is a human institution established to strengthen and spread this faith. Though at best it may represent eternal values, it possesses no ultimate, transcendental validity. But in the Middle Ages the Church had assumed such an ultimate character. The popes had continued the universalism of the Roman Empire, and had claimed supreme rule over the world. In their struggles with the German emperors they had nearly realized their claims, and had become the rulers of the world in fact as well as theory. At the end of the Middle Ages the popes were predominantly interested in presenting and extending their political, legal, economic, and financial powers.

Of course, such a Church which served the world instead of serving Christ became ever more repugnant to loyal Christians believing in the religious revelations of the Gospels. They began to demand a reform of the existing Church in keeping with its original meaning. The idea was not the destruction of ecclesiastical institutions or the establishment of a new Church. It was an honest reformation which was discussed by all the great Church councils of the fifteenth century which were called together for this purpose. The most important of them was the Church Council of Constance which took place from 1414–1418. The demand for a reformation was by no means an exclusively German demand; the British theologian John Wyclif and his Czech disciple Jan Huss gave expression to the same feeling as their German contemporaries. Huss became a martyr to the new views when in 1415 he was burned as a heretic by the Council of Constance.

In Germany the religious passions of the masses were mounting during the entire fourteenth and fifteenth centuries. They found their first outlet in the mystical movement which we have discussed. Laymen wanted to understand Christianity more deeply and wanted to live it more boldly. They began to object to the passive role which had been assigned to them during the previous centuries. The Roman Church had inherited the well-organized bureaucracy of the Roman Empire, and had kept it strictly apart from the laity by special rites and consecrations. It had consolidated this by using Latin as the official Church language. Yet to the laymen Latin was a strange idiom, and little was done by the privileged priesthood to acquaint the masses with the inner spirit of Christianity.

Several non-German nations had already taken issue with the clergy serving a foreign ruler residing in Rome. The French and Spanish churches had early become independent, and the English Church had become rebellious prior to Henry VIII. During the fifteenth century the Church in Germany also was exposed to more and more attacks from the national point of view.

Independent of the religious and national demands for a reform of the Church was the social movement that grew up during the same period. The farmers and lower urban classes were no longer satisfied with their economic and social status, and became more and more restless; they demanded consideration, if not equality, and their agitation reached an ever higher degree. They became prey to social delusions and utopian prophecies, some of which had a communistic tinge derived from early Christian ideas of communal living. From 1400 numerous pamphlets gave vent to these emotions, and local revolutions broke out in several areas. Finally in 1524–1525 there arose the great German peasant revolt which could only be put down by the most brutal measures of the princes. This peasant revolt established a certain connection with the religious movement, although Luther himself, after initial indecision, turned against it and condemned the peasants' excesses. The later uprising of the Anabaptists led to similar excesses and assumed an exclusively religious character, although it was socially motivated at least in part.

Social unrest could also be found among the lesser nobility which felt its economic and social bases circumscribed. In 1522–1523 Franz von Sickingen made a daring attempt to re-establish the broken power of the ordinary knights. Yet his uprising succeeded as little as the revolt of the peasants.

Thus Germany around the turn of that century was loaded with high tension which needed but a spark to erupt into action. This spark was provided by the ninety-five theses which Martin Luther affixed to the door of the Wittenberg Castle Church on October 10, 1517. Within a few weeks the German masses were moving, and hailed him enthusiastically as the embodiment of their dreams.

Luther was born in 1483 of Mansfield peasant stock, and was considered one of the people. Although he had become a priest and, in addition, a professor of theology, he was inspired by the same religious instinct as the masses. He was motivated by it almost to the exclusion of all else. Out of the strength of personal emotion he opposed the objective and material power of the Church, and demanded the reduction of its institutions to their original subservient function.

Of themselves Luther's protests against ecclesiastical abuses were nothing new, but they were uttered from the purity and depth of a great religious heart. It was this that captured the attention of the Germans. Luther originally just wanted to reform the old Church, and had no desire to found a new one. However, the Church paid no heed to his demands and excommunicated him, so that he was forced to act alone. With a heavy heart he decided upon founding a new Christian organization. As this was to be a worldly institution serving the interests of the spirit, it needed worldly supervision. Such supervision in Luther's age could only be exercised by the territorial princes. For Charles V, Maximilian's successor as emperor, had decided against the reformatory cause. Thus Luther had to ask the German princes to act as "emergency bishops" (Notbischöfe). By this decision Luther gave support to forces undermining the Empire. The intermediary powers had increased in power since the end of the Hohenstaufen period, and had bargained with the emperor for more and more rights and privileges. Now their selfish designs received a moral justification and a religious halo. The

The Parabolic and Didactic Style

Reformation made it possible for them to oppose the emperor with a clear conscience.

Luther did not intend to weaken the Empire, but he had to rely on the territorial princes for support. After his death the destructive tendencies increased still further. The emperor finally tried to subjugate the Protestant rebels by the force of arms, but was unsuccessful. He therefore had to compromise with their demands in the Augsburg Religious Peace of 1555. This treaty gave to the German territorial powers the right either to introduce the Reformation, or not to introduce it. The principle was formulated as *cujus regio, ejus religio*—"whoever owns the territory will also determine its creed." This formula made the territorial princes independent factors in German history, and further decreased the power of the central administration.

Religious developments determined German civilization from Luther's first appearance in 1517 until the Augsburg Religious Peace of 1555. Aesthetic interests became of such little importance that some scholars speak of the "Lutheran Pause." Literature between 1517 and 1555 represented an extreme example of that didactic tendency which characterized the whole epoch. Luther's appearance gave a new stress and also a peculiar twist to this didacticism, but did not initiate it. The Reformation was one of the characteristic expressions of the culture of the rising middle classes, but not its chief or only cause.

The Humanist scholars had initially greeted Luther with some enthusiasm as an ally. Yet they soon discovered the abyss that separated his religious irrationalism from their own classical and logical spirit, and turned away from him in ill-disguised anger. An aristocratic, conciliatory scholar like Erasmus of Rotterdam could muster little understanding for Luther's religious obsession and for the excited masses committed to him. Other Humanists found themselves isolated. Those Humanists who decided in favor of the Reformation became primarily interested in the solution of religious problems. Many found it easier to side with the Swiss reformer Huldreich Zwingli who had initiated his own independent reform movement. It continued to grow after his death in battle in 1531, and soon found a new leader in his great French disciple, John Calvin (d. 1564).

Zwingli and Luther did not remain the only reformers. Their protest against ecclesiastical abuses was followed by those of other deeply moved individuals who claimed an equal right in interpreting religious truths according to their personal experience. These so-called *Schwärmer und Täufer* ("Visionaries and Anabaptists") were critical not only of

The Reformation

the old Church, but of every kind of institutionalized religion. They relied on their personal inspiration and revelation, and they interpreted the Bible subjectively without considering the time-hallowed traditions of theology. They were exclusively concerned with their personal salvation, and paid no attention to worldly aspects and to political powers; many of these independents believed that the day of judgment was closely approaching. There were even a few radicals who made extreme communistic demands and began to practice promiscuity.

For a while there existed the danger that the reformatory movement would be drowned in the subjectivity of such sects and conventicles. When Luther realized this danger, he began to consolidate his position and to refer increasingly to the objective divine revelation laid down in the Bible. The followers of Luther and Zwingli did not accept the *Schwärmer und Täufer* as allies, and persecuted them just as ruthlessly as the Catholics; yet their sects and conventicles presented a significant sideline of the Reformation.

The Bible became the exclusive foundation of Luther's new evangelical creed. The Bible therefore had to be translated into the idiom of the common man, and Luther undertook this necessary task. He was by no means the first German to translate either single books or the complete canon of the Bible. We know of fourteen High German and three Low German Bibles extant before Luther, but all these were translations from a translation, from the Latin Vulgate employed by the Roman Church. None of them went back to the Hebrew and Greek texts of the original. And even their rendering of the Latin text was frequently incorrect. Many were also dialectal versions, and could only be understood by readers of certain regions.

Luther was the first translator to base his German version on the original text of the whole Bible, and to employ a form of German that could be understood by people everywhere. He worked at his translation for over a decade and even then continued to correct and improve it in many details. He began his work at Wartburg Castle in December 1521. In September 1522 he completed the translation of the New Testament and put it into print. The Books of the Old Testament were issued individually, until in 1534 the entire Bible could be printed as *Die Bibel oder die Heilige Schrift* ("The Bible or the Holy Writ"). But Luther did not yet consider his translation perfect, and went carefully through it in consultation with Philipp Melanchthon and other philologists and theologians. It was only in 1546, shortly before Luther's death, that his Bible translation appeared in its final form.

[99

The Parabolic and Didactic Style

It was through Luther's Bible translation that the German people received a unified language, although Luther himself was not the first to write this language. A movement had already started toward a standard written language. Especially was the imperial chancery interested in establishing general rules which could apply to its far-flung correspondence. Charles IV had stimulated this tendency; his chancery employed a Bohemian dialect which was closely related to Middle German. The printers, whose importance was increasing, were also aiming at a general German. Luther, according to his own words, took over what already existed: "I am not using my own peculiar brand of German, but employ the German standard language of the Saxon chancery which is the model for all German kings and princes." This Saxon chancery on the whole followed the imperial chancery, although to a certain extent it kept its Meissen peculiarities. Even so it was no literary language as yet. It served administrative, legal and political ends, but not those of poets or philosophers. Only when Luther utilized this chancery dialect did it become a vehicle for spiritual concerns. Luther's New High German was the first written standard language that could express the views and feelings of the common people as well as the poets and philosophers. He enriched the German vocabulary from the treasure house of the dialects, and adapted it to all the needs that he encountered in his Bible translation.

Luther was a model translator. He wanted to be as correct and as exact as possible, but avoid mere transliteration. The German version should be readable and also beautiful. He discussed his principles in his *Sendbrief vom Dolmetschen* ("Treatise on Translating," 1530). Others before him had transliterated the beautiful Latin *Ave Maria, gratia plena* into *Gegrüsset seist Du, Maria voll Gnaden* ("Greetings to you, Maria, full of grace"). This Luther rejected as un-German and changed it into: *Gegrüsset seist Du, Holdselige* ("Greetings to you, gracious Maria," cf. "Hail thou that art highly favored" in the King James version) which was more poetic and still correct. He endeavored to render the spirit of the Biblical passages in good, worthy German, and he succeeded to such a degree that his German Bible became a best seller and a constituent part of German literature. It was not only the common man who turned to the Bible for consolation and spiritual guidance. Luther's Bible also set the standard for the leading German poets and philosophers down to Goethe and Nietzsche. It can almost be said to have created the New High German literature.

The chancery language had been limited in its geographical spread.

It was only through Luther's Bible translation that it became the standard for every part of Germany. One should of course not imagine that after 1534 all German writers were dropping their dialects. The Netherlands preserved their own written standard which had developed in the thirteenth century, and also in Germany proper Luther did not succeed completely or immediately. The Swiss territories spoke dialects of a peculiar character, and could therefore adopt Luther's standard only hesitantly and after attempts to alter it somewhat. And the Low Germans also accepted it only with reservations. One can even say that the German of Luther's Bible was changing in the process. Still, on the whole it determined the further development of the German language. Luther's opponents had to employ the new Wittenberg German if they wanted to address themselves to the mass of readers. And neither are the Catholic writers of today writing Catholic German nor the Protestant writers Protestant German.

A discussion of the Bible translation does not exhaust the subject of Luther's importance for German literature. His *Catechism* was of at least equal significance. For here he explained the doctrines of his reformed Christianity in simple terms for common people. The *Catechism* was far less expensive than the Bible, and in Luther's time was read by far more people.

Of a more temporary effect were Luther's pamphlets which electrified his contemporaries. The earliest ones were the most inspired. In the pamphlet *An den christlichen Adel deutscher Nation: Von des christlichen Standes Besserung* ("To the Christian Noblemen of the German Nation: On the Improvement of Christian Practices," 1520) Luther gave the general program of his reformation. In the treatise *Von der Freiheit eines Christenmenschen* ("On Christian Liberty," 1520) he discussed his essential dogma of human charity, which was morally valuable but would not lead to salvation without the addition of Christian faith. Many of these pamphlets equal in excellence the style of the *Sendbrief vom Dolmetschen*. Luther was an admirable stylist. And he could write in more than one vein. If necessary, he used coarse language and shouted from the rooftops. He could also be gentle and delicate. None of his numerous aides and disciples could write an equally forceful German, and his opponents were far less able and appealing. Most of them fought with the ancient weapons of scholastic scholarship. The only exception was the agile and sincere Thomas Murner. His most popular pamphlet appeared in 1522, and was entitled *Von dem grossen Lutherischen Narren* ("About the Great

Lutheran Fool"). It employed the style of Murner's early fools' stories in the discussion of problems of faith which were of the deepest concern to the honest Strasbourg Franciscan and the Christian community for which he spoke.

In the pursuit of his religious mission, Luther also found it necessary to compose his own hymns. In the old Church the congregation had participated little in the service, and the few hymns that were actually sung were mostly in Latin. Luther wanted the congregation to take an active part in the service, and his preferred means for accomplishing this was the singing of hymns. These naturally had to be German hymns that could be understood and memorized by the average parishioner. There existed some *Meisterlieder* and a few spiritual folk songs which could be taken as models, but they could hardly be used as a part of the liturgy. Thus Luther had to write his own hymns. He did not intend to express his personal feelings in original poetry. His object was to lend voice to the religious feelings of the congregation, and he wrote poetry with a purpose which nevertheless often was good poetry. The hymn *Ein feste Burg ist unser Gott* ("A mighty fortress is our God") bears the unmistakable stamp of Luther's religious genius, of his depth of feeling and his steadfastness of purpose, although it was inspired by the 46th Psalm; the song became a veritable battle hymn of the Reformation. Luther's personal note can also be detected in the penitential hymn *Aus tiefer Not schrei ich zu Dir!* ("From heartfelt need I cry to Thee!"). In other songs he was less personal, especially when he took Latin songs such as *Te Deum laudamus* (*Grosser Gott wir loben Dich*, "To Thee, O God, we sing our praise") and translated them into German. Luther also took over popular texts and adapted them to his own purposes; an example is provided by the Christmas carol *Vom Himmel hoch, da komm ich her* ("From Heaven on high I come to you") which stands out as one of Luther's most intimate hymns and has become very popular. As a matter of course all of these hymns were provided with melodies which were often devised by Luther himself. The services adorned by these hymns appealed to the ear in the same sense as the service of the traditional Church had appealed to the eye. With them started the true Protestant art of playing down the visual factors and emphasizing the aural; it held more appeal for introvert Nordics.

Luther's hymns stimulated many of his followers to write similar poetry. Other Protestant groups also produced hymns of their own, and finally even Catholic poets busied themselves with such writing. Luther's example had started an important literary trend.

The Reformation

The literary genres not actually cultivated by Luther himself were cultivated by some of his co-religionists. Although Luther objected to the traditional Passion plays as blasphemous and pagan, he had no quarrel with religious and pious drama as such. Thus the dramatic tradition was not entirely broken. While on the Catholic side the old popular presentations still continued to some degree, some Humanists wrote their Latin scenes for the edification of their learned colleagues, and others who had joined the Reformation tried to employ the classical rules in German plays with a propagandist slant. One presented Judith chopping off the head of Holofernes who symbolized the Roman pope. Another treated the New Testament parable of the prodigal son in order to spread the new Protestant concept of morality founded in faith; this became one of the favorite Biblical themes of the time.

The strongest pro-Protestant play was written in Latin by Thomas Naogeorgus. In his *Pammachius* (1538) he presented the pope as the Antichrist who concluded a pact with the Devil, while Luther was changed into Theophilus, a fighter for God. Burkard Waldis wrote a Low German Shrovetide play *Vom Verlorenen Sohn* ("The Prodigal Son," 1527), and Paul Rebhun treated the apocryphal tale of *Susanna* (1536) in order to exhort his audience to Christian morality and to faith in God.

Thus the literature of the Lutherans between 1517 and 1555 presented an interesting though necessarily one-sided picture. The Catholics on the whole contributed little that was worthy of note; their dramatic efforts were few, and even these merely followed tradition. Besides the Lutherans only the writers of other Protestant sects can claim some attention.

Numerous hymns of Anabaptist origin have come down to us; they can often claim a certain freshness and originality. The prose writings of the Protestant independents sometimes anticipated later developments; in reading Kaspar Schwenkfeld one is reminded of seventeenth- and eighteenth-century Pietism. An even more interesting writer was Sebastian Franck (d. 1542 or 1543) who renewed the old ideas of German mysticism in his own original way. More than Luther he was aware of the human character of the Biblical documents; they were not written by angels but by divinely inspired men, and were also collected and transmitted by men. Religious doctrines could therefore not be established on a safe historical foundation, but had to be examined against the personal experience of the pious individual. "I would prefer a self-denying quiet heart in which God could find himself reflected gloriously." Naturally, personal experience was also removed from absolute certainty and could claim no authority. It was for this reason that Franck advocated tolerance toward other Christian sects and also toward the Jews; anti-Semitic persecutions he condemned outright. In more than one respect this independent anticipated the Enlightenment of the eighteenth century.

The Revival of Poetic Literature

THE Augsburg Religious Peace of 1555 put a temporary end to inter-denominational strife. The two factions gave up their dreams of speedy reunification and took stock of their limited gains; they also directed their attention to holding rather than increasing them. The Religious Peace made a consolidation of the denominational territories easier. The princes now had the right to insist on the religious conformity of their subjects, while nonconforming individuals had only the option to emigrate. Religious freedom had been attained primarily for the princes.

The recovery of Catholicism during the second half of the century progressed at an awesome pace. Catholicism was renewed inwardly and outwardly, and prepared for a counterattack. The doctrinal and organizational groundwork was established by the Council of Trent (1545–1563) which abolished flagrant worldly abuses of the Church's Christian name and consolidated the Catholic dogma in an imposing theological system. The new popes no longer were worldly princes in the manner of the Renaissance popes, but considered themselves guardians of the Christian religion represented by the Church; their concern was once more with matters of the spirit.

One of these popes in 1540 authorized the Order of Jesuits which had been founded by the Spaniard Ignatius of Loyola. It was a monkish order with an entirely new mission; it did not withdraw from the world, and did not primarily concern itself with preaching or with works of charity. Its aim was to further the Church as an institution by political and educational means, by mission and propaganda. Starting with a religious revival in the traditionally Catholic regions, the Order soon branched out into territories of divided allegiance and finally into solidly Protestant territories. Prudently and adroitly the Jesuits also supported pertinent movements of a secular character, and soon proved themselves important in science and education, in art and literature.

The first attempts at a Counter Reformation by the use of force were made by Spain. Here the crown had come down to Charles V's son Philip II, who in his Catholic zeal brooked no tolerance toward men of a different conviction. He continued the absolute rule of his father and his grandfather, and gave new impetus to the Inquisition against heretics and infidels. His attempt at conquering England with the supposedly invincible Armada was also partly inspired by religious motives. The Habsburg rulers of Austria were Philip's relatives and admired his example. To a gradually increasing degree they became promoters of Spanish influences upon German civilization.

From his father Philip II had also inherited the Low Countries which had early turned toward Protestantism. Since they did not conform to his concept of religion, he tried to reintroduce Catholicism by force. But the proud and independent Dutch burghers did not submit to such attempts willingly, and started an open rebellion. It began in 1568, and led to long and bloody wars which in the end were successful for the rebels of the northern Netherlands. The Westphalian treaty of 1648 recognized their independence, and severed the ties that still connected them with the Holy Roman Empire. In the final analysis this political separation affirmed the cultural separation of the Netherlands that had started several centuries before, yet it did not affect the mutual sympathies of German and Dutch Protestants.

The religious revival inspired the Catholic masses with new confidence, and contributed measurably to a cultural revival. Edifying tracts written in the enthusiastic manner of the Spanish mystics began to circulate, and the anti-Lutheran pamphlets betrayed a new vigor and a new depth. They were frequently written by Jesuits, and the Jesuits were also instrumental in reviving and modernizing religious drama. Yet this important literary manifestation can be properly appreciated only against the background of the coming period.

Protestantism in the late sixteenth century no longer took new territories by storm. It had saturated the entire northern part of Germany, and had also captured important southwestern outposts. But it was divided in itself. At the Marburg Colloquy of 1529 Luther and Zwingli had attempted to reach a theological agreement, but had not succeeded. And the Augsburg Religious Peace which had acknowledged the existence of Lutheranism did not apply to the Reformed Church. This Church was established by the followers of Zwingli and his disciple Calvin, and in Germany assumed a more peaceful and philosophical character than in Western Europe with its Reformed orthodoxy. It continued to grow in southwestern Germany, and in 1563 adopted its own confession of faith, the so-called Heidelberg Catechism.

Part of the success of German Calvinism can be explained by the fact that the Lutherans after the death of their founder became lost in petty theological quarrels which were abhorred by sensitive and deeply spiritual persons. To Luther himself the organization of a dogmatic Church had originally seemed to be of doubtful value. Then the Anabaptist movement had interpreted religious experience quite subjectively, and had sapped the strength of the reformatory movement; thus he had consciously confined himself to the authority of the Bible, and built on it a strong organization able to cope with the old Church on equal terms. Luther's successors, however, lost sight of the limitations of institutionalized religion, and became anxious slaves to the letter of the Gospels. The living religion was drowned in a sea of words. Most Lutheran pulpits of the second half of the sixteenth century resounded with acrimonious dogmatic debates and hate-inspired attacks on the Calvinists.

The same picture is presented by the Lutheran pamphlets of this time, few of which exhibited a depth and vigor comparable to the ones written by Luther himself. Only the Strasbourg author Johann Fischart (1546–1590) upheld the original cause of Protestantism, hoping against hope to sustain its purity. With the whole wonderful power of his style he attacked Jesuits and ordinary monks, Catholic doctrines and Catholic rites. Besides his, only a few edifying tracts in verse and prose showed deeper insight into the essence of religion.

There also was little originality in the hymns written in the decades following Luther's death. But a bright spot was presented by the Humanist school dramas performed at Strasbourg, which foreshadowed the style of the following period.

The Reformed literature of this time consisted of little but pamphlets—which, however, were more conciliatory than the ones written by the Lutherans.

Evidently the purely religious literature after 1555 was declining in favor of more worldly writing. The public was surfeited with theological controversies. Only didactic tracts still elicited an interested audience.

The Revival of Poetic Literature

A famous model for many satires was provided by Dedekind's Latin *Grobianus* ("Mr. Boor," 1549); it lampooned uncouth table manners which had become all too common, and which the author desired to better. Like all of the didactic writers of this age, Dedekind was more specific and positive than fifteenth-century authors of Brant's type. He appealed to city readers who wanted to improve themselves and their fellow townsmen. The Lutheran impulse increased the number of such specific satires. There arose a whole literature of deviltry. Vices and bad manners of all kinds were laid at the feet of the Devil and his many special servants. Tracts and pamphlets came out about a "Court Devil," a "Toper's Devil," a "Pants Devil," etc. Other authors blamed witches for the misbehavior of their fellow men. Witchcraft was firmly believed in, and this was the age of the vicious witch hunts and burnings at the stake of innocent victims of a religious delusion. Witch hunts continued into the eighteenth century; the superstitions of the Middle Ages were not overcome at once.

It is with a certain feeling of relief that one turns to the frankly entertaining works of sixteenth-century literature. It was hardly an accident that Hans Sachs wrote most of his Shrovetide plays during this later period of his life. Nor was it an accident when the number of anecdote collections increased by leaps and bounds. The interest of the time in short, witty satires with a practical application again made itself felt. In addition, their value as an entertainment assured them popular appeal. Pauli's *Schimpf und Ernst* had consisted of preachers' homilies. Jörg Wickram's *Rollwagenbüchlein* ("Coach-Traveler's Companion," 1555) was more outspokenly worldly. It portrayed coach travelers entertaining each other with short stories and anecdotes of multifarious origin. Successors to Wickram's book were Frey's *Gartengesellschaft* ("Garden Party"), Schumann's *Nachtbüchlein* ("Bedtime Reader") and other similar collections. These later books often told dirty stories without any feeling for decency. It was the same vulgar naturalism that had already existed in the days of Rosenplüt and Folz, and the Reformation had affected the readers of these books but superficially. Dedekind's *Grobianus* was timely indeed.

All these collections were loosely organized, without a unifying theme. Better organization could be found in the *Lalebuch* (1597) which in its second edition became the *Schildbürgerbuch* (1598). Lalen as well as Schildbürger are citizens of a fictitious rustic town who commit all possible mistakes in trying to regulate their civic affairs. They build a city hall without windows and then try to bring in

[107

the daylight by shoveling it into bags, catching it in mousetraps and packing it in boxes. In the lake where they have hidden their church bell, they indicate the spot by cutting a notch in their boat. And so on. The unknown author never fails to point out how closely folly and wisdom are interrelated, and he does not exonerate his readers from participation in similar foolishness. There is serious thought running through all these amusing tales.

The *Schildbürgerbuch* was but one of the chapbooks which after 1555 continued a literary trend well established before Luther's Reformation. A more famous example was provided by the Faust book which the Frankfurt publisher Spiess brought out in 1587; thus it is often called *Das Spieszsche Faustbuch*. Its theme was not altogether new. The whole Middle Ages had known tales about foolish sorcerers who had made a compact with the Devil. In return for consigning their immortal souls to Hell, they had received but a few years of earthly pleasure or a perishable treasure of gold and silver. Now came the tale of a sorcerer who had allied himself with the Devil in order to gain superhuman wisdom. Faust is a true son of the Renaissance who is not satisfied with the knowledge he has acquired by a study of such traditional disciplines as jurisprudence, medicine, and theology. He also longs for the passing pleasures of the world. He therefore allies himself with the Devil, who promises him forbidden wisdom and forbidden pleasures. But Faust is not able to accept all his hellish gratifications without remorse, and tries in vain to get out of the Devil's clutches. In so doing, he is ever more seduced into crime and debauchery. In the end Satan takes his due.

The unifying trend in this tale was provided by the biography of an actual scholar of the Renaissance period who combined a measure of true scholarship with roguery and charlatanry. An unknown author, a theologian, used the story of the charlatan's life in order to warn all good Christians against worldly pleasures and against the dangerous desire to attain a wisdom reserved for God. Yet he was a mediocre writer who proved himself unable to master his theme even in an elementary way. His central thought got lost in a collection of sometimes frightening, sometimes entertaining anecdotes. When his book was translated into English, his contemporary Marlowe made it into a drama and displayed a much deeper understanding of the story; although Marlowe likewise had to consign his Dr. Faustus to an eternity in Hell, he could sympathize with the doctor's daring quest for ultimate wisdom and his energetic pursuit of superhuman power. In Germany

The Revival of Poetic Literature

seventeenth-century playwrights and puppeteers superficially copied and adapted Marlowe's plot, and storytellers reworked the material of the old Faust story by adding a number of pertinent anecdotes and by elaborating on its moralizations. None of these later treatments was of any artistic value, and the possibilities of the theme were not realized. It remained for the great Goethe to grasp its true significance, and to use Faust in his drive for ultimate wisdom as a symbol of modern man.

Another chapbook of the sixteenth century tackled a theme which could have become equally fruitful if any author of consequence had taken it seriously. This was the chapbook about Ahasuerus, the wandering Jew. He had declined to aid Jesus when He collapsed under the burden of the wooden cross on His way to Golgatha, and Ahasuerus was therefore condemned to wander through the ages in eternal, restless remorse. Yet at best this theme was treated from a narrow denominational or even anti-Semitic point of view.

A few more consequential attempts at raising the contemporary entertainment level deserve special mention. There was the work of the Magdeburg schoolmaster Rollenhagen, the author of *Froschmäuseler* ("The Frogs' War against the Mice," 1595). Rollenhagen followed the example of the classical *Batrachomyomachia*, and used the fable of the war between the frogs and the mice as a mirror of human behavior. The book was a continuation of the type of literature best represented by *Reynke de Vos*.

Still more remarkable was the town secretary of Colmar, the Alsatian Jörg Wickram, who took up themes derived from the social situation of the middle classes. He was a forceful writer from whose pen also flowed *Meisterlieder*, religious plays, and didactic treatises; his *Rollwagenbüchlein* has already been mentioned. As a novelist Wickram first followed the French style and wrote romantic stories of adventure. In his *Goldfaden* ("The Golden Thread," written in 1554, but published in 1557) he became more realistic, and finally he exclusively treated tales from real life. His *Knabenspiegel* ("Mirror of Boys," 1554) contrasted a diligent, plodding boy of lowly origin with the dissipated, lazy son of a knight, and thus provided an edifying example to the rising middle classes. His last written novel, *Von guten und bösen Nachbarn* (1556), portrayed successful merchants who led a model life of prudent sobriety. The didactic elements in these stories were incidental to the intention of portraying typical exponents of the age. The language was simple and to the point, and kept away from exaggerations. It was a promising beginning which, however, was cut short by the renewed influx of foreign novels at the end of the century.

Such foreign models proved nearly fatal for the most gifted German author of the age, Johann Fischart of Mainz and Strasbourg, who has already been mentioned. His facility and versatility were astonishing. He wrote satirical pamphlets such as *Aller Praktik Grossmutter* ("The Grandmother of All Almanacs," 1572) which ridiculed the astrological superstition of his contemporaries. He furnished a delightful satirical tale in his rhymed *Flöhhatz* ("Flea Hunt," 1573), where he had as a hero a flea who jumped from the skirts of one woman to another and still another; this gave Fischart the opportunity to describe various aspects of middle-class life combined with a great display of merry humor. He also treated the Eulenspiegel story in rhyme in his *Eulenspiegel reimenweis* (1572), and achieved a satirical, more unified treatment of the popular tale. He finally wrote the verse tale *Das Glückhaffte Schiff zu Zürich* ("The Lucky Ship from Zürich," 1576), one of the sixteenth-century pieces still enjoyable today. It portrayed a Zürich boat rowed by energetic oarsmen reaching Strasbourg on the very evening of its departure, so that the porridge cooked in Zürich was still hot enough to be eaten. The tale had political significance, as it showed that the Protestants of Strasbourg were by no means isolated and could find quick support from the people of Zürich. Fischart sought to inspire his Strasbourg fellow citizens with new hope and new energy for the Protestant cause which lay close to his heart.

Then this gifted writer came into possession of Rabelais' wonderful story *Gargantua and Pantagruel*, and felt constrained to create a German counterpart breathing the same vigorous Renaissance spirit as the original. He even attempted to outdo Rabelais, but in attempting this followed an altogether esoteric conception of form. Fischart's *Geschichtklitterung* of 1575 was not superior to its model, but achieved a mere parody. Fischart's conception of lively exuberance was a surfeit of puns and allusions, of neologisms and distortions. His language became drowned in a welter of eccentric jargon. Fischart's individual inventions and deformations often were highly interesting and original, but their sum total became formless confusion. His interest in the realistic details of life was in keeping with the sober bourgeois spirit of the age, but he indulged it to an extent where the fabric of life came apart at the seams. The attempt to infuse this realism with the lifeblood of Renaissance vigor did not succeed. Rabelais' great book was distorted into some of the most monstrous gibberish in the world's literature.

CHAPTER FIVE

The Tense Style of the Baroque Period

Between Humanism and Christianity

WESTERN and Southern European civilization had taken great strides during the sixteenth century, and was measurably advancing during the seventeenth. It had originally followed Renaissance ideals, and had endeavored to revive the great and simple forms of classical antiquity as vigorously as possible. Yet the new Humanist learning was often at conflict with traditional Christian tenets, and its Renaissance rhetoric and splendor had to be applied to the expression of Christian morality and pious humility. Thus an actual revival of classical antiquity did not take place, and about the turn of that century with the churches becoming stronger and stronger, one of the problems of the day clearly became a need to adapt Roman and Greek inheritance to the prevailing Christian culture.

There evolved a new representative style which aimed at expressing Christian truths by means of classical rhetoric and the majestic forms of the Renaissance. The new style was called *baroque*, a word of Portuguese origin originally applied to irregular, oval-shaped pearls; it was used to designate a style that was no longer austere and simple. This new style sought to employ all the methods and conventions of classical rhetoric and of the architectural and decorative style of late antiquity. In literature it exhibited exuberant or exaggerated moods of tenseness and turgidity, and accentuated sensationalism and affectation in subject matter as well as in language, in the emotions of the lyrical poets and the behavior of dramatic characters. In the fine arts it was characterized by complicated lines and theatrical arrangements, by grandiose and explosive gestures, by sophisticated design and far-fetched allegories. Baroque architecture used twisted and bloated columns and broken architraves; *décor* delighted in deep, unmixed colors and irridescent gilding, heavy brocade and taffeta draperies. The century's men of fashion paraded in stately Spanish court dress, the ladies wore heavy bodices and full, weighty farthingales.

In the Catholic countries of Romance culture the new style developed quite early. Its Italian beginnings could already be discovered in the paintings of Rafaello Santi and in the frescoes and sculptures of Michelangelo Buonarroti (d. 1564), as well as in the heroic epics of Ludovico Ariosto and Torquato Tasso. The full force of the new style became apparent in the paintings of Titian and Correggio, in the façade and cupola of St. Peter's Cathedral, and in the sculptures of Bernini.

In Spain the Christian culture of the early Middle Ages had never died out, and only about—and after—1600 did it culminate in triumphant artistic and poetic expression. Cervantes created the great prose form of his *Don Quijote*, and filled it with the tragicomic conflict of absolute ideal and base reality. Later Velasquez and Murillo produced their sublime paintings, and Lope de Vega and Calderón excelled in their dramatic presentations of Christian ideals.

In France the new poetry was initiated in the sixteenth century by the energies of Pierre de Ronsard (d. 1585) and other poets united with him as the Pleiades. In prose the new style was perfected in the novels of Gauthier de La Calprenède and Madeleine de Scudéry, in the dramas of Corneille and Racine, and the comedies of Molière. French fine arts and decorative arts combined in creating a majestic setting for the mighty monarch Louis XIV and his court.

England at the end of the sixteenth century saw the dramatic revelations of William Shakespeare's (d. 1616) genius which also exhibited baroque stylistic traits. The seventeenth century was the century of Milton (d. 1674).

Finally, one of Germany's closest neighbors was producing most impressive examples of the new art and poetry. We refer to the Netherlands which until 1648 still were legally a part of the Holy Roman Empire, although in reality they had broken away and were pursuing a destiny of their own. The Netherlands was the home of the painters

Between Humanism and Christianity

Rembrandt (d. 1669) and Ruysdael (d. 1682), of the Dutch national poet Joost van den Vondel, and of the philosopher Heinsius. The southern part of the Low Countries was the home of the painters Rubens (d. 1640) and van Dyck (d. 1641).

To be sure, every one of these artists had his own individual style, and one cannot apply the term "baroque" to all of them indiscriminately. But generally speaking, art and literature in Western and Southern Europe were great beyond all doubt, and Germany about 1600 had produced nothing that equally moved the heart and the senses. For here religious developments had monopolized the first half of the sixteenth century, and when after 1555 literature and art again claimed the attention of contemporaries, they almost had to make a new start. Only in part and with difficulty was the time lag overcome by German culture, and during the whole seventeenth century Germany was more or less dependent on the celebrated foreign models. Its most original contributions to baroque style evolved around or after 1700. They were made in music, where Bach (1685–1750) created definitive masterworks. They were made in architecture, where one may point to Heidelberg Castle (started in the sixteenth century and destroyed by war and fire), to the royal palace at Berlin (razed by the East German government after 1945), to the churches of the Würzburg prince-bishops, and to the pavilions of the Dresden *Zwinger*. Finally, the German decorative arts of the baroque period could also claim the connoisseur's attention.

Only the German literature of the period did not achieve the greatness of its European contemporaries. It was too deeply involved in dogmatic and denominational quarrels, and rarely attained the spiritual freedom that characterized even such a devout Catholic as Calderón. Literature in the mother country of the Reformation never quite succeeded in shaking off the burdensome yoke of theology, and as a result its actual accomplishments seldom measured up to the laudable intentions of the poets. Quite frequently translations and rough adaptations of foreign models took the place of original German works. Yet the historical importance of this German literature was by no means slight. It brought about that modernization of the spiritual life without which subsequent German progress would have become impossible. It renewed and reorganized the German churches so that they once more became effective institutions of Christian education, and the import of that education lasted throughout the whole eighteenth and much of the nineteenth centuries; without the baroque restoration

[113

both the old and the new Churches would have meant less than they actually have meant in German life.

When the mastersinger Hans Sachs died in 1576, the new period of German culture was just beginning. It was initiated by the princes and their officials who had taken over the lead from the big cities. The south German cities which had so vigorously promoted the Reformation began losing their importance when the oriental trade no longer used the unsafe land routes, and the seaports of Spain and the Netherlands, of France and England were rising in wealth. In addition, the Reformation had increased the power of the territorial princes. They now were free to follow the long-cherished model of the Italian Renaissance states, and to develop their own states into despotically governed and efficiently administered institutions. The common subjects had little to say, and even in their religious allegiances depended on the whims of the princes and the vagaries of dynastic politics. In the case of the emperor and his Catholic allies, the model of Spain, the leading power of the Counter Reformation, further stimulated the existing tendencies.

Religious issues continued to determine princely politics until the middle of the seventeenth century. The Counter Reformation culminated in the attempt to stop the German Reformation by force through a long and bloody war that lasted thirty years. It ended in a stalemate. Germany continued to be separated into various denominational camps, and no party was powerful enough to make any essential changes. But the war also laid waste many prosperous territories, and reduced Germany to a second-rate power. It emphasized for many people the insecurity of life and the doubtful value of earthly riches, and thus generally contributed to the continuance of basic Christian attitudes. It was also accompanied by denominational broadsides and pamphlets, by battle hymns and occasional performances of allegorical plays.

The denominational and political schism manifested itself likewise in civilization as a whole. The Catholic culture of southwestern Germany moved farther away from the Protestant culture of northeastern Germany. The Catholic culture was promoted by the monastic orders and the princes of the Counter Reformation. The Protestant culture was stimulated by the princes of the Reformation and their officials who usually were noblemen. The Catholic culture could still preserve the old medieval traditions to a degree; it could still exercise a mass appeal. The Protestant culture was more esoteric and left the people largely to their own devices.

The new elements in baroque culture were not Christian but Humanistic. The new Renaissance ideals of efficient administration and justice required many learned ambassadors, governors, judges, and officials, and this brought about a marked increase in Humanist learning. Not all of the newly needed officials could be recruited from the aristocracy, and many had to be taken from the middle classes, which therefore also partook in the revived Humanist trend. Some social historians have called this age the age of the *Gelehrten,* i.e., the academically trained administrators, judges, and ministers.

The new epoch was initiated by a revival of Humanism. For a while Luther's Reformation had overshadowed this learning and used it only for theological ends. Now the new princely courts revived its splendor, which originally had been produced by middle-class scholars. But the old as well as the new Humanists kept aloof from the uneducated masses who were unacquainted with Latin, and the fact that the new Humanists mostly represented the princely powers further increased the social schism.

Reformation literature had displayed little interest in problems of form, and had instead amassed mountains of new materials and new ideas. Now the Humanists tried to bring order to this chaos, and to apply stylistic elegance to the forms of literary expression. Here the example of the Romance countries became the determining factor. For in the Romance countries the medieval tradition of Catholic Christianity had not been interrupted by the Protestant rebellion. In Spain feudal institutions were still in force, and in Italy and France no such upsurge of uncultured laymen had occurred as was characteristic of the German Reformation. Thus the new age in German literature had to begin with translations from the Romance literatures. The Spanish chivalrous prose romance of *Amadís,* as well as the Italian heroic epics of Ariosto and Tasso, were put into German and were preferred to the popular chapbooks. The delicate forms of the most recent Italian and French society lyrics were also imitated. For a whole century after the Thirty Years' War German literature and culture moved in the orbit of Romance culture to such a degree that the original character of the German language became endangered; the letters of the imperial general Wallenstein read like preposterous gibberish.

The world of classical antiquity also assumed new importance, mainly in Romance garb. The bucolic poetry of late antiquity became a desirable model, the style of Horace, of Cicero, and of Seneca again became a desirable aim. Some of the classical plots also entered by way of England through the Elizabethan materials which wandering English comedians introduced into Germany. They did not yet acquaint the

The Tense Style of the Baroque Period

Germans with the genius of Shakespeare himself, and must be primarily evaluated as the first professional actors to become known on the continent. They satisfied the new desire for splendid costumes and great gestures, and were soon imitated by native German bands of actors.

The really new aspects of the theater of the seventeenth century came from Italy. For the Italian architects were the first to apply their construction principles to the stage and to create through them the illusion of reality. Their example was soon taken up in the German south, and was followed in the performances of the school dramas which now became an indispensable part of German higher education. Originally the school dramas represented the Humanist tradition. Yet they were employed for entirely different purposes by the new Order of the Jeusits that had been founded at the beginning of the Counter Reformation. The Jesuitical school dramas treated all kinds of material from the Bible and the lives of the saints, from Church history and from secular history, and used it to demonstrate the meaning of Christian faith and the precepts of Christian morality. They juxtaposed good and evil in impressive scenes, and appealed to man to make his choice, the freedom of which God had granted to him. The right choice was shown as the intelligent and reasonable one; the wrong choice was the choice of fools and dunces. This accent on reason was typically Humanistic, but also typically baroque; for Christianity was now connected with Humanist learning.

That the Jesuit dramas employed the Latin language was another Humanist trait. Originally these plays had been conceived as learning aids in rhetoric and gentlemanly behavior. But the Latin form was less well suited for missionary purposes. Still the Jesuits continued to employ it, if only because Latin was the Church language and must therefore be upheld. On the other hand they tried to help the unlearned laymen by German program sheets and by German dramatic entr'actes. And they also helped them through the new Italian theatrical apparatus. The student actors used lively rhetoric and impressive gestures. The stage decorators put every trick of the trade into use. The stage musicians performed vigorously and effectively. The total result was truly operatic. Perhaps the pious Fathers themselves were not quite aware of how different their concept of the world was from that of the Middle Ages. The dramatic world for the first time was conceived as an autonomous unit to which pictorial and mimic arts, dance and music contributed in equal measure. Some of the Jesuit poets, like Jakob Bidermann (d. 1639), were born showmen. They were far from propagandizing Christianity in simple directness, and appealed rather to the theatrical predilections of the masses. They arranged real mass festivals, and substituted them for the earlier Passion plays. These medieval plays became old-fashioned and were only continued in rural mountain valleys. The most famous example of such a continued medieval play is the Oberammergau Passion Play which has been preserved up to the present time; but it has come down to us in a Jesuit version.

While in the German south the monastic orders were fashioning the new literature, the German north saw special societies arise for its cultivation. This was in keeping with the Humanist conception of poetry as not primarily a personal gift. Poetry was a branch of rhetoric, it could be taught and discussed in an objective, scientific way. Like the rest of rhetoric, it had public, impersonal tasks of instruction, representation or mere ornamentation. Understandably, the princes of the seventeenth century either favored poetry or wanted to become poets themselves. The first princely society for the promotion of poetry was founded in 1617, following the model of the Italian *Academia della Crusca*. Its German counterpart bore the name *Die Fruchtbringende Gesellschaft oder der Palmenorden* ("The Fruitbearing Society or the Order of Palms"). Soon similar societies arose in other parts of Germany, and their members were courtiers or were connected with the ruling classes of the free cities. All these societies were primarily concerned with linguistic standards; for poetry to them was the art of using the right words. They aimed at linguistic purity and at grammatical correctness, and thereby sustained the German language at a time when foreign influences were endangering its very substance.

The Literature of the Intellectuals

THE new literature was already in the making when in 1624 Martin Opitz published his *Buch von der Deutschen Poeterey* ("Book on German Poetry") and thereby provided the poetry of his age with its basic theory. One can often read that he created a new literature, but

[117

this is historically inaccurate. What he really did was to formulate the laws embodied in a literature already in existence. And in formulating them he drew heavily on the actual body of Latin and Neo-Latin theory. Essentially Opitz was a Humanist aiming at a German literature equal to the classical models; only such a literature could impress the French and the Dutch. Opitz was a man of the world, and attempted to draw a clear dividing line between poetry and theology. He defined poetry as a useful implementation of courtly life and culture. He described the subject matter of the various subdivisions of poetry. He pointed out ways to an enrichment of poetical language. He cleansed German verse of the faulty accentuation which had become a general nuisance in the sixteenth century. To be sure, many of these rules laid down by an administrative official were narrow and pedantic, and in his own poetic productions Opitz was merely a ridiculous rhymester. His pedestrian mind was lacking in imagination and could never produce masterpieces of art. Still, he was admired by his many sober contemporaries, and furnished them with examples in almost every field of poetry. Whether these examples were original productions or mere adaptations or translations of foreign models was not important. His word became law, and his opponents and detractors quickly lost their importance. The theories of Opitz as well as his practice became the lodestar of the baroque "school" of poetry.

The term "school" as applied to the poetry of this century is meaningful. Its poetry is representative and not at all individualistic; for a courtier to betray personal emotions would have been in bad taste. We have but a few poems alluding to that great event of the time, the Thirty Years' War. And the love lyrics of the period seldom betray the beloved damsel by her name; they speak of "Asteris" or "Chloe" or "Cynthia," i.e., an ideal figure who is celebrated in exemplary song. They are songs for society, and the model courtier is the man best able to hide his subjective emotions behind a mask of tranquil stoicism. The highest poetic achievements of the seventeenth century can be found in those fields of poetry where abstraction from individual experience is obligatory for the fulfillment of the poetic task. This holds true in all the didactic genres, and it is therefore no accident that baroque poetry has excelled in epigrams of admirable artistry.

The fame of Friedrich von Logau (1604–1655) as the greatest German epigrammatist is still unimpaired. He directed his satiric barbs against the imitators of alien customs and alien dress so characteristic of his time, and staunchly upheld the ideals of genuine noblemen and

The Literature of the Intellectuals

of German patriots. Logau's ideas were grounded in a deep personal piety to which Longfellow felt attracted enough to render some of these epigrams in English. Logau's epigram on retribution reads:

Gottes Mühlen mahlen langsam, mahlen aber trefflich klein;
Ob aus Langmut er sich säumet, bringt mit Schärf' er alles ein.

*

Though the mills of God grind slowly, yet they grind exceeding small.
Though with patience He stands waiting, with exactness grinds He all.
[LONGFELLOW]

Logau's piety is not of the denominational kind. He expresses the desire of rational eighteenth-century Enlightenment for an interdenominational religion:

Luthrisch, Päbstisch und Calvinisch—diese Glauben alle drei
Sind vorhanden; doch ist Zweifel, wo das Christentum dann sei.

*

Lutheran, Popish, Calvinistic, all these creeds and doctrines three
Extant are; but still the doubt is where Christianity may be.
[LONGFELLOW]

An equally famous epigrammatist was Johannes Scheffler (1624–1677), another of the many Silesian poets who played a dominant role in German literature of the seventeenth century; his pseudonym was "Angelus Silesius" (the Silesian Angel). Silesia was a buffer zone between the Habsburg will to carry forward the Counter Reformation and the Protestant movement toward an even greater religious individualism, and the intense battle between these opponents produced an especially vigorous literature. The beginning of the century saw the Görlitz cobbler Jakob Böhme (1575–1624) struggling for the expression of his disturbing religious experience. His deepest speculations centered around problems which still baffled the philosophers Spinoza and Leibnitz. During his whole life Böhme continued to wonder how the dreadfulness of real life could be reconciled with the idea of a merciful Creator. He tried to overcome this contradiction by a mystical identification with God. His God was conceived as a God transcending all contradictions, which were apparent only to a human mind. To be sure, man himself was full of contradictions; as Böhme once said: "Man is

[119

the book in which all secrecy is enclosed." And the world also was alive with contradictions. Yet in God they were overcome and reconciled. In a dark and groping way this unlearned cobbler anticipated the idea of evolution. Life was never at rest, but always becoming and developing. The static world of the Middle Ages no longer existed for Böhme.

Johannes Scheffler was deeply stirred by Böhme's thought, although he was a physician of the imperial court. Yet he did not achieve the solution of his inner struggles in the new Protestant manner of individual piety, but became a convert to the Catholic Church. Yet Scheffler's religious hymns can hardly be called Catholic in the denominational sense; eighteenth-century Pietists introduced many of them into the Protestant hymnbooks. And the epigrams of his *Cherubinischer Wandersmann* ("Cherubic Wanderer," 1657) seldom show a one-sided denominational attitude. To be sure, the tradition of older Catholic mysticism has been resumed by Scheffler in its entirety. But the traditional paradoxes often take on a highly personal flavor, so much so that some modern critics are tempted to describe him erroneously as an agnostic. The mystic identification of the individual with God can be expressed in baffling exaggeration:

> *Ich weiss, dass ohne mich Gott nicht ein Nu kann leben;*
> *Werd' ich zunicht, er muss vor Not den Geist aufgeben.*
>
> *
>
> *I know that without me God cannot live a moment;*
> *For otherwise His spirit would have nought to stay in.*

And Scheffler is able to write such an intimate and penetrating epigram as the following:

> *Mensch, werde wesentlich; denn wenn die Welt vergeht,*
> *So fällt der Zufall weg, das Wesen, das besteht.*
>
> *
>
> *Man, be thy essence, for the world will fall away,*
> *The accidental perish, the essence only stay.*

When such a deeply disturbed personality could find peace in the arms of the Catholic Church, one realizes how much symbols and ritual must have meant for Scheffler. To him as a man of the seventeenth century a personal religion was out of question, and the rich imagery of the traditional dogma satisfied all his longings. Still, the satisfaction was not achieved without passionate struggle. His poetry was bold. Nevertheless it met with the approval of the Catholic hierarchy. To them the hyperbolic style of Scheffler's epigrams was a fitting expression for the inscrutability of the supernatural. Certainly Opitz's Humanism appears superficial when contrasted with Scheffler's baroque paradoxy. Outwardly he stuck to an ascetic life with iron will and determination; inwardly he surrendered to the ecstasies of unbridled passions. In a later period he would have clothed his religious confessions in a personal lyrical style, and would not have used the hard, rational Alexandrine verse of French poetry. In the seventeenth century subjective mystical experiences could still be expressed in the traditional imagery of Christian mysticism.

Scheffler is one of the few German poets who can be clearly classified as baroque. With the later Silesian poets the baroque tension is not quite as strong. Hofmann von Hofmannswaldau no longer visualizes an abstract world of the spirit, but rather an abstract world of the senses, and adumbrates it in a language rich in sensations, following contemporary Italian models. However, his sensualism should not be taken too seriously. While his poems were often daring, his personal life was beyond reproach, and he exercised his senses merely in the field of the intellect.

The time for a more personal poetry had not yet arrived. However, it was being anticipated by a number of poets who had no connection with the artistic circles gathered around the princes. Some of these poets were still continuing the old tradition of the folk song, such as the Jesuit Friedrich von Spee, the profoundly pious author of *Trutznachtigall* ("In Spite of the Nightingale"). Others were pursuing the Latin tradition of the Humanists with a distinctly personal note. The greatest Neo-Latin poet of the century was the Jesuit professor Jakob Balde (d. 1668), a preacher at the Bavarian court; his odes were pervaded by a warm patriotism which later prompted Herder to translate them. Still other poets anticipated a sentimental attitude which became general only in the eighteenth century. Heinrich Albert's simple song about *Ännchen von Tharau*, which Longfellow translated, has preserved its popularity until the present time; it was originally written in East Prussian dialect. The Saxon Paul Fleming was independent enough to indicate the real name of his beloved, Elsgen (=Elsie), in the acrostic poem *Ein getreues Herze wissen* ("To know a faithful heart"); but otherwise he conformed to the Humanist tradition which inspired his Latin as well as his German verse. Fleming ably represented the Christian stoicism characteristic of the century.

With the dramatic poets we come to an artistic form which lent itself to the expression of the baroque spirit to a much greater degree. The modern stage apparatus introduced by the early Jesuit plays was taken over by baroque playwrights everywhere. Theatrical performances quenched perfectly the baroque thirst for representation and excessive accentuation. They were presented everywhere, in schools and universities, at princely coronation festivals and wedding celebrations, at receptions for foreign diplomats, and even during hours of worship. Life itself often assumed the traits of a stage play; it was the time of high-sounding titles and flowery addresses, of elaborate hoop skirts and laced cuffs.

The early Jesuit plays always showed an individual who wavered between Heaven and Hell, until he gave his undivided allegiance to one of them and thereby chose the way to eternal happiness or damnation. The later plays of the century centered mostly around an individual who had already made his choice, and then proved his strength of character in the whirl of historical events. The events were usually taken from the world of politics, especially dynastic politics, and the heroes were stoics, great in enduring the vicissitudes of life; Christian stoicism in the face of all changes of fortune evolved as the exemplary attitude. The "heroes" were always individuals of some stature, usually princes and princesses; courtly audiences could conceive of ordinary people as fit subjects only for comedies.

A typical Latin play was written by the Austrian Jesuit Avancini who portrayed the triumph of piety. A Protestant contemporary of his was the Silesian syndic Daniel Casper von Lohenstein whose view of life was far less optimistic. The triumph of Habsburg Catholicism filled him with dread, and he portrayed it allegorically as the triumph of evil. Yet he showed that man could withstand even that, and his soul need not be affected. Lohenstein's older compatriot Andreas Gryphius wrote dramas which centered around martyrs of great stature; one of his heroes was the decapitated English King Charles I.

Gryphius also made a name for himself as a writer of comedies. The two heroes of one of them bore the unpronounceable names Horribilicribrifax and Daradiridatumtarides, and were lampooned as windbags who had nothing in common with real heroes of inborn nobility (*Horribilicribrifax*, 1663). Another of his comedies ridiculed the unlearned dramas of a *Herr Peter Squenz* who in mastersinger fashion imitated the English comedians and their primitive play of Pyramus and Thisbe. Gryphius did not want to have anything to do with such rustic theatricals. He was really one of the most serious poets of his century. In his poems as well as in his personal life he displayed single-minded devotion and a passionate longing for his soul's redemption.

None of the Protestant playwrights was able to capture more than a local audience, and this very fact proves that their dramas did not completely embody the ideals of the century. It was a different type of drama in which the period found itself reflected best. Of all the literary and semi-literary genres, it is the opera which must be called the representative product of the century; for it exhibited the desired combination of the arts subservient to poetry's representative function. Martin Opitz himself furnished the model by supplying (from an Italian original) the first German opera text in 1627, and having Heinrich Schütz set it to music. Soon the Protestant courts of central Germany began to follow suit, while the courts of Munich and Vienna were satisfied with Italian operas. The best German operas were performed at Hamburg where the Atlantic trade had begun to flourish. The famous Georg Friedrich Händel (1685–1759) wrote his first operas for the Hamburg theater; when the orthodox opponents of "frivolous" amusements forced its closing, he had to go to England in order to find a new field of activity. These early German texts used by Händel were, of course, of just as little poetic value as those of his contemporaries and predecessors. The later Händel used only Italian opera texts. All these operas primarily appealed to the ear and the eye, and the inferior ones among them provided little more than ephemeral sensuous amusement. The lower classes got their share of this satisfaction through the so-called *Haupt- und Staatsaktionen*, the spectacular pageants and blood-and-thunder tragedies of the wandering troupes.

Naturally the baroque drama could not fully develop until after the end of the devastating Thirty Years' War. The same must be said of the baroque novel, although it had started early with the *Amadís* story. The amorous episodes of *Amadís* did not satisfy later readers, since love in this novel was still described in a coarse and superficial manner. A finer concept of love was introduced by the bucolic novels which derived from the shepherd romances of late antiquity. Nearly all of them were German translations from other literatures. The most original German representative of the genre was Philipp von Zesen's novel *Die Adriatische Rosemund* ("Rosemund from Venice on the Adriatic Sea,"

The Tense Style of the Baroque Period

1645); it envisioned a marriage founded upon a serious, spiritual relation and an equality of the two personalities. Zesen even dared to allude to persons from real life, and was therefore rejected by the ruling critics of his time who wanted something less personal and intimate.

When Opitz undertook to translate a foreign novel which could be used as a model for German literature, he chose John Barclay's Latin novel *Argenis* (1621), a book filled with historical and political developments. The prose writers of the Reformation period had been interested in local and personal affairs. But the new writers did not want to put love affairs and private aspirations in the center of their stories. They wanted to describe great souls who with stoic equanimity stayed true to their calling in face of the disturbing upheavals of history personified by Fortuna, the goddess of blind chance. They believed that such constancy and fortitude in the end would find their just rewards, and that fate could not ultimately deny them the crown of victory.

When the great war ended, Opitz's work was continued. A prince of Middle Germany, Duke Anton Ulrich von Braunschweig, was the greatest of the new novelists, and *Die durchläuchtige Syrerin Aramena* ("Her Highness Princess Aramena of Syria") was his most ambitious work. He offered a veritable welter of action, an astounding number of sudden changes of fortune; yet all this not merely in order to amuse his readers. The changes of fortune were supposed to represent the world of dynastic history as experienced by the heroine and her beloved, with a composure at once stoic and Christian.

A certain notoriety has clung to this very day to another baroque novel, the *Arminius* of Daniel Casper von Lohenstein. Here the multiple action no longer combined into an organic unity, and the characters were suffocated by the wealth of historical event and meaningless esoteric facts. The romantic poet Eichendorff aptly called this novel "a crazy encyclopedia" (*eine tollgewordene Realencyclopädie*). Lohenstein's realistic delight in objective facts no longer was truly baroque. A shorter novel in a similar vein was Heinrich Anselm von Ziegler und Klipphausen's *Asiatische Banise oder blutiges doch mutiges Pegu* ("Banise, an Asiatic Princess, or the Siege of Bloody yet Courageous Pegu"), the locale of which was the Malay Peninsula. A truly baroque writer would have treated her story in many more pages.

The end of the baroque period was foreshadowed in Christian Reuter's comic novel *Schelmuffsky*. In this, a Leipzig student lampooned a bourgeois who tried to imitate the nobility by relating fictitious travels and aping well-mannered behavior. Schelmuffsky was derided as a comical fraud, and the author once more affirmed his contemporaries' belief in the static nature of society. But at the same time Christian Reuter betrayed an atypical liking for popular speech and no longer played up to aristocratic readers, but rather down to the tradespeople of the cities. In another manner the social prejudices of the age were shown up by the gifted Bohemian Johann Christian Günther (d. 1723). This passionate lyricist sought satisfaction in real life and no longer was interested in the transcendental. As Goethe later said of him, he did not know how to constrain himself, and thus wasted his life and his poetry.

Some court poets at the turn of the century gave up the baroque style of exaggeration and involution, and tried to write in a more moderate and more lucid manner. Writers such as Besser and Neukirch foreshadowed a new period. Among them also belonged the Leipzig poet Pietsch who inspired Gottsched, the critical protagonist of the subsequent style.

The Popular Writers of the Seventeenth Century

IN THE previous chapter we discussed almost exclusively literary works written for the court circles of the seventeenth century which reflected the ideals of the age. But there existed masses of readers who were not reached by the writers of fashionable society. The tradespeople of the German cities had acquired their ideals from the Lutheran teachers and clergymen, and these advocated a more simple and sober style of living and thinking. The middle classes hardly shared in the strict separation of literature from life which was upheld by the intellectuals in lines like the following:

> *Das Herz ist weit von dem, was eine Feder schreibet,*
> *Wir dichten ein Gedicht, dass man die Zeit vertreibet.*
> *In uns flammt keine Brunst, obschon die Blätter brennen,*
> *Von liebender Begier. Es ist ein blosses Nennen.*

*

The Tense Style of the Baroque Period

The heart is far removed from what the pen does say.
We make a poem just to while the time away.
No passion's glow is ours, though pages are aflame
With fervent love's desire. We just provide a name.

In contrast to such views, middle-class readers favored a literature that was closer to their feelings and their personal lives, and in which everything was expressed in a natural language one could understand and enjoy. The tradespeople of the seventeenth century continued to sing the folk songs and to read the chapbooks of the Reformation period, and they attended the popular performances of the wandering troupes; occasionally they themselves acted in the traditional pieces of the sixteenth century or continued to assemble in the churches as mastersingers. Most of this unlearned literature lasted until the time of the Romantic poets who then renewed all the popular genres in their own way. Yet not all its representatives were unliterary, and some of them must be singled out as pacemakers of real culture.

Since the seventeenth century was deeply devoted to Christianity, it needed new hymns for its expression. But few of the Protestant hymn writers of the century let themselves be influenced by the ruling literary fashions. Most of them rather continued the tradition of the sixteenth century, as did Paul Gerhardt, the best-known church poet of the new age. His songs have remained favorites because of the profundity of his faith, and the straightforwardness and freshness of his language. Songs such as *Befiehl du deine Wege . . .* ("Commit your ways to God's care . . .") and *Nun ruhen alle Wälder* ("The forests now have all found rest") can be found in all German Protestant hymnbooks. In the seventeenth century they satisfied the religious as well as the literary demands of the middle classes, who were bypassed by the courtly authors.

There also existed numerous theological tracts and books of edification. Johann Arnd wrote his *Vier Bücher vom wahren Christentum* ("Four Books on True Christian Life," 1605–1609), and his disciple Valentin Andreae (d. 1654) was another author characterized by deep insight into religious realities. The ardor of their language followed the example of the old mystic writers with whom they agreed in stressing true Christian life as the natural consequence of true Christian faith. These books foreshadowed the Pietism of a somewhat later period.

Many satirists of the seventeenth century also wrote in the popular vein. Logau was not the only one to raise his voice against the imitation of foreign models. He was at least equalled by the juicy Low German verses of the north German Johann Lauremberg, and the outspoken prose tracts of Hans Michael Moscherosch. Moscherosch was a Strasbourg patrician who did not adopt the newfangled tenets of courtly circles, and preferred to stress old-fashioned virtues. In his *Gesichte Philanders von Sittewald* ("Visions of Philander von Sittewald") he continued the fools' revues of the sixteenth century, although at first he closely followed a Spanish model. But the second part of his *Gesichte* proceeded independently, and conjured up the old Teutonic heroes of the past as helpmates in the fight against foreign fashions and for a truly German civilization.

The older tradition was also alive in the Catholic priest Abraham a Sancta Clara who lived at the end of the century (d. 1709). To be sure, he used all the tricks of baroque rhetorics so that he could capture the attention even of the Viennese court. Yet the essence of his sermons differed little from those of Geiler von Kaiserberg. He could write a *Narrenspiegel* ("Fools' Mirror") like Murner's. His most important book of edification was *Judas der Erzschelm* ("Judas the Arch-rogue"), a best seller not only among Catholics. When, later, Friedrich Schiller needed a military chaplain for his play *Wallensteins Lager* ("Wallenstein's Camp"), he used Abraham a Sancta Clara as his model.

The popular didactic works of the Reformation period also inspired the great novelist Grimmelshausen. His main work *Simplicius Simplicissimus* may be called the most searching expression of the whole century. Its material was partly taken from the author's own life. Hans Christoffel von Grimmelshausen was born in Gelnhausen in Hesse in 1621 or 1622. In 1634 imperial troups attacked the city and plundered it. This was the end of Grimmelshausen's carefree boyhood. Shortly after the sack of Gelnhausen he joined some marauding soldiers. Then he was kept a prisoner by Croats for weeks. Later he became a stableboy, and still later a dragoon in the imperial army. Next we find him in a garrison in Soest in Westphalia. Then he goes to Baden and begins to advance as a professional soldier. He finally becomes regimental secretary. When the Treaty of Westphalia was signed, Grimmelshausen's regiment defended the besieged Bavarian fortress of Wasserburg on the Inn River. Thereafter he was glad to give up soldiering and return to Baden. He married and became an administrator for noble estates. Soon he could buy his own farm and his own tavern, and in 1667 he became mayor of the Strasbourg village of Renchen. In the last years of his life the poet again had personal experience of war as a consequence of the aggressive French policies of Louis XIV. Soon afterwards, in 1676, Grimmelshausen died.

The vicissitudes of his life led him to unusual observations, and set him pondering over the meaning of the world. Grimmelshausen was raised as a Protestant and later became a convert to Catholicism; but he was never intolerant toward other denominations, and was always thinking his own thoughts. He started his career as a writer with the clear intention of augmenting his meager financial resources, and therefore began with satiric stories in the manner popular since Sebastian Brant. But in the process of writing he came across the picaresque genre introduced from Spain, and remembered his own war experiences. The result was his chief work *Der abenteurliche Simplicissimus Teutsch* ("Simplicius the Vagabond," 1668). The hero of this novel is no longer a conventional fool reflecting on the follies of mankind, but a real soldier of the Thirty Years' War who in the misery of the time undergoes basic human experiences and is forced to grope for a satisfactory solution to the riddle of existence. Simplicius grows up with peasant foster parents. The war destroys his childhood home and forces him to seek refuge with a forest hermit who actually is his own father, although Simplicius does not know this at the time. After the hermit's death, the helpless boy is seized by vagrant soldiers and brought to the fortress of Hanau; here Simplicius is pressed into service as a court jester. Then he becomes a soldier, and the fortunes of war transfer him to Westphalia, where he makes himself independent and leads a comfortable life as a brigand. He undertakes a journey to France where gallant ladies employ the personable young man in sensual escapades. But smallpox afflicts the *beau Alman* ("handsome German"), and Simplicius has to return to Germany disfigured by ugly scars and devoid of earthly goods. He now makes acquaintance with another soldier of fortune, they become good friends and enter upon a pilgrimage. Simplicius, however, does not take this too seriously, and is only superficially converted to Catholicism. He then marries and tries his hand at farming. But his wife dies, and again he resumes his wanderings. The prince of the subterranean water sprites, *der Fürst vom Mummelsee*, instructs Simplicius in the rudiments of philosophy, and finally he realizes the vanity of the world and withdraws into the solitude of the Black Forest in order to become a hermit. However, his renunciation of the world is not to be taken too literally. For Simplicius still owns a spyglass with which he observes the doings of the people in the valleys, and he constructs a hearing trumpet so that he can listen to the noises of the world below.

In this half-hearted hermit's life Simplicius becomes a fitting symbol for his author's contradictory attitude to the world. Grimmelshausen too realizes the vanity of the world, and his motto is *Der Wahn betreugt* ("The world is a deceptive illusion"). Yet he cannot help living in it and even loving it. This is a typical seventeenth-century attitude which is frequently termed baroque. If one uses the term more strictly as applying to a certain literary style, Grimmelshausen is not typically baroque. For he does not aim at rhetorical elegance and at representative gestures, but rather confines himself to simple, artless narration, to earthy, popular language, and to a simple construction founded on the antithesis between the satirized world and the lasting transcendental values. His novel has neither involved style nor an involved massing of events. *Simplicissimus* cannot even be called a true novel of development; for though the stages of the hero's development are all presented in psychological sequence, the process of development itself is not described; we have almost a film of successive independent acts. Yet there is development within the acts themselves, and the structure of the work as a whole can be called contrapuntal; for every time Simplicius rises in the esteem of the world and accumulates earthly riches, he sinks low on the moral scale; and every time he loses the world's respect and is reduced to poverty, he gains in wisdom and contributes to the salvation of his soul. Grimmelhausen's hero symbolizes more than an age. The novel also reflects an ever-recurring human situation, and has therefore remained alive until today.

In summary, one can call Grimmelhausen's *Simplicissimus* a true reflection of the dichotomy of the age, and a popular novel of real stature and lasting merit. At its appearance it achieved immediate success, and the enterprising publisher quickly encouraged his author to other ventures in a similar vein. The first of these was the *Continuatio* of the story, the so-called sixth book. It takes Simplicius to new adventures, this time in the exotic world beyond the sea, and it is told rather well; but viewed from the close unity of the first five books, the *Continuatio* is merely repetitive. The next novel, the so-called seventh book, entitled *Die Landstörzerin Courasche* ("Mother Courage the Vagabond," 1670) is interesting because of its material, and represents a kind of female Simplicius, a camp follower of the rival armies, who sinks deeper and deeper into depravity until she finally becomes a queen of the gypsies. Yet the story is told without artistic pretensions and does not incorporate any deep or original philosophy; in fact, it may justly be called a seventeenth-century version of the medieval condemnation of woman as a tool of the Devil.

In the rest of his works (*Der seltsame Springinsfeld*, 1670,—"The

Curious Peg-Leg"; *Das wunderbarliche Vogelnest,* 1670,—"The Wondrous Bird's Nest," and many others), Grimmelshausen sank to the
level of a popular entertainer and even a hack. He gave up his own
earthy language in favor of the more refined, but also less colorful style
demanded by the enterprising publisher and his meticulous proofreaders;
in the final edition of *Simplicissimus* the vigorous language of the first
printing had to yield to the fashionable baroque language of the time.
But that did not make the author a fashionable poet, and he was never
recognized by the critics of his age. Yet he had literary successors among
whom we must mention Johann Beer (d. 1700), a musician of Austrian
parentage whose numerous novels portrayed the land of his youth with
robust humor. The merits of Beer as well as of Grimmelshausen have
been discovered only in our time. We now consider *Simplicissimus*
among the few lasting treasures of German seventeenth-century literature.

CHAPTER SIX

The Witty Style of the Enlightenment

The Spirit of the Eighteenth Century

TOWARD the end of the seventeenth century the nobility gradually lost its spiritual leadership and yielded it to the bourgeoisie. The reasons were not solely of an economic nature, although the worst consequences of the Thirty Years' War had by this time been overcome. Larger political groups such as Prussia were developing out of the confused welter of small German states, and were giving more strength to middle-class industry. But a genuine economic upswing was still prevented by the many wars that took place at the end of the seventeenth and at the beginning of the eighteenth centuries. Shortly before 1700 the Holy Roman Empire fought off the Turks, then the new century was opened by the Nordic War and the War of the Spanish Succession, and after Frederick the Great's ascension to the throne in 1740, Germany was prevented from developing by the three Silesian Wars.

Thus the strengthening of the middle classes must be attributed primarily to cultural causes. All important spiritual developments after 1700 had their roots in the Reformation which was carried by the bourgeoisie of the sixteenth century. The nobility took little part in it and on the whole remained absorbed in politics. Yet this very concern in the Reformation also prevented the German bourgeoisie from immediately absorbing the worldly learning of Humanism and entering into the spirit of reawakened antiquity. On account of the strong religious currents of the seventeenth century, the German bourgeoisie remained fifty years behind in its development. It was only around 1700 that it caught up with French and English culture and began to enter into the Age of Enlightenment.

The Enlightenment developed as a consequence of Humanism. Humanism had only partly freed thinking from the authority of dogma and tradition. The Enlightenment now attempted to make reason completely autonomous and to derive all the other authorities from it. The Church no longer kept its dominating position, and even ideas of God, freedom, and immortality were interpreted as postulates of logical thinking. Only the Dutch Jew, Spinoza, and the German Leibnitz (d. 1716), the two greatest philosophers of the Enlightenment, sensed that God can be only believed and not proved, and therefore avoided absolute rationalism. The latter was most clearly represented by the Frenchman, Descartes, the father of rationalism, and by the German, Wolff, the most popular of Leibnitz's disciples. Descartes with his penetrating logic acknowledged man only as a reasoning being, and assumed that reason and existence are identical: *Cogito, ergo sum* ("I think, and therefore I am"). By the same deductive method, the Wolffians in Germany tried to discover the reasons for all the processes and facts of life, and collected their definitions in ponderous dictionaries.

To the same degree that reason shook off its churchly fetters, it also became less concerned about churchly dogma. The beliefs of the individual became less important than his thoughts and actions. Thus people became tolerant, and the quarrels between the denominations which in the seventeenth century had been supercharged now became less violent and less fatal. The realm of the supernatural lost its power over the philosophical mind. Rules were given for moral life, and practical ethics constituted the first concern of Christians. Life in this world, as it was or as it should be, now became the important factor. Leibnitz went so far as to assert that the world we live in was the best of all possible worlds. Everything in this world expressed a reasonable purpose and was the instrument of a benevolent divine will. The ideal man for this century was no longer the hermit who escaped from the world, but the practical hero who obeyed God's command to abolish the injustices of human organization and to lead a reasonable life in the present. This attitude was throughout optimistic and quite different from the ascetic resignation of the seventeenth century. It also was not merely theoretical, but was seriously concerned with the practical application of Christian principles. It was the eighteenth-century Enlightenment that in spirited battles erased many traces of medieval retardation. The Enlightenment did away with trials for witchcraft and with torture chambers; it pleaded for dignified living conditions for the Jews and other minorities. It fostered the education of women and started the emancipation of the colored races. After the twentieth-century revival of medieval torture methods in Russia and in Nazi Germany one must look at the ridiculed Enlightenment with different eyes.

The later development of the German Enlightenment took place chiefly under the influence of English philosophers such as Locke and Hume. They too knew only the one authority of reason, but they based reason upon experience and are therefore called empiricists. Instead of starting with general principles, they began by the observation of detailed objects, and only inductively derived their few ultimate principles. Another Englishman, Shaftesbury, applied empirical methods to the fine arts, and became an important influence in the development of an original German literature.

The most important representative of German empiricism was the poet and critic Gotthold Ephraim Lessing. His younger contemporary, Johann Gottfried Herder, could likewise be called an empiricist, although in his observations he also considered emotional and historical attitudes and conditions. Herder, therefore, no longer looked upon the world from the exclusive standpoint of reason, and must indeed be counted among the protagonists of the age to follow. But interpreted from the basis of the eighteenth century only, his philosophy could also be described as an original form of the Enlightenment. A similar assessment can be made of the Königsberg philosopher, Immanuel Kant, in whose works is partly found the culmination of German empiricism. But in other respects he opened a new chapter in philosophy, and must therefore be discussed later.

Both rationalism and empiricism were ways of understanding the world as a meaningful order obeying its own laws and embodying them as constituent elements. To be sure, neither the existence of God nor His creation of the world were explicitly denied. Yet His role was interpreted in a different light. He created the world, but afterwards left it to its own devices: that was the formula of the deists. Or, He developed the world as His own body according to the perfect laws conceived by Him: that was the formula of the pantheists. In both cases God no longer interfered with the daily processes of orderly life by sudden, unexplainable miracles, and life no longer received immediate transcendental directives. Man's destiny now fulfilled itself within the framework of an autonomous universe, and the laws of this universe functioned without exceptions.

Thus not only philosophical attitudes were changing, but also religious ones. The rise of subjective reasoning was accompanied by a rise of subjective feeling. The personal attitude toward the Christian creed and the practical realization of that attitude occupied the center of attention. This new wave of personal feeling could be noticed in every nation of Western Europe. France had Pascal and the Jansenists. England had its Independents, who later on became the Congregationalists; it had John Fox and the Quakers, and John Wesley, the founder of Methodism. In Germany the movement developed under the name of Pietism.

Historically speaking, German Pietism revived the thought of the old German mystics of the fourteenth century, thought that had never disappeared entirely. In the sixteenth century it was taken up by the small Protestant sects, and found its way into the writings of Sebastian Franck. In the early seventeenth century it was reflected by Jacob Böhme. In the decades after the Thirty Years' War, mystic thought was kept alive by Catholic mystics such as Angelus Silesius, and by scattered Protestant thinkers. Finally there arose the big movement of Lutheran Pietism.

The name Pietism itself was taken from the pastor Philipp Jacob Spener's influential treatise *Pia desideria* ("Pious Wishes") of 1675; the Alsatian author demanded family worship and an active Christian attitude toward all the problems of everyday life. A few years later August Hermann Francke delivered his first Biblical lectures at the University of Leipzig; but they displeased the orthodox theologians, and he had to leave for Erfurt. Soon thereafter he founded the model orphanage at Halle an der Saale. While Spener's views came close to those of the Congregationalists, Francke's ideas can be described as a kind of Methodism. Both emphasized the importance of personal religious experience; superficial, conforming church attendance was a very poor substitute.

Pietism also led to a new form of religious organization. In 1722 Count Zinzendorf founded the Church of the Moravian Brethren, with its strong stress on personal piety, on the singing of hymns, and on a mystical adoration of Jesus, the sweet Lamb of God. Although the Moravians devised no new theology, they often criticized abuses of the established Churches; they also generally revived the old Christian traditions and practices that had fallen into neglect. They reorganized Christian missionary work in India and in the New World; courageous

The Spirit of the Eighteenth Century

missionaries such as Zeisberger and Heckewelder tried to bring the Gospel to the North American Indians. In their search for religious freedom some Moravians emigrated to Pennsylvania, where Bethlehem and other towns were founded by them. Many Pietist activities were inspired by the quiet hope that man could indeed improve his lot and make this earth a better place to live in.

Pietism with its emphasis on personal piety and on emotional religion marked the end of the institutionalized and intellectualized religion of the Baroque period. Its practical Christianity became a mighty force in German everyday life, and has continued its influence up to the present time. In general German culture, Pietism must be called the first form of modern individualism. Its religious individualism directly prepared the way for the literary individualism that started with Goethe and the *Sturm und Drang* ("Storm and Stress") Movement. To be sure, individualism had already been initiated by the Reformation and by Humanism. But the seventeenth century had seen a revival of medieval feudalism which tended to suppress all individual assertions in a hostile manner. This feudalistic civilization still continued in the eighteenth century, and only now found its political expression in the absolutist form of government. Princely absolutism following the model of the great French king Louis XIV was the dominating form of the eighteenth-century state. Yet this absolutism could no longer suppress the mind. To be sure, it tyrannized individual authors, but it was powerless against the general spirit of the time. Educated people could not condone the more radical forms of despotism, but they could understand it in its enlightened form as it was represented by the Prussian king Frederick the Great (1740–1786) and his Austrian disciple, Emperor Josef II. For truly enlightened absolutism was a reasonable organization of the state, and was quite compatible with the general spirit of the eighteenth century. The despotic form of absolutism made its decisions out of irrational and arbitrary impulses, and was therefore abhorred. Yet the disciples of Enlightenment would just as much have abhorred the nineteenth-century state founded on irrational impulses of nationality and tradition. They were international in their outlook, and although Rousseau's theory of the state as a rational social contract (*Le contrat social*) lacked historical proof, it was shared by the rationalists as a justified ideal. The modern Western concept of a state organized and governed by reason, the modern vision of an international network of free, peaceful exchange between the nations was directly derived from the practical idealism of Enlightenment.

The Witty Style of the Enlightenment

The new middle-class individual felt free and independent even toward an enlightened monarch. And he also felt definitely at home in the contemporary world. Hofmannswaldau and Lohenstein had dared to be sensuous, but in doing so they had still revealed a bad conscience. Now the average lyric poet praised without scruple the joys of living. As a result the baroque tension between asceticism and worldliness dissolved, and the individuals of the eighteenth century were much more harmonious and vigorous. Only to a later, more sophisticated age could they appear to be commonplace and too simple.

The Literature of Wit

THE new concept of a well-ordered universe and of man as an autonomous contributor to the perfection of its design also necessitated a different literary style. An example of this new style could only be found in seventeenth-century French literature, and the literature of the German Enlightenment in its first phase could do little better than follow it. English literature became important only by stages, and the English model could replace French literature only in the second half of the century when philosophical empiricism had routed the forces of early rationalism. In 1700, however, French literature appeared as the only Western literature which gave full recognition to newly enthroned reason by its style of clarity, orderliness, and emotional balance. The imitation and reception of the French models led to the new German style of wit and good taste. *Guter Geschmack* (good taste) became the watchword of the new writers, and *Belustigungen des Verstandes und des Witzes* ("Delights of Reason and Wit") stood at the masthead of their most important magazine.

Among the early protagonists of the new literature Christian Weise, Gottfried Arnold, and Christian Thomasius were of the greatest influence. Weise was still impressed by Spanish literature, and in his own literary productions had not yet achieved a particularly new form. His novels read like rationalistic counterparts to the older fools' revues of Brant and Murner. But like Weise's influential school comedies and his rather pedestrian lyrics, his novels too served the development of a pragmatic morality and of courteous manners among the rising bourgeoisie. As the rector of the Zittau Latin School, Weise took over the educational ideal of baroque nobility, and made it attainable for his own social class. In the process it lost some of its transcendence and gained in sobriety. Weise was among the first writers who avoided baroque involutions and expressed themselves clearly and succinctly.

Arnold's *Unparteiische Kirchen- und Ketzerhistorie* ("Impartial History of Churches and Heresies," 1699–1700) was another sign of the changing times. This book no longer evaluated heretics by the objective standards of orthodoxy, but by the sincerity of their subjective convictions; thus it propagated tolerance and a piety not limited to a belief in correct dogma.

Thomasius was a Leipzig professor of law who was singularly public-spirited. He founded the first German periodicals in order to promote the enlightenment of the intellectuals. Here Thomasius set forth a philosophy no longer derived from transcendental revelation. Although, of course, he did not deny revelation, he thought little of its practical value. He stressed everything that could be useful to man in his desire for earthly happiness and in his fight against pain and premature death. In 1687 Thomasius formally renounced Latin as the vehicle of university instruction, and gave the first lectures in the German language, for he wanted to broaden the education of the middle classes and therefore had to speak to them in a language they could understand. His aim was a general cultural refinement, and he was also aware of the high attainments of other nations. Still, he wanted culture of a home-grown variety, and in his period German had become a language "of soldiers and horses," to employ a later witticism of Voltaire. The scientists, as in the Middle Ages, still spoke and wrote Latin. The nobility was bedazzled by the brilliant court of Louis XIV, and was aping the French in language and manners. The French wig and the French surcoat became the customary dress of the eighteenth-century German.

Weise, Arnold, and Thomasius prepared the ground for the general intellectual upheaval which started with Johann Christoph Gottsched's inauguration as professor at Leipzig in 1730. He came from East Prussia where rationalist thought had always found fertile soil (as, in earlier times, had mystical thought). Like Weise and Thomasius, Gottsched endeavored to introduce Humanism to the middle classes. Quite naturally, therefore, he fought the baroque literature of feudalistic representation. Gottsched shared the philosophy of Wolff and conceived of poetry within the limits of sober reason. He also loved to fight, and he fought with the stubborn passion of an essentially limited personality. He waged war against the preciousness (*Schwulst*) of late baroque style. By means of a solemn stage ceremony he abolished poor Punch (*Hanswurst*) who had been introduced by the English comedians.

Gottsched quite rightly wanted to elevate German drama above the level of burlesque horseplay, and therefore emulated French and English classicism. An additional reason was his search for a style interpreting human life as man's primary concern, and replacing the baroque metaphorical style expressing a transcendental view of life. If Gottsched had been a gifted poet, he might have supplied the prototype of a new German drama. But his gifts did not lie in that direction, and thus his model drama *Sterbender Cato* ("The Dying Cato," performed in 1731, an adaptation of *Cato*, a play by Addison) unfortunately became a model of boredom. Even worse, Gottsched had little critical insight into poetry. In his *Versuch einer Critischen Dichtkunst* ("Attempt at a Critical Art of Poetry," 1729), he fought with the stubbornness of a mule against poetic imagination; his rationalistic guide, the French critic Boileau, had been wise enough to presuppose this quality by silence. By such narrow views Gottsched finally drew upon himself the enmity of every German writer of distinction, and became a ready butt of ridicule. His dictatorship over German taste had even less chance of succeeding than the dictatorship of Opitz.

Yet it would be unfair to Gottsched if one did not also point out his merits. His rejection of crude acting and obscenity on the stage was a step in the right direction, and his sponsoring of good actors and actresses required moral courage; for the age considered them vagabonds and outcasts, and commonly denied them Christian burial. Gottsched also founded *Deutsche Gesellschaften* ("German Societies") to combat provincialism in manners and language. He published important collections of older German literature, and thus paved the way for the scientific study of German literary history. Finally, he advocated better education for women, an effort in which he was supported by his wife, a poet in her own right. Feminine education up to that time had been largely neglected, and Gottsched here, as everywhere, fought ignorance and obscurantism. But praiseworthy as his endeavors often were, they also betrayed an astonishing lack of discrimination.

Thus only enlightened empiricism became of real importance for German literature. Empiricism first turned to the study of poetry in the writings of Gottsched's Swiss opponents Bodmer and Breitinger. They were Milton enthusiasts, and the epics of the English poet opened their eyes to an understanding of the irrational elements of poetry.

The Literature of Wit

The theories of the Swiss ("*die Schweizer*") were put into practice independently by the nature poets of the turn of the century. There was the Hamburg alderman Brockes (d. 1747) who published his *Irdisches Vergnügen in Gott* ("Earthly Delight in God"), in which the beauty of the earth was considered in the light of a rational purpose, and was interpreted as a reflection of heavenly beauty. Yet in spite of these theological limitations, Brockes also succeeded in adumbrating impressionistic pictures. Another nature poet was the Swiss scientist Albrecht von Haller, who in 1729 published his epic *Die Alpen* ("The Alps") in which he anticipated the ideas of a fellow countryman, the empiricist philosopher Rousseau. Haller discovered the beauty of the high mountains, which up to that time had been despised as ugly, and thus became the father of modern mountaineering, although his rejection of artificial urban civilization and the concomitant praise of the naturalness of the mountaineers was purely utilitarian in character. Haller valued nature for its own sake as little as his successors. Most of the nature poets were strongly influenced by English models. Thus the poet Ewald von Kleist was inspired by Thomson's "Spring" (the first part of his *Seasons*) to write his own German *Frühling*.

Poetic empiricism can further be found in the so-called Anacreontic poets. This designation was derived from the fact that they imitated the Greek songs supposedly written by Anacreon in praise of love, friendship, wine, and festive occasions. In defense of the German Anacreontic poets one might say that at least they recognized the claims of the senses as well as those of the intellectual faculties. Yet they still believed that they could control the senses by morality and reasoning. Everything had to submit to good taste as the final arbiter; violent emotions and passions were simply unreasonable and *not* in good taste.

> Der Weise kann das Glück betrügen,
> Auch wahres Übel fühlt er kaum;
> Und macht sich's leicht und macht es zum Vergnügen.
>
> JOHANN PETER UZ, 1720–1796.

*

> The sage is happy in a moderate measure;
> He also hardly feels true misery
> And takes it lightly, changing it to pleasure.

The carousers of Anacreontic poetry never got drunk. Its amorous lads were merely skirting love, and their loving lasses were never too deeply engaged and could easily be swayed; they were for the most part charming and graceful, but also flippant, vain, and slightly stupid. Love was mere play which must not be taken too seriously. In fact, the poets themselves could not afford to be even suspected of any serious affair, for that would have harmed the moral reputation of staid public officers and professors such as Hagedorn, Gleim, Lichtwer, or Uz. Even the very young Goethe of 1767 believed it witty to contrast the realities of poetry and life in the following manner:

> Von kalten Weisen rings umgeben
> Sing' ich, was heisse Liebe sei;
> Ich sing' vom süssen Saft der Reben,
> Und Wasser trink' ich oft dabei.

*

> While sages cold have conversation,
> I forge of love a red-hot link;
> Of dulcet wine's intoxication
> I sing with water for my drink.

Finally there were the satirists of the eighteenth century, who often excelled in the observation of real life. Yet even Rabener, one of the best of them, produced no great work.

At the same time that empiricism began to affect German literature, Pietism too expressed itself significantly. Pietistic influences developed the emotional life of the Germans and unfolded its hidden powers. They greatly contributed to real poetry which did more than put philosophy into rhyme.

The work of Brockes, who was no Pietist in the strict sense, already showed a strong emotional life that was not of an exclusively religious tinge. A more pronounced emotionalism is found in Schnabel's novel *Die Insel Felsenburg* ("Felsenburg Island"), the best of the Robinson Crusoe stories written in emulation of Defoe's masterpiece. Schnabel as a boy enjoyed a Pietist education. His novel energetically rejected the feudal world of intrigue, and confronted it with the ideal picture of an island republic of virtuous patriarchs.

Pietist sentiments were popularized by the poems and lectures of the Leipzig Professor Christian Fürchtegott Gellert. This son of a poor preacher from the bleak Erzgebirge (the Saxon Ore Mountains) was originally under the influence of Gottsched. But soon he could be found among the writers of the so-called *Bremer Beiträge*, the chief organ of Gottsched's opponents. (The actual title of the Bremen periodical was

The Literature of Wit

Neue Beiträge zum Vergnügen des Verstandes und Witzes ["New Contributions to the Delights of Reason and Wit"].)

Gellert's *Fabeln* ("Fables," 1746–1748) were still written under a strong French influence, especially the influence of the celebrated La Fontaine. Like Hagedorn before him, and a host of minor talents after him, Gellert tried to coin useful rules of life into pleasing verses. It was exactly what his contemporaries desired. Frederick the Great, who was saturated with French literature, singled out Gellert as the only German writer worthy of notice. From our point of view Gellert's church hymns (1757) are of a much superior quality. They continued the best traditions of the seventeenth century. Six of them were set to music by Ludwig van Beethoven. Hymns such as *Die Himmel rühmen des Ewigen Ehre* ("The heavens proclaim the honor of the Lord"), and *Gott, deine Güte reicht so weit, so weit die Wolken gehen* ("God, Thy mercy extends as far as do the clouds") are assured of a permanent place in German Protestant hymnbooks. The convincing strength of their feeling is not to be denied.

Gellert also wrote the novel *Das Leben der schwedischen Gräfin von G**** ("Life of the Swedish Countess G***," 1746), and here too endeavored to express genuine sentiments. Using the letter form, but not very intelligently, this followed the example of Richardson; it ushered in a succession of German sentimental novels that culminated in Goethe's *Werther*.

Gellert's philosophy in part was still rationalistic, as any reader of his fables could attest. In this respect he differed from Friedrich Gottlieb Klopstock (1724–1803), the first poet of the century who could be described as essentially emotional. When Klopstock published the first cantos of his epic *Der Messias* ("The Messiah") in 1748 in the *Bremer Beiträge*, his contemporaries sensed an entirely new note, and the impression overwhelmed them.

Klopstock's talent was lyrical. His odes (1771) displayed a strength of subjective feeling that had not existed in German poetry before. Klopstock's God was exclusively transcendental; no human adjective sufficed to describe His personality. The poet never tired of expressing his boundless awe of the Infinite. In order to be able to project this awe, he must reject all sensuous imagery, and thus Klopstock's poetry assumed a seraphic and ecstatic character that sometimes anticipates the style of modern expressionism. This poet was infinitely more serious than the Anacreontic poets, and did not avoid coming to grips with the problem of death. Admittedly, in singing of friendship or love Klopstock

[141

usually became pathetic and sentimental; yet even in these lyrics Klopstock displayed a singular boldness of style and language. When he expressed his hope of seeing his beloved "Fanny" again in the Beyond, he wrote with a convincing religious fervor. He was not afraid of using incomplete or abbreviated periods, and he ventured into free rhythms as a matter of course. Nearly all his odes and hymns were written without the use of rhyme, and in most of them he tried to emulate the varied meters of Horace, which seemed to offer a more adequate vehicle than conventional verse forms for the transmission of a natural flow of the emotions. Klopstock represented a new force in German literature, and prepared the way for the personal lyrics of Johann Wolfgang Goethe. Only his Humanist rhetoric and his Christian transcendentalism still marked him as a poet of the older generation; almost no trace remained of the style of wit and good taste.

To his contemporaries, Klopstock was the poet of *Der Messias* (1748–1773). The theme of this epic was suggested by Bodmer, and Milton was adopted as Klopstock's model. *Der Messias* is written in hexameters, and describes the last days of Jesus' life. In powerful visions the poet depicts the struggle between Heaven and Hell, and every trace of reality is washed away by the glowing passion of religious sentiment. Klopstock attempts to preserve a consistent spiritual note, and in this respect shows himself influenced by the musical oratorios which came into fashion at the end of the seventeenth century. These oratorios no longer tried to represent the divine by theatrical means addressing themselves to the senses, but by musical means speaking to the soul. The style of the oratorios was brought to its zenith in Johann Sebastian Bach's *Matthäus-Passion* ("The Passion According to St. Matthew," 1729). Klopstock's poems can sometimes be described as poetic fugues, and his *Messiah* displays the same baroque pathos as Bach's (1685–1750) oratorios and organ music. Unfortunately it also contains weak passages, and inspiration is often lacking. In addition, the style does not fully express Klopstock's spirit. For his attitude is no longer unequivocally ascetic. His theme is not the Lost Paradise of Milton, but the salvation of mankind. He never tires of praising the humanity of Jesus: *Singe, unsterbliche Seele, der sündigen Menschen Erlösung* ("Sing, my immortal soul, of sinful mankind's redemption") *Die der Erlöser dereinst in seiner Menschheit vollendet* ("which the Savior did accomplish in his human form").

Klopstock's dramas were of ephemeral interest. Some of them used historical topics from the German past, and thus anticipated the revival of the Middle Ages by authors of the later Storm and Stress school. Klopstock also wrote a theoretical work *Die deutsche Gelehrtenrepublik* ("The Republic of German Scholars," 1774). Here, among other things, he demanded that the poet be original and beware of mere imitation, and this treatise too evoked the approval of the Storm and Stress period.

Gotthold Ephraim Lessing

I N Lessing and Wieland, the German Enlightenment finds its highest poetic expression. Lessing as critic makes empiricism the ruling philosophy, and thereby liberates new creative forces. Lessing as poet fashions an enlightened model drama which rests on a knowledge of real man, and therefore comes closer to life than Gottsched's drama. Wieland, on the other hand, in verse and prose narratives aims at a solution of the empiricist moral problem. Both poets, as far as possible, also go back to the age of classical antiquity, and thus foreshadow German classicism which achieves the ultimate synthesis of Pietist, empiricist, and classical elements.

Like Gottsched, Gotthold Ephraim Lessing (1729–1781) came from the German east; like Gellert he was a Saxon. He belonged to a family in which the inclination to literary studies was hereditary. Consequently, Lessing made excellent progress in the school of his native village and at the age of twelve was admitted to the Fürstenschule ("Princely School") at Meissen, then one of the seats of classical learning. Here the young student thoroughly absorbed the language and literature of the ancients; but the curriculum did not neglect the German language and literature either, and one of the lecturers encouraged Lessing to independent reading in contemporary European letters. The young man was such an omnivorous reader that his principal spoke of him as "a horse requiring double fodder." The school also countenanced poetic composition by the students as a legitimate part of true Humanist tradition, and thus it became the scene of Lessing's first poetic attempts.

From Meissen the young poet went to the University of Leipzig where he was supposed to round out his education and to study theology. But another attraction proved stronger for him as he became acquainted with the troupe of Frau Neuber, the celebrated actress and former ally of Gottsched's reformatory attempts. Perceiving Lessing's dramatic talent, she greatly encouraged him, and it was for her stage that the young writer finished his comedy *Der junge Gelehrte* ("The Young Savant") which he had begun at Meissen. The piece was an immediate success, and Lessing wrote other comedies, none of which, however, attained the success of the first one, which had aroused in Lessing the attempt to become the German Molière. Indeed, all these early plays still betrayed much French influence, generally centering around one principal personage. Yet Lessing was determined to become more than an imitator, and thus he could derive much good from a change of residence. In 1748, after less than two years at Leipzig, he left for Berlin and established himself as a journalist; he had already published some famous reviews. Although young Lessing by no means found it easy to get rewarding employment, he was finally appointed literary critic for the *Vossische Zeitung* ("Voss's *Times*"). As such he would write on some of the most important German and French books of his day; even early reviews show the learning, judgment, and wit for which he became celebrated. Then he acceded to the urgent wish of his parents and took his master's degree at Wittenberg. After his return, he became more firmly settled in Berlin and wrote, together with his friends Mendelssohn and Nicolai, *Briefe die Neueste Literature betreffend* ("Letters on the Most Recent Literature"); they discussed the principal works that had appeared since the beginning of the Seven Years' War (1756–1763), and laid down critical principles, later generally recognized as basic.

In 1755, before the outbreak of the war, the publication of *Miss Sara Sampson* had marked another milestone in Lessing's development. It showed that the writer had not given up the idea of reforming German literature by actual example, in addition to his critical efforts. It also indicated a certain break with French influence and a greater leaning toward English models. Above all, it was the first serious German drama since the Renaissance which took its material from the actual daily life of the middle classes; heretofore this had been reserved for comedies. The heroes of *Miss Sara Sampson* were no longer statesmen, kings or generals, as in the baroque dramas. They were average people, and made a direct appeal to the audience. At the same time their fate became an individual fate, and no longer implicated whole cities or nations; so it lost in representativeness what it gained in intimacy. The introduction of middle-class heroes was therefore a decisive innovation; it had first been made in England in Lillo's *George Barnwell* (1731), but had also been adopted by French dramatists such as Diderot. Subsequent German dramatists accepted Lessing's innovation. It was continued in Schiller's tragedy, *Kabale und Liebe* ("Love and Intrigue"), which employed German characters for Lessing's English ones. And it was followed by a host of nineteenth- and twentieth-century plays.

The war years from 1760 to 1764 Lessing spent in Breslau as secretary to General Tauentzien, in Prussian military surroundings. He drew upon these experiences for his important comedy *Minna von Barnhelm*. Shortly afterwards there appeared the aesthetic treatise *Laokoon oder über die Grenzen der Malerei und Dichtung* ("Laocöon or the Limitations of Poetry and Painting"). Both works attested to these five years as a most busy and fruitful period in Lessing's career.

Lessing had now assumed a leading prominence in German literature. When he resigned as secretary, he was not allowed to take a long rest. Patrons interested in the development of the German stage attempted to found, in Hamburg, a German National Theater, and called on Lessing to accept the position of "critic of the plays and actors." He moved there in April 1767; but the theater closed in November of the following year. Want of public appreciation, jealousies among the actors, mismanagement, and downright blunders caused the failure. Yet Lessing's criticisms were collected under the title of *Hamburgische Dramaturgie* ("Dramatic Notes from Hamburg"), and it was here that he formulated general criteria for dramatists and actors. To be sure, the Hamburg experience also made Lessing take a dislike to all theatrical work; but his theatrical learning soon reasserted itself, and in 1772 another of his tragedies appeared. It was *Emilia Galotti*, in which Lessing sharply criticized the licentious life of the contemporary princes and the helpless state of their subjects. Again, Schiller later followed Lessing's lead in his own *Kabale und Liebe*.

In 1770 Lessing was appointed court librarian at Wolfenbüttel, where he looked forward to a period of settling down and recuperating from the unrest of his earlier life. But in his library he discovered a manuscript of the late Professor Reimarus. The publication of these so-called *Wolfenbüttel Fragments* in 1774 led to sharp controversies with the orthodox fundamentalists, and soon Lessing had again become the focal point of fierce intellectual battles. For Reimarus was a deist who did not admit miracles, and attempted to explain the Bible historically; he frankly did not believe in "a divine revelation intended for all men and credible in all ages." Lessing, though not agreeing with Reimarus in every detail, came very close to his views. He fought at least for tolerance toward Reimarus, and the battle became so heated that finally Lessing was forbidden to publish any further theological pamphlets. There was nothing for Lessing to do but to answer his adversaries on the stage. He did this in *Nathan der Weise* ("Nathan the Wise"), the most important dramatic production of German Enlightenment. Another fruit of the theological controversy was the treatise *Die Erziehung des Menschengeschlechts* ("The Education of the Human Race") which became Lessing's chief work as a philosopher.

Lessing met with sudden death in the fateful year (1781) which also witnessed the appearance of Schiller's *Die Räuber* ("The Robbers") and of Kant's *Kritik der reinen Vernunft* ("Critique of Pure Reason"). Goethe was planning to visit the older poet, and when he was informed of his death remained despondent for several days.

Lessing's position as a critic cannot be understood without an examination of his relation to classical French drama and the drama of Shakespeare. Classical French drama of the seventeenth century had first dramatized the idea of man behaving logically within the framework of a definite period and in a definite locality. This was a new idea beyond the scope of Italian opera which, though it had presented a coherent universe, yet had assigned to man a merely decorative role. One can therefore understand why French plays were eagerly welcomed by the audiences of Enlightenment, and why they were praised as models by the leading critics of the time. But French drama had also confined the period of action to a rather short limit, and had restricted locality within each play to a single room. Lessing believed that the French conception of the unities of space and time was too superficial. The only unity that mattered was the unity of action which derived directly from the singularity of the dramatic character. His actions, to be sure, had to happen within a definite time and within a limited space; yet the time was not necessarily defined by the length of a theater evening, nor was the space necessarily limited by the walls of a single room or a single house.

Lessing's better realization of the potentialities of modern drama not only led to a revision of the somewhat pedantic French rule of the three unities, but also opened the way to an understanding of the differently constructed Elizabethan drama and its greatest representative, Shakespeare. For Shakespeare's dramas exemplified continuous action within the framework of a given human character, and free treatment of time and space could only be understood from that premise. Lessing especially admired dramas such as *Othello, King Lear, Hamlet,* and *Romeo and Juliet.* He saw that these plays deeply moved their audiences, but did not instruct them in the schoolmasterly fashion of the rationalist playwrights. He also observed that Shakespeare took his characters from history, but treated their development quite freely. By means of these and other pertinent observations, Lessing freed German drama from a too-slavish dependence upon French models, and encouraged playwrights to follow the more congenial English example. However, it must also be stated that in his critical attacks on French drama, Lessing did not do full justice to its greatest exponents, Corneille and Racine; he was right only in regard to the less important dramas of Voltaire and his eighteenth-century contemporaries.

Lessing's observations on the drama were contained in his *Hamburgische Dramaturgie.* In his *Laokoon,* the critic tried to do something similar for epic poetry. He proved that the epic poet was different from the painter in not devoting himself to description, but in resolving everything by action. In this connection Lessing gave beautiful expression to his admiration for the greatness of Homer. But the critic was hindered by the still-rampant prejudice that the poet could be guided by rules, and thus his *Laokoon* at times makes rather a pedantic impression. The same limitation is revealed by the fact that Lessing also devoted a very detailed treatise to the animal fable, a relatively unimportant genre of epic poetry.

Lessing did least for lyric poetry, since its subjective and musical character could not be reduced to rules. But he was an empiricist, and therefore often acknowledged realities which did not exactly fit into his scheme. Thus he was able to give an unprejudiced account of Greek civilization. Yet being a son of his century, he saw in it an eternally obligatory example. The word of Aristotle still was law for him. In this respect Lessing did not differ so much from the often berated French, while he differed strongly in his interpretation of the classics. Thus it remained for Lessing's great contemporary, Winckelmann, to impress upon the Germans a freer attitude toward Greek antiquity. It was he and not Lessing who became the founder of genuine German classicism.

The Witty Style of the Enlightenment

In his own dramatic efforts, Lessing reached the limits of his period. Although in his most mature creations he no longer imitated the French in the slavish fashion of Gottsched in his *Sterbender Cato*, he still believed with his enlightened contemporaries in the power of reason over passion, and therefore presented heroes and heroines overcoming their blind impulses and obeying the eternal laws of ethical conduct. It is only in the light of this concept of an orderly arranged world that the external structure of his dramas becomes coherent; though they deviate from the French rules, they do so only to a moderate degree. It was only hesitantly that Lessing changed the scenery in his *Minna von Barnhelm* and his *Nathan der Weise*. He was not yet inclined to a full imitation of Shakespeare by portraying human beings under the impact of an all-consuming passion, and he nowhere took the liberties that later characterized Goethe's *Götz von Berlichingen*.

It is highly instructive to compare *Minna von Barnhelm* with the contemporary comedies of Diderot and Destouches, for they too want to teach a lesson. Lessing shows that a good officer must not be haughty, and through the ridiculous personality of Riccaut de la Marlinière he seeks to prick German national pride. Yet Lessing's dramatic thesis has to be taken with a large grain of salt, for the hero of the play often behaves all too exemplarily. It is well that Lessing does not hold him up entirely as a model—he also smiles at him; and it is not so much Lessing the Saxon who smiles at Prussian stiffness, but Lessing the man who smiles at his own manhood; he possesses enough self-awareness not to take himself too seriously.

The hero Tellheim's inner conflict results from his fighting the promptings of his heart. Resisting to the utmost, he does not wish to continue his engagement to Minna when he becomes poor. It is only through devious stratagems that Minna can make him aware of the fact that she would not marry him for money anyway, but only for love; Tellheim must learn to swallow his pride and to prove his own love. Meanwhile it turns out that the circumstances of the lovers are not so bad after all, and the play which at times comes close to tragedy at last ends happily.

Thus Lessing illustrates the right of passion. He succeeds perfectly in holding his audience. What splendid figures are his Tellheim and Minna, his Werner and his Franziska! It is a distinctly German comedy, the first one of lasting value.

But Lessing's greatest achievement is his last drama, *Nathan der Weise* (1779). Here, with philosophical calm, he presents his noble view of life. Theological disputes in the last analysis do not matter for him; he fights merely for an active form of Christianity. To an astonishing degree Lessing lacks comprehension of the mystic and metaphysical aspects of religion. Yet although this drama owes its existence to a theological controversy which he continued on a different level, it is more than a mere pamphlet; it is more than a mere plea for the Jews; it wants to do more than merely spread the doctrine of tolerance, which it illustrates by a fable taken from Boccaccio's *Decameron*.

Lessing leads us to Jerusalem during the time of the Crusades. Representatives of Judaism, of Christianity, and of Mohammedanism meet on common ground. The Christians prove to be more intolerant and more superstitious than the Mohammedans and the Jews. Nathan, the representative of Judaism, exhibits a kindness and wisdom which are disarming. Modeled after Lessing's philosophic friend Mendelssohn, he exhorts the audience to believe that only the Last Judgment will show which religion is the true one, and that until then we can do nothing but perfect our own religion as far as possible. It is not the obstinate upholder of a dogma who possesses the true religion, but the man exercising the highest virtue, which endears him equally to God and his fellows.

Thus the play, far from extolling any definite religion, only demands from all religions that they put their doctrines to proof by applying them to life. But neither does it exclude any religion from attaining the highest validity; neither Judaism, nor Christianity, nor Mohammedanism as such are rejected. It is tolerance that Lessing demands; he demands it from and for all religions. And tolerance to this eminently masculine mind is not an effeminate endurance of all wrongs committed in the name of so-called religions; it is rather an active, courageous assertion of Christian love.

Just as *Nathan der Weise* in its theme fights for harmony, so it aims for harmony in its dramatic form. Its verse is no longer the French Alexandrines employed by Gryphius, Lohenstein, Gottsched, and Gellert. Instead, Lessing uses blank verse as did Shakespeare, although his blank verse is more uniform and monotonous than Shakespeare's. The end of the play is harmonious; all misunderstandings are dissolved, and the characters separated by fate are reunited.

Lessing's dramas still portray a world governed by reason, and the language spoken by his characters is still the language of wit and good taste. But the characters are taken from real life, and they are no longer set against idealized surroundings. Lessing's empiricist drama

[149

therefore comes close to the drama of personal experience that dominated the period to come, and has indeed prepared the way for it.

Johann Christoph Martin Wieland

LESSING illustrated Enlightenment by his vision of a harmonious world established through the application of reason. Wieland, too, longed for harmony, but he was primarily concerned with harmony within himself; his problem was more subjective. In other words, Lessing was primarily a philosopher, Wieland primarily a creative artist. He did not merely discuss passion and sensuality, he experienced them. To be sure, he fought hard for a balance between reason and sensuality, yet he almost never attained it. He was too impressionable and too complicated. His reasoning was never very convincing, and his emotions were easily excited. Wieland as a Southern German could not quite believe in the force of reason as did Lessing, the Central German. So his works ended either with an open victory of the natural instincts, or they recognized reason in a somewhat forced and roundabout way. The empiricism of Enlightenment led Wieland very close to the borders of scepticism and irrationalism. His aim was classicistic, but his achievements were often romantic, although to his last breath he fought romanticism.

Historians are wont to term Wieland the poet of German Rococo, and indeed his style is essentially related to the rococo style of the fine arts. Rococo everywhere softened the baroque tension into playfulness and easy, natural grace; it aimed at an inobtrusive harmony. Where Bach's music overwhelms us with massive polyphony, Mozart (1756–1791) flatters our ear with gracious euphony. Where Baroque delighted in brilliantly gilded ornaments, Rococo preferred the softly veiled radiancy of silk. It shunned heavy contrasts and severe disharmonies, and always dissolved them after the Chinese model. Thus Rococo was the pertinent expression of enlightened empiricism in the fine arts.

Johann Christoph Martin Wieland was born in Swabia in 1733, the son of a Pietist parson. To begin with he underwent an education completely antagonistic to his artistic sensuality. In a Pietist educational institution, Wieland was early vexed by religious doubts. And yet Klopstock and Bodmer became the first models to whom the young poet paid homage. Bodmer even invited him to share his house at Zürich, and for a while Wieland's work bore the spiritual stamp both of his host and of Klopstock. After he left Zürich, Wieland went so far as to experiment with monkish ecstasies.

However, this unnatural extremism soon turned upon itself. The young man's suppressed sensuality broke through in amorous adventures which ended only with Wieland's marriage. Shortly before this, in 1760, the poet had become senator of the Rhenish free town of Biberach, and here he tried for a while to live the narrowly circumscribed family life of a provincial bourgeois. Yet he did not wholly succeed, preferring instead to visit the nearby castle of Warthausen, the residence of the Mainz Chancellor, Count Stadion. Here Wieland again met Sophie Gutermann, his childhood sweetheart; she had meanwhile married the court counselor Laroche, administrator of Count Stadion's estates. Wieland later helped her to publish her substantial first novel, which opened the way to countless subsequent women novelists.

Wieland and his friends paid homage to French elegance, and read French writers presenting the views of men of the world. In his novel *Agathon* (1766–1767) the Swabian poet described his conversion to a graceful cultivation of the senses. As a result of this book he became a professor at Erfurt, where he wrote *Die Abenteuer des Don Sylvio von Rosalva* ("The Adventures of Don Sylvio of Rosalva," 1772), a novel paying tribute to "the victory of common sense over exaltation." At the same time he published *Der goldene Spiegel* ("The Golden Mirror"), in which he advocated enlightened absolutism. This novel was instrumental in procuring for Wieland the position of tutor to the Weimar princes; he in turn was of assistance to Goethe in bringing him to Weimar. Wieland now fully considered himself a classicist, solving the classical problem in *Oberon* in his own way. He became a prolific author, but could not refrain from repeating and exhausting himself, especially after the publication of *Oberon*. Still, he experienced a serene old age, and in his last novels he showed enough vigor to combat the new romanticism until, in 1813, death overtook him.

Wieland's works were the result of a life rich in changes and movement, and were therefore of different kinds and of varying caliber. The religious ramblings of the youth can be contrasted with the often frivolous tales of the mature man and the translations and philosophical writings of the old man. Yet all of them were real contributions to German literature, and many became popular enough to wean educated Germans away from the fashionable literature of the French writers. Today only three or four of Wieland's works remain alive: the short verse tale *Musarion* (1768), the novel *Agathon* (1766–1767), the verse epic *Oberon* (1780), and perhaps the humorous story *Die Abderiten* ("The People of Abdera," 1776).

In *Musarion* and *Agathon* Wieland treated the central problem of his life, the reconciliation of reason and sensuality. *Agathon* was his chief work. It was started in 1761, but did not receive its final form until 1794. Its hero Agathon grows up in lonely country surroundings; far from urban temptations, he knows only the ravishments of the heart. When he goes out into the world, the philosopher Hippias teaches him materialism and individualism, and the courtesan Danae ensnares him with her wiles. From now on Agathon's head is in continuous conflict with his heart. Only in the harmony of senses and spirit can he find true perfection. But this solution is unattainable for a fragile human being. Wieland himself did not fully experience it, and his reason often yielded to his artistic sensibilities. Therefore the style of the novel is never wholly serious, but always hangs in the balance. Wieland treats Agathon's achievement of a harmonious personality with sceptical reserve, and when at the end of the story he goes beyond this sceptical reserve in order to reach a synthesis of his hero's character, the result is more philosophical than poetic.

In the main body of his work Wieland is a true representative of the style of wit and good taste, always elegantly combining the extremes, yet never quite committing himself to a definite stand. But he is the most urbane and most intelligent, as well as the most artistic, representative of that style. Agathon is sincere in aiming at harmony, and is quite serious in trying to find himself. This is no longer a mere adventure story like so many novels of the seventeenth and early eighteenth centuries. It can rather be called the first successful psychological novel in German literature. In this respect Wieland largely attained what Grimmelshausen in his *Simplicissimus* only attempted.

The ideal presented in *Agathon* comes close to the ideal presented by Goethe and Schiller in their classical period, and in his personal attitude toward Goethe, Wieland never wavered in appreciation. He came equally close to classicism in his political views. In the second part of *Agathon*, the hero flees to the court of the Syracuse tyrant Dionysius, and shows considerable interest in republican principles of self-government. The long story *Die Abderiten* develops the picture of a small-town community and its political vagaries. Thus Wieland displays his interest in the realities of social and political life. For although *Die Abderiten* ridicules the foibles of provincial nepotism, bigotry, and narrowness, yet it does this in a spirit of sympathetic understanding and not of aristocratic arrogance. The story is a humorous collection of Greek small-town anecdotes, and even today can be enjoyed for its wit and elegance of style. Wieland scarcely believed in the possibility of enlightening the masses, but he did not despise them either, and did not treat community affairs with sovereign disdain. This story was a precursor to the social ideal portrayed in Goethe's *Wilhelm Meister*.

In his artistic sensualism Wieland also approached German romanticism. From 1762 to 1766 he published the first German translations of Shakespeare, and thus prepared for the deeper influence of the Bard which started with Herder. And around 1780 he published his charming *Oberon*, which begins with the verse:

> *Noch einmal sattelt mir den Hippogryphen, ihr Musen,*
> *Zum Ritt ins alte romantische Land!*

> *

> *Again the Hippogriff, ye Muses, bring*
> *For one more journey to romantic land!*

as rendered in the admirable translation of John Quincy Adams, the sixth President of the United States. "Romantic" here means "romance-like," fantastic. The material has been taken from legends and fairy tales, but there is order in this realm of fancy.

The knight Hüon, so the story goes, kills the knight to the left of the Babylonian Caliph, robs the Caliph himself of four of his molars and a handful of whiskers, and kidnaps his daughter Rezia. In all this he is helped by Oberon, the king of the elves. Oberon likewise profits by Hüon's actions, for Hüon's persevering love for Rezia helps Oberon regain the affection of his estranged wife Titania. Thus romantic elements have here been used for the decoration of a theme characteristic of the age of reason: the reunion of two lovers. And we not only have figures from Shakespeare's *A Midsummer Night's Dream* and details from Arabian fairy tales, but also elements from Old French epics and from classical antiquity. Add to this the god Amor and the oft-appearing rosy fingers of dawn, add thereto the absence of any trace of historical sense, and you will admit that *Oberon* is certainly

[153

no romantic epic. It is a delightful rococo fable illuminating a theme of Enlightenment. But through its metrical virtuosity and its imaginative fancy a door seems to open to the deeper and more basic irrationalism of the coming *Sturm und Drang* and of German romanticism.

CHAPTER SEVEN

The Style of Personal Experience in the Age of Goethe

The Age of Revolution

ABOUT 1775 new cultural trends become evident which finally come to their full fruition in the nineteenth century. Individualism which had been furthered by the Pietist cultivation of the soul and the critical attitude of the Enlightenment increases and begins to disturb the traditional cultural alignments.

In the economic field the age of machine industry and of modern commerce began. In 1775 Watt's steam engine was first installed on German soil. A few years later, in France, the first balloon rose into the air. The initial decades of the new century saw Fulton's steamboat and Stephenson's locomotive. Production and commerce were generally stimulated and accelerated.

Great progress was also made in hygiene and medicine. Edward Jenner in 1796 demonstrated the first successful vaccination against smallpox. Modern street lighting and modern sewage systems were introduced, and began to reduce the virulence of the epidemics that had plagued Europe since the Middle Ages. Individual man could look forward to a longer life span as well as to more permanent employment, and the population of Western Europe began to increase. Then suddenly employment and dislocation problems arose. Working conditions and labor unrest became subjects of discussion. Emigration and colonization became practical necessities. And the world began to shrink.

The new tendencies were at first hardly noticed. But as their signs multiplied, the resulting economic and social unrest could no longer be ignored. It soon took on distinct political forms. New liberal and democratic ideas that had originated in England and France were officially formulated in the American Declaration of Independence of 1776, and put into practice by the American Constitution of 1787. In Europe the new ideas became important through the French Revolution of 1789, for which philosophers such as Montesquieu, Voltaire, and Rousseau had paved the way. The state no longer appeared as a transcendental entity resting on its own eternal foundation, but as a temporary contract between independent individuals.

Parallel with this process, the national state arose as the most suitable form of political organization. In Germany princely absolutism had produced impossible conditions. The national domain was divided into hundreds of big and small principalities and imperial cities, which sharply differed in administration and economy, religious and educational systems. When in 1806 the Napoleonic Wars erased the last shadow of the "Holy Roman Empire," it was not interpreted as an epochal change. In fact, more orderly political organizations had already started in individual territories. When the Prussians fought their wars of liberation against Napoleon from 1813 to 1815, they were certain of the approval of all German patriots.

Many of the changes were so sweeping that contemporaries resisted them, and at the first opportune moment started a reaction. In France the wild excesses of the Revolution led to the rule of Napoleon who once more dreamed the medieval dream of a universal empire which the Habsburg rulers were finally to abandon. His victorious reaction set into motion the new forces of nationalism by which the visionary plan was defeated in the end.

In Germany, reaction took spiritual forms. Here between 1775 and 1830 art and music, literature and philosophy were the major concerns, since political organization remained largely intact. The fields of spiritual endeavor no longer were in an ancillary position, as during the baroque period and the Enlightenment, but followed their own laws and led all the other activities of life. In this realm the new, radical impulses were all accepted. But they were also checked by comparison with the culture that was in existence. Thus there arose great figures of enduring stature who embodied the values of the old as well as the new.

In philosophy it was the age of Herder and Kant, in music of Haydn (1732–1809) and Mozart, of Beethoven (1770–1827) and the romantic composers, in literature of Goethe and Schiller, Hölderlin and Kleist. The fine arts of the period employed many interesting talents but produced no outstanding personalities of the caliber of Goethe or Beethoven.

In literature proper our period begins with the tempestuous individualism of the Storm and Stress Movement, which for the first time brings to the fore the centrifugal tendencies hidden in Enlightenment. Then follows a reaction which leads to the balance and moderation of German classicism. But the new forces can be checked only for a short period, and in German romanticism the individualistic and realistic tendencies finally become dominant. The nineteenth century is completely under their sway.

The details of this development are complicated, and classicism and romanticism cannot be clearly separated to everyone's satisfaction. Seen from the point of view of the previous age, they are merely different artistic manifestations of the new individualism. The new writers no longer acknowledge general poetic rules derived from philosophical principles, but base their forms on personal experience. Poetry now becomes an individual expression, and has remained so almost to the present day. It blossoms in a great variety of styles. Poets differ in their interpretation of the nature of personal experience, and they differ in their mode of expressing it. They agree only in their individualistic approach to experience and style.

The new approach first became manifest in the life and works of Johann Wolfgang Goethe, and modern scholarship has often given the term Goethe Period (*Goethezeit*) to the initial decades of the new age. Others have more conservatively called it the Period of Classicism and Romanticism. But the actual wealth of personalities and movements in the period from 1772 to 1832 can hardly be compressed into a simplified classification. Nobody will deny the central position of Goethe in his age as well as in German culture in general. Yet he had great contemporaries in Schiller and Hölderlin, Jean Paul and Heinrich von Kleist, who should not be reduced to minor proportions.

Hamann and Herder

THE new age began with a revolutionary break with the previous age through the literary movement known as *Sturm und Drang* ("Storm and Stress"). But Storm and Stress had certain philosophical antecedents. Rationalism as well as empiricism had believed in the existence of absolute metaphysical ideas. Rationalism had derived them from pure reason, empiricism from experience. Now the possible consequence of drawing conclusions from experience alone was the denial of the existence of absolute ideas altogether. All metaphysics would be rejected as unscientific, all other philosophy would be restricted to realism or pragmatism. Radical realism could even deny the rationality of experience, and could claim that experience may be fathomed only by instinctive intuition. Such intuition was the prerogative of the individual, and no longer derived from a common social consciousness, from the traditional *consensus omnium* ("universal opinion") of the empiricists. Individualism also frequently led to naturalism, i.e., the aim of an individual life free from strangling inhibitions. Thus a whole new tendency was introduced by the more radical empiricists, and Enlightenment was turning against itself. The breakthrough came with the irrationalist philosophies of Hamann and Herder. Both were East Prussians, and represented a region which since the end of the Middle Ages had favored philosophical irrationalism.

Johann Georg Hamann (1730–1788) lived as well as reasoned in complete disagreement with rationalistic tenets. Descartes based his whole premise on a single statement, and achieved a lucidly balanced system. But for Hamann every system as such was an obstacle to truth. His *Sokratische Denkwürdigkeiten* ("Socratic Thoughts," 1759) and his *Kreuzzüge eines Philologen* ("Crusades of a Philologist," 1762) did not present continuous exposition, but merely disconnected revelations; it was not always easy to understand this *Magus des Nordens* (Seer of the North), as he was called. Hamann proceeded from Pietist foundations which he expressed very forcibly. "Everything that appears improbable and ridiculous to earthly reasoning is irrevocably and uniquely certain and comforting to Christians." Yet Hamann recognized empiricism, and did not therefore withdraw entirely into his labyrinthine soul. God also revealed Himself in nature and history. They were a part of Him and were just as unfathomable. Hamann acknowledged no separation of body and soul, of inner meaning and outward appearance. Like a primitive, he intensely experienced the world and God as an indissoluble unity approachable not by reason, but only by religious intuition.

As a writer Hamann attempted to free the reader's imagination, and therefore did not employ logical abstractions but images and symbols. They were not always clear, and he often consciously destroyed them again in order to open the reader's mind to the intangible. Thus Hamann anticipated the later style of German romanticism, with its cherished romantic irony. He also anticipated the humor of Jean Paul in his attempts to combine the sublime and the ridiculous, in order to express directly the unity of "God and World." Hamann found the religious passages of the Old Testament and the primitive chants of the ancient Orient to his liking. And he discovered that they were also beautiful poetry. Unspoiled mankind was always poetic as well as religious. "Poetry is the mother tongue of the human race."

Johann Gottfried Herder (1744–1803) took over this and many other ideas from Hamann, but he found clearer and less restricted expression for them. He also avoided a rationalistic system, yet he achieved a consistent, unified view of history and life, and codified important fundamentals of poetry. On general terms Herder might be compared with the French Swiss Rousseau (1712–1778) who likewise fought rationalism. But Herder was more radical than Rousseau, and rejected rationalism completely. For the abstract *consensus omnium* he did not substitute the isolated individual, but the wholeness of life, sensuous as well as spiritual, individual as well as national and international. Herder in no way compromised with Enlightenment, and became one of the most original thinkers of German philosophy.

He too was raised in Pietist surroundings, and in the beginning aimed at the ministry. As a Königsberg student he made the acquaintance of Hamann and also of Kant. Kant at that time was an empiricist who criticized rationalism and had an important influence on Herder. Then Hamann obtained a teaching position for Herder in the Latvian city of Riga, which at that time still had a predominantly German character. Here Herder became acquainted with Russian civilization, and was made aware of the importance of national feeling. He began to see that poetry was the mother tongue not only of mankind, but also of a national community. Whereas Hamann had discovered the irrational character of language, Herder now discovered the irrational character of nations. Nations were living, indivisible organisms, but they contradicted reason just as little as the various animals and plants, and they likewise could not be fully understood by abstract reasoning. Herder saw that nations were not deductions of ratiocination, but realities of history that could only be grasped intuitively.

Yet Herder's views had little in common with the extreme nationalism that hailed any particular nationhood as an ultimate. For Herder also spoke of the spirit of mankind which grew out of the totality of different national cultures just as white light results from the various colors of the spectrum. Herder did not favor an erasure of national differences, and welcomed the thought that each individual nation in its own way contributed to the greater whole. This spirited German enthusiastically described the ancient Hebrews and the old Irish, the young Baltic and the young Slavic nations; some scholars have gratefully called him *apostolus slavorum* ("the Apostle of the Slavs"). Herder himself was basically a Humanist, but he was easily misunderstood by disciples who lacked wisdom and restraint, and made him the father of nineteenth-century nationalism.

When irrationalism was applied to poetic literature, it led to an emphasis on the poet's originality and independence from foreign influences. Herder pointed to examples of ancient oriental poetry and of folk poetry, but he did not uphold them as models to be slavishly imitated. The German poets rather should proceed from the center of their national consciousness in a like manner. Such demands were first made in his *Fragmente über neuere deutsche Literatur* ("Fragments on Modern German Literature," 1766–1767) and then further developed in *Kritische Wälder* ("Forests of Criticism," 1769). In the latter work Herder took exception to the common classicistic prejudice that Greek culture had provided the universal standard for all time, and asserted his own view that this culture was an astonishing historical accident that could never be repeated.

Herder's ideas were corroborated by his travels in France, Holland, and Belgium, and soon became important for German poetry. When Johann Wolfgang Goethe met Herder in Strasbourg in the fall of 1770, his attention was directed to Homer and Pindar, to Shakespeare, to Macpherson's *Fingal* (1762) and *Temora* (1763), purporting to be translations of the Gaelic poet Ossian, and to German folk song. A new vista arose before Goethe's eyes; thereafter he gave up writing in the conventional rococo manner, and developed a style of his own. The first product of the conversations between Herder and the young Goethe was the booklet Von deutscher Art und Kunst ("On German Character and German Art," 1773); Goethe's hymnlike description of Strasbourg Cathedral and Herder's paean of praise to Shakespeare's genius stand side by side. Goethe also contributed to Herder's collection of folk songs originally called Volkslieder (1778–1779) and only later dubbed Stimmen der Völker in Liedern ("The Voices of the Nations in Songs"). This was inspired by Bishop Percy's Reliques of Ancient English Poetry (1756) and contained folk songs and popular poems of all nations, most of them translated and edited by Herder himself. In a similar vein a later book by Herder, Vom Geist der Ebräischen Poesie ("The Spirit of Hebrew Poetry," 1782–1785), praised the style of the Psalms. However, the mature Herder could not retain all of his youthful enthusiasm, and developed in a peculiar manner that will be treated later.

Storm and Stress

HAMANN and Herder expressed the spirit of a whole new generation which reached physical maturity around 1770. Like so many of the young generations before and after them, they rejected the culture of their parents and wanted to be independent at any price. They walked and dressed differently, they let their hair grow, and they affected the strong language of adolescents. The older critics dubbed them Originalgenies or Kraftgenies ("original or forced geniuses"). Modern critics are often reminded of the German youth movement before the First World War. Both movements indulged in ridiculous exaggeration, and both voiced a strong demand for an all-embracing pattern of life.

While in France the young generation's revolt resulted in the Revolution, in Germany it spawned a literary movement. Besides worshipping the German idols Hamann and Herder, the movement also paid homage to the Geneva sage Jean-Jacques Rousseau, with his contempt for the prevailing rococo culture and his recall to nature; and it venerated Shakespeare as the supreme poetic expression of originality. But the new movement was not quite as literary as it seemed. The young people demanded action, and to them literature was only a substitute for it. It is easier to say what these young poets were fighting against than what they were fighting for, and it was appropriate that the movement was called *Sturm und Drang* after the title of a typical drama written by one of their number, Friedrich Maximilian Klinger.

The spirit of Storm and Stress was essentially liberal. It fought vigorously against the absolutism of the princes, and against the artificial culture supported by them. By contrast it upheld the world of the common people, who were unspoiled by education and who expressed themselves in quite different forms of literature. Additional inspiration came from the German past; here the writings of the Westphalian patriot Justus Möser became an important stimulus.

The Storm and Stress poets wanted to live spontaneously like the great figures of the Middle Ages, under which term they included the sixteenth century. They wanted to follow the commands of their guardian *Genius*: where Enlightenment deified reason, they deified feeling and believed that it provided a secure basis for all vital decisions. Goethe later expressed it thus:

> *Ein guter Mensch, in seinem dunklen Drange,*
> *Ist sich des rechten Weges wohl bewusst.*
>
> *
>
> *A good man, in his uncertain groping,*
> *Is well aware of the right way.*

Enlightenment supported law and order, Storm and Stress hated the guardians of control and police regulations. These poets admired the great criminals and revolutionaries. Some representatives of Storm and Stress revolted against time-hallowed monogamy; passion was the slogan of the day; poetry was to reflect passion and emotional experience.

Some of these tenets represented a healthy reaction against the artificiality of rococo. Yet mere passion was often destructive, and only mature education could open the way to a rediscovery of nature and of the simple people. Immature minds were not equal to the stress, and were often destroyed by their own excesses. Others overcame the dangers of extremism by entering into practical life. After 1780 the revolution of a stormy decade had practically passed.

Storm and Stress

The most important documents of Storm and Stress were Goethe's drama *Götz von Berlichingen* (1773) and his novel *Die Leiden des jungen Werthers* ("The Sufferings of Young Werther," 1774), which initiated the movement, and Schiller's drama *Die Räuber* ("The Robbers," 1781), which terminated it. But all these works owed their importance to the fact that they were less one-sided than those of their contemporaries. They also understood the old world of the Enlightenment, which they in most respects attacked.

In Goethe's *Götz von Berlichingen* the influence of Shakespeare is all-pervading. Young Goethe does not bother about time and locality; his shifts of scene are more numerous even than those employed by Shakespeare. His action is complicated and often confusing; a great number of persons are involved. The language is forceful and earthy; verse form is dispensed with.

Götz himself is a true hero of Storm and Stress. As the last representative of a healthy, unspoiled generation he fights against the approaching era with its dark intrigues and emaciated lawyers. He rebels against princely immorality and social artificiality. He sides with the rebellious peasants, and seeks refuge with those social outcasts the gypsies. "Freedom" is his watchword. Leading critics of the older generation, such as Frederick the Great in his treatise *De la littérature allemande* ("On German Literature," 1780), denounced the play as destructive radicalism in content and form, while the young generation saw in Götz the inspiration for its fight against an artificial culture of hypocritical refinement.

It should not be forgotten that the struggle of Götz is a volcanic one; he stands alone, and he employs questionable methods; for all his pure and unselfish idealism, he merely produces disturbance and bloodshed. Goethe already sensed that unbridled individualism could not bring lasting satisfaction and could not endure.

Was life at all worth living? In *Die Leiden des jungen Werthers* Goethe presents an individual of his time. Young Werther is wrapped up in his own emotions, and is little interested in objective facts or in other personalities. He has no real attachment to his mother or to his closest friend. He addresses simple people in a condescending manner. He does not seek nature, but rather its reflection in his personal mood. Yet self-isolation does not bring happiness, and Werther looks for life's meaning elsewhere. Neither religion nor art can provide it for him, and he cannot adapt himself to the demands of a vocation. Finally, he is even unable to overcome his ego in love. Werther meets Lotte, and feels that all his being centers around this charming, beloved girl. She seems to be responsive to his feelings, she accepts him as a friend; but she is engaged to another man, and Werther will have to sacrifice his emotions for the happiness of another human being. This he is unable to do. He is less and less concerned with his adored girl's happiness and more and more with his own sensual gratification. He risks her displeasure by intruding upon her seclusion, and finally kisses Lotte with complete disregard for her feelings. His so-called love now stands revealed in its selfishness, and Werther in his isolation is at last man enough to face the consequences and end his futile existence by suicide.

This novel made Goethe famous overnight. A real Werther fever began. Everyone read the novel, translators made it known all over Europe, and imitations and commentaries abounded. Young men dressed themselves like Werther in sky-blue frock coat, yellow breeches, and jackboots. A few eccentrics even excused their own suicides by quoting the example of Werther, so that Goethe had to preface his second edition with a warning. He had succeeded in expressing the innermost impulse of his time—a desire to break with all social conventions and to live according to the dictates of one's heart. Indeed, "heart" was one of the most frequent words in the novel. But few people realized that Goethe had also questioned this sentimental subjectivism. Werther's suicide was an empty victory over isolation. As Goethe saw it, man needed the objective institutions of culture for his complete fulfillment. To his creator *Werther* signified the end of a period of subjective sentimentality, and the beginning of a search for a more objective basis of existence.

Werther rounded out the history of the European psychological novel in letter form which began with Samuel Richardson and continued with Rousseau's *Nouvelle Héloïse*. Goethe perfected the form, and made it the necessary vehicle of an asocial subjective passion that ran its natural course. All the letters in the novel are written by Werther. Only in the last phases of the story did Goethe find it necessary to interpose himself as the interpreter; for here the hero became incoherent and even unable to communicate. Goethe's artistic achievement was definitive.

Schiller's play *Die Räuber* likewise represented but a passing phase of his literary development. Externally, of course, the play was a product of Storm and Stress. Its language was unbridled and exaggerated, it violated all the rules of good taste, its characters were youthful abstractions and caricatures. The second edition of the play bore an attacking lion on the title page, and was inscribed *In tirannos* ("Against the tyrants").

164]

Storm and Stress

(The first edition had appeared in the significant year 1781, which also saw the death of Lessing, the foremost representative of the Enlightenment, and witnessed the appearance of Kant's *Critique of Pure Reason*, the book which refuted all rationalistic philosophy.)

The hero of Schiller's drama is the student Karl Moor. Disgusted with depraved contemporary society, he flees into the Bohemian forests to organize a gang of robbers. Like Robin Hood, he wants to replace right with wrong, but in the end he has to surrender to the authorities, and confesses that he has only destroyed and not created anything new. Thus *Die Räuber* also partially contradicted the creed of Storm and Stress.

The other authors of this literary group were distinctly inferior to Schiller and Goethe, but they too denounced the worship of reason and opened the way for literary movements to come. A most important personality was Friedrich Maximilian Klinger. His dramas were typical of the whole movement, dramas such as *Die Zwillinge* ("The Twins"), *Das leidende Weib* ("The Suffering Woman"), and *Sturm und Drang*. In later years Klinger became an officer in Russia, and wrote philosophical novels which aimed at a more objective view of the world. One of his early narratives was entitled *Fausts Leben, Taten und Höllenfahrt* ("Faust's Life, Actions, and Descent to Hell"). The same theme was treated by the poet Müller in his *Situation aus Fausts Leben* ("Situations from the Life of Faust"). Müller was also talented as painter, and has therefore become known as Maler Müller. He excelled in the writing of idylls in dialogue form, in which he came close to real folk poetry. In his idylls *Das Nusskernen* and *Die Schafschur* ("Nut Shelling," "Sheep Shearing") he portrayed genuine peasants who were quite different from the bewigged and well-groomed shepherds of fashionable rococo authors.

Other narrative endeavors of Storm and Stress were of an autobiographical nature, which is easily understandable in such a subjective movement. As an example, one can point to the life story of Heinrich Jung, called Stilling, which was set in Pietist circles. Karl Philipp Moritz, the intelligent author of the autobiographical novel *Anton Reiser*, also came from this group. But there is only one novel that can be mentioned in the same breath as *Werthers Leiden*, namely Johann Karl Wezel's novel *Hermann und Ulrike* (1780). These lovers remain faithful to their feelings and thus defeat the intrigues of rationalism. The novel originated under the influence of Fielding, but excelled all similar productions by its independent power of observation. Wezel was intelligent enough to reject mere adolescent ravings and realize the merits of reasonable living. Such an attitude was not easily achieved in this stormy period, as can be proved by a glance at Wilhelm Heinse's novel *Ardinghello oder die glücklichen Inseln* ("Ardinghello or the Islands of Happiness," 1787). This belated product of Storm and Stress advocated nudism and promiscuity, and had for its hero a Renaissance superman; his female counterpart advocated the same promiscuity, and demanded woman's suffrage.

Closer to Herder's idea of a religious and national poetry came the poets of the *Hainbund*, the "Grove Association," that was formed in 1772 in a grove near Göttingen. They were followers of Klopstock, and revolted vigorously against all foreign influences and tried to uphold national traditions. Unlike the poets of Storm and Stress proper, they excelled in lyric rather than dramatic forms. Loosely allied to them was the magistrate Gottfried August Bürger, the first great ballad poet of Germany. In his life he exhibited complete contempt for social conventions, so that the outer as well as the inner circumstances of his life became more and more entangled, and he died brokenhearted. This same primitivism, however, made him immortal as a writer. Bürger's free and congenial translation of his fellow countryman Rudolf Erich Raspe's *Baron Münchhausen's Narrative of his Marvellous Travels* (1785) as *Wunderbare Reisen zu Wasser und zu Lande* (1786) made the show-off Münchhausen a household figure of German folklore. Bürger's ballads could evoke the mysterious charm of unspoiled nature. In his *Wilder Jäger* ("The Wild Hunter") one hears the raging storm itself. In his convivial song *Vagantenbeichte* ("A Vagabond's Confession," based on a poem by the Archipoeta of the twelfth century) one senses a deep passion that shocked the puritans of his time. And in his *Lenore*, which appeared in 1774, he succeeded in endowing ghosts with an uncanny vitality. This ballad alone would suffice to make its author famous. English romanticists such as Sir Walter Scott were deeply impressed by him; after all, Bürger's ballads were inspired by Bishop Percy's *Reliques of Ancient English Poetry*. Other English influences molded the thinking of the professor Georg Friedrich Lichtenberg, whose colleague at Göttingen University Bürger became in his later years. Lichtenberg was equally unconventional in his life and philosophic attitude. His aphorisms were published after his death (1799), and made him famous as one of the best German stylists.

While Bürger was born in central Germany, Lichtenberg was a south German, as was Christian Friedrich Schubart, the unfortunate author of *Die Fürstengruft* ("The Tomb of Princes"). He too supported the ideas of the Grove group. His longing for freedom was distinctly political, and the Württemberg duke whom Schubart's verses attacked was autocratic enough to have the poet arrested and imprisoned in a fortress for ten years. When Schubart was freed, his health was completely broken.

Some north German poets also must be counted among the sympathizers of the Grove Group. The most important of them was Matthias Claudius, who edited the periodical *Der Wandsbecker Bote* ("The Wandsbeck Messenger") from 1771 to 1775. Claudius' lyrics have a more subdued, quiet character, and his inclination for contemplation is a typical north German trait; these people think twice before they speak. Claudius' songs have a warm, popular tone:

> *Der Mond ist aufgegangen,*
> *Die goldnen Sternlein prangen*
> *Am Himmel hell und klar.*

> *

> *The moon is slowly climbing,*
> *The golden stars are shining*
> *In skies so clear and bright.*

Such lines characterize the whole Claudius with his simple, unaffected language and his deep, heartfelt emotions. The same poet can also display robust humor of an earthbound quality:

> *Schön rötlich die Kartoffeln sind,*
> *Und weiss wie Alabaster,*
> *Sie sind für Mann und Weib und Kind*
> *Ein rechtes Magenpflaster.*

> *

> *The pink potatoes look so nice*
> *And white as alabaster,*
> *They are for man and wife and child*
> *A real stomach poultice.*

Or:

> *Der Winter ist ein harter Mann,*
> *Kernfest und auf die Dauer.*

> *

[167

Winter is a doughty man,
Tough to the core and lasting.

Such verses express another side of the north German character.

All the themes of the *Hainbund* and of Storm and Stress were to be taken up again by romanticism and the realism of the nineteenth century. But the foreground of the literary stage now belongs to the two classicists Goethe and Schiller.

German Classicism

GERMAN classicism was a countermovement to Storm and Stress irrationalism, and therefore of necessity was quite different from French classicism with its rationalistic basis and English classicism with its empirical basis. It is preferable to describe German classicism as a special form of German Humanism.

Like the poets of Storm and Stress, the representatives of German classicism also wanted to live a full life, but full in every sense of the word. Every human being must develop all his potentialities in harmony with himself; otherwise he will end in chaos. And he must develop these in harmony with society; otherwise all will end in destruction. Every individual needs society for his continuation and his field of action; he can reach his ultimate goals only through society. Schiller at one time expressed this belief in the often quoted verse:

Vor dem Tode erschrickst du? Du wünschest unsterblich zu leben?
Leb' im Ganzen! Wenn du lange dahin bist, es bleibt.

*

Are you afraid, then, of death and wish to continue forever?
Live for the whole! Long after you have passed, the whole still remains.

Thus by consistently following the tenets of Storm and Stress, German classicism reached a new ideal of life; the next question was how to transform this ideal into reality. The answer was: through art! Art better than anything can present our vision of the new man of harmonious character as a member of an integrated society. For this new man is a living ideal and no mere logical postulate. By visualizing this ideal through art we are stimulated toward imitating it; thus art becomes the great instructor of mankind. Art serves culture in a very general but decisive capacity. It is no longer self-sufficient, but neither is it utilitarian in a narrow sense. Whereas the culture of Enlightenment was a scientific one, German classicism visualized an aesthetic culture.

The symbols needed by German classicism for embodying its ideals were provided by contemporary culture, and this culture was largely Humanist. The first recourse of German classicism was to antiquity, and then it seemed to resume the classicism of Wieland and Lessing. Many critics also understood German classicism in this reactionary sense, and the second rate dramatists all through the nineteenth century wrote dull academic plays in the mistaken belief that they were following Schiller and Goethe. Likewise during this time teachers in many mediocre German *Gymnasien* misinterpreted German Humanism as the rule of dry philology, the exclusion of music and the fine arts, the deprecation of gymnastics and athletics.

But the real idea behind Goethe's and Schiller's Humanism was quite different; it did not derive from the conventional concept of classical antiquity, but from the inspired vision of Johann Joachim Winckelmann (1717–1768). As Goethe himself later emphasized in his essay *Winckelmann und sein Jahrhundert* ("Winckelmann and his Century"), Winckelmann's *Geschichte der Kunst des Altertums* ("History of the Art of Antiquity," 1764) again opened up the sources from which Greek art derived its origins. It directed the eyes of his contemporaries to the live Greek human being who had long been neglected in favor of the technical and theoretical aspects of art. Winckelmann was a disciple of Shaftesbury, and conceived of art as the embodiment of enthusiastic observation and imagination. Yet art was far from "imitating nature" in the traditional sense; it rather attempted to invest the spirit of nature with its proper form. It attempted an imitation of nature that was aesthetically satisfying. The genuine work of art combined sensual as well as spiritual elements, beauty as well as moral ideals, into one sublime form. This form was realized for the first time by Greek art, which was characterized by "noble simplicity and calm grandeur" (*edle Einfalt und stille Grösse*). This formula, which Winckelmann used as early as 1755, was later greatly misunderstood. For its author it still implied a divine sublimity and serenity. He longed for an ideal fully satisfying to his senses, while at the same time keeping them within bounds.

[169

The Style of Personal Experience

It was Winckelmann's truly humane conception of life which became of decisive importance for German classicism. Its aim was the resuscitation of Greek man, not of all the historical trappings of Greek civilization. The narrowly classicist phase therefore soon passed, and the essence of the new Humanism was not exclusively expressed in works of classical origin. Goethe's *Wilhelm Meister* and *Faust*, and Schiller's *Wallenstein, Maria Stuart,* and *Wilhelm Tell* were works of German or northern European origin; Goethe's *West-östlicher Divan* even employed oriental symbols. For Goethe and Schiller were not only influenced by the Humanist traditions of German culture, but by its Christian traditions as well. The interest of German classicism in the individual soul went deeper than that of Sophocles and Euripides, and no Greek ever wrote an autobiography such as Goethe attempted. This side of German individualism went back beyond Storm and Stress to German Pietism, and personal piety was a very important element of the Humanism conceived by the classicists. True, this piety had little use for religious dogma and institutions, and it could hardly be called Christian in the churchly sense of the word. For where the traditional believer felt utterly dependent on God, the German Humanist stressed individual autonomy and responsibility. Still, even these ideas were not entirely foreign to Christian theology, and one could not call Goethe's and Schiller's faith unchristian.

Some of the mature works of the German classicists have been adequately understood only in our time, and it was therefore perhaps excusable that most of their contemporaries, including men of the stature of Klopstock, failed to grasp their meaning. Goethe's and Schiller's conviction of the paramount value of earthly life, and their vision of a beauty at once spiritual and physical, confounded all orthodox Christians. Their conception of life as an irrational movement not wholly approachable through intellectual reasoning confounded all the narrow rationalists. And their insistence on man's reasoning powers, limited though they were, confounded all the old and new irrationalists. Elements of all these three strains of thought were combined in the ideas of the mature Herder, who at the turn of the century became something like a leader of the opposition to German classicism.

From the year 1776 Herder was *Generalsuperintendent* and court preacher at Weimar, where he had gone at Goethe's behest. His theological views had become stricter, and he soon felt repelled by the free-and-easy Weimar atmosphere. Yet his *Ideen zur Philosophie der Geschichte der Menschheit* ("Ideas on a Philosophy of Human History," after 1784) still proved him to be one of the leading Humanists. *Humanität* ("Humanity") was declared to be the essence of man's character as well as the irrevocable aim of history; the term was used at once descriptively and teleologically, and was a product of intuition rather than of logical reasoning. *Humanität* for Herder meant voluntary submission of man to the reasonable, though not always rational, laws of nature, and led directly to religion as its natural consequence. Herder combined scientific, philosophic, and religious ideas in a manner that lent general support to the ideas underlying Goethe's and Schiller's German classicism. Yet a closer inspection also uncovers some disquieting differences. Herder's views were dynamic and could not easily be adapted to existing conditions. His *Humanität* had a national coloration, and he could therefore sympathize with the ideas behind the French Revolution which started in 1789. He dreamed at that time of a German revolution bringing about a German national state. Goethe and Schiller for their part saw in the French Revolution a disturbance of mankind's slow progress toward genuine human culture, and therefore rejected it.

In 1795 Herder demanded a new German poetry in unmistakably nationalistic terms; he repudiated Greek mythology, and asked for a restoration of Germanic mythology. Schiller, to whom art had become an instrument of universal human education, could no longer agree, and accused Herder of an irresponsible realism. Goethe also eventually broke with his old friend. For while in *Wilhelm Meister* Goethe visualized an aesthetic education of mankind, Herder in his old age insisted more and more on a narrowly moral and denominational education, and agreement was no longer possible. Herder's last years were spent in bitterness. He felt that he had been misjudged, and that his efforts for German culture had been frustrated. Only a few gifted individuals went along with him, particularly Jean Paul. Herder died in 1803.

To be sure, Goethe and Schiller were not the only cultural leaders opposed by Herder. Another was Immanuel Kant (1724–1804), his erstwhile teacher at Königsberg. Kant had started as an empiricist, and had been deeply influenced by the English philosopher Hume. In his criticism of metaphysical speculation he had finally proved to most philosophers' satisfaction that metaphysics was never derived from experience and could not be logically deduced from it. In his *Critique of Pure Reason* Kant dealt the death blow to traditional methods of proving God's existence, and to many contemporaries he therefore appeared as an atheist and a dangerous radical.

The Style of Personal Experience

Actually he was far from it. For Kant's intelligence was profound enough to realize that reason is not man's only approach to a perception of the outside world. In his *Kritik der praktischen Vernunft* ("Critique of Practical Reason," 1788) Kant taught that moral laws presupposed the existence of God, and that therefore the belief in Him was an irrefutable postulate of practical reasoning. Nevertheless belief was not knowledge, and the *Ding-an-sich*, the "thing-in-itself" of metaphysics, remained inscrutable. Metaphysical speculations were possible only as long as they remained aware of their limitations. These arguments made Kant the founder of philosophical idealism, and resulted in the great German philosophical systems of Fichte, Schelling, Hegel, and Schopenhauer. Not until after 1830 was metaphysics avoided by the average German philosopher.

The third of Kant's critiques was called *Kritik der Urteilskraft* ("Critique of Judgment," 1790); it discussed the validity of aesthetic judgments, and led to the aesthetic speculations of the mature Schiller.

Perhaps Herder did not quite understand Kant. His criticism was directed chiefly against Kant's heuristic separation of spirit and matter, of abstract idea and concrete appearance. For Herder there existed only the experienced world of sensuous-spiritual totality, and his philosophy could perhaps be described as vitalism. This vitalism has been a recurrent feature of German thinking, and instances of it will be met throughout the nineteenth and twentieth centuries.

It was this emotional vitalism which prevented many Germans from grasping the full significance of Goethe's and Schiller's lucid new Humanism. The two great poets became isolated like Herder, although in a less pronounced sense. The German public at large was unable to plumb Goethe's last works, and achieved only a narrow interpretation of the mature Schiller. In spite of all the lip service to German classicism, its wonderful Humanism remained the possession of only a few, and throughout the nineteenth century a different spirit ruled from that visualized by the two contemporary leaders of German culture.

A third German poet was even more isolated from his contemporaries, and was hardly known during the whole of the following century. The Humanism of this great poet, Friedrich Hölderlin, has been understood only since the second decade of the twentieth century. For in many ways his Humanism was the most modern and least traditional of all. Interpretation of his poetry today has finally driven home the point that German classicism in spirit as well as in form attempted something quite different from ordinary classicism.

172]

Johann Wolfgang Goethe

JOHANN WOLFGANG GOETHE was a delicately built individual endowed with an almost morbid sensitivity which during the years of Storm and Stress threatened to engulf him. Yet he early discovered the way to restraint and balance that was offered by Winckelmann's reinterpretation of classical antiquity. The ideal toward whose realization Goethe worked hard and successfully was the fully developed, mature personality. In aspiring to it, the poet had to relinquish none of his rich gifts, and in his long life of over eighty years he participated in all changes of the German *Zeitgeist* from the rococo to romanticism and beyond. Thus, Goethe in his works belongs among the few who have successfully achieved a harmony between the two opposing strains of the German character, the dark, emotional strain and the lucid, reasoning strain. The harmony is so hard to achieve because the conflict is so profound. Goethe was thoroughly familiar with the pitfalls of emotionalism, he knew the dark longings of our animal nature, he was conversant with the power of primitive magic and fully appreciated the role of the demoniac in history and in nature. And still he did not succumb to the lure of the depths, but stayed on the side of the sane and the serene; he gave the day its due, and had an encouraging word for the practical business of workaday life. In his most mature works we find a harmony and simple humanity that is all the more engaging since it has been built on the brink of an abyss and still lets us sense something of the egoistic ebullience it has so successfully subdued.

Yet it would be wrong to consider Goethe's solution a merely personal or German solution. For the problem which disturbed him was a general European problem. The French Revolution and the concomitant revolt of feeling everywhere set free forces of cultural destruction and negation which it was important to control. If that was to be done at all, it could only be done by a recourse to the Renaissance ideal of man, which allowed a free range to the individual at the same time that it directed him to a noble ideal of his humanity. Goethe gave his answer to this problem in Humanist terms, and actually achieved that universality of the European, if not of the human, spirit, for which the whole West was secretly longing. Whoever in Western culture is seeking a specific

[173

answer to the ills besetting modern man must of necessity turn to Goethe. This is not always realized, for Goethe, like Dante and other great writers, is but imperfectly known to many who write about our culture. Even in Germany Goethe is often criticized by pedants and glib *literati*. Yet whoever makes the effort really to study his genius will find himself richly rewarded.

Johann Wolfgang Goethe was born at Frankfurt-am-Main on August 28, 1749, the middle of the eighteenth century. Frankfurt was still a free imperial city, and was the place where the rulers of the Holy Roman Empire were crowned. The Empire itself lingered on until 1806, when Goethe was fifty-seven years old. In his social and political attitude he remained a man of the eighteenth century with its many small principalities and its aristocratic society, but also with its rising middle classes and its dreams of human rights and of world government. One should never lose sight of the fact that Goethe was a scion of the patrician families governing a small German city state, and that therefore conservative ways of thinking came just as naturally to him as liberal ways.

When Goethe was young, rococo culture was still flourishing in Germany. When the boy started his studies, he still followed its French models and their German imitators. At the end of 1765 he went to Leipzig in order to study law. The city was called "Little Paris" and aspired to the graceful manner of the life of fashion which left its traces in Goethe's shepherd play *Die Laune des Verliebten* ("The Wayward Lover"), and in a number of charming but unoriginal poems. In his personal life the Leipzig student enjoyed his independence from parental supervision and had little regard for his health. As a consequence he suffered a breakdown, and in 1768 had to return to Frankfurt and give up further studying for almost a year. He now had time to reflect and began to think more lucidly.

Soon the young student again felt his full powers, and set out for the University of Strasbourg in order to complete his studies. On April 2, 1770, he arrived in the capital of Alsace, and in September made the acquaintance of Herder. Herder accelerated the younger poet's development to intellectual independence. He brought to full realization Goethe's feelings of personal immaturity, and of the shallowness of the easy rococo manner. He directed Goethe's attention to genuine poetry as it could be found in the Bible, in Shakespeare, and in the folk songs of all nations. Goethe in return helped Herder to collect the material for the latter's folk-song collection, and soon himself began to write in the new style. Lyrical gems such as *Heidenröslein* ("Rose Among the Heather"), *Mailied* ("May Song"), *Willkommen und Abschied* ("Welcome and Farewell") began to flow from Goethe's pen. The poet had finally discovered his own manner, and henceforth gave direct expression to his spontaneous personal feelings. From now on original lyrics accompany Goethe's life in all its changing moods and phases as "fragments of a great confession," and Goethe thus introduces into literature the new poetry of personal expression.

In looking at the Strasbourg Cathedral with its late Gothic ornamentation, Goethe became aware of the German Middle Ages, and in roaming through the beautiful Alsatian countryside he experienced nature. In the center of these experiences stood a charming young girl, Friederike Brion, the parson's daughter from Sesenheim. For the first time Goethe felt the joys of real love, but also its pangs. For he was not yet ready for a lasting union, and suffered from awakened hopes that he could not fulfill. When he returned to Frankfurt with a license to practice law, he left behind him a charming idyll that forever had to remain a dream. The young man realized now that life is passing and fragmentary, and that man cannot help but cause suffering and confusion, however noble his motivation may be. Some of this feeling went into Goethe's first tragedy *Götz von Berlichingen*, which he completed in the fall of 1771, and which appeared in print, somewhat amended, in 1773.

In this, Goethe definitely broke with the Age of Enlightenment and became the acknowledged leader of Storm and Stress. In his lyrics of that time he asserted his independence and threw a challenge to the gods, like Prometheus of whom he sang in rapturous free verse. But he also had moods when he wanted to forget himself and submerge his identity in the overwhelming wave of the universe; then he would sing perhaps of Ganymede who longingly rose upward to the bosom of the all-loving deity. In these contrasting themes of self-assertion and self-renunciation, much of the mature Goethe was to be found.

The months from May to September 1772 were spent at Wetzlar, where Goethe was supposed to acquire practical experience as a juridical observer at the Supreme Court of the Holy Roman Empire (*Reichskammergericht*). But the young author hardly visited the courts, instead enjoying life among a convivial circle of friends. One of them was engaged to a young lady called Charlotte Buff, and Goethe too was soon passionately in love with the spirited girl. But how should he proceed? Should he claim the superior rights of genius and simply ride roughshod

The Style of Personal Experience

over friendship, as did Dr. Faustus who at that time frequently occupied his thoughts? Should he give in to hated social convention? Or should he even destroy himself, in order to be spared a personal decision? In the end Goethe manfully took hold on himself and abruptly left Wetzlar, without taking leave of his beloved.

His passion was supposed to consume itself through lack of an object, but it took ample time in doing this. Goethe became entirely free from it only when he expressed the attitude he had taken in a novel. *Die Leiden des jungen Werthers* ("The Sufferings of Young Werther") appeared in 1774, and freed Goethe from a personal way of life that could only lead to his destruction. His own attitude differed from his hero's and was entirely compatible with, nay even required, identification with the rest of mankind. In writing *Werther* the irresponsible emotionalism of Goethe's youthful contemporaries was implicitly rejected, and the Storm and Stress movement, in which most of them lingered on for a considerable while, was rejected too. Goethe now felt the need to come to grips with practical life, and to counterbalance his subjective sensibility by an objective knowledge of the realms of nature and of human affairs.

There followed a brief engagement to the daughter of a Frankfurt banker which was finally broken off because it did not really satisfy Goethe's aspirations. Then, in the fall of 1775, Goethe was summoned to the court of the young Duke of Weimar, and taking this as a call of fate, the poet accepted the invitation.

Though at first hardly envisioning a long stay at Weimar, Goethe actually remained there for the rest of his life. To pay homage to art and poetry was customary for the princes of the period. But the Weimar court was not merely observing custom. Here Goethe lived among a circle of friends who went along with the young generation and accepted his unusual character. He found in the young Duke Karl August a man who fully appreciated him, and in whose native tact and sensibility he could fully confide; Goethe sagely guided the younger man during his years of development to maturity. How different was this court from the court of Frederick the Great who only a few years later denounced the young poets in his treatise already mentioned, *De la littérature allemande.*

Above all, Weimar offered young Goethe the welcome opportunity to overcome his egocentricity by taking part in political activities. Soon after his arrival he became one of Karl August's councillors, and took a hand in administrative affairs. He helped to reorganize the Ilmenau mines, and concerned himself with the living conditions of the Apolda hosiery workers; he assisted in the drafting of soldiers, and rearranged the state's financial accounts. Last but not least, he set an example for the duke in the observance of his duties as a ruler. When they both returned from a journey to Switzerland, Karl August had matured into a conscientious nobleman who could safely be trusted to perform those duties.

Goethe's lyric poetry of his first Weimar decade also shows a preponderance of objective insights. An ode such as *Gesang der Geister über den Wassern* ("Song of the Spirits over the Waters") hints at the limitations of human existence, and in *Grenzen der Menschheit* ("Limits of Man") Goethe warned man against overestimating himself.

Denn mit Göttern	*For with the Gods*
Soll sich nicht messen	*Should not contend*
Irgend ein Mensch.	*Any mere mortal.*

Still, man's fate is not devoid of hope. If he humbly accepts the place assigned to him, he gains access to the godhead and can find happiness in trying to live out his destiny. In the poem *Das Göttliche* ("The Godlike") Goethe phrases this destiny as follows:

Edel sei der Mensch,	*Let man be noble,*
Hilfreich und gut!	*Helpful and good!*

In philosophic and scientific studies Goethe also corroborated his conviction that the single individual was only part of a great harmonious whole. He took up anatomy and discovered the existence in the human skeleton of the intermaxillary bone, the *os intermaxillare*, thus linking man structurally with his animal forbears. He studied plants and tried to trace their manifold shapes from a common ideal prototype, the *Urpflanze*. He became a mineralogist, and looked for the bedrock supporting all subsequent strata. Through these studies Goethe developed an interesting idealistic concept of evolution. He found similar ideas in the works of Plato and Leibnitz who conceived of all nature from a few simple fundamentals. And he found some of his basic tenets reflected in the writings of Baruch Spinoza, with whom he believed in the essential unity, though not identity, of God and nature.

The Style of Personal Experience

In his personal affairs Goethe also learned to respect the objective institutions of society. Shortly after his arrival at Weimar he made the acquaintance of Charlotte von Stein, a married lady and the mother of a family. Goethe fell passionately in love with her, and she herself did not remain unaffected. But there could not be any question of a love affair, and Charlotte made this clear from the beginning. She was Goethe's senior by seven years and had acquired a serenity and maturity that could not be seriously shaken. He gradually yielded to the calming influence of her friendship, and acquired an understanding of the necessity for and beneficial effect of social conventions.

But the lesson was not learned easily, and the relationship between Goethe and Frau von Stein did not run its course without friction. The longing for peace which the two poems entitled *Wanderers Nachtlied* ("Wanderer's Night Song") express was real enough. And it was increased by the many demands of court life and official duties; as a poet, Goethe in his first Weimar years accomplished comparatively little. A feeling of dissatisfaction grew in him, and he came to the point where he had either to yield completely to convention or assert his independence. He chose the latter course, and in the fall of 1786 suddenly left Weimar. Neither Charlotte nor the Duke were informed that Goethe was fleeing to Italy.

In addition to his personal reasons Goethe also felt a more objective compulsion to go to the fountainhead of Western culture: to see the classical heritage with his own eyes. He hurried through northern Italy, and felt at ease only when he came to Rome. Following in the footsteps of Winckelmann, Goethe studied all its classical and Renaissance monuments. He also delighted in association with creative contemporaries, and enjoyed the genial friendship of the common people of Rome. Then he took up drawing and continued his scientific studies. Later he visited Naples, climbed Mount Vesuvius, and took a trip to Sicily. Here too the sunny climate, the majestic landscape, and the friendly people charmed him. Thus he rid himself of unhealthy inhibitions, and acquired a freer, more wholesome attitude toward art and life. The great Humanist tradition of German culture now became rooted in his personal life, and during all the years to come it continued to nourish his daily work and his everyday decisions. In Italy he began to put the finishing touches to the works that had been gestated in Weimar. The year 1787 saw the completion of his *Iphigenie*, 1788 the completion of *Egmont*, 1789 the completion of *Tasso*.

When the poet returned to Weimar in June 1788, he gave up most of his public offices and withdrew from the social life of the court, henceforth confining himself to activities for which he felt a definite calling. He also brought order into his emotional affairs by disengaging himself from Charlotte von Stein and starting a less complicated union with Christiane Vulpius. This quiet and simple young girl gave him the peace he had desired so long. At first they lived together in a so-called union of conscience (*Gewissensehe*); but in 1806 the union was consecrated by a church ceremony.

Of the three dramas just mentioned, *Egmont* still belongs in part to his Storm and Stress period. Contrary to historical facts, Egmont is portrayed as a dashing, carefree youth and a gallant lover; he relies entirely upon his own genius and pays no heed to the counsel of reason and experience. But like the equally well-meaning and equally childlike Götz, Egmont also ends in confusion. At the end of the tragedy we see him needlessly walking to his doom, yet presaging a rise of his beloved Dutch people to freedom.

Torquato Tasso presents the same tragic conflict of life in the fate of a poet, and more explicitly indicates a solution. Tasso is emotionally unbalanced and certainly presents no ideal human character. Yet his faults spring from his poetic vocation, and even help to establish it. He is the equal of any actual hero, and has a legitimate place in life. His poetic task is to represent by symbols the many individual facets of existence in their true proportion, and to make them appear as parts of a meaningful whole. But the fulfillment of this task is denied Tasso by his antagonist, the statesman Antonio, who sees poetry merely as decorative. When Antonio, in a fit of jealousy, insults Tasso, the poet withdraws into himself and believes himself completely bereft. Blindly groping for some human assurance, he loses touch with reality and becomes impossible at the court where he has been living. We see him wander into a lonely fate. But the rejected man arouses deep sympathy in Antonio, who now realizes that Tasso never sought an escape from life. The poet is revealed as cursed with the loneliness of the creative genius, which makes him yearn vainly for real fulfillment. His fate symbolizes the tragedy of man who longs for the absolute, yet always fails to attain it.

Since Goethe's tragedy unfolds in the highly cultured setting of Italian Renaissance society, its language is subdued and refined. There is a minimum of plot, the number of characters is small, and the action is concentrated. Yet there is scope for the feminine charms of the princess, one of Goethe's most lovable female characters, and the verse rings with singularly beautiful metaphor. The tragedy of Tasso constitutes one of the highlights of Goethe's classicism.

The twofold dramatic action of *Iphigenie auf Tauris* is the second highlight. Here for the first time Goethe expresses his belief that the tragedy of man's existence does not defy solution altogether. But still there are very real obstacles to fulfillment. Both Orestes, the hero, and Iphigenia have to overcome great tribulations, and Pylades, Orestes' pragmatic friend, cannot envision any possible solution. Orestes has revenged his father Agamemnon's murder by his mother through taking her life in turn; but in thus meting out justice he has taken upon himself the prerogative of the immortal gods, and has called down the wrath of the furies. The curse upon him is only lifted when he is ready to acquiesce to the will of the gods, however inscrutable it may be.

Orestes' sister Iphigenia comes to doubt the gods in a different way. She has been brought to Tauris by the goddess Diana, and as her priestess has been instrumental in abolishing human sacrifice. When the incensed King Thoas threatens to reintroduce it, Iphigenia is ready to resort to lies in order to save her fellow Greeks. But this would deny her faith in the mercy of the gods and would betray the king's trust. Iphigenia also realizes that lying is unworthy of her, and she submits to the will of the gods by confessing her intentions to Thoas and by appealing to his innate sense of justice. Hearing that Orestes and Iphigenia are brother and sister, Thoas desists from human sacrifice and permits the Greeks to return to their homeland. But he does this grudgingly, and only when Iphigenia tells him how well she will receive strangers from Tauris and how she considers him a friend does his attitude change, and he dismisses the Greeks with his blessing. The audience feels that Thoas has been won over from barbarism to a higher level of culture.

Goethe's play nowhere specifically mentions Christian myth or dogma, and yet it must be called Christian, for a classical Greek would have loudly protested against the injustice of fate, and would not have trusted so implicitly in the mercy of the gods. The accent of the play is on pious humility without regard to the consequences, and on meeting life's challenges instead of evading them by lies and trickery. But by clothing this basically Christian morality in an antique garb, Goethe has lent it a human appeal transcending any specific belief or religion. The Christian religion here has become the religion of Humanism, and *Iphigenie auf Tauris* can almost be classified as a religious play. It is no wonder that its action moves on a very high plane. There are only five speaking parts and no distracting realistic details. The setting remains the same during the whole action, and strict unity of time is enforced. The form is blank verse, with but few diversions necessitated by passing changes of mood. The language is generally subdued, although clear and imaginative.

If *Iphigenie auf Tauris* adumbrated a new social ideal and redefined morality in terms of the new individual responsibility, it also fulfilled one of the needs of the age. For in 1789 the outbreak of the French Revolution put the old European culture to a test. Goethe was deeply disturbed by the Revolution. In 1792 he accompanied his duke in a campaign of the German princes for the restoration of the French monarchy. When this campaign was halted by the cannon duel of Valmy, Goethe at once recognized the fatal importance of this historical moment. He himself was no democrat—how so could he have acquiesced to his elevation to the nobility in 1782?—yet he was enough of a political realist to understand that the old monarchical order was doomed.

Still, political events could not alter Goethe's primary objectives. He pursued the development of his old concept of man's place in the evolution of nature. At the time of the French campaign he was deeply occupied with the problem of a botanical prototype, and it was a discussion of this problem which led to Goethe's friendship with Schiller. The two had met before, but only now, at the end of 1794, did they become intimate. In their correspondence they revealed the deepest mutual understanding. They discussed each other's plans and stimulated each other's minds. And together they worked out their classical philosophy. Goethe often accepted the literary advice of Schiller, who was ten years his junior, and Schiller respectfully listened to the advice of the elder genius.

In 1796 Goethe completed his novel *Wilhelm Meisters Lehrjahre* (translated by Carlyle as "Wilhelm Meister's Apprenticeship") with Schiller's helpful assistance. During the same year the two poets combined in the authorship of *Xenien* (literally, "Gifts of Hospitality"), a series of epigrams mercilessly criticizing the whole of contemporary literature, and judging it according to the ideals of classicism. But contemporaries could not be brought to conform to their ideals.

In 1797 Goethe completed his idyllic epic *Hermann und Dorothea*. It treated a story of almost Biblical simplicity, and afforded Goethe an excellent opportunity to unfold his own views concerning the most epochal political event of his day and concerning the structure of society in general. His attitude toward the French Revolution can best be described as moderate and conservative. Goethe did not object to change as such, and did not want to preserve all external manifestations of the passing era. He wanted only to retain essential elements of culture, and to proceed by peaceful evolution. He was especially concerned with strengthening the family ties upon which civilization was founded, and he makes Hermann and the Alsatian refugee girl Dorothea unite in a marriage that rests not on fleeting passion, but on a sober, healthy respect for one another's rights to a personal life. This attitude represented a liberal point of view, and Goethe's further development amply proved that he continued to uphold it.

In 1798 the two poets published a literary almanac which for the most part contained ballads. Goethe contributed such excellent poems as *Der Zauberlehrling* ("The Sorcerer's Apprentice"), *Der Türmer* ("The Warder"), and *Die Braut von Korinth* ("The Bride of Corinth"). They all betray a deep awareness of the demonic forces of life.

Finally, the two poets devoted no small part of their efforts to the Weimar stage. Goethe, as its director, supervised performances of Schiller's dramas, and also commissioned Schiller to write translations and adaptations of foreign plays. Schiller in return prevailed upon Goethe to continue his work on *Faust*. Through their combined efforts, Weimar became a cultural center which for a long time overshadowed Berlin, the center of Enlightenment.

When Schiller died on May 9, 1805, Goethe was shaken to his inmost being. When his grief subsided, he composed a worthy monument to his friend in his *Epilog zu Schillers Glocke* ("Epilogue to Schiller's 'Lay of the Bell' ").

Of Goethe's works completed during his friendship with Schiller, the novel *Wilhelm Meisters Lehrjahre* deserves special comment. It applies to German culture specifically the general principles developed in *Iphigenie auf Tauris*. The hero operates fully in all the spheres of life for which he is suited. But he can do this only by meeting the responsibilities that go with the prerogatives. In contrast to the medieval way of life, Wilhelm starts out as a modern man who wants to take his place in the world of reality. He develops all his gifts through actual experience. The parents who raised him, the women with whom he falls in love, the friends with whom he associates, are not his only teachers. He is also matured by his efforts in the theater, by the intellectual currents of the time, and by the social tradition of that time among German nobility. Gradually he frees himself from the shackles of his small-town past, and becomes a free individual; as such he is conscious of his limitations, and is willing to adjust his own expectations to those of society.

Johann Wolfgang Goethe

In the end Wilhelm unites in marriage with an equally mature woman, and chooses the responsible profession of surgery.

Wilhelm's original predilection for the stage remains but a passing phase, during which he is introduced to the dramas of Shakespeare. In them he recognizes a perfect illumination of life and its conflicts. Especially does *Hamlet* provide Wilhelm with a clearer perception of the world. Yet in the end art is but a magic mirror of life and demands a changed attitude toward reality. In like manner, all other aspects of life are placed in their right perspective, be they the noble world of high society, the introspective world of Pietist reverence, or the world of love. Life is accepted in its many facets, and even a certain lightheartedness and frivolity are seen as necessary correctives to Wilhelm's early pedantry. In the end Wilhelm has become a well-balanced individual who can take his place in practical endeavor. Yet Goethe has not subscribed to a harmless meliorism. His novel also includes questionable and foundering characters. Some of these are attractive poetic creations, like Mignon, the passionate Italian adolescent, or her father, the old harpist, who bypasses life in guilty, self-inflicted seclusion.

The novel also holds the reader's attention by means of its many interesting events and its lively discussions of philosophical and artistic problems. One can derive from it a colorful picture of German life around 1775. Yet gross realism is avoided, and all the incidents are aesthetically meaningful. In certain formal aspects the novel could even be hailed as a forerunner of romanticism. Inner necessities and a few twilight figures determine the course of action, narrative parts intersperse lyrical ones, and the charm of the latter is occasionally enhanced by such deeply felt verses as *Wer nie sein Brot mit Tränen ass* ("Who never ate his bread with tears") or *Kennst du das Land, wo die Zitronen blühn?* ("Know'st thou the land where the lemon trees bloom?"). Even a whole diary is found in *Wilhelm Meister*. It is the first German novel since the baroque period that has succeeded in combining many diverse elements. Its influence on contemporary and succeeding German generations was decisive, and it started a whole new type of German prose literature, the educational novel.

Meanwhile the old order continued to collapse. On October 14, 1806, the destiny of the state created by Frederick the Great was sealed on the battlefield of Jena. Goethe, like most Germans of his generation, was not too deeply affected by this event. He had grown up under the shadow of the Holy Roman Empire, and he therefore understood the gigantic attempt of Napoleon to renew the empire of Charlemagne. Goethe in 1808 paid homage to the victorious emperor. And Napoleon, who had looked down on so many crowned heads and heroes of the battlefield, summarized his judgment of the German poet in the words: *Voilà un homme* ("At last a real man"), a phrase that from his mouth was no mean praise.

Otherwise the years after Schiller's death were poor for Goethe in external events. From the standpoint of the writer they were more productive. In 1804 his novel *Die Wahlverwandtschaften* ("Elective Affinities") appeared. Once more Goethe was concerned with the problems of marriage. The title employs a chemical term as a symbol for the centrifugal tendencies represented by individual passions. We become deeply aware of the precariousness of the monogamous ideal. Nevertheless the ideal is upheld, and is invested with religious authority. *Die Wahlverwandtschaften* is one of Goethe's deepest novels, but it is difficult of access as the events are treated symbolically.

In 1810 Goethe published his *Zur Farbenlehre* ("Contributions to the Theory of Color"), in which he attacked the optical theories of Newton. Goethe believed this work to be one of his main achievements. But it met with little understanding on the part of contemporary scientists, and while its scientific value is not established, it arouses some interest even today.

In the following years the poet wrote his autobiography: *Aus meinem Leben, Dichtung und Wahrheit* ("Fiction and Truth Relating to My Life"). It became one of the most influential German autobiographies. But it should not be interpreted as factually correct, concerned as it is with the general theme of the interplay of poetic creation and subjective experience, of personal development, and objective tendencies of the time.

The fact that Goethe started an autobiography seems to stamp him definitely as an old man. One can also point to other instances where he loses touch with the young generation. The victory of nationalism to him did not signify unquestionable progress, and in Napoleon's downfall he saw only the triumph of the masses. He did not quite sympathize with the radical young protagonists of the new liberal movement. At times he was weary of European complexity, and expressed a strong preference for the new culture rising on the other side of the Atlantic:

> *Amerika, du hast es besser*
> *Als unser Kontinent, das alte . . .*
> *Dich stoert nicht im Innern*

Johann Wolfgang Goethe

Zu lebendiger Zeit
Unnützes Erinnern,
Vergeblicher Streit.

*

America, you are better off
Than our old continent . . .
You are not inwardly disturbed
In the living present
By useless memories
And vain strife.

Thus, the oriental predilections of the old Goethe must be partly explained as a welcome escape from the turbulent Europe of his time. Translations from Persian, Indian, and Chinese sources came to his attention when once more he was eagerly looking for the true humanity that he had already adumbrated in *Iphigenie*, in *Wilhelm Meister*, and in *Hermann und Dorothea*. In Eastern garb he discovered a strangely invigorating combination of delightful sensuality and deep, mystical philosophy. Goethe was happy losing himself in this new excitement, which was enhanced by a return trip to his Rhenish homeland and by his acquaintance with a uniquely fascinating young woman. Marianne von Willemer seemed to have stepped from the pages of a Persian manuscript; she combined sensuous attractiveness and spiritual animation. Goethe relived his youth in her company, and for a while forgot his wife, who had remained in Weimar. He wrote some of the most carefree and subtle of his poems for Marianne, whom he addressed as *Suleika*, and for the first time in his life he met with equal female response: Marianne wrote poems of such beauty that they could be included in Goethe's own collection. This astonishing collection is called *West-östlicher Divan* ("West-Eastern Divan"), 1819. It contains some of the gayest and some of the most spiritualized love songs in the German language, and its last part, the "Book of Paradise," contains some poems worthy to be compared with stanzas of Dante. Both poets unite in praising divine love as the ultimate mover of the universe.

The philosopher as well as the poet Goethe have an equal share in the poems of the *West-östlicher Divan*, as indeed in all the poetry of his old age. As a youth, he had expressed himself in a subjective, completely unrestrained manner. As a man he had achieved the balanced harmony of classical style which placed subjective experience into its objective setting. Now he made the subjective experience even more representative and translucent by interpreting it in metaphor or by means of symbols. Each poem begins by citing a special case or some well-defined reality, but by interpreting it symbolically, Goethe transcends mere subjectivism or realism. The poetry of his old age often takes on a magic quality.

But such ecstasies were reserved for the rare moment, and Goethe was aware that at his age he could not simply turn his back on all his responsibilities. He chose tragic resignation rather than total abandon, and withdrew from Marianne's longing arms into the loneliness of his old age. Though to the very end he never forgot her, he never returned to her and never invited her to Weimar. He seemed to face final years of joyless isolation.

As to the literary scene, Goethe had not much in common with the Romantic Movement which during these years held more and more sway over German youth. To the old sage the young poets appeared turbulent and devoid of principles. For his part Goethe preferred to praise the poets of German dialect, such as the Alemannic Hebel, or the popular poets of foreign nations. Goethe's favorite during these years was Byron, who to him appeared to be the only poet as thoroughly alive and modern as he himself, being neither a classicist nor a romantic. Goethe likewise had good relations with Sir Walter Scott and Thomas Carlyle, other great Englishmen of his time. In France also Goethe was not unknown. In 1804 he had met Madame de Staël, and this meeting introduced Goethe as a living force into French literature. Her *De l'Allemagne* ("On Germany") made Goethe and Schiller the guiding stars of French romanticism.

During this period Goethe became a phenomenon of international literature. His home was a mecca visited by admirers both from Germany and from foreign countries. Many of them recorded their conversations with him more or less faithfully, and gradually volumes of Goethe's conversations with his contemporaries appeared in print. The most important one of these was Eckermann's *Gespräche mit Goethe* ("Conversations with Goethe," 1836–1848), a treasure chamber of the wisdom of Goethe's old age.

But grand old man of letters that he was, Goethe's fire was not dead and at times could blaze up threateningly. As a man of seventy-two he took the baths at Karlsbad, and was seized by a violent passion for a seventeen-year-old girl, Ulrike von Levetzow. Inevitably he had to tear himself away from her as he had from Marianne von Willemer.

Johann Wolfgang Goethe

But when he bowed to the separation, he wrote the moving *Marien-bader Elegie* ("Marienbad Elegy"), one of the most mature love poems in the German language. In this, Goethe touchingly expresses the necessity for resignation.

Resignation was also the key to Goethe's last novel *Wilhelm Meisters Wanderjahre oder Die Entsagenden* (translated by Carlyle as "Wilhelm Meister, Journeyman, or The Renouncers"). In 1821 it appeared in its first version, and in 1829 in a second revised and enlarged edition. Goethe put an astonishing amount of material and effort into his work. He was no longer concerned with man as an individual, but with modern society as a whole. In the thirty years that had passed since *Wilhelm Meisters Lehrjahre*, the Industrial Revolution had begun and presented its vast new problems. Goethe was among the first Europeans to recognize the new situation. *Wanderjahre* deals with the doomed domestic industry of overpopulated mountain regions and with the slum conditions of the new industrial regions. The novel shows a group of disinterested organizers directing the uprooted craftsmen and farmers to the few open spaces of Europe and the vast possibilities of the New World. Wilhelm and his co-workers select and train emigrants for new lives in America, aware that emigrants have to sacrifice much and have to realize their limitations. But the prospect is not hopeless. The end of the novel includes an optimistic marching song sung by the newly constituted emigrant society. Goethe's answer to the social ills of his time was therefore cosmopolitan, and could not hope for intelligent reception by an age that had turned toward nationalism. Nor could its potent wisdom find understanding with a public that continued to prefer sensational adventure stories and sentimental trash. The vast universality and many-sided reflectiveness of *Wanderjahre* is still appreciated only by a few critics, and these few critics are mostly men advanced in years.

Now signs of the end became more numerous. Goethe collected the forty volumes of his literary legacy into a last edition (*Ausgabe letzter Hand*); later there followed twenty more volumes of posthumous writings. The fall of 1831 saw the completion of *Faust*. In the spring of the following year, on March 22, 1832, the poet died. Tradition has it that his last words were: *Mehr Licht!* ("More light!").

The gestation of the great tragedy of *Faust* occupied a good part of Goethe's life. It could have been brought to birth only by a man who lived a many-sided life through successive ages. The drama of *Faust* presents human existence under the aspects of youth and old age, of manhood and womanhood, of the student and the courtier, the poet and the merchant, the sheltered townsman and the rapacious colonizer. It presents existence in the experience of mortal man and in the perspective of the eternal God. Through this wide lens the drama achieves a singular self-awareness of Western man in a crucial period of awakening individualism. This is a complete vision of the modern ego, standing in marked contrast to the incomplete visions of all romantic and post-romantic subjectivists. In *Faust*, man is exposed in the reality of his limitations.

The hero of the drama is not an ideal or perfect character, but rather a representative one. His redeeming feature is his awareness of his imperfections. Faust seeks to overcome them and to gain access to the absolute. Finally he casts his lot with the Devil in the shape of Mephistopheles, who tries to turn Faust's dissatisfaction with life into a negation of all higher values and a reduction of existence to momentary lust. But Mephistopheles, the great Destroyer, cannot see that he is but a part of creation, and that Faust's alter ego belongs to the constructive and positive elements of the universe. Faust can never find complete satisfaction in momentary sensual enjoyment. But neither can he become completely identified with the supreme good, and the base part of his make-up furnishes the Devil with his well-taken points of attack. In its essential human aspects Faust's life is indeed a tragic sequence of half-successes and part-failures.

In this sequence there seems to be little development. Faust never seems to learn from his experiences and never outgrows them. In Part One, Faust falls in love with the sweet, innocent Gretchen. Mephistopheles almost manages to turn Faust's sublime, self-forgetful emotion into mere sensual lust and shameful abuse. Yet when Faust becomes a murderer and an accessory to murder, his motives are not entirely corrupt, and he does not in the least enjoy his evil deeds. Only by force can the Devil tear him away from the victimized girl in a scene which ranks with the greatest in all literature.

In the second part of Goethe's drama, Faust enters the impersonal world of politics and achieves a short-lived triumph through his invention of paper money. He then demands to experience the aesthetic satisfaction of supreme beauty, which Goethe lets him find in a symbolic marriage to Helen of Troy; but the idyll cannot last. At the end of his life Faust helps the Roman emperor to win a civil war, and is rewarded with being granted sovereignty over a stretch of shoreland, which he quickly dams up and colonizes. He attains his ends by brute force and scheming trickery, and only in his last moments does he reject his gains and find happiness in unselfish though never successful activity. Faust ends his life with a grandiose vision of happy colonizers united by civic virtues in an industrious endeavor for the common good. The Devil has not succeeded in killing his divine spark.

Of course, Faust has not realized perfection, and his soul which the angels carry off to Heaven must yet grow and be slowly cleansed of all its mortal shortcomings. Only after a long heavenly evolution can the depersonalized eternal spirit of Faust combine again with its divine origin. The attainment of this hoped-for, ultimate redemption is possible only through Divine Love which in Goethe's wisdom is here symbolized as Eternal Womanhood. Merely mortal life in *Faust* is thus represented as a never-ending struggle, and the designation of the play as a tragedy is fully justified. But the epilogue in the transcendental world visualizes this struggle as meaningful and hopeful.

A complete, detailed discussion of all the many aspects of Goethe's supreme achievement would fill the pages of a substantial book. The complexity of his tragedy has often baffled interpreters and led to one-sided criticism, but it is not incompatible with the open, effusive structure which *Faust* shares with the religious dramas of the Hindus, the Passion plays of the Middle Ages, the historical dramas of Shakespeare, and the processional plays of Strindberg. The setting in such dramas is a constituent part of the whole, and without the surrounding world of beauty and of knowledge, of politics and of society Faust would hardly be the representative man that he is, for he would represent exactly nothing.

To be sure, some *Faust* passages, especially in the second part, are characterized by evasiveness and excessive allusion. By his own admission, Goethe at times lost himself in his effusiveness, and inserted some scenes which have but a slight connection with the main theme. But an intelligent reader will not be unduly disturbed by these stylistic imperfections, and theater audiences have always been captured by the many scenes of singular power and beauty, the scenes in Heaven and the Gretchen scenes, the Helena scenes and the scenes on the dunes. They are equally entranced by the majestic sweep of the angels' voices in the Prologue, by the philosophic depth of Faust's monologues, by the chilling chorus of human and inhuman demons, by the biting wit and humorous worldly wisdom of Mephistopheles. It is not enough to pay one's tribute to the deep philosophy expressed in *Faust*; let us also consider that in its form and language *Faust* must be adjudged the greatest attempt of the German genius to portray the meaning of human life in aesthetic symbols appealing to modern man. In world literature it ranks with Shakespeare's *Hamlet* and *King Lear* and with Dante's *Divina Commedia*, with the Hindu *Bhagavadgita* and with the *Tao te King* of Laotzu.

Friedrich Schiller

ON THE whole, Goethe's life was a quiet process of growth. With unerring artistic instinct he enmeshed his many gifts into a harmonious personality. And his personal experiences seemed to spring from the necessities of his development. Contrasted with Goethe's life, Friedrich Schiller's was not the life of a universal genius. His talent was typically one-sided, and from the beginning he found himself in painful antagonism to the totality of existence. At times the poet believed in his ability to overcome this antagonism, and he courageously challenged an unsympathetic world and a lazy century: *Es ist der Geist, der sich den Körper baut* ("It is the mind that builds itself the body"). At other times the problem seemed to defy solution, and Schiller despairingly called a halt to his spirit: *Steh, du segelst umsonst!* ("Stop, you sailor to nowhere").

To be sure, the conflict between art and life decreased in the course of Schiller's development, and in his mature period the poet learned to enjoy the fleeting moment. Yet the basic tension *zwischen Sinnen-glück und Seelenfrieden* ("between sensuous joy and peace of mind") was never entirely absent. Even for Goethe, who knew Schiller intimately, the prevailing impression was of a continuous fight against nature, a heroic attempt to overcome the limitations of his ego and of the whole contemporary culture by fighting for the ideal. Goethe and Schiller may be said to have their last aims in common, but not their presuppositions.

Goethe in his fight for personal balance preferred to express himself in lyrics, and to unfold his whole mind in epic succession. Schiller, on the other hand, was a man of will who had an affinity for the drama. He fought within himself and he fought against the outer world.

Friedrich Schiller

The mutual opposition of ideal and reality in the last analysis was what he could not overcome. Thus he became not only a dramatist, but a tragedian.

This tragedian presented German-speaking people with an impressive treasure of great dramas and powerful ballads. In a few popular quotations he may appear childishly naïve or rhetorically empty. He is weak as a lyricist, and has been superseded as a historian. Yet Schiller at his best can still inspire us by the nobility of his mind that so impressed Carlyle and Coleridge. And in the performances of great actors, Schiller's heroes and heroines become wondrously alive and arouse our highest sympathies. Unfortunately, one usually takes Schiller's measure from the hands of popularizers and schoolmasters. One should rather read interpretations by fellow artists such as Thomas Mann, who in his last lecture convincingly demonstrated Schiller's greatness in face of all his minor flaws.

Even Schiller's personal life was a constant fight against hostile circumstances. While Goethe came from a ruling patrician family, Schiller's family was still fighting its way up. The boy Friedrich was born at Marbach in Württemberg on November 10, 1759. His father began his career as a Bavarian regimental surgeon, then campaigned with the Württemberg army, and later on was stationed in several places as garrison officer and recruiting officer. In 1775 he was retired, and given the position of garden superintendent at the Duke of Württemberg's castle Solitude near Stuttgart.

At this time fate put an end to the carefree school years of his young son Friedrich. The lad was just ready to leave the Latin school, and to start the theological studies for which he had shown an early inclination, when in 1773 Duke Karl Eugen drafted him into the military academy for able officers' sons which he had just founded at Solitude. The Duke's interest was a special favor which Schiller's family could not afford to decline, and since only law was taught at Solitude, Friedrich had to change to this subject, which he did not like. Two years later the academy was transferred to Stuttgart, and was enlarged by the addition of a medical school. Again Schiller changed his plans and took up the study of medicine, as his father had done before him. In later years the ducal academy was known as *Karlsschule*. Its method of education was military, and Schiller smarted under its strict regulations. Still, he found ways to satisfy his finer sensitivities, and became acquainted with the most recent German poetry. He closely studied Klopstock's *Messias* and himself attempted to write a *Moses*. Soon,

The Style of Personal Experience

however, he was attracted by contemporary dramas such as Gerstenberg's *Ugolino* or Goethe's *Götz*, and by Shakespeare's *Othello*, and discovered through them the language of passion. His new poetic attempts followed this direction until in 1777 he found the material on which he could base his *Die Räuber* ("The Robbers") which was completed while he was still at the academy. In this, Schiller challenged the world of the Enlightenment with its princely despotism, and gave expression to personal feelings in the passionate manner of Storm and Stress. However, the hero of the play ultimately arrived at the realization that mere revolutionary radicalism would by no means solve the ills of the world.

Young Schiller hardly realized all the implications of his stand. He was still fighting against reality, and looked for philosophical confirmation to Rousseau's writings against the unnaturalness of his age, and to Plutarch's anti-democratic biographies. When in 1779 Goethe visited the *Karlsschule* with the Weimar duke Karl August, Schiller must have been painfully aware of his own unsatisfactory position. In 1780 he obtained his license for the practice of medicine, and could look forward to better years. But the authorities tried to dampen his fiery spirit by giving him a position as physician to an inferior regiment. Now that the discipline of the school had passed, however, Schiller enjoyed greater freedom and could attend to the printing of *Die Räuber* at his own expense. When the play appeared in 1781 it immediately caught the attention of the contemporaries. The following year the Mannheim National Theater produced Schiller's play in a somewhat weakened version, and the production achieved overwhelming plaudits. Soon thereafter Schiller's *Anthologie auf das Jahr 1782* ("Anthology for 1782") appeared, which with all its youthful extremism still foreshadowed the future poet. The Duke of Württemberg did not at first pay much attention to his pupil's writings, but when Schiller absented himself without leave to attend a second performance of *Die Räuber*, the Duke put him under arrest and forbade him to write. Schiller protested, but this only aggravated the Duke, and so the poet decided to escape; in September 1782 he left Stuttgart for good. By his flight Schiller gave up his modest claim to economic security, and his fight against contemporary society began now in earnest. No longer could the young poet simply take a negative view, and the easy radicalism of Storm and Stress was out of the question. Even his own Karl Moor in *Die Räuber* had arrived at the realization that unbridled individualism led to the destruction of civilization.

192]

Friedrich Schiller

Years of vagabondage began, often years of bitter want and dependence upon charity. The need was aggravated by the first signs of the tuberculosis which in the end became fatal to the poet. Schiller at first tried to make a living as official poet to the Mannheim theater. In 1784 his *Fiesco* had a poor première; contrary to his original intentions, Schiller had provided the tragedy with a happy end. He also wrote a third play, *Louise Millerin*, which became later known as *Kabale und Liebe* ("Love and Intrigue"). He then began his blank-verse drama *Don Carlos*. But a gap yawned between Schiller's ideals and the contemporary stage, and soon the poet was again without a position and found himself facing life alone.

The drama *Kabale und Liebe* most purely reflects the young Schiller with all his noble aspirations and his amateurish shortcomings. Fortunately the tasteless title of the play was not of the poet's own choosing. Like Lessing's *Emilia Galotti*, Schiller's drama reflects the spirit of a self-conscious middle class. Yet Lessing's play still had an Italian setting, while Schiller drops the mask and shows us German, or more exactly Württemberg, conditions. We hear of a duke who sells his subjects to the British Crown as mercenaries in the American War of Independence, and who uses the money thus obtained to give costly presents to his British mistress. In the background looms a meretricious court supervised by a President, Walter, who has acquired his position by criminal means. Walter's son Ferdinand is supposed to inherit the exalted position of his father. But Ferdinand is in love with a girl of the middle classes, the daughter of the musician Miller. Louise herself fancies her love to be a crime against the established order of things, and even Ferdinand does not quite believe in the possibility of breaking through the barriers of caste. The lovers successfully defend themselves against brute force, but when the court starts intrigues against their union, they do not know how to ward them off. Louise is induced to sign a love letter to a high personality and to keep this secret from Ferdinand. And Ferdinand is trapped into belief in her disloyalty, and makes her drink poison before taking it himself. Only a brief while before his death he discovers the truth. This end is rather arbitrary and does not measure up to the unavoidable, tragic entanglement which it was supposed to be. In addition some traits in Schiller's characters and in the situations seem exaggerated. Yet the exaggerations are not as great as they were in *Die Räuber*, which also was a prose play. Miller and his family are no angels, and the court people are no devils. On the whole, *Kabale und Liebe* is more probable and closer to life. The play signifies a considerable step away from mere Storm and Stress toward a more balanced view of the world. *Kabale und Liebe* can be understood on its own human terms, and even in our time the play is frequently performed.

When Schiller's contract as stage poet was not renewed, he at first did not know what to do. Then the German upper class became interested in the promising young Swabian. He was invited to Weimar by Charlotte von Kalb who was connected with the Weimar court; again a lady was instrumental in educating a Storm and Stress radical. Charlotte polished Schiller's manners, she polished his speech, and she personally introduced him to the Duke of Weimar, who appointed Schiller an honorary councillor without pay. Then the coquettish Charlotte showed signs of a fiery passion for him, and although Schiller did not remain unaffected, he did not want to yield to her. So they separated, and again Schiller was alone.

Fate, however, favored him once more. An invitation came from Councillor (Oberappellationsgerichtsrat) Körner at Leipzig, who had become an enthusiastic admirer of Schiller's poetry. Schiller spent happy days on Körner's little estate and later on at Dresden. Körner's devoted friendship helped the young poet to overcome his financial worries, and he could now resume his work with new vigor. In 1787 the drama *Don Carlos* appeared in print, and the *Lied an die Freude* ("Ode to Joy") was written, whose exuberance later provided a fitting vocal finale for Beethoven's Ninth Symphony. Schiller also started important philosophical studies.

However, in spite of all his efforts the poet had not yet gained mature insight into life, and was still wanting security. His acquaintance with Körner made him painfully aware of this, and Schiller began to look for an office or position of some sort. Naturally his thoughts turned to Weimar where he already had some connections, and in July 1787, he left Dresden and traveled to the Thuringian abode of the muses.

He did not immediately find what he wanted. Finally he was appointed associate professor of philosophy at Jena University. He settled there in 1789, and in the same year married Charlotte von Lengefeld. Schiller's external circumstances were now easier; yet he still had not solved his problem as a creative artist. Goethe had finally found himself in Italy: Goethe who had to experience everything through the immediacy of his senses. Schiller always fought against reality, and had to establish harmony within himself before he could discover it in external life. For the next few years he therefore became engrossed in

Friedrich Schiller

philosophical and historical studies. In 1787–1788 his *Geschichte des Abfalls der vereinigten Niederlande* ("History of the Secession of the United Netherlands") appeared; the work was written in quest for the meaning of history, and no longer displayed a belief in revolution but rather in the progressive reform of human existence. Immediately after this Schiller mustered his forces to write *Geschichte des Dreiszigjährigen Krieges* ("History of the Thirty Years' War"). But he had overtaxed himself. He suffered a dangerous attack of pneumonia which brought him to the threshold of death. Recovery was slow, and was complicated by serious financial worries. Then unexpectedly two Danish admirers relieved the poet by magnanimous gifts; they were the Duke of Holstein-Augustenburg and the Count Schimmelmann. The Danish bounty provided much-needed relaxation for the next three years. Schiller now had an opportunity to study Kant at his leisure. Although he did not accept it in every detail, Kant's basic dualistic distinction between appearance and reality, duty and inclination was shared by Schiller, since it appealed to the dramatist in him. Yet it was somewhat attenuated for Schiller the artist, who longed for harmony of form and idea. In 1793–1795 his *Briefe über die ästhetische Erziehung des Menschen* ("Letters on the Aesthetic Education of Man") was published, and was dedicated to the Duke of Augustenburg. In this Schiller accepted Kant's unsentimental insistence on selfless duty, but he also stressed the value of moral emotions. Schiller's point of view was less rigorous and less theoretical than Kant's, for he could not stop being an artist. Man ought to do his duty, but he could do it to his emotional satisfaction. His true progress consisted in his total spiritual and mental growth, not in cold obedience to an intellectual command. Man was also not furthered by sudden revolutions. Schiller turned his back on the French Revolution and insisted on man's gradual total and political education. Nothing could better advance it than art, and in Schiller's philosophy art assumed the same central role in culture which during the Middle Ages had been given to religion. He did not yet envision the "art for art's sake" of later critics, which merely served subjective expression. Art with Schiller had a task to perform, and this task was best served by a harmonious form. A slavish imitation of reality would not do, and Schiller spoke out with acid clearness against pure realism. On the other hand, he did not want to lose all connection with life, and likewise turned against an all-too-abstract idealism. The secret of the artistic form to him seemed to lie in a healthy middle road between the extremes, in *Realidealismus*. In the essay *Über naive und*

The Style of Personal Experience

sentimentalische Dichtung ("On Naïve and Sentimental Poetry") Schiller attempted to elucidate his thoughts still further.

After this last philosophical writing Schiller returned to his own field of poetry. In the final analysis all his studies were only a preparation for new dramatic endeavors, the first of which was the *Wallenstein* trilogy. Indeed, even the *History of the Thirty Years' War* of 1792 read like a drama with Gustavus Adolphus and Wallenstein as the principal actors. In the summer of 1794, when his new period of creative activity started, Schiller also came to know Goethe more intimately and this new friendship greatly aided his artistic efforts. Yet Schiller did not turn away from philosophy immediately, for during the following years he wrote his most important philosophical poems, among them *Das Ideal und das Leben* ("Ideal and Life") and *Der Spaziergang* ("The Walk"). And along with Goethe he defined and defended his idea of art against contemporaries in the *Xenien* printed in 1797. Soon afterwards there appeared a ballad collection written by the two poets together. While Goethe's ballads made the reader aware of the demonic elements in nature, Schiller's ballads were versified dramas in lucid language. As examples one may mention *Der Handschuh* ("The Glove"), *Der Ring des Polykrates* ("The Ring of Polycrates"), *Die Kraniche des Ibykus* ("The Cranes of Ibykus"). In 1799 Schiller completed his *Lied von der Glocke* ("Lay of the Bell"), which could not of course be classified as ballad. In clear images and versatile forms it presented the whole of human existence. The philosophic narrative verses of the bell-founder accompany and connect the pictures, but by no means destroy their sensuous charm.

Still, the most important result of his association with Goethe was for Schiller his resumption of dramatic poetry. In 1799 in Jena he completed his *Wallenstein*, which was published in 1800. Ten years had elapsed since Schiller's *Don Carlos* had appeared in print, the uneven product of a period of transition.

Wallenstein was the most important Catholic general of the Thirty Years' War, and in addition a man with ambitions of his own who turned traitor against the Habsburg emperor and was therefore murdered. Schiller's play interprets Wallenstein's actions as those of a German patriot who wants to stop the civil war between the religious factions and restore peace. Thus we once more have as a hero a noble criminal of the type of Karl Moor. Schiller has not gone beyond Storm and Stress in this, yet the picture is less one-sided. Octavio Piccolomini, the emissary of the Roman emperor and therefore the opponent of the traitorous general, becomes humanly understandable and arouses our sympathy. The collision of a great individual with the state becomes an unavoidable tragedy where light and shadow can be found on both sides.

The *Wallenstein* trilogy was the result of long, persistent effort, and the three parts form a distinct unity and should not be staged separately. *Wallensteins Lager* ("Wallenstein's Camp") depicts Wallenstein's army and makes the general's actions understandable: *Sein Lager nur erkläret sein Verbrechen* ("Only his camp explains his crime to us"). This part of the play is written in lively couplets often pervaded by a felicitous humor. The two other parts, *Die Piccolomini* and *Wallensteins Tod* ("The Piccolominis" and "Wallenstein's Death"), are written in blank verse which serves to set off the action from historical actuality, and also better fits the degree of culture represented by the great general. The action itself is intense. By concentrating his army, Wallenstein has made the first step toward the betrayal of his emperor. Yet already Octavio Piccolomini has taken countermeasures. Wallenstein knows of them, but in his astrological delusion does not encompass Octavio's defection. Thus the general goes to his doom in blind trust. He literally represents his own fate: *In deiner Brust sind deines Schicksals Sterne* ("Within your breast are found your fatal stars"). From these premises the action proceeds swiftly and with few interruptions. Only the love scenes between Max Piccolomini, the son of Octavio, and Wallenstein's daughter Thekla seem to disturb the unity of the whole. Yet in these scenes Wallenstein's guilt becomes transparently clear; his tragic choice involves even innocent bystanders. Schiller has rarely portrayed dramatic heroes in more lucid style, and a good theatrical performance of his trilogy reveals a majestic sweep which in a reading one cannot fully visualize.

With *Wallenstein* Schiller had returned to dramatic art. This made it desirable for him to get into closer contact with the actual theater, and in 1799 he moved to Weimar. Here he completed *Maria Stuart* (in 1800) and *Die Jungfrau von Orleans* ("The Maid of Orleans," 1801). But besides his own productions Schiller also contributed to the general development of the Weimar stage. Goethe took a hand in the education of the actors, and Schiller assisted his friend in enlarging the repertory. Schiller wrote stage adaptations of Shakespeare's *Macbeth*, Gozzi's *Turandot*, Racine's *Phèdre*, and a few French comedies, and in all of them he tried to limit theatrical realism. His intention to achieve a more elevated style can also be seen in his own tragedy *Die*

The Style of Personal Experience

Braut von Messina ("The Bride of Messina"), which was finished in 1803. The drama of *Wilhelm Tell* followed in the next year, and later Schiller began a *Demetrius* which was never completed. His last drama was an inconsequential festival play in honor of the Crown Prince of Weimar. (Schiller also had become a court poet and been elevated to nobility in 1802.) Soon after the completion of the festival play, Schiller was beset with the fever attacks which he had had since 1790. The spring of 1805 brought him great suffering, and he finally died on May 9th at the early age of 45. The death of the dramatist left a wound in Goethe's innermost depths.

We cannot here evaluate every one of Schiller's dramas. Yet that does not necessarily mean that those but mentioned summarily are of little value. Even *Die Braut von Messina,* which is rarely performed on the stage, is a lofty work of art. Here Schiller tried his utmost to re-awaken the tragedy of classical antiquity to new life. He introduced a chorus, he condensed the dramatic action to its bare essentials, he kept the rhythmical language at a high uniform level. Yet he could not revive the classical idea of capricious, inhuman fate; the destiny of his heroes derives solely from their character.

Equally transparent is the action of *Maria Stuart,* perhaps the most soul-searching of Schiller's dramas. Here we have none of the theatrical sensationalism which can be found in *Don Carlos.* Even before the curtain rises, the fate of Maria Stuart has been decided, and the play only presents the last three days of the doomed queen. The issue therefore is not political or historical, but strictly moral and even religious in a sense affecting every human being. How is one to cope with an inexorable fate, especially when it appears unjust and undeserved? Mary Queen of Scots solves this question by accepting her execution as a just atonement for the misdeeds of her youth. She thus changes a dire exigency into a free act of submission, and upholds her belief in the justice of God. The central scene is a meeting between Mary Stuart and Queen Elizabeth, in which Mary appears as Elizabeth's moral superior. Schiller shows Elizabeth as a cold, scheming, conceited, and jealous female. Mary, too, though good and noble in her intentions, is no paragon of virtue, and the insufficiency of human aspirations is brought out clearly. Guilt and noble-mindedness here are perhaps more closely connected than in Schiller's other plays.

The most popular of his dramas are *Die Jungfrau von Orleans* and *Wilhelm Tell.* The subtitle of *Die Jungfrau von Orleans* is *Eine romantische Tragödie* ("A Romantic Tragedy"). Schiller wanted to indicate that the events of the drama appear to us romancelike and unreal. For the play takes place during the Middle Ages, when religious concepts could inspire human beings to the greatest deeds. The whole action occurs within the souls of the characters, and the style of the drama is lyrical and musical. There are abundant monologues, and they are mostly of great length.

Schiller has not conformed to historical truth in essential details. While the historical Jeanne d'Arc was captured by the British and burned at the stake, Schiller's heroine experiences a fate more in keeping with her mission and dies in battle. Thus in the place of historic accuracy the drama moves us by its inner consistency. The theme is the conflict between ideal and reality which for Schiller is the basic issue of human life. The Jeanne d'Arc of the play is a simple French peasant girl who with her inner ear hears the voice of the Virgin Mary; the Virgin commands her to chase the enemy out of the country, and this after they have conquered the greater part of France. Jeanne follows the voice, and instills new courage into the wavering soldiers. The English are routed, and the triumphant Jeanne leads the French king to Reims for his coronation. But at this juncture her womanly feelings rise, she shows pity and love, and violates the commands of the Virgin as she has conceived them. In despair she falters. She feels remorse, and begs for a chance of atonement of her guilt. Miraculously breaking through her prison walls, she seeks her death at the head of the French army.

Jeanne d'Arc's guilt lies in her having become faithless to her inner voice, even though she has sinned only in thought. Instead of living for the whole, she has momentarily lived for herself. But such sorry moments of betrayal cannot be avoided. According to Schiller, no lasting reconciliation is possible between ideal and reality.

If *Die Jungfrau von Orleans* is a romantic tragedy, *Wilhelm Tell* is a romantic ballad. In this drama, tragic guilt and inner atonement are hardly discussed at all. Everything is told straightforwardly without digressions. Schiller now no longer seems to conceive of life as unavoidably tragic.

Wilhelm Tell is based on a Swiss legend, and the characters of the play have become legendary heroes. There is the tyrannical Habsburg governor Gessler who despises the simple people and treads their rights underfoot. His opponent is the archer Wilhelm Tell, a plain man, a provident father to his family. Tell would not have thought of murder if Gessler had not provoked him by demanding that he shoot an apple from the head of his beloved son. The hero hesitates on the brink before his liberating action. Yet he sees that the tyrant not only oppresses one individual, but all the people of Switzerland. And for the sake of the whole Tell shoots Gessler down and frees the Swiss nation.

Tell also can be classified as a noble criminal, like Karl Moor or Wallenstein. Yet he is different from them in that he represents the eternal right of national rebellion that is written in the stars. He does not act from a personal desire for revenge, and thus his individual action does not become a tragic personal constriction. Tell's figure is Schiller's poetic answer to the French Revolution, whose pure intention appeared to him to have been disfigured by egotistic individuals.

The bold, forceful characterizations of the drama explain why *Wilhelm Tell* continues to have a real appeal for youthful audiences. Yet adults also are attracted by the charming local color of the play. Schiller had never seen the Swiss Alpine regions, and yet managed to depict them with astonishing realism. Their luminous colors, their quick weather changes, their homely inhabitants come to life. Alpine atmosphere surrounds the audience from the opening dialogue of the fisherman and the hunter down to the last words describing the reaction to Tell's liberating shot. The action of the hero grows out of this landscape and is justified by it. In *Wilhelm Tell* perhaps more than in any other of his plays we have the whole Schiller with his almost boyish belief in simple virtue, his love for homely proverbs and catch phrases (*Die Axt im Haus erspart den Zimmermann*—"The axe at home saves us the carpenter"), but also his noble enthusiasm for right and freedom. *Wilhelm Tell* has endeared Schiller to his nation and has inspired many fighters for popular rights and decent government. For the Swiss people it has become a national play.

Friedrich Hölderlin

DURING the nineteenth century the greatness of Schiller and Goethe was generally appreciated. Yet it took German critics a hundred years to arrive at an equal estimate of Friedrich Hölderlin. The reasons

Friedrich Hölderlin

are partly to be found in his unfortunate fate, but are mostly connected with the prevailing positivistic approach to literature and art. This approach could be used with most of Goethe's and Schiller's poetry, yet did not provide the slightest clue to Hölderlin's. His poems also were based on personal experience, only his was quite different from young Goethe's spontaneous experience; for Hölderlin was always groping for the ultimate elements in all momentary experience, and visualizing them as gods. Schiller occasionally had similar visions and tried to portray them in poems such as *Die Götter Griechenlands* ("The Gods of Greece") or *Das Eleusische Fest* ("The Eleusinian Festival"), but with him the visions rarely came alive and were often obscured by rhetoric. In the reading of Hölderlin's mature poems one is actually meeting the gods whom he has conjured up; they become radiant, ravishing reality.

Hölderlin, who was born in 1770, was twenty years younger than Goethe, and more than ten years younger than Schiller; his development was therefore not disturbed by the Storm and Stress Movement. Yet parallels to the life of Schiller, his Swabian compatriot, are not wanting. Hölderlin had also originally intended to become a minister. From 1788 he studied theology at the Tübingen Seminary. His fellow students included Schelling and Hegel, who later became philosophers, and Hölderlin freely exchanged ideas with them. When his studies were finished, he was at odds with orthodox religion and preferred the life of an independent private tutor. Now a period of wandering began for young Hölderlin just as it had for young Schiller, and this time, too, the aim of the quest was the recovery of ancient Greece.

First, Hölderlin became tutor to the son of the same Charlotte von Kalb who had played such a fateful role in the life of the elder Swabian. Then he moved to Frankfurt am Main to educate the children of a banker by the name of Gontard. Gontard's wife Susette became Hölderlin's intimate friend and confidante; her role in his life was similar to the role of Charlotte von Stein in Goethe's. The poet called her "Diotima" and paid her poetic homage. Her own feeling in the beginning was motherly and friendly; but later she responded to his sublime language and shared his transports. When this state of affairs became known to Diotima's husband, Hölderlin was no longer welcome in the family and had to leave Frankfurt. In the neighboring town of Homburg he completed his novel *Hyperion* and worked at his drama *Empedokles* which was never finished.

The Style of Personal Experience

Hölderlin felt profoundly misunderstood by society and withdrew into himself. From about 1800 on he no longer gave an impression of normality, and when in 1802 he was informed of Diotima's death, his emotional response was absolutely cold. Hölderlin became a schizophrenic whose contact with life grew more and more tenuous. Loyal friends tried their best to change his outlook, and Hölderlin made repeated attempts to find another position. Yet the mental disease continued, and made his poems more and more inscrutable. Finally he had to be confined in the Tübingen insane asylum. In 1808 his condition had subsided into a permanent stupor, and in accordance with the medical practice of the time he was farmed out. For many years he lived in an old tower under the supervision of a cabinetmaker. Death came in 1843.

In contrast to Schiller, the born dramatist, Hölderlin excelled as a pure lyricist. At first he was a protégé of his older fellow countryman, and contributed to Schiller's magazine *Neue Thalia* ("New Thalia"). Hölderlin's youthful *Hymnen an die Ideale der Menschheit* ("Hymns to the Ideals of Mankind") read almost like Schiller's own verses; they employed the same meters and the same poetic devices. Still, even at that time Hölderlin's attitude to Greek antiquity was different. In Schiller's poem *Die Götter Griechenlands* the beautiful world of antiquity was described as past; it had yielded forever to the empty, colorless "Heaven" of Christianity and could only be revived in song. For Hölderlin, on the other hand, the divine was continuously revealing itself in concrete shapes and appearances, in the youthful exuberance of spring and the Pandean magic of noontime, in inspired poets and heroes, in divine women. Hölderlin could not conceive of the Greek gods as dead and historical; they had merely transferred their abode from Greece to Germany. His later *Gesang des Deutschen* ("German Ode") addressed itself to a Greece ever present. This Greece had merely been asleep, and there would come a time when it would be reawakened in German form; Hölderlin visualized a nation of poets, musicians, and philosophers joyfully competing for the highest prizes of peace. A similar vision was set down in more elaborate form in the novel *Hyperion*; no one who has read the harsh criticism of German realities at the end of this novel would call it nationalistic.

Yet the divine was not at all times equally accessible. Human beings were not always properly alive to it, and could only grasp it partially and fleetingly. Whoever tried to bridge the profound abyss between the divine and the human was in danger of losing himself and of being

Friedrich Hölderlin

extinguished by death or insanity. Occasionally Hölderlin wrote purely antithetic poems which might be interpreted as romantic. Indeed, romantic poets and critics were the first to appreciate Hölderlin's achievements. They could point to *Hyperions Schicksalslied* ("Hyperion's Song of Fate") with its emphasis on the dichotomy between the blessed divinities clothed in heavenly raiments and the human beings below condemned to an uncertain and arbitrary fate. In the love poem *Abbitte* ("Atonement") a harmonious union between the poet and Diotima is deemed impossible, and the poet is described as merely a passing cloud on the serene face of the moon.

Still, it would be a mistake to call Hölderlin a romantic. He cannot even be called a sentimental idealist; Schiller in the end could not understand him. Hölderlin had implicit faith in the harmony of life, and most of his hymns were hymns of praise. In early poems he often expressed the triumphant belief in an all-pervading divinity. In *Heidelberg* he speaks of the old ruins of the castle having been completely destroyed by a thunderbolt from Heaven, yet this is only the dark setting for a jubilant trust in the healing powers of nature; joy predominates at the end of the poem. In a later ode, one of Hölderlin's greatest by the name of *Brot und Wein* ("Bread and Wine"), the romantic propensity for night and death and dream moods is explicitly rejected, and the ideal attitude is described as *wachend zu bleiben bei Nacht* ("staying awake in the midst of the night"). In the singular elegy *Menons Klagen um Diotima* ("Menon's Laments for Diotima") Hölderlin applied the same resolution to his personal love problems. He compared himself to a wounded deer straying through the woods in the vain hope of finding relief:

Nicht die Wärme des Lichts, und nicht die Kühle der Nacht hilft,
Und in Wogen des Stroms taucht es die Wunden umsonst.
Und wie ihm vergebens die Erd' ihr fröhliches Heilkraut
Reicht, und das gärende Blut keiner der Zephire stillt,
So, ihr Lieben, auch mir, so will es scheinen, und niemand
Kann von der Stirne mir nehmen den traurigen Traum?

*

Neither the warmth of the day nor the coolness of nightfall is soothing,
And the waves of the river seek to be healing in vain.
And as its curative herbs to no good purpose the earth now
Hands him, and none of the zephyrs stills the exuding blood,

The Style of Personal Experience

Thus, oh friends and beloved, not one appears to be able
To remove from my forehead the harrowing dream.

Yet in the end the poet finds courage to accept his fate, and to live on in spite of the blow that has struck him:

Komm! es war wie ein Traum! die blutenden Fittiche sind ja
Schon genesen, verjüngt leben die Hoffnungen all.
Grosses zu finden, ist viel, ist viel noch übrig, und wer so
Liebe, gehet, er muss, gehet zu Göttern die Bahn . . .
Wo die Gesänge wahr, und länger die Frühlinge schön sind,
Und von neuem ein Jahr unserer Seele beginnt!

*

Come! It was but a dream! The bleeding wings are already
Mended and all our hopes doubled by quickening pulse.
Many great things still remain to be found, and whoever thus loved
To the gods is finding his path, as necessity bids him. . . .
Where the songs are all true, and longer the spring season's beauties,
And a year of our soul, a new year, commences again.

One should always read Hölderlin as a whole and not quote his poems out of context. He never was satisfied with the passing mood, but always waited for the backswing of the pendulum. He was not out to write ordinary poems, but Pindaric odes and hymns. He aimed at balance even in his rhythms, matching ascending units with descending ones and uniting many voices into a symphony. The total effect of his classical meters is one of complete harmony, achieved without the device of rhyme. The great Klopstock partly anticipated Hölderlin in his visionary attitude and his sweeping style. Yet the younger poet was no longer concerned with a special Christian mythology or theology. He rather invented a new mythology of his own.

At the end of his poetic career Hölderlin embodied his vision in great odes. He dreamed of a new Golden Age, a future harmony between the conflicting forces of life. Nature and spirit will no longer fight each other, but combine in an idyllic state of peace that is at once new and ancient, since it brings back the patriarchal conditions pertaining at the beginning of history. No longer will the nations nor the various religions fight each other. Divine forces will rule mankind, gods will again converse with men. Hölderlin visualized the coming Golden Age as a festival time to which the whole Olympic Pantheon was bidden, and

Friedrich Hölderlin

among the Greek gods he placed Christ as the god whose gentle ways he loved most. This view, of course, was not orthodox, and actually amalgamated Christian and classical mythology in a manner akin to the classicist religion of Schiller and Goethe. Hölderlin also emphasized the speciousness of all mythology, e.g., at the beginning of the great hymn *Patmos:*

Nah ist	*Close by*
Und schwer zu fassen der Gott.	*And hard to approach is God.*
Wo aber Gefahr ist, wächst	*Yet where danger is, waxes*
Das Rettende auch.	*The saving grace also.*

This quotation shows that the dark undertones of anxiety and awe are certainly not lacking in Hölderlin's religion. However, it would be wrong to call it Chthonian or Dionysiac. Hölderlin did not yield to frenzied intoxication, but described his visionary state as *heilignüchtern* ("holy and sober").

Hölderlin's thought is not always easy to grasp, and he has added to our difficulties by using a language which avoids ornamental comparisons and tends toward the absolute metaphor characteristic of the moderns. In addition it tries to combine German words with Greek style and sentence structure. Hölderlin acquired his idiom by translating the poetry of Pindar and Sophocles. Because of this style he could never become popular with the mass of German readers. But since Nietzsche and George have grasped Hölderlin's significance, he has become a guidepost for many moderns. They are hailing him as a predecessor of their own poetic idiom, and Hölderlin's vision of a German culture fusing classical and Christian elements is commanding the respect of latter-day Humanists. What an inspiration for a poet to see himself described as the ruler of living history, *der stille Gott der Zeit* ("the quiet god of the times"), destined to play the decisive role in initiating a new era!

Jean Paul

THE works of the Franconian writer Jean Paul may appear puzzling to a reader accustomed to the stately balance of Goethe, Schiller, and Hölderlin. Yet they contrast it with German reality around 1800, and draw their main strength from the deeply experienced, almost desperate antagonism of that reality to the ideals proclaimed by the leaders of German classicism. Jean Paul knew intimately the petty limitations under which most of his fellow countrymen lived; he also knew how hard he himself had come by his rich education. Thus he became a natural sceptic about chances for improvement, and was disposed to view existing conditions with humor and toleration or to discover meaning and hidden values in the poverty and narrowness of ordinary German circumstances.

The poet's full name was Johannes Paul Friedrich Richter, and he was born in 1763 at Wunsiedel in the Fir Mountains (*Fichtelgebirge*), located in one of the small principalities of eighteenth-century Germany. His father was an underpaid schoolteacher, and later became an equally underpaid country parson. The poet as a child was no better off than other village children, except that he came into closer contact with the world of the spirit. In 1780 Richter was able to register at Leipzig University as a student of theology, but he had to study in the most depressing surroundings. Soon he exchanged the miseries of a theology student for the uncertainties of a free-lance writer. In 1783, at twenty years of age, he published his first work, *Grönländische Prozesse* ("Greenland Lawsuits"). The income from it did not better his circumstances in the least. Additional income from tutoring also meant no real financial security, yet he became more outspoken in his convictions and expressed this by proudly assuming the pen name "Jean Paul," which he adopted in imitation of the name of Jean Jacques Rousseau.

Jean Paul succeeded with the public only when he started to write long novels. *Die Unsichtbare Loge* ("The Invisible Lodge") appeared in 1793, his *Hesperus* in 1795; this second novel became a literary sensation. Jean Paul himself considered *Titan* (1800–1803) as his masterpiece, a novel in which he was somewhat influenced by classicism. Yet the world of Weimar did not attract him permanently, and he kept up contact only with Herder. In the end Jean Paul's own destiny became sim-

Jean Paul

ilar to Herder's. The poet showed himself pitifully unable to distinguish between the central core and the lunatic fringe of the Weimar group, between Goethe's and Schiller's timeless visions and their contemporaries' misinterpretations and local gossip. Baffled and frustrated by the literary activities of Weimar, soft, impressionable Jean Paul decided not to settle there permanently. In 1804 he withdrew to Bayreuth in the center of his home region. None of his later works approached the extraordinary success of *Hesperus*, neither his novel *Flegeljahre* ("Pangs of Adolescence," 1804), nor his numerous short idylls and stories, neither his important artistic confession, the *Vorschule der Aesthetik* ("Aesthetic Propaedeutics," 1804), nor his pedagogic confession, *Levana* (1807). Yet he continued to be a favorite of the German public, and in 1817 received an honorary doctor's degree from the University of Heidelberg. Even young students honored the elderly Jean Paul for his progressive political ideas, and when he died in 1825, their representatives mournfully followed his coffin.

Jean Paul as a writer was a product of the sentimental period. His inner life was rich to overflowing, and during his whole lifetime made him distrustful of the rigid demands of formal perfectionism. Jean Paul loved the grotesque and bizarre in the extreme, and even in his quieter moods was fascinated by the irrationality of life. His early eighteenth-century style of farfetched wit and analogy he later adapted to purposes hardly compatible with arid "good taste," and the example of Lawrence Sterne confirmed him in his ways. Jean Paul's novels are rarely divided into chapters, but rather into "Dog-mail days" (*Hundsposttage*), "Jobel periods" (*Jobelperioden*), or labeled as items from a naturalist's cabinet. They abound in lengthy digressions and footnotes, in overgrown prefaces and appendices without seeming connection with the main topic. Often the real action is hidden away amongst details, and the mere number of his writings is legion. Gottfried Keller once called Jean Paul a pyrotechnist. And indeed Jean Paul delights in elaborate displays of dazzling brilliancy. It is as if the free spirit in his writings continuously fights with the base matter. Their fanciful outer form frequently buries truly poetic ideas under a mountain of trivia, of undigested learned quotations, or of *aperçus* copied from random notebooks. Jean Paul sometimes comes close to modern surrealistic montage.

But all this is merely the superficial impression. For Jean Paul's vagaries have a meaning. He always renders adequately the discrepancy between ideal and reality, and always somehow carries the reader away into the magic world of the spirit. Even in his most abstruse concoctions and his obvious command performances one can find at least a few paragraphs of admirable poetic fullness. In his best passages Jean Paul expresses incomparably the magic of human imagination, for which reality is mere inert matter to be overcome or to be transcended. Jean Paul's world is in fact the world of the soul. His individuals do not limit themselves, but transfuse into the universe, thus fulfilling the very spirit of Storm and Stress. Goethe and Schiller knew also the necessity of limitations, and Goethe in his old age never tired of directing German dreamers to the concrete and the practical. Inasmuch as Jean Paul represented the acme of the German dreamer, he was the very opposite of the two great Weimar poets.

Nevertheless he was strangely attracted to the world of Weimar, and in his *Titan* he attempted to emulate the purity of the classicist form. He restrained some of his wildest excesses, and narrated in strictly epical fashion. In a way Albano, the hero of *Titan*, parallels Wilhelm Meister's development into a useful member of society. His antagonist Roquairol, the unrestrained pursuer of sensual as well as intellectual pleasures, ends his life by suicide, while Albano becomes the responsible ruler of a small German principality. Yet different from Wilhelm Meister, Albano is of a more political and national bent, and his religion clearly approaches orthodox Christianity. The novel also gives great prominence to inspired descriptions of seasonal and musical moods. All of this distinctly betrays romantic predilections.

Jean Paul's essential affinity to romanticism also explains why in spite of serious attempts this poet simply could not keep to the pure form of German classicism. His *Flegeljahre* no longer found an unambiguous formula for the abundance of his spirit. Like the earlier writings of the poet, this novel again got caught between humorous contrasts. In the twin brothers Walt and Vult, ideal prerequisites and real suppositions oppose each other just as in Eichendorff's *Aus dem Leben eines Taugenichts* ("From the Life of a Good-for-Nothing") the artists oppose the Philistines. And no common denominator can be found for their differences. Jean Paul in artistic honesty could arrive at no compromise between ideal and life, between heart and world, and thus his novel remained a fragment. The influence of Weimar ideals can be found only in the greater conciseness of the tale.

Jean Paul refused to accept the antagonism between ideal and life in its tragic aspect, and continued to believe in the power of the soul. He therefore smiled at the dichotomy of the universe, and became Germany's greatest humorist. To be sure, this humor was not absent from the writings of Goethe, but there it was not given the leading part. Jean Paul presented an important modification of Goethe's vitalism, and certainly a necessary correction of the oppressive seriousness of Schiller and Hölderlin. It was this that Carlyle meant when he referred to "that giant Jean Paul," and that the New England transcendentalists found worthy of their special attention. A present-day reader can most appreciate Jean Paul's greatness in some of his charming idylls, of which the best known is entitled *Leben des vergnügten Schulmeisterleins Maria Wuz in Auenthal* ("Life of the Happy Little Schoolmaster Maria Wuz in Auenthal"); here the author has endowed a humdrum German existence with humor, and has transfigured poverty and misery by the magic wand of poetry. Once one has realized Jean Paul's abundance of soul, one can understand how difficult the problem of form must have been for this mind. One also understands why the classical solution to the problem of expression could be but a temporary one. When it was no longer felt as adequate, the field was free for romanticism.

The Founders of German Romanticism

GERMAN romanticism was a direct development from the Storm and Stress Movement. Storm and Stress poets had discovered an individual approach to life which did not accept the common values of tradition and endow them with objective forms. The poets now found their own interpretations of life and gave them subjective expression. German classicism then tried a voluntary fusion of this new individualism with the existing culture, and an individual validation of objective artistic form. But this could work only as long as the tradition was not completely shattered. Through the French Revolution and its stormy aftermath an uncritical acceptance of existing values became more and more impossible. The Holy Roman Empire came to an end, the German territories west of the Rhine were temporarily lost, the old Prussian state collapsed, and out of these ruins there finally emerged a conglomeration of independent German states which had little more than a common geographical denominator. The same centrifugal tendencies were discernible in commerce and industry, in philosophy and theology, and the generations growing up after 1800 found themselves in something of a void. An individual approach to life now appeared to be the only one possible, and was promulgated by the German romanticists. This German romanticism was of course only a late form of the general European Romantic Movement. From a European perspective, the poets of Storm and Stress no less than those of German classicism could be called romantic. However, in this chapter and following ones, the term romanticism will apply only to German poets coming of age between 1795 and 1830.

Individualism to these young poets did not yet represent a source of pure joy. They still had before them a great tradition which had not yet altogether faded, and thus they suffered, as had the classicists, from their individual limitations, and aimed to overcome them. Yet the conquest of individuality in terms of life rarely succeeded. In spite of all efforts there remained an ineradicable emotional tension. The romantic mood can be described as ceaseless longing, seeking and aiming for harmony, without the possibility of ever attaining it permanently. Only for brief moments were the contradictions of life overcome, and these moments were the moments of artistic creation. Only in the imaginative world of poetry could the romanticists forget themselves and experience that fullness of life which the classicists could still find in practical activity.

The romantic world of the imagination everywhere betrays its origins. The classicists could still see their ideal in the classical culture as Winckelmann had reinterpreted it for them; their world was unified, clear, and serene. The romanticists, on the other hand, always discerned the many separate voices contributing to the world symphony. Classicism isolated its heroes and stressed their few permanent characteristics, thus achieving the effect of statuary. Romanticism with its abundance of overtones was related to music. It aimed at an infinite melody, and individual works of art were mere fragments in an everlasting stream. They were fragmentary in their conception and often in their execution.

The world of romantic imagination was colorful, rich in figures and associations, and incessantly changing. It preferred the imagery of ever-changing nature, of the variegated Middle Ages, of the fabulous Orient, of the ocean of history. When Herder uncovered the individuality of historical periods and nations, he laid one of the important foundations for romanticism. Yet to be wholly satisfied with the singular and the individual would amount to realism, and although romanticism later on was connected with realism, it aimed at something different. It proposed to blend interesting individual details into a common basic mood. It was attracted by the atmosphere of the dream, of the fairy tale, of forest or nocturnal scenes, of the voyage, and themes taken from these fields are indeed characteristically romantic.

Yet even in his imagination the romantic poet could not get lost. His world was better and more perfect, yet it always differed from the reality of everyday life. So he contrasted the two worlds and set his world of imagination against a world less complete, less colorful, and less purely tuned. The romantic idealist isolated this world of fancy and looked down upon so-called "reality." Here his attitude was different from that of classicism and, of course, also from the Enlightenment. The real world, as seen by members of these schools, to him appeared unpoetic and distasteful. It had to be transmuted into the world of poetry if it was to acquire any validity at all. Practical life appeared unessential and unimportant, and this fitted in nicely with the attitude of Christian asceticism. Romanticism often felt itself akin to Christianity. Art almost became a revelation of the true, genuine world adumbrated by religious doctrine. The romantics stressed the transcendental experience of religion that was unfathomable to mere logic. The Protestant theologian Schleiermacher in his *Reden über die Religion* ("Lectures on Religion") defined it as the feeling of absolute dependency. That romanticism could combine such a feeling with the experience of individual independence is highly revealing of its contrapuntal character.

Romantic poetry employs a number of special methods in order to create its world of fancy. It dissolves and diffuses all compact forms and rigid outlines. Romantic lyricism no longer submits to the discipline of classical metrics. If it employs antique meters at all, it employs them as one element among others of equal importance. Romantic stories combine poetry and prose to achieve variegated effects. In order to contrast the work of art with reality, romanticism also employs its so-called romantic "irony," i.e., the artist consciously destroys the artistic illusion himself, or he deliberately changes a mood into its opposite. The artist wants to remind the reader that he has to do with a product of fancy and not with a slavish imitation of reality.

Of course, our general characterization of romanticism does not apply to every romantic author. There is a certain difference between an older and a later group of authors. The older group seeks possibly to over-

The Style of Personal Experience

come the contrast of reality and imagination. Like classicism, it aims at a unified interpretation of the world. In all seriousness it attempts to redeem the world by poetry. The later group has finally become reconciled to the contrast of poetry and reality. It is compromising with despised practical life, and builds up its gay world of fancy in competition rather than opposition. It no longer tries to achieve an impossible balance.

In surveying the older group, one starts best with Wilhelm Wackenroder's *Herzensergiessungen eines kunstliebenden Klosterbruders* ("Effusions of an Art-loving Friar," 1797). In this earliest document of German romanticism we first meet with the desire to elevate reality through art. Artistic creation appears as a distinctly pious activity, and the artists of the Middle Ages are described as saints who painted and built and sang to the glory of God. One result of this book was the discovery of the beauty of historic Nuremberg with its city walls and moats, its towers and churches, which at that time had not yet been destroyed by aerial bombardment. On a vacation trip through the German south, Wackenroder "experienced" the historic city with Ludwig Tieck, his friend and fellow student from early Berlin days. Wackenroder opened the eyes of the easily excitable Tieck to the different artistic culture which had produced ancient Nuremberg, and after Wackenroder's early death (1798), Tieck continued to enhance the new view.

Tieck (1773–1853) was the least philosophical of the older romanticists. Basically he cared little for poeticizing life. He was satisfied with the creation of a beautiful world of imagination, and thus really belongs to the later group. He took his writing none too seriously, and in his youth could already lend his pen to rationalist projects. Under the influence of Wackenroder he found himself and became a romantic. Then he wrote the fairy tale *Der blonde Eckbert* ("Fair Eckbert," 1796) where nature was described as weird and mysterious, since poetry had not yet redeemed it. Thereafter he published his novel *Franz Sternbalds Wanderungen* ("Franz Sternbald's Wanderings," 1798) which had a disciple of Dürer for its hero, a young artist roaming the world and producing a symphony of emotions. Tieck also adapted for the stage the fairy tale of *Der Gestiefelte Kater* ("Puss in Boots") and in so doing continuously and consistently took pains to destroy the illusion: the audience, the author, the stagehands took a part in this comedy of a comedy. Then again he rewrote an old chapbook into the so-called comedy *Kaiser Oktavianus* ("Emperor Octavianus," 1804). Here Tieck intentionally mixed the most different verse forms in order to achieve a superlatively gay impression of change. But this galaxy of meters fell apart, and there remained only fragmentary details, like the famous definition of the romantic mood as "moonlit nocturnal magic holding the mind in captivity" (*mondbeglänzte Zaubernacht, die den Sinn gefangen hält*).

Tieck was forever discovering poetry in other European literatures. His special predilection was Shakespeare, whose comedies and imaginative plays he was the first German critic to appreciate. He also put into German Cervantes' *Don Quixote* (1799–1801) which he interpreted as a model romantic work.

Through *Franz Sternbalds Wanderungen* Tieck became associated with the brothers August Wilhelm and Friedrich Schlegel who both were more serious than he. It was they who emerged as the critical pioneers of the new poetry. Endeavoring to acquire a unified philosophy, the Schlegel brothers at first became disciples of classicism. Friedrich Schlegel (1772–1829) was inspired by Schiller's essay *Über naive und sentimentalische Dichtung* ("On Naïve and Sentimental Poetry"). To this was later added the influence of Johann Gottlieb Fichte, who made Friedrich Schlegel essentially independent. In his *Wissenschaftslehre* ("The Foundations of All Scientific Theories," 1794) Fichte took exception to Kant's assumption of the existence of a reality outside our consciousness. He wanted to derive even experience from what he labeled "the Ego." The world in every sense came into being by means of an "autonomous action" (*Tathandlung*) of the spirit which was conceived as a mysterious absolute entity. In Friedrich Schlegel's uncritical interpretation Fichte's "Ego" simply became the poet's individual ego, and now the task seemed to be the progressive development of one's inner soul. Romantic poetry was defined as "progressive universal poetry" (*progressive Universalpoesie*), and irony was postulated as the chief method to be applied in its execution.

The older brother, August Wilhelm Schlegel (1767–1845) was the more balanced of the two. He early came under the influence of Herder whose idea of world literature aroused his enthusiasm. He pleaded for a translation of Dante and Shakespeare, and as early as 1797 published the first volume of his own translation of Shakespeare. It later constituted August Wilhelm's chief claim to fame.

The Schlegel brothers had moved to the Thuringian university town of Jena. Soon Jena became the center of the new literary movement which was establishing its independence from classicism. In 1798 the brothers decided to launch a critical periodical called *Athenaeum*. In

The Style of Personal Experience

this they laid down a program for the new romantic "school" in a series of so-called "fragments." The *Athenaeum* did not come out regularly and did not continue for long. Still, it succeeded in raising the banner of German romanticism. The brothers also published model reviews of a character at that time new. They aimed at construing poetic and artistic works in a sympathetic spirit, and avoided measuring them by abstract yardsticks. These eminent critics fell short only in their own poetry. Friedrich in *Lucinde* attempted to report his own confused philanderings in the form of a novel. The "novel" is little more than a shapeless succession of interesting fragments and tactless confessions, but it is an important historical document. For it points to the role played in the new movement by deeply emotional women such as August Wilhelm's wife Caroline, and by intellectual women like Friedrich's wife Dorothea, the daughter of the philosopher Mendelssohn. It also foreshadows the fateful replacement of the motherly ideal of womanhood by the ideal of the emancipated woman for whom emotions are an end in themselves.

A great part of the "Fragmente" of the *Athenaeum* were written by Novalis (1772–1801) who expressed the intentions of the older group in pure poetry. He was a Saxon, and his real name was Friedrich Leopold, Freiherr (baron) von Hardenberg; his family thus was a noble family as the Schlegels' had originally been. Novalis became a poet because of personal experience. The untimely death of his first fiancée wounded him so deeply that he was filled with a longing to follow her. This longing produced the *Hymnen an die Nacht* ("Hymns to Night," existing in manuscript form by 1799) in which Novalis dreams of an infinity combining the world of light with the world of night, and centering around the creative power of love. It is Christ who has opened this existence to us. The *Hymns* are a Christian myth of redemption. However, this redemption belongs to the future, and the poet has to prepare the way for it by overcoming the contrasts of the visible world. Poetry's magic wand unveils world and nature as they really are, as a "universal metaphor of the spirit" (*Universaltropus des Geistes*), as a "magic city turned into stone"; but at some time nature no longer will be. It will change gradually into a world of spirits. Thoughts such as these are found in the *Athenaeum* under the poetic title *Blütenstaub* ("Pollen"). They were written under the strong influence of Fichte's *Wissenschaftslehre*, but also of the identity philosophy of Schelling who aimed at understanding nature as a gradual manifestation of the spirit.

In his novel *Heinrich von Ofterdingen* Novalis once more tried to express his thoughts in poetic form. In this, according to the poet's own words, "the world of the fairy tale becomes wholly visible while the real world is visualized as a fairy tale." Poetry, represented by the medieval singer Heinrich von Ofterdingen, is destined to bring about this union of reality and imagination. The poet is to overcome the rule of arrogant reason and to resuscitate the Golden Age. Novalis' symbol for the Golden Age is the "Blue Flower" under whose sign all the contrasts of life should fuse into one great whole. But the early death of the poet (1801) prevented him from finishing his novel in the manner intended, and it remained a fragment. If *Heinrich von Ofterdingen* had been completed, it would have become a romantic parallel to Goethe's *Wilhelm Meister*. While Goethe's hero overcame his subjectivity by active participation in practical life, Novalis' hero was to find redemption in the world of imagination. But this world of imagination had to be worked for and not merely to be dreamed of. Novalis in real life was a reliable official and no visionary. The older group in general worked hard for a redemption of the world, so that *Wilhelm Meister* to Novalis and his friends originally appeared to be a romantic novel. Goethe's book had inspired the Schlegel brothers to enthusiastic reviews, and had influenced Tieck in his *Sternbald*. Few other books had had such a decisive importance for romanticism.

Heinrich von Kleist

THERE was one poet whose isolated efforts were inclined in the same direction as those of the older romanticists with whom he had no personal contact. This poet was Heinrich von Kleist, a Prussian nobleman characterized by an unrestrained, almost primitive spontaneity. More profoundly than anybody he experienced the tragedy of his generation, the ever-widening gap between individual and society. In desperate loneliness he approached the classicists' attempt to bridge it, but in the main arrived at a romantic solution much against his will. Only a few of his works overcame the isolation of the individual and let him find the social response for which he was longing.

Heinrich von Kleist was born at Frankfurt-an-der-Oder on October 18, 1777. His ancestors had been soldiers in the changing fortunes of

[215

war, and had early shown signs of good mental caliber. Kleist at first followed the tradition of his family and entered the Prussian army; he served in the campaigns against the French Revolutionary armies, and in 1797 became a lieutenant. Yet the prospect of years of mere spit-and-polish made military life unbearable for a man of Kleist's fitful temperament. Suddenly he threw off the shackles of discipline, and registered at the university of his home town. He hoped that searching studies would give a clearer direction to his life. At twenty-two years of age it seemed justifiable to start all over again.

Kleist's first choice was rationalistic science, but his restlessness did not allow him to pursue it too long. He was carried away by the exuberance of an early engagement. Then, in 1800, a depressive mania drove him to Würzburg. The young man suffered in body and soul, and his imagination painted his condition in the most dreadful colors. When the emotional storm had passed, he felt painfully the necessity for objective limitation and certainty. He still hoped that he might find it in science, but that hope was shattered. Kleist became acquainted with Kant's philosophy, probably through Fichte's treatise on *Die Bestimmung des Menschen* ("The Destiny of Man," 1800). Kant taught that all our judgments refer only to the world of appearances, and Fichte concluded that they refer but to shadows and dreams, while the real world was the creation of our will. Before Kleist's impressionable eyes the world was dashed to pieces, and there remained only the individual in his abysmal loneliness. It seemed impossible to build certainty on such shifting ground. Kleist fled from his native Prussian surroundings, and in 1801 traveled to Paris. His only companion was his beloved sister Ulrike; he could endure no other human being. Yet Paris only increased Kleist's hatred of society and civilization. He embraced Rousseau's ideal of a return to nature, and dreamed of becoming a farmer. But his fiancée would not follow him, and he soon asked her to spare him the trouble of reading her letters.

Kleist's isolation was growing, but it also set free his genius. He began to work at his *Robert Guiskard*, and for a while he sought out the company of other writers. To Swiss fellow poets he read his first play, *Die Familie Ghonorez* ("The Ghonorez Family"), a tragedy in five acts. It appeared anonymously in 1803, and was published by one of his friends; the title was changed to *Die Familie Schroffenstein*. It commanded respect through its style with its explosive, disrupted sentences expressing the wildest fury; there was no trace of classical restraint and even-measured blank verse. Yet it was a fitting style for the concept of a world diseased to its core. The plot itself was not original. Just as in *Romeo and Juliet,* two related noble houses are fighting each other in furious hate. Even the purity of a love arising between two children of the hostile houses cannot stop the senseless slaughter. Both young people perish, and at their biers stand the heads of the opposing factions. No way seems to lead out of this world of raving lawlessness.

Still, Kleist for a while felt relieved by his production. He rented an island cottage on the Lake of Thun, and engaged a fisherman's daughter as his housekeeper. In quiet contemplation he seemed to live entirely for his poetic creations. But the idyll was soon interrupted by illness, and the unsafe political conditions also forced Kleist to leave Switzerland. In Germany he found refuge on the estate of old Wieland who understood and admired him, yet this too was only a temporary refuge, and finally Kleist was but a restless nomad. Only the correspondence with Ulrike gave him some measure of the inner peace which even his poetic work could no longer provide. The planned *Robert Guiskard* overtaxed his strength, and on a sudden trip to Paris he burned the manuscript in a fit of blackest despair. Kleist came close to insanity and by that time might easily have committed suicide.

In a later moment of tranquillity the poet restored the opening scenes of *Robert Guiskard* from memory, and thus we can form some idea of Kleist's astonishing plan. The scenes portray the Norman duke Robert Guiskard at the summit of his power; he is entrenched before the city of Constantinople which appears willing to surrender. But the plague has attacked Guiskard's army, and has even seized the duke himself. Fate has thrown up a barrier against his superhuman will power, and he must fall on account of *hubris.* Yet so must his nation which has followed the arrogant usurper Guiskard instead of enthroning the legitimate heir. Thus *Guiskard* embodied an individual as well as a national tragedy. And it was also supposed to be a classical as well as a modern tragedy. As a classical tragedy it was to show man perishing by his own lack of restraint, as a modern tragedy it was to show a usurper who had violated the rights of legitimacy. It was Kleist's firm intention to combine and to supersede all dramatic patterns in existence. Yet his plan led to insoluble contradictions and ended in failure. Only the fact that in 1808 Kleist could still reconstruct his draft makes one wonder whether his resignation was final.

When the *Guiskard* manuscript had been destroyed, the poet was sobered and hastened home. Humbly he presented himself to his relatives and accepted the position of a petty official at Königsberg. Yet his engagement with bureaucracy could not last long. He found his wings again, and completed the comedies *Der zerbrochene Krug* ("The Broken Jug") and *Amphitryon*, and concluded his first prose work, e.g., *Das Erdbeben in Chili* ("The Earthquake in Chile").

Like Kleist's *Schroffenstein* play, *Der zerbrochene Krug* portrays a world of lawless individuals. Yet this time fate interferes and makes possible the salvation of innocent victims. Kleist seems to have removed himself from the dissolution of his times and to have overcome his own hopeless despair. The action of *Der zerbrochene Krug* centers around the village judge Adam, a crafty rascal who has pursued innocent little Eve with a net of lies and has broken a jug when he suddenly had to flee from her. So far she has escaped her pursuer, but he insists on estranging the innocent girl from her fiancé. The audience knows from the beginning that his schemes will not succeed, that it was Adam who broke the jug when he harbored designs against Evchen's virtue. Yet the facts come out only gradually in a lengthy court session which it is Adam's duty to hold on account of the damaged vessel. So the judge presiding over the trial is actually the defendant, and in the end ignominiously flees his office. Eve's innocence is established, wrong is still wrong, and right is still right. The audience feels a healthy relief, and its laughter derives from a moral and almost religious basis.

The conciseness of *Der zerbrochene Krug* is exemplary in the history of the German juridical comedy that has come down from the Middle Ages. The play should be performed at a fast pace, and the audience should not be allowed to regain its breath. Good staging will convince one that this is one of the few German comedies measuring up to Shakespearean standards. It is also a truly poetic play in which external actions are wholly subjugated to the dialectics of words. Kleist never surpassed its excellence.

His other comedy, *Amphitryon*, can be called a comedy of ambiguity. It is far more disturbing than *Der zerbrochene Krug*, and opens our eyes to an abysmal depth of existence. It achieves this effect by using the well-known story of Jupiter seducing a defenseless human woman. Under the reign of absolutism Molière had treated it frivolously as the story of an absolute monarch exercising his royal prerogatives. Now Kleist, in reworking Molière's comedy, discovered a deeper meaning. Jupiter, the supreme deity, has seduced Alkmene by assuming the form of her husband Amphitryon. Whom will she love when the betrayal is discovered? Will it be her everyday husband Amphitryon, from whom her thoughts have never strayed before, or will it be the god in the form of Amphitryon? Kleist here probes the certainty of individual feeling, the basic question of every marriage: can a wife still love her husband after his company has become a daily habit? Alkmene's answer is: she can. In Amphitryon she has always loved a human form of the divine, and when Jupiter approached her, it was the same husband to whom her innermost self had always responded. She fails to see any problem of identity and is unconscious of any guilt; in the depth of her love she does not have to choose between god and man, and the god realizes: "And everything that comes close to you is Amphitryon" (*Und alles, was sich dir nahet, ist Amphitryon*).

Tentatively, *Amphitryon* admits individual feeling as a possible foundation for existence, and Kleist must have felt sure of himself when he left Königsberg. But once again the uncertainties of life were brought near to him, this time by the events of history. On October 14, 1806, the Prussian army had been decisively defeated in the battle of Jena. When the poet on a trip to Dresden was passing through Berlin he was made prisoner and taken to France as a suspected spy. Prison surroundings seemed hardly conducive to creative writing, but he started to write the play *Penthesilea* and had it finished when through Ulrike's personal efforts he finally regained freedom.

Again the reliability of individual feeling forms the question underlying a Kleist play; but this time it is answered in the negative, and we are witnessing tragedy. Penthesilea lives in a feminine world, she is the queen of the Amazons and, like all her subjects, has first to conquer her lover in battle before she is permitted to marry him; moreover, she is not to choose him individually. Yet she has met Achilles, the most masculine of the Greeks, and immediately Penthesilea forgets the laws of her state. Achilles also forgets his extreme masculinity; he is seized by sudden love, and decides to surrender to his opponent without weapons. This, however, makes no sense to Penthesilea who is still rooted in her Amazonian femininity, and when Achilles for the sake of appearances challenges her to a duel, she believes herself rejected. In a paroxysm of rage the queen of the Amazons attacks him with her bloodhounds and they tear him to pieces; love has turned into demonic passion. Then Penthesilea comes to her senses and realizes that one-sided femininity has led to destruction: *Ich sage vom Gesetz der Fraun mich los* ("I renounce the feminine laws"). By a sheer strength of will, Penthesilea destroys herself; it is the only way out for her, once she has acknowledged the different law that governed Achilles.

Penthesilea in her raging fury is the equal of Kriemhild in the *Nibelungenlied*, and the play comes close to a rehabilitation of Germanic primitivism. The same impression is left by its blank verse which does

[219

not stride smoothly like the verse of *Iphigenie*, but bursts with the wild energy of spluttering sentences. And the traditional scheme of five acts is superseded by an undivided sweep of words and action. Elemental forces shake Goethe's world to its very foundations, the harmonious, restrained world presented in *Iphigenie*. It is small wonder that the Weimar poet rejected *Penthesilea* as undisciplined, and sensed in Kleist the absolute antagonist. Yet Goethe overlooked the fact that Kleist's play showed that feminine passion stood in need of masculine reasoning. The poet's final word was hardly a return to primitivism.

In his next play *Käthchen von Heilbronn* ("Käthchen from Heilbronn," 1808) the poet again places a woman in the center, and again he lets her rely on feminine instinct. Kate is a woman of the Middle Ages who follows her beloved knight with single-minded devotion and lets nothing stand in her way. Her Ritter vom Strahl (the name signifies radiancy) yields to her and accepts her as his wife. In contrast to *Penthesilea* Kleist here portrays the effectiveness of feminine feeling. Yet he puts Kate into fairy-tale surroundings, in the end making her the illegitimate daughter of an emperor. She walks as if in a trance, and it takes a sentimental audience to fully appreciate this most romantic of Kleist's plays. To a more critical spectator the story is not entirely convincing, and Kleist himself was not too sure of it either; consequently he paid too much attention to the demands of the stage, and thereby confused the issue in several respects. *Käthchen von Heilbronn* is Kleist's most popular play, but not his best.

Meanwhile some Dresden friends of the poet had seen *Amphitryon* into print, and *Der zerbrochene Krug* had been performed under Goethe's direction. However, the Weimar poet did not understand the play and cut it up into three acts; in this form it naturally became a failure. To this were added other failures, the most notable one a short-lived journal which Kleist had edited with the philosopher Adam H. Müller.

In that journal Kleist still differentiated between politics and poetry. Shortly thereafter he completely reversed himself and found the solution to all his troubles by submerging his individuality in a worship of the state. A patriotic frenzy came over him that was just as uncontrolled as his previous passions. Kleist displayed hate for Napoleon that overstepped the borders of sanity. He adopted the form of Schiller's *Lied an die Freude* ("Ode to Joy"), that most universal of German poems, and distorted it into a pathological hymn of hate entitled *Germania an ihre Kinder* ("Germany to her Children"), calling on the Germans to hunt Napoleon to death like a wild animal:

Heinrich von Kleist

Schlagt ihn tot! Das Weltgericht
Fragt euch nach den Gründen nicht!

*

Strike him dead! The Last Judgment
Will not ask for your reasons.

Here we have the very opposite to Goethe's political and cultural
views. Kleist saw in Napoleon and in the French culture which he represented the embodiment of aboriginal evil, not expressions of the
spirit of Western man. He became more nationalistic than Friedrich
Schlegel and most of the younger romanticists who at that time also
turned to politics. His *Hermannsschlacht* ("Hermann's Battle in Teuto-
burg Forest") of 1808 was an avowed piece of psychological warfare.
Kleist took it to Austria which in 1809 was rising against the Corsican.
Yet the officials of that international state were afraid of the play's
demoniac passions, and Kleist had to depart from Vienna without the
hope of a performance.

In the beginning of 1810 he arrived in Berlin, ridden by debts. He
founded a newspaper to which important contemporaries contributed,
but it failed to find readers. The poet's last drama, *Der Prinz von Homburg*, was not even appreciated by the Prussian court. Kleist again saw
his poetic hopes shattered, and applied for readmission into the army.
The application was granted but only in case of war, and thus Kleist
was faced with ruin. In this final crisis of his life friends who might
have helped him were not at hand, and he found an unexpected companion of his last journey, a Mrs. Vogel, who was incurably ill. On
November 21, 1811, Kleist first shot her, and then himself, by the shore
of Lake Wannsee. His search for certainty had ended in annihilation.

Kleist's two posthumous tragedies were only printed in 1821 when
contemporary conditions no longer favored an enthusiastic reception.
This was especially true of *Hermannsschlacht*. *Der Prinz von Homburg*
claimed more lasting attention. Its central figure is a great individual
in all his admirable singularity, which, however, also makes him willful
and unreliable. Against him stands the law which in its inhuman cruelty
is no respecter of individuals, but nevertheless is endowed with majesty.
Life oscillates between these two poles. The author himself stands above
his characters and must not be identified with any of them. Here, Kleist
has indeed reached the balance between romantic and classical elements
that had been his lifelong goal.

[221

The Style of Personal Experience

Prince Homburg, the hero of this Prussian play, has disobeyed an order of the Great Elector (Friedrich Wilhelm von Brandenburg, 1640–1688), but has thereby won a battle and thus believes himself justified. In spite of this, the Elector has the prince imprisoned and condemned to death. The prince is terrified, and the once-brave hero becomes a groveling coward; his youthful world of glorious dreams has been shattered. The Elector himself teaches the prince to judge him more fairly, and the hero accepts his fate and rejects all attempts to liberate him. Only then can the Elector pardon the prince. For he has demonstrated the unreliability even of exceptional individuality and the necessity of law, although at times it may seem pedantic. The individual only finds himself by giving himself up. This solution brings together several elements: the radical, severe rationalism of the Calvinistic tradition in which Kleist was reared, the Prussian atmosphere which surrounded his manhood, and finally the Prussian idea of the supremacy of the state. The play is a distinct confession of Kleist's faith in that idea, ending, as it does, with the patriotic line: *In Staub mit allen Feinden Brandenburgs!* ("Into the dust with all the enemies of Brandenburg!"). Of course, in Kleist's time the Prussian idea was still the moral idea that had developed under the Great Elector and under Frederick the Great; it must not be confused with the misunderstood forms it assumed at the end of the nineteenth century.

Nobody can say whether Kleist would have adopted the solution of this play as final had he continued to live. *Der Prinz von Homburg* paints the charms of individuality alluringly, and the poet before had not found the severe Prussian discipline to his liking. Was the play more than a romantic reaction to the historical necessity for the fight against Napoleon? In any case, Kleist here posed an absolute question and gave an absolute answer, and his play could be called a great representation of a decision against individualism. In its style *Der Prinz von Homburg* is, next to *Der Zerbrochene Krug*, the most accomplished play ever written by Kleist. Romantic emotionalism and classical sobriety have balanced each other admirably. The first scene shows the prince's dream of glory, the last one its fulfillment, but the scenes in between have been filled with reality and the dream has taken on great meaning. The characters of the play are outlined clearly, even the secondary figures come alive. And the language no longer is erratic, but tamed and musical. This play by itself would establish Kleist's claim to lasting fame. It is hard to understand why he had to wait so long for national (and finally even European) recognition.

In his last years of life Kleist also published a volume of stories which he himself considered secondary works only written for a hungry public. Yet in the estimate of competent critics these *Novellen* are masterpieces ranking with the best of Cervantes or Boccaccio. An example is *Michael Kohlhaas* which may be called an epic counterpart to *Der Prinz von Homburg*. Kohlhaas is another individual who believes he stands above the law; he also is able to defend his actions plausibly. Kohlhaas is a horse trader who has been maltreated by Junker Wenzel von Tronka, but gets no redress through the courts and thereafter loses his confidence in the just order of the world. Thereupon he engages in a private campaign for justice and harasses the countryside until he is assured of a fair trial. As a result of the court's verdict, Wenzel von Tronka has to expiate his arrogance. But Kohlhaas has meanwhile committed crimes against peace and order, and therefore has to pay the supreme penalty of death. In the beginning he was perhaps right and pointed out real weaknesses of the law, but he also attacked its very substance by his willful actions. He can therefore not be pardoned like Prince Homburg who came to a voluntary acknowledgment of law.

Here too Kleist has treated a Brandenburg theme, and he has done it as a real artist. The action affects us with the force of a natural catastrophe. Kohlhaas' crimes grow like an avalanche until he no longer differentiates between right and wrong. Add to this the breathless tempo of the tale and its passionate language, and it can readily be acknowledged as one of the most impressive of German stories. However, its art was lost on contemporaries, and the public turned to lesser authors who could be understood more easily. These authors were the later German romanticists.

The Harvest Time of Romanticism

WHEN the original romantic circle in Jena dissolved, the movement lost its unity. Berlin never became a satisfactory substitute. Friedrich Schlegel went to Paris. He began to age quickly and soon little was left of the exuberant, witty youth of the Jena period. Perhaps there were still traces of the young Schlegel in the book *Über die Sprache und Weisheit der Inder* ("On the Language and Wisdom of the Hindus," 1808), which persuasively called the attention of German intellectuals to India. But the Friedrich Schlegel of these years was a tired writer looking for security. In 1808 he became a convert to Catholicism; he accepted the traditional answers of the Church and yielded to a ritual satisfying his senses. In 1809 Friedrich Schlegel settled in Catholic Vienna and became more and more closely associated with political and religious reaction. He gave lectures on modern history (1810) and developed the idea of an alliance of European princes on a common Christian foundation, the very idea that later became the foundation stone of Metternich's Holy Alliance. Romanticism from its beginnings had envisaged a rebirth of the Holy Roman Empire. Now it was sponsoring a political system which sacrificed the future of Europe to its past.

August Wilhelm Schlegel always preferred to develop the ideas of his brother rather than think along independent lines. In his later years he became more and more the scholar. He revised his important lectures on literary history. He also completed his translation of Shakespeare's plays with the help of Tieck's daughter, Dorothea, and Count Baudissin. The translation made Shakespeare a constituent of German literature. Finally August Wilhelm became a professor of Sanskrit philology in Bonn; as such he edited the classical works of Indian literature in critical editions and translations, and thus laid the foundation for German Sanskrit philology.

It was Tieck who perhaps underwent the more significant change. There had been a noticeable trend toward realism in him from the beginning, and only now this trend reached its fullest development. The old Tieck became a protagonist of the German *Novelle*. He would portray the most various characters in the most varied combinations, and would indulge to his heart's content in the representation of the unusual and interesting as such. The *Novelle Des Lebens Überfluss* ("Life's Luxuries") is perhaps Tieck's most brilliant performance in the romantic mixture of fairy tale and reality. Other stories take their characteristic color from a realistic delight in the portrayal of variegated reality. This is especially true of the historical tales of which the unfinished *Der Aufruhr in den Cevennen* ("Revolt in the Cevennes") can claim to be a masterpiece. Tieck's late novel *Vittoria Accorombona* (1840) also impresses as a realistic portrait of history. It brings to life the world of the Italian Renaissance.

The Harvest Time of Romanticism

Thus the founders of German romanticism gave up their original tenets. From its beginnings the later group did not feel so tense and unbalanced; rather, like Tieck, it enjoyed the charming world of fancy and tasted knowingly of an infinite variety of delightful sensations. For the older group the poetic world was the only one in which one could live. The later poets were never slow in compromising with reality, and visibly thrived upon the contrast between imagination and everyday life. The main task of art now appeared to be the adequate portrayal of the rich world of imagination.

Romanticism spread over the whole of Germany after it had originated as a predominantly Eastern movement. The first center of later romanticism was the old university town of Heidelberg. Here Arnim and Brentano in the summer of 1805 edited the first volume of *Des Knaben Wunderhorn* ("The Boy's Magic Horn"). From old prints and oral tradition they collected the folk songs despised by rationalism, and brought them into the light of day. They sometimes modernized them, or recast them entirely, if they did not please. And occasionally they even added some of their own. Yet on the whole their book offered genuine popular tradition in the sense of Herder. It unlocked a treasure of common national heritage which aroused the enthusiasm of romantic poets trying to escape the curse of individualism. And the *Wunderhorn* was not the only collection that helped to give new life to the national tradition. In 1807 there appeared the *Deutsche Volksbücher* ("German Chapbooks") of the Rhenish publicist Josef Görres who had also come to Heidelberg. In 1812 the brothers Grimm edited their *Kinder- und Hausmärchen* ("Household Tales") which were destined to become one of the German books most internationally known. The Grimms too were loosely connected with the Heidelberg circle.

The patriotic sentiments aroused by all these collections distinctly contributed to the great political movement taking hold on the Germans between 1806 and 1813. Germany during this period was ruled by Napoleon either directly or through his intermediaries. Nevertheless, this was but the external reason for the rise of German national feeling. Actually this rise had begun much earlier. It had first become apparent with Klopstock and Herder and the poets of Storm and Stress. Napoleon only forced it into different channels. The Germans demanded the liberation of their country from the yoke of the foreign conqueror, and they were also thinking of a revived national culture in forms more timely than those of the Holy Roman Empire. Most romantic poets contributed their share to the psychological warfare against Napoleon, and a special group became proverbially known as poets of freedom.

[225

The Style of Personal Experience

By means of this political movement Germany was moving away from the traditional unity of European culture toward the modern multiplicity of national cultures. For the movement was by no means exclusively German. In fact, it had started with the *levée en masse* (1792) of the French Revolution; but in the Romance countries the relation to the Latin past was no problem, and could never become as tenuous as in Germany. Here, nationalistic thought presented an actual danger, as Goethe saw very early. But to it belonged the near future. After the Wars of Liberation (1813–1815) romantic thought continued to stay alive, and contributed to the political movements of the nineteenth century, which culminated in the new German Empire of 1871. It also contributed, in much changed and often distorted form, to the ill-starred episode of National Socialism.

The national movement was paralleled by an intellectual movement which also started in Heidelberg. The life work of the Grimm brothers stemmed directly from Heidelberg romanticism. It laid the foundations of modern German philology with a historical German grammar and a comprehensive German dictionary (*Deutsches Wörterbuch*, begun in 1852 and still uncompleted). German historical scholarship received an important impetus from the publication of the *Monumenta Germaniae Historica* ("German Historical Monuments"), which was started in 1820 by the baron and statesman vom und zum Stein and the historian G. H. Pertz. The *Monumenta* aimed at reliable and critical editions of the sources of German history, and thus fitted in with the rise of nationalistic thinking that was displayed in so many popular and semipopular books and speeches. We can but mention the well-meant but not always well-reasoned works of Ernst Moritz Arndt, the brilliant though prejudiced *Reden an die deutsche Nation* ("Addresses to the German Nation") of the philosopher Fichte, and the somewhat exaggerated *Deutsches Volkstum* ("German Nationality") of Friedrich Ludwig Jahn, the founder of German athletics.

Yet however popular such ideas were among German youth, the spirit of universality was not wanting. The *Vorlesungen über die Philosophie der Weltgeschichte* ("Lectures on the Philosophy of the World's History") of the philosopher Hegel (1770–1831) found their public too, and inspired it by their brilliant summarization of the romantic view of history. And a host of romantic scholars devoted themselves to the sciences of aesthetics, of comparative religion, and of the physical world. Universalism was also displayed by the numerous translations following Schlegel's and Tieck's renditions of Shakespeare and Cervantes. The versatile poet Friedrich Rückert unlocked the treasures of oriental literature and acquainted his readers with Arabic, Indian, Persian, and Chinese works. And he was only one of the new translators.

In the field of literature proper the typical contrast between realistic and imaginative tendencies was expressed by characteristic motifs and figures. In lyrics, the poems of Brentano are no longer pure, unearthly music. They owe their effect to a sensuous element represented by the sound of the words; when Brentano in his later years recaptured the Catholic tradition of his childhood, he lost that sensuous power. In his best verse, such as *Abendständchen* ("Serenade") or *Wiegenlied* ("Lullaby") he could achieve an almost bewitching charm; yet it is the charm of mysterious transcendence:

> *Sprich aus der Ferne,*   *Speak from the distance,*
> *Heimliche Welt,*   *Secretive world,*
> *Die sich so gerne*   *Which ever so gladly*
> *Zu mir gesellt.*   *Comes to join me.*

Romantic transcendental longing has also found a lasting form in the poems of Eichendorff. Of all the romantic poets who have proceeded from folk song, he is without doubt the most intimate. A sad feeling of strangeness in this world, of ever having to wander and roam, permeates his poems:

> *In einem kühlen Grunde*
> *Da geht ein Mühlenrad,*
> *Mein' Liebste ist verschwunden,*
> *Die dort gewohnet hat . . .*
>
> *Hör' ich das Mühlrad gehen,*
> *Ich weiss nicht, was ich will—*
> *Ich möcht' am liebsten sterben,*
> *Da wär's auf einmal still!*
>
> *
>
> *A mill wheel*
> *Is turning in a cool vale,*
> *My love*
> *Who once was living there has vanished . . .*
>
> *When I hear the mill wheel going,*
> *I do not know what I want—*

[227]

The Style of Personal Experience

Rather would I die, and
Then at once everything would be still.

Yet this feeling is no longer always reaching for the infinite, it can also find consolation in finite nature. And nature often is described quite objectively. At times the longing can be satisfied, and ends in a note of fresh cheerfulness:

Wem Gott will rechte Gunst erweisen,
Den schickt er in die weite Welt,
Dem will er seine Wunder weisen
In Berg und Strom und Wald und Feld.

*

He upon whom God bestows especial favors—
Him He sends to roam over the world,
To him He shows all His wonders
In vale and wood, in field and stream.

And in a quiet moonlit night the poet can find peace and the blissful assurance of God's love:

Und meine Seele spannte   *And my soul far extended*
Weit ihre Flügel aus,   *Its wings and*
Flog durch die stillen Lande,   *Flew through the silent lands,*
Als flöge sie nach Haus.   *As though it flew home.*

Eichendorff's lyric poetry is not exactly rich in motifs, and typical moods occur again and again. Yet it is exquisitely pure and intimate. As a pious Catholic Eichendorff was never able to feel the desolate loneliness of the modern individual as deeply as the Protestant poets.

A downright realistic tone is often found in the lyric poetry of the so-called Swabian romanticists. The most important among them was Ludwig Uhland (1787–1862). He excelled in ballads where he gave firm, lucid expression to romantic themes; thus *Das Glück von Edenhall* ("The Luck of Edenhall"), which Longfellow translated, let a fairy's prophecy become a family's destiny. Uhland also wrote purely lyrical poems and here often happily found the tune of folk song. Uhland's poem *Der gute Kamerad* ("The Good Comrade") has indeed become a folk song. If one compares Uhland's lyrics with those of Novalis and other similar poets, one discovers a distinctly masculine trait in them. And the later Uhland turned more and more to the masculine ideal of the "fighting singer" (*streitbarer Sänger*). In Uhland's poetry even the shepherd on the mountainside swings his sword, and as his human ideal he venerates Bertran de Born, the Provençal troubadour who defied his king with his lyre in his hand. To be sure, Uhland's verse sometimes betrays the professor; still, he knew how to take an active part in life. In 1848 he was elected a representative to the German National Diet, and displayed admirable courage in fighting for his principles.

A related figure was the Saxon Wilhelm Müller, the author of such popular, healthy songs as *Am Brunnen vor dem Tore* ("At the Well by the Gate"), *Im Krug zum grünen Kranze* ("At the Green Wreath Inn"), *Das Wandern ist des Müllers Lust* ("To Wander is the Miller's Joy"), etc. They inspired Heinrich Heine, who later made the significant transition from romanticism to realism. They also found a congenial composer in Franz Schubert, who extended their fame in setting them as *Lieder*.

In the narrative prose of later romanticism one meets the same distinct tendency toward the objective expression of characteristic motifs. The narrative art of Brentano and Eichendorff almost could be called atmospheric. It owes its peculiar charm to the power of a prevailing mood. Brentano's *Geschichte vom braven Kasperl und dem schönen Annerl* ("The Story of Just Caspar and Fair Annie," 1817) has some of the touching qualities of an old folk song. Eichendorff's immortal story *Aus dem Leben eines Taugenichts* ("From the Life of a Good-for-Nothing," 1821) is the story of a wandering artist like Tieck's Sternbald. Here nature and human experience, musical and lyrical elements combine harmoniously and achieve a singularly beautiful mood. To be sure, the world of fancy is carefully set off from the world of the Philistines, the "lazybones lying at home," and the critical reader cannot help but observe that at the end of this tale, Taugenichts has also become a homebody with a *Hausfrau* and children. But then, why should we not sometimes forget the drudgeries of daily existence and roam for a while with this gay, irresponsible youth?

The charming tale of the Germanized Frenchman Chamisso, *Peter Schlemihl* (1814), is also the story of a wanderer. Peter Schlemihl has sold his shadow and now feels at home in no country in the world. This is actually more than another romantic tale, for it symbolizes the psychological plight of the emigrant who for political reasons had to leave his French homeland and in spite of honest effort can still not feel quite assimilated into German culture. *Peter Schlemihl* is also characteristically romantic in its use of fairy-tale motifs. One finds them used everywhere by the writers of later romanticism. An example of a modernized fairy tale is *Undine* by Baron de la Motte Fouqué, the scion of another family of French refugees. Undine is a water sprite longing to become a human being, and yet not quite able to immerse herself in human life. Brentano's friend Arnim also employed many fairy-tale figures and motifs. He was best when he concentrated on a single case as in *Der tolle Invalide auf dem Fort Ratonneau* ("The Mad Invalid of Fort Ratonneau"), a peculiar story of war neurosis.

The most important narrator of later romanticism was E. T. A. Hoffmann (1776–1822). He was a very unstable character continuously going from one extreme to the other. Starting as a conscientious Prussian bureaucrat, he suddenly became an artist, partly out of inner compulsion, partly on account of circumstantial necessity. In Bamberg he made a living as composer and conductor, as stage manager and painter of scenery. In all these fields Hoffmann displayed unusual although not unique gifts. After the Wars of Liberation he again sought refuge in the social security of Berlin officialdom. To be sure, he used every one of his free hours for his literary creations, which became increasingly serious. But to conform was not satisfying to this neurotic poet, and alcoholism destroyed Hoffmann's life before its natural end.

Hoffmann's works are just as questionable as his life. Some of his tales have made him internationally known as a writer of mystery and horror stories. Yet most of these mystery stories were written with an eye to mass appeal, in order to make money, and they hardly possess a distinct literary value. Hoffmann in such stories showed no compunction about his means and methods, and freely indulged in crassly realistic portrayal of the wild effusions of his imagination. He readily prostituted his talent. Yet occasionally such minor works rise to poetic heights. As an example we mention *Das Fräulein von Scudery*, the story of a goldsmith who loves his jewelry so passionately that he always is killing the human beings who wear it. In his fate the artist's jealous passion for his works has found a symbolical expression.

Hoffmann's most considerable works all portray the artist possessed by demons and struggling forever in vain with the unpoetic world of everyday reality. There is the masterful *Nachtstück* ("night piece") *Ritter Gluck* ("Chevalier Gluck"), in which the dead German composer Gluck appears once more among the living who do not understand him. A similar plot is presented in the fairy tale *Klein Zaches* ("Little

Zaches"). But here the representatives of unbridled imagination finally defeat the machinations of their enlightened opponents who may seem shrewd but in reality are witless. In hours of optimism Hoffmann still hoped to overcome the extremes of real life. In the charming fairy tale *Der goldene Topf* ("The Golden Pot") nature and spirit became unified. And in *Prinzessin Brambilla* their unity is at least achieved in a work of art.

Yet such hours of optimism were rare, and Hoffmann's most characteristic creations only expressed an unappeased longing for a beloved predestined to him from eternity. Such a longing formed the core of Hoffmann's opera *Undine*, which was completed in 1814 and had its first performance in 1816. It was his most important musical work, and was based on Fouqué's tale already mentioned. However, it was soon superseded by Weber's *Der Freischütz*, which for the first time treated a romantic theme in a new musical style.

The problem of Hoffmann's unfulfilled love was also brought out in the witty imaginative novel *Die Elixiere des Teufels* ("The Devil's Elixirs"). Here mysterious blood relationships were adduced in order to explain away Hoffmann's peculiar fate. No such explanation can be found in *Kater Murr* ("Murr the Tomcat"). In this bizarre piece of writing the world of the Philistine was represented through the autobiography of an unreasoning animal, a tomcat by the name of Murr. The cat tears pages from an old book and inserts them as blotters between the written pages of his diary. Yet the printer sets these torn pages in type and prints them along with Murr's own chapters. So we get interspersed fragments from the life of the conductor Kreisler, a demoniac musician whose extremism knows no bounds. It is seldom that the late romantic attitude toward the world has found such a powerful form which is throughout consistent in its inconsistency.

In dramatic literature the only interesting figure of the later romantic group was the East Prussian poet Zacharias Werner. He was attracted by exceptional and abnormal human beings in mysterious historic contexts which seemed to embody the transcendental. He was interested in the forms and sects of religion, in the complex psychology of priestly mountebanks, in the fateful relation of religious intoxication to sensual passion. Werner probed into forbidden nooks and recesses of the soul; thus his characters often display a surprising depth and remind one of more modern dramatists. Yet none of Werner's dramas was more than externally completed, and they all fell short of perfection. Unfortunately the only drama which continues to bring

[231

his name before the public is his tragedy *Der 24. Februar* ("The Twenty-fourth of February"). Here a date and a dagger have assumed the role of fate, and fate has become rigidly localized in time and place. Through such devices Werner tried to make visible uncanny influences, and from the limited viewpoint of the stage he has indeed achieved an unusual effect. Werner found a number of imitators, whose "tragedies of destiny" localized fate in an even more ludicrous manner. In one of them the role of fate is assumed by a picture on the wall; but perhaps one should not blame Werner for such excesses.

CHAPTER EIGHT

The Style of Personal Experience in the Nineteenth Century

The Spirit of the Nineteenth Century

GERMAN classicism and romanticism represent the last important attempts to master once more the divergent forces of culture and to combine them in a balanced view of the world. Unfortunately this attempt met with only temporary success. In the course of the nineteenth century, the unified attitude toward the world degenerated into mere pretense, if it was not given up altogether. Replacing this unified attitude is a predominantly anti-metaphysical mood, with occasional overtones of scepticism and despair. Ethical laws and cultural obligations gradually change into mere conventions or, worse, mere conveniences, and each individual lives a life of his own. Individual personalities and individual projects rule the age. They no longer contribute to one unifying theme, but become eclectic or materialistic. The natural sciences achieve unheard-of progress.

The last universal system of philosophical idealism was the system of Hegel. Here the world was viewed in a romantic manner. It was permeated by the World-Spirit, which unfolded itself in historical progression. After Hegel the philosophy is no longer universal, it becomes specialized. It is isolated psychology or aesthetics or logic or philosophy of history. One often witnesses a revival of the same rationalism that romanticism had so persistently fought. Only one idealist late-comer, Arthur Schopenhauer, tried to build a universal system in his work *Die Welt als Wille und Vorstellung* ("The World as Will and Idea," 1819), which became a success only in its second edition of 1844. Accepting the critical side of Kant only, Schopenhauer no longer believed in the validity of prevailing cultural pursuits. He turned away from them in disgust and advised in pessimistic despair a negation of the will to live.

The sciences of the nineteenth century still preserve noteworthy remnants of an idealistic interpretation of life. The scientists wished to interpret everything materialistically, by the chance interplay of forces and substances. But they did not achieve an uncontested ascendency over the humanities which still managed to uphold the traditions of the great past. Yet representatives of idealism fought a losing battle against the dominant mood of the times.

No longer held in check by ethical and religious obligations, the individual could now enjoy his liberty to the utmost, flexing his muscles in the fields of industry and politics. The nineteenth century became the Golden Age of German industry. Inventive ingenuity and organizational achievement bloomed as never before. The year of 1835 saw the opening of the first German railroad. In 1847 Alfred Krupp began to build his first cannon foundry. In 1859 Friedrich Siemens invented his steel smelter. And in 1867 Werner (von) Siemens constructed the first electric motor.

In politics, the age of *Realpolitik* was dawning. Political romanticism still wanted to fashion reality after a spiritual model. Now the opposite was undertaken, and wonderful romantic "dreams" must yield to the demands of reality. Real progress was made toward greater political freedom for the individual. Where Storm and Stress raised rather general demands, the nineteenth century translated them into political practice. Liberalism broke through with the French Revolution of 1830, the so-called July Revolution. It conceived of the individual as sovereign master of his own destiny and emancipated him from all tradition. Everywhere in Europe the individual citizen became a strong factor in the formulation of a political will. Yet pure liberalism was predominantly negative, it always wished to be free from something. As such, it was quite different from the democratic attitude, which demands a responsible participation of the individual in actual

The Spirit of the Nineteenth Century

government. Democratic ideologies also came to the fore in the nine-teenth century, but they were felt to be rather imposing, and their idealistic will to achieve the perfect state went against the grain of the period. Only a few stalwart German democrats took up the cudgels, but they lacked popular support. The average individual preferred a state that interfered as little as possible with its newly gained freedom. In practice this liberal attitude led to little more than speeches and to a *laisser-faire* attitude in economics and social legislation. In political theory, democracy and liberalism were not always differentiated.

The other political idea of the nineteenth century was of a more definite romantic progeny. This was the idea of nationality. All European countries during this period became conscious of their national character; outside of the Germanies the Greeks and Italians, the Poles and Czechs, the Hungarians and Bulgarians were fighting for their national independence. German history of the nineteenth century revolved around the national problem. Something had to replace the Holy Roman Empire, and nobody questioned the economic urgency of a new organization of the Germanies; but should it be strong or loose? Should it be federalized or centralized? Should it be strictly national or include other geographically related areas? Should it be under Prussian or under Austrian leadership? And should it be republican or monarchical? All such detailed questions were subjects of spirited discussion and of wide disagreement. In the sense of older romanticism the solution should have been universal. In the spirit of the new realism it became narrowly Prussian. Prussia, through its Customs Union of 1833, achieved an abolition of all inner German customs barriers outside of Austria. Though this was definitely an economical step forward, it prevented an even more desirable European customs union which might have been initiated by the inclusion of Austria. Then in 1848 and 1849 the liberal and democratic elements attempted vainly to unite the Germanies on a democratic or at least parliamentary basis. Finally Bismarck brought the national movement to a momentous conclusion. But his conclusion was distinctly Prussian and centralized, and it was also reactionary. For Bismarck achieved his success by the negation of the democratic forces, although he used the liberals as his allies when opportunity advised it, and gave a democratic façade to the new German Empire of 1871. His strongest support came from the Prussian junkers, and the ultimate rationale of his *Realpolitik* was "blood and iron."

Most of the German nationalists were blinded by Bismarck's success. Yet even in their camp not everybody was satisfied. Bismarck's *Reich* did not include all Germans, and it did include some Frenchmen in the west and some Poles in the east. Behind the imposing external façade an inwardly weak and therefore loud-mouthed spirit predominated. "German" after 1871 often became synonymous with "Prussian" and "reactionary," and lost the universal and European connotations of classical Humanism and romanticism. After all, the same Austria that had been forcibly excluded was also a German nation, and the Germans of Switzerland, who had no desire to be joined to Germany politically, also represented a different shade of culture. By strengthening its powers and by organizing so skillfully, Germany after 1871 was endangering its soul.

Literary achievement around 1800 had constituted events of major importance. Now political developments crowded the stage, and were pushing literature into the background. What survived was more often than not a literature without a philosophy. It was a literature of writers who were no longer servants of the nation, but lived their personal lives and expressed them subjectively. Literature became a specialized trade and an individual chattel, *geistiges Eigentum* or "intellectual possession." As early as 1794 Prussia had recognized authors' copyright and had thus translated the new concept into law. The average writer of the nineteenth century seemed to exist solely as a mirror of the times, whose function it was to entertain or divert his contemporaries. The fine arts often followed suit.

To be sure, other, older forces continued to thrive in secret; it was primarily because of them that the continuity of national culture was preserved into the twentieth century. Herder and the romantics had discovered folk life, and consequently German regionalism began to flourish. Many of the important literary works of the nineteenth century originated in a regional atmosphere: Bohemia or Switzerland, the atmosphere of the northern plains, or of the central woods and hills. Here the poets lived in close affinity to the elemental forces of nature and of folk life, and did not discover their characters in urban isolation. To be sure, many of these poetic figures lacked universality, but they often exhibited an awareness of the limitations of individual existence and of its obligations toward the community. The heroes of this regional literature were still representative heroes to some degree.

All literature of this time, whether of a regional or an urban character, endeavored to be "realistic." It tried to describe reality for its own sake instead of as a sheath for a transcendent meaning. Only weak imitators or exceptional rebels still measured reality by eternal standards. The average writer did not look for spirit beyond reality.

Socially, most writers of nineteenth-century literature represent the same proud bourgeoisie that also led in the field of industry and to some extent in politics. Few of the writers hailed from the nobility, and princely patronage played a less important role.

The new period begins about 1830 with the death of Goethe (1832) and Hegel (1831). Until 1880 this middle-class literature is devoted exclusively to middle-class problems. The decades from 1880 to about 1910 are interested in the problems of the rising new class of industrial workers, and are influenced by their different perspective.

Between Romanticism and Realism

GERMAN realism of the nineteenth century was rooted in the previous romanticism. The late romantic interest in the curious and anomalous was the earliest form of the new realism. The turn toward it could first be discerned in a few romanticists such as Tieck. A more decided trend in the same direction was taken by the Westphalian Immermann (1796–1840) who was no longer satisfied with the romantic view of things. His play *Merlin* he termed significantly a "tragedy of contradiction" (*Tragödie des Widerspruchs*). His novel *Die Epigonen* ("The Inheritors") displayed a disharmonious and melancholy attitude toward life: the poet lived in the shadow of his great predecessors, and did not feel quite able to achieve new independent creations of his own. Still, in his other novel *Münchhausen* (1838–1839) Immermann inserted an episode that started an important new trend. Several chapters of *Münchhausen* take place on the *Oberhof*, one of the old Westphalian farms with which the author was familiar. And here is related the first German village story; its robust, rugged characters still strike us like a gust of fresh air amid all the unhealthy fantastic haze of late romanticism. Immermann shared the enthusiasm of his Westphalian compatriot Justus Möser for the genuine and the natural,

[237

and found in it an antidote to the vagaries of subjective imagination.

Immermann's literary opponent was August Count von Platen-Hallermünde (1796–1835). He too began writing under the influence of romanticism. He imitated oriental verse forms and wrote fairy-tale comedies in the manner of Tieck. His best-known poem is *Das Grab im Busento* ("The Grave in the Busento River"), a typical romantic nocturne. Yet the same Platen also tried to overcome the romantic weakness for the fanciful; he even tried to satirize it. He finally sought refuge in a hardened, crystal-clear form of classical antecedents, which he applied to public and impersonal themes. Platen must be described as a rather weak and unstable personality who, in an age of threatening dissolution, vainly aspired to order and discipline.

The most important poet in whom one can observe the transition from romanticism to realism is the dramatist Franz Grillparzer (1791–1872). His peculiar character is best understood if one keeps in mind his thoroughly Austrian background. He had a warm, sensuous, almost Mediterranean feeling for nature; forces of nature and forces of fate were to him something objective. On the other hand, he also had Austrian Catholicism in his blood. He did not feel quite at home in the world, and most of his characters perished in collisions with reality. The beginnings of his dramatic career were determined by this inherited Christian, and also romantic, feeling of being a stranger on this earth; he started with the tragedy of fate *Die Ahnfrau* ("The Ancestress," 1817). Later, Grillparzer represented more and more the real forces of life, and in the end he approached realism. But he never yielded wholly to the spirit of the new age, and even fought it. For his was an extraordinary complex personality. Besides romantic and classical elements his make-up also comprised traces of Austrian Enlightenment and, especially, Austrian baroque. In Austria the Christian and late Roman tradition of German culture was never broken, and the disruptive forces of modern industrialism and nationalism were unable to conquer wholly the Austrian past. It was certainly no accident that Grillparzer learned so much from the Spanish dramatists of the seventeenth century, and it was also no accident that the personal motto of his later years had a strange baroque sound: *In Selbstbewahrung liegt zuletzt die Ruh* ("Self-preservation yields the final peace").

Die Ahnfrau does not yet show the characteristic style of Grillparzer. That becomes more clearly defined in his second tragedy, *Sappho*, which was first produced in 1818. Its heroine is the famous Greek poetess Sappho, whom Grillparzer portrays as longing for life and its whole, beautiful sensuousness. Yet the poetess cannot totally yield to it, she must knowingly resign herself and find peace in voluntary death. The same gloomy view pervades the tragedy *Des Meeres und der Liebe Wellen* (literally, "The Waves of the Sea and of Love"), which appeared on the stage in 1831. Here the theme is the old legend of Hero and Leander, the lovers separated by the sea and destroyed by a capricious fate. And here, just as in *Sappho*, we have a picturesque, melodious language that achieves without effort a fusion of classical harmony and romantic warmth. Its simplicity is never strident, its ornamentation never overdone.

Another classical theme was treated in the trilogy *Das goldene Vliess* ("The Golden Fleece," 1821). Its third part, *Medea*, achieved European theatrical fame, although it can be properly understood only in the context of the whole. The trilogy traces the ruinous consequences of Jason's and Medea's past hypocrisies. Jason made Medea his wife from pure love of adventure, not from love of her. And Medea followed the scion of a foreign nation against the dictates of her own conscience. Jason dreamed of tearing her from the night of paganism into the radiant brightness of Greek culture, but this proved impossible. Medea could not shed her native inheritance. Culture, even life itself, are almost a curse to the poet:

> *Was ist der Erde Glück?—Ein Schatten!*
> *Was ist der Erde Ruhm?—Ein Traum!*
>
> *
>
> *What is earth's happiness?—A shadow!*
> *What is earth's glory?—But a dream!*

These early plays of Grillparzer present to us a tired world. But it is also a world alive with sparkling, beautiful detail described in noble, colorful blank verse. The problems of this world are very delicate, and can be fully understood only at a distance from the noise of the day. Yet even in Austria developments were afoot toward a better form of actual life. To be sure, the government of Prince Metternich tried to suppress all liberal movements inside and outside of the Danube Monarchy, in order to preserve its very existence. Yet he was unable to quell the growing unrest among its constituent nationalities.

Grillparzer's quiet conservatism found little sympathy with his contemporaries, who finally rejected his fine comedy *Weh dem, der lügt* ("Thou Shalt not Lie") at its first presentation in 1838. The play portrayed a youth's struggle for purity of heart; but this struggle struck no responsive note in the superficial theatergoers. Thereupon the oversensitive poet withdrew from the stage in angry despair, and did not publish anything thereafter.

But Grillparzer was no simple escapist. Even before the failure of his comedy he had begun to take part in the political movements of his time. As an ardent patriot, he tried to stimulate the Austrians by presenting scenes from their great past. Thus in his rich play *König Ottokars Glück und Ende* ("King Ottokar, His Rise and Fall," 1825) he portrayed the rise to power of Rudolf von Habsburg, the founder of Austria's dynasty. Here an Austrian national poet was emerging, and one might have expected the government to support him. But Metternich's petty bureaucrats were afraid of any show of intellectuality. The most important Austrian poet of his day was merely allowed to eke out a living as a minor official.

Still Grillparzer continued to write in the quiet of his study. He added many a fine play to the type which he had begun with *König Ottokars Glück und Ende*. Now that he had given up the struggle for the stage, he transcended individualism more and more. Among his later plays the posthumous drama *Libussa* should occupy a special niche with its astonishing intuitive grasp of problems of social organization. Grillparzer shows how the primitive matriarchal world is replaced by the male world of activity, matriarchal peace and sheltered happiness being meant for service and not for rule. To rule and promote justice is the prerogative of the masculine world. Grillparzer poses the question whether the gain of a harder, more extended and rougher world was worth the sacrifice; for it resulted in a loss of vision and of direct harmony with the forces of nature. Yet the poet realizes that all economic and political progress has been bought at this price. His tragedy ends with the founding of the city of Prague. The plot itself is based on a Czech legend, and all the more lovable characters of the play are Czech, a clear indication of the universality of Grillparzer's Austrian nationalism and its far removal from any narrow Teutonism. The same universality also led him to sympathetic understanding of Jewish characters, as is evinced by his posthumous tragedy *Die Jüdin von Toledo* ("The Jewess of Toledo"). The Spanish king who is the hero of the play is consumed with his passion for a Jewess abundantly endowed with sensuous charm. His councillors believe that the state is in danger and order the royal mistress to be murdered. The king almost loses his senses and can never forget her, yet he manages to find his

Between Romanticism and Realism

way back to sovereign leadership. The play clearly speaks for the rights of a great passion although they are denied in an ending characteristic of Grillparzer. The poet has not given up his Austrian peculiarities, but the realistic elements have become predominant and a positive view of culture is achieved. It is no wonder that Grillparzer was one of the few German poets of his time who exerted an international appeal. Lord Byron was deeply impressed by his *Sappho*, and only recently Arthur Burkhard and Henry H. Stevens' congenial American translation of his plays has again attested to their universal attraction.

Yet for all his universalism Grillparzer was thoroughly Austrian, and in several respects his achievements were based upon the tradition of the Vienna folk play. Its delight in theatrical display should not be interpreted as a romantic trait, as it actually continues the old stage tradition of baroque times. Baroque culture has never died in the German South, and has given a distinct character to its popular art and culture. Austrian, Bavarian, and Swiss native costumes are largely baroque, the home-made furniture and the village churches constructed and decorated by local craftsmen are baroque. Baroque are the horses on the merry-go-rounds, and baroque are the *Kasperletheater*, the Punch and Judy shows of all the Southern country fairs. The Viennese magic comedies (*Zauberpossen*) of the beginning of the nineteenth century were a faithful continuation of the familiar style of the Jesuit dramas and the operas of the seventeenth century. As of old, gay masquerading and fanciful stage play served for the revelation of serious moral teaching.

The most charming exponent of the Vienna folk play was the self-educated confectioner Ferdinand Raimund (1790–1836). His best plays achieved a sympathetic depiction of human life in terms of Christian morality. His most popular drama was *Der Verschwender* ("The Spendthrift," 1834); it showed up the petty ambition of mere fortune hunters. Raimund's successor Johann Nepomuk Nestroy did not capture the same freshness and honest simplicity. His *Lumpazivagabundus* (1833) was hardly more than a glorification of vagabondage.

Heinrich Heine

Heinrich Heine's singular standing in German literature derives only in part from his poetic achievements, though they were by no means unimpressive. It rather signifies him as the first German poet to become aware of the modern European dilemma of conflicting standards of values. The resultant complexity of his character has made him a most controversial figure. It is easier to criticize than to understand and appreciate him.

Heine was born in the Rhenish city of Düsseldorf in 1797, and grew up in respectable Jewish circumstances at a time when Jewish traditions had begun to falter. As a student in Bonn, Heine drew equal nourishment from German popular culture and from the works of Goethe, whose greatness at once impressed the young man. He participated in the romantic vagaries of German youth, yet he also suffered early from material and spiritual want. His father became bankrupt, and young Heine henceforth depended on the grudging generosity of his uncle, a Hamburg banker with the uncouthness and lack of culture characteristic of the *nouveau riche*. Heine had to find his way in an age that was drifting toward a materialism which could not be reconciled with the ruling romantic sentimentality. Yet the spiritual tradition was still alive, and in Berlin Heine frequented the parlors of highly cultured Jewish society leaders such as Rahel von Varnhagen (nee Levin). He himself submitted to baptism when he was acquiring his law degree from the University of Göttingen; yet only a short while before he had eagerly joined a small group of scholars interested in Jewish folklore and history.

Heine's early writings brought him into conflict with the prevailing reactionary censorship, ultimately forcing him to leave Germany. He emigrated to Paris, where he had justifiable hopes of earning a livelihood. As a correspondent for German newspapers he did indeed reap some financial rewards. But increasing difficulties with the censors and severe illness prematurely ended his affluence. The favorite poet of the contemporary public soon had to depend on the grudging handouts of his uncle's family and what additional income he could scrape up by painfully laborious writing. After 1848 Heine was completely paralyzed and never left his bed which in joking despair he called his "mattress grave."

Heinrich Heine

Heine found Paris congenial from its constitutional government down through all its strata. He struck up acquaintances with most of the leading Frenchmen of his time. He married a Frenchwoman who loved him like a dutiful wife, but did not understand a word of his poetry. Still, he never became a Frenchman in spirit, and was proud of his mission as a German poet. His verses were filled with longing for Germany, although he could not stomach the policies of German reaction and occasionally vented his wrath at the stolidity of the German character. In prose and verse Heine consistently upheld the liberal in politics. He was often cynical, and the vitriolic sharpness of his pen knew no bounds. But Heine needed his wit to defend himself against the anti-Semitism and the reactionary smugness of so many of his contemporaries. He needed it too as a guard against his own romantic sentimentality, for behind the cynical façade of Heine the merciless scoffer there beat the almost too-gentle heart of Heine the believer in justice and charity. In the excruciating sufferings of his final years he expressed a belief in life after death and an awareness of the existence of an almighty God. In his last verses he confessed a spiritual love for a female visitor (Elise Krinitz, the "Mouche") who had come to brighten his dreary days. Heine's death in 1856 came as a long-desired release.

Heine became a poet through unhappy love experiences that wounded his sensitive heart to the core. When his youthful dreams faded, the awkward, penniless youth found himself confronted by an antagonistic world whose values seemed to him both base and material. In an earlier decade Heine would have become a romanticist, scorning the unpoetic world of the Philistines and perhaps even scorning life itself. The temptation was great, and the poet occasionally succumbed to it. His first important collection, *Buch der Lieder* ("Book of Songs," 1827), and his last one, *Romanzero* (1851), are full of dreamy romantic moods. He visualizes a fairy-tale India of lotus flowers and holy gazelles to which he might carry his beloved "on wings of song" (*Auf Flügeln des Gesanges*); he pictures her as a saint in a medieval cathedral (cf. *Im Rhein, im schönen Strome*, "In the beautiful Rhine river"). He can while away radiant evening hours at the seashore (*Wir sassen am Fischerhause*, "We were sitting by the fisher's hut"), and he enjoys the warmth of wonderful May days (*Im wunderschönen Monat Mai*, "In the wonderful month of May"). But these sentimental poems are not Heine's most characteristic and they are not his best. His prevailing mood is one of bitterness from which the poet is by no means anxious

[243

to escape. With effortless ease he conjures up the mythical river siren, the *Lorelei,* who would lure all boatmen onto dangerous shoals and exult at their death. He can write the grandiose ballad *Die Wallfahrt nach Kevlaar* ("The Pilgrimage to Kevlaar") with its melancholy description of a love faithful to the end, and he does the same kind of thing in an oriental setting in the haunting lines of *Der Asra* ("The Asra"). He can write of the patriotic lament of French soldiers for their dead emperor Napoleon (*Die zwei Grenadiere,* "The Two Grenadiers").

Heine's bitterness is caused by the poet's awareness of the realities of a situation, and by his equal awareness that his own role in it has not been entirely heroic or inspiring. He feels the justification of the world's judgment, and he frequently rails against his own sentimentality. Heine's irony is peculiar in its tendency to destroy the subjective world of his dreams, where romantic irony strove to destroy the objective world of everyday reality. This Byronesque mood comes to the fore in poems where, for instance, he ridicules a girl waxing sentimental over the setting of the sun (*Das Fräulein stand am Meere,* "The maiden stood by the sea"), or where he utters a despairing prayer that a sweet, innocent young girl may always remain so sweet and innocent (*Du bist wie eine Blume,* "To me you're like a flower"). It can increase to the bitter sarcasm of the *Neue Gedichte* ("New Songs"), which Heine wrote during the beginning of his stay in Paris, and which among other things deal with purely sensual and mercenary love experiences. One of Heine's most effective buffooneries tells of the wife or mistress of a jailbird who makes merry only an hour after his death on the gallows (*Ein Weib,* "A Woman").

No responsible critic will deny that Heine has written numerous pieces of a merely superficial brilliancy, of jingling rhymes and dazzling puns. He has also often indulged in expressing the trite and commonplace with nauseating directness. Yet a good number of his poems are lasting additions to the permanent treasury of German lyrics. Aside from some of the poems already mentioned (*Du bist wie eine Blume, Die zwei Grenadiere, Die Wallfahrt nach Kevlaar, Der Asra*) the Heine section of this treasury would also include *Schattenküsse Schattenliebe* ("Shadow kisses, shadow love"), *Nicht gedacht soll seiner werden* ("He shall not even be remembered"), *An die Jungen* ("To Youth"), and *Doktrin* ("Doctrine"). It would include such fine ballads as *Belsatzar* ("Balshazzar"), *Der alte König* ("The Old King") and *Frau Mette* ("Mrs. Mette"). Together, these poems represent a rich variety of mood and form. Heine very often employs the most simple schemes of rhymed

Heinrich Heine

folk poetry that stand in poignant contrast to the complexity of his moods; yet he has written poems in free verse (*Die Nordsee,* "The North Sea," 1826) and in trochees (*Atta Troll*). The haunting charm of his best verses has been acknowledged by great composers such as Schubert (d. 1828) and Schumann (d. 1856) in their setting them to music. As Heine has often been upbraided as the mere scoffer, the fact should also be emphasized that a strain of religious belief leads from the early *Belsatzar* to his last poetic utterances expressing a faith in transcendental existence.

The complexity of Heine's make-up is likewise reflected in his prose writings. The earliest ones contain little more than journalistic observations. They show Heine as a charming *causeur,* the forerunner of the later columnists. Their form is the romantic mixture of poetry and prose and the equally romantic frame of an excursion or a trip. The most lively of these early writings is *Die Harzreise* ("The Journey to the Hartz") of 1826. It is characterized by the incessant change of romantic and realistic moods typical of Heine. Here, descriptions of nature and of the wanderers met on the way occupy the foreground; later, in the *Buch Le Grand* ("Boyhood Days") or in *Englische Fragmente* ("English Fragments"), political discussions predominate. After Heine had moved to Paris, he wrote many more essays. His style improved, and his insight deepened. The essays collected in *Lutezia* contain numerous pertinent observations on French life as well as amazing scraps of wisdom and political prophecy. In another of his essays Heine took up arms against his journalistic contemporary, Ludwig Börne (d. 1837), a staunch fighter for liberal theories. And finally Heine's fine essay on Ludwig Markus should not be entirely forgotten. Less appealing are his epic poems *Atta Troll* (completed in 1846) and *Deutschland ein Wintermärchen* ("Germany, a Winter's Tale," 1844) which must be included among his journalistic writings in spite of their poetic form.

Heine was primarily a liberal for whom the state in every form was a necessary evil, and who saw individual freedom best guaranteed by a constitutional monarchy. He naturally opposed traditionalism and nationalism as forms of coercion. Yet he likewise saw with deep misgivings the rise of a democratic coercion and a communistic autocracy. His vision of the future was a common European culture to which all nations and religions contributed their share. A century later the achievement of such a culture must still be called unfulfilled.

[245

Between Poetry and
Journalism

HEINE's manner was soon taken up by the Young Germans, a loosely knit group of journalistic poets. The important developments of the nineteenth century were of an economical or political nature, so it appeared to be the task of the poet to take an active part in such movements and to be a fighter in the political battles. The poet became a partisan, and his poetry became political and tendentious, sometimes in a rather narrow sense. Or the poet became simply a journalist. Journalism profited considerably by the technical progress of the age and generally increased in importance. Only since the middle of the nineteenth century has Germany had a modern press.

In certain respects Heinrich Heine could be called the first of the journalistic poets. The influence of his forms and ideas was felt almost everywhere in the literature of the period. It was strange that Heine embroiled himself with his Young German devotees. These Young Germans were liberals, and in the true spirit of liberalism originally worked independently of each other, without forming a distinct party. They felt themselves spiritually akin to similar movements that were sprouting in other parts of Europe. But these other movements often crystallized into actual political parties; such a revolutionary group was the so-called Young Italy. It was understandable, then, when the reactionary police of Austria and other German states suspected the existence of a German party of dangerous intellectuals. Then a hostile critic indicted the whole Young German group, and the Austrian chancellor, Prince Metternich, thereupon set the German Confederation to investigate them. The outcome of the investigation was a special decree of 1835, which enjoined the group from writing. The authors chiefly affected by this decree were Heinrich Laube (1806–1884) and Karl Gutzkow (1811–1878), both bourgeois writers of liberal tendencies. However, they were not very courageous and lacked the stuff of martyrdom, so they did not defend themselves too vigorously and began to tune down their radicalism. They learned restraint and gradually developed into harmless representatives of political and literary mediocrity. Heinrich Laube produced a host of dramas that showed him as a weak imitator of Schiller, and he finally became the influential director of the Vienna Burgtheater, the main pillar of German classical tradition. Gutzkow was less amenable to political blandishments and retained a little more of his fiery radical temperament. His novels and dramas continued to fight for liberalism. *Uriel Acosta*, his best drama, pleads for freedom of thought and deserves to be rescued from oblivion.

Of greater importance than the writers of Young Germany were the political lyricists who helped to prepare the ground for the German Revolution of 1848. They were more outspoken and often enjoyed a quick popularity. Strictly speaking, the poets of the Wars of Liberation (1813–1815) had already expressed political ideas, but their programs had been rather nebulous. Now the poets became more specific in their demands—poets such as Hoffmann von Fallersleben, the author of the German national anthem *Deutschland über Alles*, or Georg Herwegh, the author of the stirring lines:

> Reisst die Kreuze aus der Erden,
> Alle sollen Schwerter werden!

> *

> *Tear the crosses from the graveyards,*
> *So that swords they shall become!*

The number of political poets of the forties was very large. For the German Revolution deeply excited the German imagination, and the excitement was not only restricted to the progressives. Conservatism too had its poets in Strachwitz and Scherenberg. Of the political poets of outstanding merit one must name Ferdinand Freiligrath (1810–1876). He had started writing in a romantically exotic vein reminiscent of Victor Hugo, but the political trends of the time were working against such escapism and compelled him to redirect his energies. He suddenly became a political activist and embraced more and more radical ideas. In the end he became almost communistic and could no longer stay in Germany. He fled to England where he began to translate English lyric poetry. Among the English and American poets who aroused his attention was one Walt Whitman.

The most important figure of this whole group, however, was Georg Büchner, the brother of the materialist philosopher Ludwig Büchner (*Kraft und Stoff*, "Force and Matter"). If he had lived to a more mature age, he might have become the real leader of the liberals and might have continued in the dramatic tradition of Heinrich von Kleist. He knew that a renovation of Germany could only come from the lower strata of the nation, while Heine and the representatives of Young Germany cast their lot with the educated classes and tried to arouse them to greater political activity. Büchner had no faith in the intellectuals; he hated ideologies and a priori explanations of life. In the end his scientific studies and his reflections on history led him to an almost nihilistic scepticism of man's ability to overcome his predicament. The hero of his original tragedy *Dantons Tod* ("Danton's Death") fails in his resistance to Robespierre's fanaticism because of his apathetic passivity; but Robespierre too is destroyed by the Revolution. What remains is a true concern with mental and spiritual suffering; political action is no panacea. Büchner's unfinished drama *Woyzeck*, with its disturbing scenes from lower-class life, revealed the naked state of man, the reality of his suffering. Büchner here was no rhetorical agitator; he sharply and mercilessly documented the social conditions of the masses. No other German dramatist of the period attempted a similar setting; the dramas of young Gerhart Hauptmann came over forty years later and, indeed, paved the way for the earlier Büchner's success on the German stage. Büchner was a passionate realist and in *Dantons Tod* made use of actual documents. Still, he was moved by compassion and could not entirely break loose from romanticism. This other side of the poet came out in his witty comedy *Leonce und Lena*. Büchner died in 1837, when he was only 23 years old.

After the defeat of the revolution of 1848, people generally sobered or made their peace with the regime. Radical political poems became rare. Only the longing for national unity continued without abatement. But the leading authors no longer expressed their thoughts in openly tendentious works; they turned again to genuine artistic tasks. In the works discussed in this chapter realistic traits can often be discerned. Now they became more and more predominant.

Friedrich Hebbel

BEFORE Büchner, Christian Dietrich Grabbe (1801–1836) had attempted to write realistic dramas. He hailed from Düsseldorf, and
his ambition was to become a German Shakespeare. He suffered deeply
from the confusion of the period, and in the beginning tried to express
it boldly in dramas full of contradictions; one of them bore the characteristic title *Don Juan und Faust* (1829). Yet the contrasts were too
great, and Grabbe did not succeed in writing unified tragedies. His later
dramas became a mere series of individual scenes. Grabbe met with no
public response to this early dramatic impressionism, and finally drank
himself to death.

The North German dramatist Friedrich Hebbel (1813–1863) had far
greater gifts than Grabbe and approached realism more closely. As the
son of a bricklayer and a servant girl he represented the new *petite
bourgeoisie* struggling for recognition. His education was patchy and he
was chiefly self-taught. Hebbel's early dramas were written in a desperate
fight against abject poverty and moral disintegration, although he was
temporarily helped by meager stipends. Only when he found his way to
Vienna did Hebbel's life become secure, and he could straighten himself
out, both economically and morally. Though his later dramas were not
an uninterrupted series of successes, the poetic fame of Hebbel and the
acting fame of his wife sufficed to keep the family going. Had his earlier
years of want not undermined his health, Hebbel might have reached
full fruition.

Most of Hebbel's dramas were written in blank verse, and might
therefore remind one superficially of the dramas of Schiller. But Hebbel's tragic concepts differed from the idealistic tradition. Where Schiller
believed in absolute moral values, Hebbel knew only relative ones. All
his dramas point up their own intrinsic relativity. In each of them two
sets of values are fighting for supremacy. One of them is usually doomed,
while the other gains ascendancy. The values marked for destruction
are the traditional values of society, the rising values are represented
through an outstanding individual. But this individual cannot yet maintain his different standards, and succumbs fighting for them. Hegel in
his *Vorlesungen über die Philosophie der Weltgeschichte* ("Lectures
on the Philosophy of History") described this process as the essence of

[249

The Style of Personal Experience

history. Hebbel now enacted it in drama. His world was essentially historical, and represented the final consequence of romanticism for which the world was a continuous oscillation between contrasts that had equal privileges. But Hebbel's world was also tragic to the core; it did not become tragic merely by accident. For in Hebbel's view, no individual is absolutely right, even though he may temporarily triumph. It is only because of its philosophic formulation that this attitude appears less realistic than it is. To some extent Hebbel anticipated Ibsen.

In Hebbel's first drama, *Judith* (1840), the ephemeral values are represented by oriental despotism, the transcendent values by the deeper insights of the Jewish religion, which bases action on divine inspiration. When Judith cuts off the head of Holofernes, the Jewish values apparently triumph. Yet the heroine is made to realize that she has acted for egotistic reasons and has succumbed to the very attitude she believed she had conquered. The drama dismisses us with the depressing feeling of the ambiguity of all human deeds.

In *Maria Magdalene* (1844) the heroine also comes to a tragic end. Yet the reason is not that like Judith she has been born too soon, but too late. She is following the stolid, antiquated traditions of the *petite bourgeoisie* and is drawn into their bankruptcy. Klara's father, Master Anton, clearly expresses the downfall of bourgeois values: "I no longer understand life" (*Ich verstehe die Welt nicht mehr*). But new, emerging moral values are nowhere to be found. *Maria Magdalene* is the most gloomy and also the most unified of Hebbel's dramas.

Herodes und Mariamne ("Herod and Mariamne," 1850) has a more complicated structure and a more artificial form. While the earlier dramas are written in prose, this one employs blank verse. Herod represents the ancient oriental tradition where woman is the absolute property of the husband. Mariamne fights for a world where husband and wife are held together by their own free consent. Yet Herod cannot understand her, and so she despairs of a meaningful married life and contrives her own death. She makes him believe that she has committed adultery, and he has to kill her. Only then does he realize that he has put credence in appearances, while in reality his wife has remained faithful. He is left with the awesome feeling that a new world with new values is approaching. They will be the superior values of Christianity.

It would be possible to find "guilt" in any of the three dramas just discussed. In *Agnes Bernauer* (1855) such guilt cannot be established. For Agnes dies because she is exceptionally beautiful, and we cannot hold her responsible for that. But her distinction has disturbed the peace of the world. She has endangered the existence of the state and must be sacrificed to it. Her ducal husband and her father-in-law also have to sacrifice their inner peace on the altar of the state. The play takes place in Germany at the end of the Middle Ages, and shows the replacement of Christian feudalism by the modern self-centered state. Perhaps this drama expresses most clearly Hebbel's conviction of the relativity of the individual to his circumstances. But one should not deduce from it that Hebbel believes in the supremacy of the state.

Gyges und sein Ring ("Gyges and His Ring," 1856) is a less satisfactory play. Its problem is too remote for a modern audience, and can no longer stir the emotions. *Die Nibelungen* (1862) is more impressive. It is the last work Hebbel completed. But on the stage this trilogy is less effective than in print. On the whole one might call it an able dramatization of the *Nibelungenlied*.

With the *Nibelungen* and *Maria Magdalene* almost the only exceptions, Hebbel's dramas often suffer from unpoetic abstractions. Yet only in minor works does the author completely give in to his weakness. In his better dramas it is compensated for by a natural gift for exposing valid contradictions. The least Hegelian speculation is expressed in Hebbel's poems, the best of which are nowadays acquiring fuller recognition. *Sommerbild* ("Summer Image") and *Herbstbild* ("Autumn Image") are wonderfully concise. *Sie sehn sich nicht wieder* ("They will not meet again") expresses a powerful passion. *Nachtlied* ("Night Song") is an impressive expression of romantic awe. *Gebet* ("Prayer") is entirely personal, and yet by its pure form reminds one of Hölderlin.

Richard Wagner

BECAUSE of their very special German, Austrian, or Swiss antecedents, most of the great writers discussed in previous sections have become little known outside of the Germanies. The same is anything but true of the musical dramas of Richard Wagner whose energetic fusion of romantic and realistic tendencies has rightfully won international renown. His early works may be called the consummation of the romantic drama. His later ones show an original awareness of

The Style of Personal Experience

the problems of bourgeois society, and accordingly should not be dismissed as mere pageants of old Germanic legendry.

Richard Wagner was born at Leipzig in 1813, and like his contemporary, Hebbel, came from a humble background. His enthusiasm for the people's rights was natural, and showed to advantage in his first successful opera *Rienzi* (1842), where the hero is the leader of a popular revolution. In subsequent years Wagner was occupied with the opera *Jesus von Nazareth*, in which Jesus was pictured as a social reformer. Yet in romantic fashion the people were seen as incorporating mythical, elemental forces, and the more important works of the young liberal were imbued with the spirit of romanticism. During his first stay in Paris, from 1839 to 1842, Wagner composed *Der fliegende Holländer* ("The Flying Dutchman"). He then became music director of the Saxon Court, and while holding this position completed *Tannhäuser* (1845), *Lohengrin* (completed 1848), and conceived the text of *Die Meistersinger* (score completed in 1867). When the liberal revolution of 1848 broke out, Wagner's democratic sympathies prompted him to take an active part in it, and consequently he had to flee from Dresden. He went first to Paris, taking with him all his manuscripts. Then he moved to Zürich, and from 1850–1858 directed the Zürich Musical Society. During this time he completed the text of *Der Ring des Nibelungen* ("The Ring of the Nibelungs," composition completed 1874). *Tristan und Isolde* was also started in Zürich and was finished in 1857. Soon thereafter the romantic Bavarian King, Ludwig II, began to become Wagner's sympathetic patron. The number of Wagner enthusiasts throughout the world now increased rapidly, and from funds subscribed by them a special theater for the performance of Wagner's operas was erected in Bayreuth, where Wagner moved in 1872. Here he wrote *Parsifal*, which was performed for the first time in 1882. Shortly afterwards, in February 1883, the composer died in Venice.

Wagner's musical dramas show unmistakable romantic features in form as well as in content. As a mixed genre, opera caught the fancy of the romanticists, who dreamed of a combination of all the arts in a common effect. They also tried to raise the literary level of opera texts, and attempted to make the opera at home in Germany by giving preference to German national subjects. Wagner continued these efforts and first established the principle of an uninterrupted union between text and melody. He defined his aim as a *Gesamtkunstwerk*, a "total work of art" produced by the parallel endeavors of poetry, music, painting, architecture, and choreography. Yet in practice it was always one field of art that predominated. In his librettos Wagner had to submit to the demands of musical composition, and many of them could be described simply as free verse rhythms. But his ideal was the alliterative verse of the *Edda*, and he used alliteration wherever he could. In *Der Ring des Nibelungen* Wagner even drew from the Middle High German language, with the result that some of his most famous arias employ a curiously grotesque Wagnerian German that is paralleled nowhere else in German literature; it is doubtful whether this was such a great improvement over earlier opera texts. On the whole, the musician in Wagner was superior to the poet in him. Yet even this musician began as a dyed-in-the-wool romantic, who endeavored to express in sound the dark, mysterious core of life.

In traditional German fashion Wagner was convinced of the poet's leading role in culture, and in his personal dynamism he was thoroughly conscious of his own value. He chose the subjects of his operas from German legends and stories of the past, preferring those which had found poetic form before. Most of Wagner's sources were medieval material flowing from the pens of Heine, E. T. A. Hoffmann and the minor romantic writer August Hagen (*Norica*, 1827). The last two furnished most of the details of *Die Meistersinger*. Yet all the old stories were modernized by Wagner and changed into myths of salvation. For, like other great contemporaries, like Gotthelf, like Keller and Raabe, he was not fully satisfied with the materialistic culture of the bourgeoisie, even though he personally profited from it in generous measure. *Der Ring des Nibelungen* employed Teutonic myths to illustrate the curse of earthly existence. The voluptuousness that swelled the Paris overture to *Tannhäuser* yielded no lasting satisfaction. *Tristan und Isolde* conceived of love as a desire for self-effacement and death in the midst of its deepest fulfillment; indeed, *Liebestod* ("love-death") was its proper designation. Wagner was deeply influenced by the Buddhistic thought that he found in the works of Arthur Schopenhauer. He ultimately tried to combine this with Christian elements in *Parsifal*, which became a drama of personal salvation through the emergence of compassion.

Die Meistersinger is less serious and less heavy than Wagner's other works. Here Wagner sings his songs of praise for genuine folk art coming from the heart and not following the dictates of laborious reasoning. Of course, this romantic conception of medieval German poetry is not correct in every detail, although it can be upheld in its general outlines. One cannot characterize such a complex modern personality by the single adjective "romantic." Of the staging of his dramas Wagner thought in quite realistic terms, and it was this operatic realism that made them popular with many sentimental contemporaries. Our modern taste can no longer accept Wagner's stage realism; his grandson Wieland in recent Bayreuth stage versions has done his utmost to tone it down. Of more lasting importance are the realistic elements in Wagner's music. Every one of his personalities, and sometimes every side of one personality, is characterized by a special configuration of sounds called *Leitmotif* ("leading motif"), which recurs at every appropriate moment; this is the very opposite of pure, absolute music. And the strictly tonal qualities of Wagner's music have an unmistakably sensuous, at times even voluptuous, flavor. The sounds in his operas can only rarely be called seraphic or angelic.

Wagner's interest in German national art culminated in his efforts to create a special center for it. The cornerstone for the Bayreuth Festival Theater was finally laid in 1872. Here every summer operas were supposed to be performed for the purpose of uniting the leading spirits of the German nation in common worship of artistic revelation. Wagner deeply felt the lack of a central spirit in the German nation of his time, and wanted to close this gap by his "total work of art"; *Der Ring des Nibelungen* was intended to become for the Germans what Aeschylus' and Sophocles' tragedies had been for the Greeks. When in 1876 *Der Ring* was performed for the first time before the emperors and kings assembled in Bayreuth, Wagner could indeed believe he had achieved the supreme national ambition of his art. No doubt this performance was the best artistic expression of the unification of the German people.

But from a more traditional point of view, this substitution of artistic for religious values was also a dangerous sign of the progressive evaporation of spiritual substance. There was something ominous in the wide popular acclaim heaped upon Wagner's operas, and his erstwhile friend Friedrich Nietzsche was quick to realize this. Nietzsche's criticism of Wagner also deserves to be reread in the light of the frivolous Wagner cult of Adolf Hitler. It will hardly be possible any longer to consider Wagner's art as the timeless culmination of German music; even his own period had other masters in Hugo Wolf and Johannes Brahms. But whatever the final verdict of fearless criticism, nobody will deny Richard Wagner's great historical importance nor overlook the intensity of his all-embracing artistic effort.

Narrative and Lyrical Realism

T HE German drama of the nineteenth century could not be described as wholly realistic. It is only when we come to narrative and lyrical literature that we find a more decided turn toward realism. This realism differed from the individualism of Heine and the Young Germans who had started by rejecting romanticism and instead had embraced actuality. For realists such as Stifter and Keller concentrated on the great, lasting forces of life, the forces of nature, of landscape and climate, and on human beings as they always had been and as they had shaped history. The writers of German realism were not rooted in any abstract contemporary philosophy, but were linked with the region in which they grew up and were living; or at least they discovered this connection as they worked. It is therefore easy for a foreign critic to dismiss them as mere regionalists, and one cannot refute his contention that some peculiarities of these realists can be understood only by German readers familiar with their provincial background.

The disintegration of German political and social life during the nineteenth century has produced an astonishing richness of personalities and sceneries, but has also made it difficult for the outsider to appreciate this literature as it deserves. For only the minor writers of passing fame were satisfied with the local and provincial. The important ones had not yet lost the feeling for the lasting values of total German civilization, and did not yet attempt to look at man as a mere biological species. In portraying regional cultures they often portrayed only regional forms of Western Christian culture, and thereby prevented the century from drowning in subjectivity. While none of the important realists measured up to Goethe, many were fine representatives of German culture, and a few could be called almost great.

The heroes of the realistic narratives were everyday people, store clerks and roofers, cobblers and farmhands, ladies' maids and ballerinas, lonely spinsters and widows eking out a living. These people were not exceptionally gifted nor were they good-looking or attractive, but they were respectable and virtuous and had a healthy philosophy. In the end they always achieved a mastery of life that was out of reach for the snobs and arrogant climbers against whom they were matching their wits.

The Style of Personal Experience

Strident individualists with their pretentions and egotistic demands were always the losers, for they were lacking in substance. Of course, this contrasting of the healthy average with empty pretenders might impress one as romantic, and in fact no amount of nineteenth-century realism could deny the romantic heritage altogether. It would even be possible to interpret the literature of the nineteenth century as a contest between the romantic and the realistic.

Realism had already appeared in Immermann's *Oberhof* of 1838–1839, yet it came into its own only after 1848 when the Young German individualism had become questionable and had shown its inability to change the existing order. The search for new foundations for living continued, but its field now became traditional, and evolution instead of revolution seemed the order of the day. It was ably represented by three great conservatives, namely, the Austrian Adalbert Stifter, the Westphalian Annette von Droste-Hülshoff, and the Swabian Eduard Mörike.

Adalbert Stifter (1805–1868) was a devout Bohemian Catholic. He subscribed to the traditional view that literature must serve the ends of religion. Yet that did not lessen its importance; art and poetry Stifter described as "the highest earthly activities next to religion, so that I have never assumed my writings to be pure poetic creations, nor will I ever presume it. There are few poets in the world; they are the high priests and benefactors of the human race; but there are very many false prophets." Such sentences attest to Stifter's humility which is only partly contradicted by his artistic self-consciousness. For Stifter knew that his style was different from the style of the average writer. He was a devoted friend of the apparently insignificant which he believed to be the really important. "The flow of the air, the rippling of the water, the growth of the grain, the undulation of the sea, the verdure of the earth, the radiance of the sky, the effulgence of the stars I believe to be great. The glorious thunderstorm, the stroke of lightning that destroys houses, the storm that chases the breakers, the fiery volcano, the earthquake that buries countries—these I do not believe to be greater than the other phenomena; I even deem them the lesser because they are mere consequences of higher laws. They only occur in specific places and are the results of singular causes." Such was Stifter's interpretation of his characteristic brand of realism. It was upheld by the example of Goethe, for Goethe in his old age had often displayed the same detachment as Stifter; he once wrote a poem on a gnat. Still, Goethe never lost the feeling for the dynamic, the tragic, and soul-stirring passions. Stifter, on the other hand, was anxious to avoid them. One rarely meets with erotic relations in his works. Whenever he speaks of love, he restricts it to elegiac and conventionally permissible feelings.

This avoidance was deeply personal. Stifter in real life was a school supervisor and an example of probity. He suffered early from cirrhosis of the liver and fought a losing battle against the ever-growing despondency caused by his illness; he died in a comatose state wherein he no longer quite knew what he was doing. Stifter's narratives were a continuous self-defense against the dark aspects of life, a search for consolation in the many-sided aspects of nature, perhaps a kind of self-education. They were not a free, autonomous self-expression. In spite of his independent, almost impressionistic observation Stifter could not be classified as a modern individualist.

His story collections bear unassuming titles such as *Studien* ("Studies," 1844–1850) or *Bunte Steine* ("Stones of Many Colors," 1853), but they hide an astonishing richness. This German from Bohemia is a real master of landscape description and, to repeat a remark of Nietzsche's, one of the finest representatives of German style. In the story *Granit* of his *Bunte Steine* he describes a journey by foot through the Bohemian forest that surpasses similar attempts by Jean Paul. In the story *Bergkristall* ("Rock Crystal") he draws a memorable picture of winter in the mountains. In the delightful tale *Der Waldsteig* ("The Forest Path," 1845) he presents a hypochondriac who is cured by the healing powers of nature; the man gets lost one day on a forest trail, and this simple trail teaches him a splendor of life and nature which until that time he had not known. The most comprehensive panorama of nature ever drawn by Stifter can be found in the story *Der Hochwald* ("The Virgin Forest," 1842), which takes place during the Thirty Years' War. Here the forest itself becomes the protagonist, the virgin forest in its undisturbed beauty and majesty that has scarcely been entered by man. Stifter describes the life of this primeval forest over the seasons, and introduces into these surroundings a story of unrequited love between the daughter of a Bohemian nobleman and a Swedish aristocrat. Human destiny here is inextricably interwoven with the divinely guided destiny of the surrounding fauna and flora.

Among the most beautiful chapters of *Der Hochwald* are those on the *Nachsommer*, a kind of Indian Summer between the German hot season and the autumn. Stifter also chose *Der Nachsommer* (1857) as the title of one of his long novels. Here he has achieved a complete serenity of spirit expressing itself in an admirably pure style and an almost unnoticeable epical tempo. Modern readers usually reject this novel as tedious, and miss in it the sensations they are used to deriving from novel reading. To a somewhat more patient critic the slowness of Stifter's style does not stem from a lack of artistic ability, but from an intentional concentration on the drawn-out, imperceptibly slow pace of natural growth. Similar criticisms could be leveled at Stifter's great historical novel *Witiko* (1865–1867). One cannot deny that the view of this writer is one-sided and even severely limited, but within his limitations he must be classified as great.

Another great Catholic among Stifter's contemporaries was the Westphalian poet Annette von Droste-Hülshoff (1797–1848). She was not only devout, but full of humility and resignation; she bowed before the narrow customs of her aristocratic family, and allowed her mother to read every letter she received. Annette literally had to hide her creative self from her relatives. But in one area at least she could assert herself. She had strong feelings demanding uncompromising expression; and she remained true to her personal vision with singular energy. Annette was literal and examined things minutely in order to draw them into her vision, but for that very reason her impressions were intimate, although never trivial. Thus she insisted that swans' voices were a wheezing, and rejected the classical poetic tradition that had always insisted on swans "singing."

Her keen gifts of observation enabled Annette to uncover the subtle lure of the ordinary. She could grow lyrical over a gravel pit, describing it in minute detail. But she never allowed herself to get lost in mere impressions. Her poems were always held together by a singular, cogent mood. She could evoke a warm summer's mood in the poem *Im Grase* ("In the Grass"), and she could describe the rising moon in the dreamlike verses entitled *Mondesaufgang* ("Moon Rise"). She used vowel symbolism expertly, and her words are always chosen with a feeling for the unusual, powerful, and characteristic. Annette's style is an almost masculine style, and the poem *Am Turme* ("On the Tower") actually expresses a fervent wish to be a man.

The poet found it hard to fit her passionate soul into the Procrustean bed of convention, and she had no easy time in making her independent emotions conform to the doctrines of the Catholic Church. She nevertheless tried to do this in her poetic collection *Das geistliche Jahr* ("The Spiritual Year"). Her attempt was only partly successful, and often she felt lost and alone, waiting for God's blessing. Here a great and honest soul wrestled with the deepest problems of existence. The same depth

Narrative and Lyrical Realism

characterizes Annette's tale *Die Judenbuche* ("The Jew's Beech Tree"), which is one of the best German stories. Its central figure is the day laborer Friedrich Mergel who gets more and more deeply involved in guilt, and finally murders a Jewish pawnbroker. Inept political officials cannot lay hands on him, but retribution is not to be avoided. Slowly but inexorably his guilt catches up with the murderer, until he hangs himself from the same beech tree under which he has killed the Jew. "Mine is the revenge, says the Lord" could stand at the end of the story, which calls itself a "picture of morals in the mountainous parts of Westphalia." The landscape here becomes mythically personified and takes part in a story that moves us to our innermost being.

Along with these two Catholic writers must be named a Protestant, the Swabian Eduard Mörike (1804–1875); until 1843 he was a country parson, but only a few of his poems can be characterized as denominational. His deep feeling of quiet resignation is common to many religions:

> *Herr, schicke, was du willt,*
> *Ein Liebes oder Leides!*
> *Ich bin vergnügt, dass beides*
> *Aus deinen Händen quillt.*
>
> *
>
> *Lord, send whatever is your pleasure,*
> *Delight or smart.*
> *I am sure that both in equal measure*
> *From Thy hands start.*

In strange contrast to such lines stand verse expressing a frivolous mood or even a pagan defiance. *Jung Volkers Lied* ("Young Volker's Song") describes the feelings of an unwed mother who has yielded to a handsome stranger in inspired abandon; in the security of her natural instincts she has defied society, and is happy to have given birth to a bouncing baby. Mörike knew the world of the senses well and occasionally even expressed sexual humor. But usually he sublimated the earthy world of the senses into playful dreams. Ballads such as *Der Gärtner* ("The Gardener") or *Schön-Rohtraut* ("Beautiful Rohtraut") belong to the most bewitching German verse, and their secret lies in their rhythm as well as their imagery. At other times Mörike conjures up the elemental forces in striking mythical images:

[259

The Style of Personal Experience

Gelassen stieg die Nacht ans Land,
Lehnt träumend an der Berge Wand;
Ihr Auge sieht die goldne Wage nun
Der Zeit in gleichen Schalen stille ruhn.
Und kecker rauschen die Quellen hervor,
Sie singen der Mutter, der Nacht, ins Ohr
Vom Tage,
Vom heute gewesenen Tage.

*

The night has leisurely climbed ashore
And now in dreams rests against the wall of the mountains;
Its eye sees the golden scales
Of time quietly suspended in perfect balance.
And the springs are bubbling forth more boldly
And are singing into the ear of
Mother Night
Songs of the daytime that has just passed.

This combination of charming sensuousness and dreamy spirituality makes Mörike one of the most important exponents of lyrical realism. His poem *Das Verlassene Mägdlein* ("The Deserted Maiden") is full of heartbreaking emotion, and his *Gesang Weylas* ("Weyla's Song") gives expression to romantic musings. Yet the same poet can write a dewy, fresh spring poem such as *Er ist's!* ("It Has Come!"), and can ridicule modish sentimentality in verses addressed by the lover to the hot springs of B (*Der Liebhaber an die heisse Quelle zu B.*). Spirituality and sensuality contended in Mörike. He tried to find a balance between them in his novel *Maler Nolten* ("Nolten the Painter," 1832), but he was not a very able storyteller. As a prose writer he was best in charming idylls such as *Mozart auf der Reise nach Prag* ("Mozart on the Journey to Prague," 1856), one of the most readable of German historical pieces.

The three poets just discussed all succeeded in some fashion in achieving a balance between their conflicting emotions. The same could not be said of Nikolaus Lenau (actually Nikolaus Niembsch von Strehlenau, 1802–1850). This Hungarian German lived a restless and unsettled life; in no way could he achieve satisfaction. His daemon drove him from his Hungarian homeland to Stuttgart, and from there to the United States. But Lenau was too much wrapped up in himself to approach the New World with an open mind. After a short stay he leased his American possessions and returned to Germany a disappointed *Amerikamüder* ("one tired of America"). Lenau's disturbed mind was incurably at odds with the world. Finally an unhappy love affair with a married woman drove him insane.

Lenau's inner dissatisfaction and self-centeredness characterize him as a late romantic subjectivist in fervent search for the peace of his soul. But he was not completely romantic, and possessed a rare ability to fathom the moods of nature in its most mysterious moments. In his *Schilflieder* ("Songs in the Bullrushes") nature provides a perfect symbolism for the poet's own emotions; external observations and internal feelings have achieved singular harmony. Lenau's power of observation was strong enough to move him to write poems on purely external phenomena, cf. his poems *Niagara* and *Die drei Indianer* ("The Three Indians"). However, pure realism was for Lenau only an occasional achievement. He most strongly expressed the feeling of homelessness. He could feel akin to the gypsies (*Drei Zigeuner*) who taught him three ways of enduring a wretched existence: one could spend one's life in smoking, in sleeping, and in violin playing, and equally despise it in all three:

> *Wie man das Leben verraucht, verschläft, vergeigt*
> *Und es dreimal verachtet.*

Or the poet could be moved by the melancholy horn of the postillion who regularly greeted a dead fellow postillion by playing his favorite song (*Der Postillion*).

Lenau also tried to express his view of the world in connected epical form, but he got lost in individual impressions and only achieved extended monologues somehow reminding one of the manner of Byron's *Don Juan*.

A Sudeten German contemporary of Lenau proved that a positive approach to experiences in America was entirely possible for a German writer of the thirties. He was the renegade priest Karl Anton Postl who had fled to America and assumed the new name of Charles Sealsfield. His numerous stories give an astonishingly faithful picture of America in the thirties and forties of the nineteenth century, and today still make interesting reading; the collection *Das Kajütenbuch* ("The Cabin Book," 1841) has achieved deserved popularity. The exhilarating experiences of frontier life and of homespun democracy prevented Postl from withdrawing into the quietism that often caused people to shrink from political and social reality, an attitude which became known by the nickname *Biedermeier*, or pseudo-classical.

His was not the only active approach to the problems of bourgeois society. Democratic and social consciousness was a part of the tradition of Switzerland, and could be applied readily to contemporary problems. The Swiss Protestant parson Jeremias Gotthelf (pseudonym for Albert Bitzius, 1797–1854) occupies the same place in German literature as Dickens and Trollope in English and Balzac in French literature. Like his more famous contemporaries, Gotthelf attempted to portray real human beings with all their shortcomings and deficiencies. As Dickens and Trollope took their figures from definite walks of life, so Gotthelf limited himself to the region he knew best, the Swiss Bernbiet ("Berne region") with its farming population. As Dickens had a weakness for moralizing, so Gotthelf made his writings a powerful vehicle for social criticism. But because he always remained somewhat of a preacher or a prude, he could never have written *Contes drôlatiques* ("Droll Stories") in the manner of Balzac.

Some of Gotthelf's stories, such as *Uli der Pächter* ("Ulrich the Tenant") might be called plainly didactic. But even in his better works Gotthelf seldom refrained from sermonizing. He wanted to revive the good old farmers' customs, and poured venom on those of his countrymen who aped foreign fashions or gave up their ancient religion. Neither did he spare the intellectuals, be they teachers or physicians or even parsons, and his criticism was blunt. Gotthelf always bore in mind that his village readers would never accept evasive words.

Still, he was an artist. He tried at least once to portray a materialist impartially, and his best novels possessed a high degree of organic unity. After all, the parson and the church were important features in Bernese village life, and Gotthelf, as a faithful chronicler of reality, could not simply ignore them; perhaps modern agnostics are unduly disturbed by his sermons. But one must not overlook the fact that Gotthelf is a storyteller of the first rank, and never skimps his descriptions of rural life. One of his most impressive stories is *Die schwarze Spinne* ("The Black Spider"), which opens with a colorful picture of a banquet whose expansiveness reminds one of a Homeric idyll. But this humorous description of the present is soon interrupted by an eruption from the solemn past as an old farmer tells the story of his family, which has achieved prosperity by fighting the Black Spider. This spider was the progeny of a woman who had called on the

Devil for help, and had defaulted on her promise to repay him by send-ing him a soul. The vengeful spider had thereupon killed everything in his way until a pious farmer caught it and imprisoned it in a hole in a beam. But if any generation should become too arrogant, the spider will find its way to freedom. Thus in mythical manner and without direct sermonizing Gotthelf points to piety as the basis of the village's present prosperity. And he gains depth and perspective for his picture of well-to-do farmers by bringing in past crises and temptations. The story is short, but substantial and meaningful. A whole people is pre-sented in its dependence on the heavenly powers. There are few equals to this German story.

Das Erdbeeri-Mareili ("Strawberry Mary") and *Elsie, die seltsame Magd* ("Elsie, the Strange Farm Servant") are the titles of two other masterpieces from Gotthelf's pen. Of his longer stories one could mention the *Bauernspiegel* ("Farm Life"), which employs the auto-biographical form, and the novel *Anne Bäbie Jowager*, which Gotthelf wrote in his old age. His most popular work has always been *Uli der Knecht* ("Ulrich the Farmhand," 1841). Uli is a poor farmhand who, by diligence and study, becomes the tenant manager of a rich farm. His patron and teacher is Meister Johannes, one of those naturally intelli-gent people who are the salt of the earth. Contrasted to him is the weak and indecisive Joggeli, whose farm is later taken over by Uli. The story also has an interesting array of female characters from the sensible Vreneli and her kind but resigned cousin, down to the not-too-intelli-gent Elisi and the slovenly Ursi. There are serious digressions in the form of exhortations by Uli's master and, later on, by the parson, and there are scenes of earthy humor such as the battle of the servant girls for the possession of Uli, a passage that reminds one of a similar scene of Fielding. Gotthelf's ambitions as a reformer and an artist were high, but his reach exceeded his grasp. His compatriot Gottfried Keller had similar aims and was fully successful, though in a somewhat lower key.

Much narrower ambitions characterized the South German Berthold Auerbach, whose village stories were popular with his contemporaries. But the farmers whom he depicted in *Diethelm von Buchenberg* and other tales were too refined; Auerbach took pains to avoid coarseness and rough language. His half-hearted realism was soon forgotten, while the genuineness of Otto Ludwig's (1813–1865) village stories gradually won the public. In his *Heitherethei* Ludwig described a village beauty who preserved her good reputation in spite of gossiping neighbors, and finally gained security. In the story *Vom Regen in die Traufe* ("Out of the Frying Pan into the Fire") Ludwig had as his hero an undersized master tailor who was ridiculed by all until he wedded a good wife. Ludwig's most ambitious work was the novel, *Zwischen Himmel und Erde* (" 'Twixt Heaven and Earth," 1855), which gave an unexcelled picture of the life of a German craftsman in the nineteenth century; it was his most integrated work. Ludwig derived the psychology of his heroes from their surroundings as well as their inheritance, and could convincingly develop it in his quietly moving stories. In his dramas he became either tendentious or oversubtle, and all his admiration of Shakespeare was of no avail. Ludwig's best dramatic effort was *Der Erbförster* ("The Hereditary Forester"). Finally the gifted poet lost his self-assurance through psychological and technical case studies, which later appeared in a collection called *Shakespeare-Studien*.

While Ludwig came from central Germany, Fritz Reuter was a North German. Unfortunately he wrote his farm novels in Low German dialect, and thus prevented them from becoming known beyond Germany. For although Low German had always possessed a literature of its own, it had an exclusively local appeal. Then in 1803 Johann Peter Hebel published his *Alemannische Gedichte* ("Alemannic Poems") and thereby set the example for further poems in other German dialects. In 1852 Klaus Groth published his Low German *Quickborn* ("Fountain of Life"); the best of his poems exude a warmth comparable to the poems of Claudius, and are sometimes better integrated. Fritz Reuter (1810–1874) also wrote lyrics; but he excelled as a storyteller. He began with *Läuschen un Riemels* ("Tales and Rhymes," 1853), a collection of pleasantly rhymed but innocuous stories. He improved in the affectionate rhymes of *Hanne Nüte un de lütte Pudel* ("Johnny and His Little Poodle," 1859), which he termed a "Tale of Men and Birds." But his great prose novels were his outstanding achievement. *Ut mine Festungstid* ("My Prison Years," 1863) was based upon the author's experiences as a political prisoner held for allegedly treasonable activities. A typical Young German would have made this experience the theme of a tendentious novel. But Reuter was not typical. He could not avoid occasional bitterness, but in the end he achieved a balanced view colored by genuine humor. He had every right to hurl accusations against a judicial system that was able to pronounce a suspended death sentence against a harmless student (his crime consisted in wearing the prohibited German colors). Yet Reuter voiced his accusations implicitly and nowhere violated artistic form. His main aim was to describe human beings. In doing this he came close to his model Dickens.

Reuter's masterpiece was his second novel *Ut mine Stromtid* ("My Apprenticeship," 1862–1864). In this he has created an unforgettable picture of life on a big Mecklenburg farm. All his numerous characters are true to life; the homespun tenant farmer Habermann, the windy supervisor Fritz Triddelfitz, the earthy inspector Bräsig and his three *Brautens* ("ladyloves"), all go through their own experiences, some happy and some sad. The many threads are held together by the warmth of Reuter's humor, a humor based on a deep awareness of man's imperfections. Reuter was more than a jokesmith who could irresponsibly gloss over problems of life and society. To be sure, he could laugh at human follies and foibles. But he was also able to castigate the insidiousness of country serfdom in his story *Kein Hüsung* ("Homeless," 1858).

Reuter's criticism of his era's materialism and his opposition to an inhuman government gave expression to the innate piety and love of freedom characteristic of provincial tradition. Unfortunately his Low German stories defy translation even into High German. His dialect permitted him a liberty of expression and a directness of comparison that was no longer possible in the more stylized High German. A High German translation would have to employ a great number of conventional expressions and would thereby achieve a triteness never intended by Reuter. A translation into American farmer's slang might be surer of success.

The still greater realism of Gottfried Keller (1819–1890) derived its strength from another German provincial tradition that had not been broken by modern developments. From the secure foothold of the ancient Swiss democracy, he could view the political and social struggles of the other German states with equanimity, and could show his contemporaries the example of a bourgeois culture at once fearless in its conservatism and liberal in its application to the contemporary scene. Keller was typically Swiss in his sober attention to the details of everyday life. He was most influenced by the Hegelian philosopher Feuerbach, the celebrated author of *Das Wesen des Christentums* ("The Nature of Christianity," 1841), who had declared that all religions conceived of God in man's own image, and later pronounced an unequivocal materialism: "Man is what he eats" (the German original is an untranslatable pun: *Der Mensch ist, was er isst*). Keller differed

[265

The Style of Personal Experience

from his artistic predecessor Gotthelf in being a realist without compromise or reservation. But within his self-imposed limits he achieved a Goethean depth and a Goethean intensity. He could never have created a mythical symbol in the manner of Gotthelf's *Schwarze Spinne*, yet on a lower plane he did create a picture of life rounded out with loving care and unrestricted in its perspectives. It was a live picture and was meant to reflect on the life of the Swiss nation. Keller rarely sermonized as obviously as Gotthelf, but he was equally aware of the need of the Swiss to be educated in the judicious exercise of their liberties. Art for him never existed for its own sake; it was a part, though a necessary one, of the great complexity of life, which it portrayed and which it served. Just as Goethe had combined his great poetic calling with political offices, Keller found satisfaction in serving as a Zürich state secretary from 1861–1876; it was the highest office that his home canton could bestow.

For the expression of his fervent Swiss patriotism Keller always used artistic means, and he used them in a disarmingly natural and expertly simple way. It is hard to believe that the author needed any long or painful education to arrive at stylistic mastery. Keller could not easily choose between poetry and painting; he was thirty-five years old before he could decide that his tool was the pen rather than the brush.

The novel *Der grüne Heinrich* ("Green Henry") was the impressive outcome of Keller's personal conflict. It was first published in 1854–1855, but later went through a complete recasting and was printed in final form in 1879–1880. Essentially an autobiographical work, it ended with the same turn toward practical life that Keller himself took as a Zürich state secretary. His experiences in that office Keller described at the end of his life in his second novel *Martin Salander* (1886), which might be called a continuation of *Der grüne Heinrich*; it was the work of a wise old man for whom the conclusions to be drawn from experience were more interesting than experience as such.

But perhaps Keller's stories will outlast his *Der grüne Heinrich* in fame. They are collected under the titles *Die Leute von Seldwyla* ("Seldwyla Folk," I, 1856; II, 1874), *Züricher Novellen* ("Zürich Tales," 1878), and *Das Sinngedicht* ("The Epigram," 1882) and the connection between them is by no means tenuous. Keller pays more than passing attention to the frame in which he presents his stories, and he keeps in mind a genuine narrative situation.

Die Leute von Seldwyla surveys the foolish strivings of ambitious social climbers and pretenders from a serious, almost moralizing standpoint which is only toned down by sympathetic humor. Keller really enjoys depicting these queer people without ever indulging in cheap caricature. There is the little tailor of *Kleider machen Leute* ("Clothes Make the Man") who knows how to profit handsomely from a case of mistaken identity, yet is so droll in his awkwardness that even the author can pardon him in the end. There are the pretentious scribblers of *Die missbrauchten Liebesbriefe* ("The Abused Love Letters") who exchange love letters for the sake of literary ambition, while conveniently forgetting the sacredness of each other's personal feelings. There are also more serious sinners, who show Keller as a searching social critic. His masterpiece is the story *Romeo und Julia auf dem Dorfe* ("A Village Romeo and Juliet," 1876), which tells of the tragic fate of two youthful lovers who are prevented from making an honest marriage by the sins of their fathers.

The best story of *Züricher Novellen* bears the title *Das Fähnlein der sieben Aufrechten* ("The Banner of the Upright Seven"), a story full of sincere though by no means blind and uncritical Swiss patriotism, and a masterpiece of quiet, constructive humor. Keller's patriotism was not without historic roots, though he observed the past just as critically and unsentimentally as the present. Keller's best historical piece is *Hadlaub* (in *Züricher Novellen*), which describes the origin of the Manesse manuscript of Middle High German minnesingers. More romantic are the whimsical tales in *Sieben Legenden* ("The Seven Legends," 1872) which treat medieval material from a modern point of view. All in all, Keller must be called the most consistent representative of bourgeois realism. He attests to this most clearly in some of his lyrics. He greeted the coming of railroads with hearty enthusiasm, he delighted in dreams of sailing through the air in a dirigible, and he admonished himself to enjoy existence to the utmost:

> *Trinkt ihr Augen, was die Wimper hält,*
> *Von dem goldnen Überfluss der Welt.*
>
> *
>
> *Drink, my eyes, as much as lashes hold*
> *Of the golden abundance of the world.*

As Keller approached the problems of his period from a firmly rooted Swiss tradition, so Ferdinand von Saar and Marie von Ebner-Eschenbach upheld the equally venerable Austrian tradition. Both wrote their best stories as mature writers, and both achieved a rare balance of style.

[267

The Style of Personal Experience

Ferdinand von Saar was a Viennese, Marie von Ebner-Eschenbach came from Moravia and was born Countess Dubsky. In the course of a long life (1830–1916) she developed slowly under the initial inspiration of Grillparzer and Keller, though she was also well acquainted with non-German writers such as Mérimée, George Sand, George Eliot, and Turgenev. The village and castle stories (*Dorf- und Schlossgeschichten*, 1884) of this Moravian noblewoman offer a faithful portrait of rural conditions in the first half of the nineteenth century. She is equally at home in the castles of the nobility, the homes of the priests, the taverns of the peasants, and the huts of the day laborers. Yet she is far from indulging in nostalgic reminiscence and is moved rather by a warm, womanly sympathy for the poor, the misunderstood, and the persecuted. She wrote some of the best animal stories of German literature (*Krambambuli*, 1884) and she portrayed amiable vagabonds with a rare understanding for their weaknesses (*Unverbesserlich*, "A Hopeless Case," 1910). Her Catholicism was open to the true Humanistic tradition, and embraced a social consciousness that was only later emphasized by the official spokesmen of the Church.

Thus the realistic trends of the nineteenth century were expressed by German writers of considerable stature. Yet they were not the century's only trends, and the attempt to answer its problems on a historical basis continued unabated. Contemporary with Gottfried Keller was his great antipode Conrad Ferdinand Meyer (1825–1898), another Swiss fiction writer from Zürich. He did not relish the realistic emphasis on workaday life, and instead upheld a style of strict, formal lucidity in the German classical tradition. But he had little in common with the sentimental writers of pseudo-historical novels that were the vogue of his day. Even such a charming tale as Joseph Viktor von Scheffel's *Ekkehard* (1862) must be called second-rate fiction, and the same poet's hugely successful *Trompeter von Säckingen* ("The Trumpeter of Saeckingen," 1854) now merely serves as a model of nineteenth-century tearfulness. Meyer's historical world was infinitely harder, even brutal, and he conceived of the great figures of the past as elements of the living present.

Meyer's novels and stories: *Jürg Jenatsch*, 1874; *Der Heilige* ("The Saint," a treatment of the murder of Thomas à Becket, 1880); *Die Richterin* ("The Woman Judge," 1885) appear to embody an exemplary masculinity. But the author himself was almost the opposite, for he was highly sensitive and vulnerable. He suffered from manic depressions, and had to exert himself to the utmost to restore his mental

268]

balance. His overt masculinity was an overcompensation for an impressionability which is betrayed in the rich color and sensuous charm of his sometimes overly rigid narratives. The difficulty with which he achieved his crystalline style becomes clear to anyone with knowledge of the various versions of his poems which appeared in 1882 in their definitive form. But the Swiss poet had then really succeeded in integrating complex events and moods in a few telling verbal gestures and substantial symbols. Ballads such as *Michelangelo, Die Karyatide, Die Füsse im Feuer* ("Feet in the Fire") rank with the best balladry produced by Schiller or Goethe. Meyer is equally convincing in terse lyrical poems such as *Nachtgeräusche* ("Night Noises"), *Säerspruch* ("Sower's Motto"), *Lied der Toten* ("Chorus of the Dead") and in epigrammatical pieces such as *Der römische Brunnen* ("The Roman Fountain"). His rhymed narrative *Huttens letzte Tage* ("The Last Days of Hutten," 1871) became popular by reason of a few clearly formulated propositions; it shows the influence of the Franco-German War.

Meyer succeeded at least partly in his artistic endeavor to combine realistic and romantic elements. He was not the only poet pursuing this aim but the others were his inferiors in style. One could point to the Munich circle of poets led by Emanuel Geibel, who tried to express sensuous passion in lines of charming beauty. This whole group of poets impresses one as somewhat effeminate. Geibel's friend Paul Heyse, who once was honored by the Nobel Prize for literature, now appears as a clever romantic virtuoso rather than as a forceful artist of classical substance. The whole world of political and commercial life was closed to him.

This cannot be said of the North Germans Gustav Freytag and Friedrich Spielhagen. Gustav Freytag (1816–1895) was actively interested in national and liberal policies, and wrote his *Bilder aus deutscher Vergangenheit* ("Pictures from the German Past," 1859–1867) for the express enlightenment of the German public. His most popular novel *Soll und Haben* ("Debit and Credit," 1855) dealt with the life of a German merchant in the first half of the nineteenth century. But Freytag's optimistic belief in progress has proved too shallow for the continuing satisfaction of modern readers.

The same could be said of the numerous novels of Friedrich Spielhagen (1829–1911), which in their day enlightened a middle-class public on contemporary political and social problems. The same public also delighted in the comic verse stories of Wilhelm Busch (1832–

The Style of Personal Experience

1908), though it failed to understand fully the acidity of his satire. Busch's *Max und Moritz* (1865) told of bad boys in witty, ear-catching jingles and in superb drawings; it became the prototype of American comic strips of which the perennial Katzenjammer Kids most closely approach it. Although there was a streak of Schopenhauerian pessimism and even nihilism in the foolish tale, this was conveniently overlooked by an admiring public. Neither was its sleep disturbed by the cultural criticism of *Die fromme Helene* ("Pious Helen," 1872), or of *Herr und Frau Knopp* ("Mr. and Mrs. Knopp," 1877), two other illustrated verse stories by Busch, and it awakened only slowly to the merits of his witty epigrammatical poems (*Kritik des Herzens,* "Critique of the Heart," 1874, and others).

The same public did not do full justice to the only North German novelist (except for Reuter) of a stature comparable to that of Dickens and Balzac, namely Wilhelm Raabe of Brunswick (1831–1910). His first novel *Die Chronik der Sperlingsgasse* ("The Chronicle of Sparrow Lane," 1857) achieved quick fame, but his more profound and better-written mature stories at first convinced only a few readers. And yet Raabe was the most wide-awake author of the second half of the nineteenth century. He apprehended the slow destruction of all traditional values with great alarm, and almost equalled Schopenhauer in his pessimism; it would appear that he despaired of finding any meaning in life and history. Yet Raabe sided bravely with the defenders of lost causes, and never gave up the fight against heartless opportunism and hypocritical crookedness. He knew there was merit in faithful devotion to timeless ideals, and he knew that this devotion was occasionally successful. He could see it at work in the liberal and social movements of his time and therefore took part in them. He was German to the core, and sincerely acclaimed the movement toward national unification. But he was deeply critical of Prussian power politics and of the ruthless efficiency of industrial and financial speculators. The passing of so many old customs and old neighborhoods filled him with dismay, and the deterioration of Humanism with horror. His feelings toward Jewish fellow citizens were not different from those he had toward Christians.

In the end the many complexities in Raabe's feelings were dissolved by his humor. It could be sentimental but it was mostly quizzical, and occasionally acid and sharp. Raabe found his stylistic ideals in Thackeray, Sterne, Dickens, and also in Jean Paul. He employed the methods of romantic irony in order to destroy romantic illusions; he could deliberately mislead his public, could interrupt his tale by didactic digressions and by seemingly pointless interpolations. Yet ultimately he always revealed his warm love for youthful or gray-haired fighters for untimely causes, for cranks and crackpots who had fled the market place, for misunderstood heroes living in uncongenial times.

Not all of Raabe's many works were of the same caliber. Perhaps a reading of his so-called trilogy may serve as an introduction to his writings. It consists of the three novels *Der Hungerpastor* ("The Hungry Parson," 1864), *Abu Telfan* (1867) and *Der Schüdderump* ("The Plague Cart," 1870), and becomes more deeply symbolic with each successive instalment. *Der Hungerpastor* describes the rise of a poor cobbler's son into the ranks of the clergy; he achieves serenity at the price of a precarious existence. *Abu Telfan* centers around the return of a liberal Forty-eighter into a homeland that has little understanding and almost no place for him. And *Der Schüdderump* shows the destructive effect of the new industrial era on a girl raised by old standards of morality.

Raabe's attitude toward his own time was conservative, but not in a negative way. *Schüdderump* was the dialect term for the horrible plague cart which transported the disfigured victims of medieval epidemics to mass graves without respect for social or economic position; Raabe used this vehicle as his symbol for history. The hero in *Schüdderump* was the old chevalier von Glaubigern who pressed the deadly sick Antonie Häusler to his fatherly heart. Thus Raabe shed Schopenhauer's pessimism in favor of an active Christian Humanism which in his later works showed up as a reverence for life deepened by an awareness of cruel realities. Perhaps the most mature and artistically unique of these later works is *Stopfkuchen* ("Cake-Eater"), which a present-day German Catholic philosopher (Romano Guardini) has honored by a detailed interpretation. In its slow inexorable progress toward a final affirmation of eternal moral values, it is a gem of German literature.

In a minor key an attitude similar to Raabe's was expressed by the Holstein storyteller Theodor Storm (1817–1888). He was more lyrical and also somewhat less critical than Raabe. Rather than go along with the contemporary money-chasing rabble, he withdrew into his parental city of Husum. Yet he also loved life and did not yield to occasional dark moods. An affirmative undercurrent runs through all the romantic poetry of Storm, and makes it most appealing. Some of it ranks with the best of Mörike's poetry, such as *Das macht es hat die Nachtigall* . . . ("The Nightingale has sung throughout the night"),

Schliesse mir die Augen beide . . . ("Cover both my eyes . . ."), or the joyful *Oktoberlied*.

Storm's early prose tales make a somewhat romantic and lyrical impression. *Immensee* ("Bees' Lake," 1849), which used to be a favorite of American classes in German, describes in retrospect an old man's once-promising youth. But in later stories Storm describes the individual tragedies of his heroes without concession to sentimental bourgeois taste. *Aquis submersus* ("Drowned," 1875–1876) is a powerful tale of a love that has become guilty. The historical setting does not affect the basic issue, which is also treated in a contemporary setting in the masterful *Carsten Curator* (1877). No less excellent is the later story *Der Schimmelreiter* ("The Rider on the White Horse," 1888), which uses old superstitions as symbols. In a lighter vein, *Pole Poppenspäler* ("Paul the Puppeteer," 1875) and the charming fairy tale *Der kleine Häwelmann* ("Little Haewelmann") tell of children and young people. Storm was opposed to conventional Christianity and believed in the elemental forces of nature. He sought in the individual's energetic devotion to selfless standards of probity and purity the ideal solution to the problems of life. In his nature descriptions he was so true to reality that later writers have found it difficult to surpass them.

Naturalism and Impressionism

THE founding of the new German Empire in 1871 liberated German energy, which could now turn more exclusively to technical, industrial, and economic fields. Inventors became important, engineers built factories and cities, bankers and export merchants made or lost fortunes. Medicine changed completely after Robert Koch's discovery of bacteria and Konrad Röntgen's discovery of X-rays, and human life became longer and safer. An era of unheard-of prosperity began, and the big cities expanded by leaps and bounds. It bedazzled the bourgeoisie into the founding of German colonies and into dreams of *Weltpolitik*. When their exponent, the youthful and willful Emperor Wilhelm II, took over the reins of government, he soon dismissed the old chancellor Otto von Bismarck, who was questioning these dreams from the wisdom of his experience.

Naturalism and Impressionism

Bismarck's fears derived not only from geographical but also from social realities. German prosperity was breeding a new social class, the growing class of industrial laborers without property and without savings. They lived in slums and shared little in the fruits of their labors. They did not participate in the national dreams, and instead expected a world revolution to change their lot; the *Kommunistisches Manifest* ("Communist Manifesto," 1848) of the Rhenish journalist Karl Marx provided them with a vision of their own. Bismarck was realistic enough to recognize the seriousness of this threat to established values; he tried to suppress it by a series of laws providing for retirement pensions, and sickness compensation (from 1883). But the proletarians were not placated and still remained outside the accepted social order. They were keenly aware of the breakdown of bourgeois culture, which its heirs were still upholding, while they became more and more materialistic.

German writers after 1880 were also aware of the changing social atmosphere. They began to pay heed to the problems of the workers, they became sensitive to the degeneration of the middle classes and the doubtfulness of traditional values. And they were groping for a new style. Popular writers continued the eclectic manner of previous decades; their numbers increased in direct proportion to the general rise in population and the development of cheap publishing processes. The *avant-garde* was acquainted with the achievements of Ibsen, Björnson, and Dostoevski, and under their influence noisily inaugurated the style of naturalism, which demanded that reality be rendered without embellishments and that poetic emotions be sacrificed to scientific objectivity. The best writers turned to impressionism, a style created by French painters of the eighteen sixties and seventies. Under the influence of a new sensualism this style cultivated atmospheric elements, and under the influence of Far Eastern art it cultivated the pure line. Literary impressionism also emphasized atmosphere and irregularity of rhythmical lines. This gave new possibilities to the poetic individual and led to interesting personal styles. It represented an important modification of the traditional style, but not yet an entirely new approach.

Early German impressionism was best represented by two North German writers, Detlev von Liliencron and Theodor Fontane. Both were conservatives at heart, but at the same time realized that times were changing. Detlev von Liliencron (1844–1909) was a baron without patrimony who had drifted into the profession of free-lance writing. His first book of poetry was called *Adjutantenritte* ("Reconnaissance

Rides," 1883), and he also elicited attention by his pessimistic *Novellen*. His experience of life had left him with a low opinion of mankind, and rather than dwell on present misfortunes he preferred to indulge in happy memories of his years as a soldier, a huntsman, a dashing cavalier. He revived them in his poems with great splashes of color and bursts of sound; the brilliant onomatopoeia of *Die Musik kommt* ("Music Sounding") was new in German literature. In his subject matter Liliencron was conventional, though he could express in a fresh, dynamic way the loneliness of life in a metropolis (*In einer grossen Stadt*), the disrespectfulness of the rising working class (*Die neue Eisenbahn*, "The New Railroad"), or the speed of an express train hell-bent for destruction (*Der Blitzzug*, "Lightning Express").

Theodor Fontane (1819–1898), the other major North German impressionist, was older than Liliencron and actually belonged to the generation of Hebbel and Wagner. As a reporter, he became acquainted with the realities of modern life. Mature ballads of his described a railroad catastrophe (*Die Brück' am Tay*, "The Bridge o'er the Tay") or a steamboat conflagration on Lake Erie (*John Maynard*). As a reporter Fontane also developed an eye for striking details and a flair for panoramic effects that stood him in good stead when at sixty he began to write Berlin society novels. He introduced his people in spirited conversations at picnics and banquets, and developed a broad and yet intimate perspective of background conditions; he was less interested in plots, and often would make a point by silence. Novels such as *Irrungen, Wirrungen* ("Trials and Tribulations"), *L'Adultera* ("The Adultress"), and *Frau Jenny Treibel* provide a wonderfully balanced portrait of Fontane's time. They maintain a conservative mood that resigns itself to the inevitable destruction of the old culture, but still has its reservations against the dawning new day of industrialization and socialization. *Effi Briest* is Fontane's intimate portrait of a victim of the old standards. His last novel *Der Stechlin* is a personal picture of the world he knew.

Fontane was independent enough to realize greatness in the first dramatic attempts of the leading poet of the younger generation, the Silesian Gerhart Hauptmann (1862–1946). Hauptmann first attracted the attention of his contemporaries when his unconventional play *Vor Sonnenaufgang* ("Before Dawn") was privately performed in 1889. The play exposed the ugly conditions in the poor Silesian mining districts, and advocated social reforms. In following plays the young author explored the role of heredity in the genesis of modern tension, and the drive of the independent individual for a full life of his own. He made a more lasting contribution with his great play *Die Weber* ("The Weavers," 1892), which treated the historical revolt of the Silesian weavers in 1842. Hauptmann portrayed intolerable working conditions and the callous ignorance of employers, but also the helplessness and lack of leadership among the workers; the revolt ended in failure. Hauptmann's scenes were vivid and dramatic in their earthy dialectal language, their emotional tension, their portrayal of inarticulate characters. In comedies like *Der Biberpelz* ("The Beaver Coat," 1894) Hauptmann proved himself an equally outstanding social satirist. Ironically he let the thieves triumph over the petty and prejudiced officials of the Wilhelmian era, and chose as his heroine a shrewd washerwoman by the name of Mother Wolff.

Hauptmann soon broke away from the narrowness of the naturalistic formula. He tried to adapt naturalist technique to historical subjects, and he included dream figures among his characters. These experiments resulted in the charm of *Hanneles Himmelfahrt* ("Hannele," 1892), in which the poor daughter of a brutal mason, dying of cold, dreams in her last feverish moments of fairy-tale figures, of angels, and of the Lord Jesus. With the introduction of such figures Hauptmann embarked on a singularly individual career. Yet his new style was not intended to replace the naturalistic approach completely. On the contrary, after this "breakthrough," Hauptmann wrote in *Fuhrmann Henschel* ("Drayman Henschel," 1899) and in *Rose Bernd* (1903) two of his most impressive naturalistic plays. *Fuhrmann Henschel* portrays in powerful dialectal prose the helplessness of a robust wagoner who cannot resist the wiles of a scheming she-devil and is too weak to face the issue; he solves it by evasion and commits suicide. *Rose Bernd*, another Silesian tragedy, draws the compassionate portrait of an unwed mother who against her will becomes a prey to her strong sexual impulses and to the unscrupulous men attracted by them. Both plays attack social problems in terms of general human significance, and no longer try to convey a direct social or political message. Hauptmann's tragi-comedy *Die Ratten* ("The Rats") of 1911 must also be mentioned as one of the finest examples of naturalistic style in its portrayal of man's personal and social obtuseness.

In the verse plays of this period man appears as a helpless pawn of fate, predestined for tragedy, for whom the poet can only express pity and sympathy. This existed in Hauptmann from the beginning, but in the nineties was intensified by a harrowing divorce. His fairy-tale play

The Style of Personal Experience

Die versunkene Glocke ("The Sunken Bell," 1896) was partly based on Hauptmann's personal life and was not quite clear in its symbolism, although it achieved fairy-tale scenes of great beauty. Another blank-verse play, *Der arme Heinrich* ("Henry of Aue," 1902), was based on Hartmann von Aue's twelfth-century legend; it was indeed a wonderful poetic creation, but was unconvincing as a stage play. Hauptmann often was uncertain in his style and, outside of the dramas mentioned, experimented with many different stylistic devices. On the whole, at the beginning of the twentieth century he had not succeeded in breaking away from bourgeois individualism. The social attitude displayed in his dramas still was the attitude of personal pity that could be found in earlier literature. Moreover, Hauptmann's style was not completely new but must rather be described as a modification of nineteenth-century style. His break with traditional moral and stylistic values occurred much later.

The success of Hermann Sudermann's (1857–1928) dramas and novels was far more definite with his contemporaries. But they substituted sensationalism for unbiased observation, and sentimentality for an honest approach to modern problems. The novels of Clara Viebig (1860–1952, married to the publisher Fritz Cohen) were far more accurate in their rendering of social conditions, franker in their acknowledgment of the needs of the human animal, and more artistic in the treatment of mass emotions, a technique which she learned from Emile Zola. But she too offered little beyond a conventional compassion for the victims of modern civilization.

A more outspoken impressionism was cultivated in Vienna. As the capital of sovereign Austria-Hungary it could afford an independent development. Here lived Peter Altenberg, the coffeehouse writer with the sympathetic attention for minute details of fleeting existence, who collected his sketches in books such as *Wie ich es sehe* ("The Way I See It," 1896); he was not interested in great questions of general import. In Vienna too lived the physician Dr. Arthur Schnitzler (1862–1931), who became one of the fashionable playwrights and storytellers of the period. His impressionism was based on the feeling of futility that seized much of the Old Austria in the days before the First World War. Schnitzler portrayed his characters with keen psychological empathy, for he was a romanticist at heart who was still searching for the ideal. But he never found it, and portrayed characters too tired to exert themselves or to make any positive contribution to life. They were playing a meaningless game and calling it existence; even love was but a momentary ecstasy that made no lasting change in the lonely individual. Like his great colleague and compatriot Sigmund Freud (1856–1939), the founder of psychoanalysis, Schnitzler was a saddened and discerning diagnostician of cultural decay; he recorded it in many brilliant one-act plays and intimate narrative studies, but he did not really enjoy recording it.

Of the host of other impressionist storytellers few have justified the reputation they at one time enjoyed. A sincere approach to philosophical materialism was represented by Carl Hauptmann, the older brother of Gerhart Hauptmann, who is still remembered for his Silesian novel *Einhart der Lächler* ("Smiling Einhart," 1907). But already his fame has been eclipsed by that of Ricarda Huch, the leading woman novelist of the time. She was born at Brunswick, but settled in South Germany where she remained even when the policies of the Third Reich went against her convictions. She was not only gifted, but also exceptionally educated. The novel *Erinnerungen von Ludolf Ursleu dem Jüngeren* ("Recollections of Ludolf Ursleu the Younger," 1893) made her known as a master of autumnal moods of cultural decay. There was a romantic element in this, and Ricarda Huch wrote a significant interpretation of German romanticism (*Die Romantik*, 1899–1902). But she overcame her early pessimism, and in the stories in *Aus der Triumphgasse* ("Triumph Alley," 1902) she described the social problems of Italians of the lower classes with feminine insight and sympathy. She also studied the narrative artistry of Gottfried Keller, and let herself be inspired by his humorous stories. He also confirmed her democratic convictions, which led her to study Italian and German popular movements. She ultimately wrote a popular German history from an excellently democratic point of view. Keeping the Christian tradition alive, she also wrote unorthodox essays on the meaning of the Bible and on Martin Luther's creed. Both her religious and her historical interests combined in Ricarda Huch's epic tale of the Thirty Years' War (*Der grosse Krieg in Deutschland*, 1912–1914), which presaged the European conflagration of 1914.

Of the lyric poets of German impressionism, Richard Dehmel and Max Dauthendey deserve brief mention. Both were endowed with a fine sensitivity and a natural feeling for rhythm, but both in typical German fashion let philosophic speculation intrude upon their poetic production. Far too much of Richard Dehmel's (1863–1920) lyric poetry must be described as tour de force, and he can be enjoyed only in his purely impressionistic pieces. In *Manche Nacht* ("Many a Night") he describes the twilight zone between daylight and darkness with vivid nuances of color. In *Die stille Stadt* ("The Silent Town") he works magic with atmospheric values; a light fog and its concomitant psychological mood in the wandering poet determine the unity of the poem. Dehmel's poetry at its best can be compared with the pictorial impressionism of German painters such as Max Liebermann or Count Leopold von Kalckreuth. Of his more philosophical poems only *Der Arbeitsmann* ("The Workingman") is still remembered for the fervent sincerity of its social message.

Max Dauthendey (1867–1918) was the son of a Würzburg photographer and outdid Richard Dehmel in his feeling for color. Dauthendey's lyric collection *Ultra-Violett* (1893) manifested his early preoccupation with unusual color sensations. He later sought satisfaction in the Far East, of which he wrote highly flavored exotic stories. The blinding brightness of the tropical sun and the mysteries of the primeval forest attracted him to the same degree as Somerset Maugham, and like him, Dauthendey gave a voice to the brown and yellow natives of Malaya and Japan, to whom he felt deeply akin. Dauthendey died during the First World War in Javanese exile.

CHAPTER NINE

The Dissociative and Surrealistic Style of the Twentieth Century

The Crisis of Individualism

THE beginning of the twentieth century marked the high point of bourgeois individualistic culture. Man's reason and inventiveness, which since the eighteenth century had been in continuous ascendance, seemed to have triumphed. International commerce and machine industry were producing a hitherto unequalled prosperity. Middle-class merchants and manufacturers became rich, and the new suburbs and fashionable vacation centers assumed a look of comfortable solidity. Well-conducted concerts and brilliant theater performances filled the leisure time between energetic hours of work, museums were rearranged or newly founded, and publishers made fortunes. The German masses were on their way to a brighter future. Twentieth-century enlightenment seemed to have enchained the demons of want and disease, and an era of world peace appeared to loom around the corner.

But this prosperity was bought at a high price. The new technological culture more and more disrupted man's natural ties and associations. Metropolitan man's working life became separated from his family life in theme and location. He began to live in an unnatural climate of artificial light and harnessed power. He dressed in synthetic fibers and ate processed foods; he relaxed before movie screens, radios, and television sets or took walks in the landscaped parks which had replaced the natural forests. With each new decade of the twentieth century a world completely remade by man in his own image became a more attainable and for many a desirable vision. It would be a world of artifacts far removed from primitive nature.

Man himself tended to become an artifact. Mechanical and electronic calculators took the place of mental operations; liberal education was superseded by vocational training. The social body was more and more composed of men and women doing specialized work with specialized tools, pursuing highly selected careers, and investigating bits and fragments of present life and past history. The feeling for the natural proportions of life and society began to become nebulous, and the individual's responsibility for the whole became weaker and weaker.

This climate proved dangerous for religion and morals. Blind trust in human reason led to doubts about Christian dogma and about religion in general, and these doubts were augmented by new historical, biological, and psychological discoveries. Darwin's theory of evolution, Freud's exploration of the unconscious, excavations in the ancient Orient seemed to make religion obsolete, and Einstein's theory of relativity and the discovery of the atomic structure of the universe argued convincingly against the traditional image of God. Objective reality was ultimately resolved into movements of minute particles beyond human vision. Man's prized intellect was at the mercy of all sorts of inherited, subconscious, and irrational drives. The vaunted Western culture lost its central significance, and became a mere incident in an endless stream of human history that appeared to have no recognizable aim or meaning. Traditional views of the world grew obsolescent after 1910, and had become hopelessly old-fashioned by 1920. Naturally traditional morality also found it hard to survive. Human life seemed to be without transcendent significance, and the individual could only enjoy his existence to the utmost. National and family ties became strained. An obtuse, ruthless materialism appeared to many as the only practical conclusion.

It was a conclusion that carried its own retribution. The new regard for personal health and well-being led to wonderful medical advances, but also to a population increase that intensified competition and necessitated an expansion of industry and commerce. The increase in German commerce intensified international rivalries, and resulted in protective policies that finally became imperialistic adventures. The international equivalent of individualism was a glorification of one's nation or at least of the white man and his Western culture. Colonial exploitation was carried on by all Western nations, including Germany. But German geography made imperialism an unwise policy. The growing German navy could be bottled up, and German international trade could be cut off at any time. Sober prudence should have dictated a policy of restraint and international co-operation. Yet official utterances were dominated by arrogant boasting and irresponsible saber rattling, which, though it was seldom supported by convincing action, sufficed to make the name of Germany hated. The international horizon between 1871 and 1914 became increasingly cloudy.

Finally the storm of the First World War (1914–1918) broke loose and ended the existing organization of Europe. By means of the Versailles Peace Treaty (1919) and its corollaries, Austria-Hungary was dissolved, and Germany was reduced to a second-rate power. But even the victorious British Empire was passing its zenith, and France emerged as a victor in name only. In the East the war had acted in part as a catalyst for the October Revolution of 1917, from which emerged a new power, that of Communist Russia.

The end of the fighting could not be the end of an unrest that had much deeper roots than temporary political alignments and miscalculations. After 1918 Germany tried to transform itself into a modern democracy, but the attempt was frustrated by the short-sightedness of the guardians of tradition and by unfavorable developments in industry and international trade. About 1930, German democracy had degenerated into a government by presidential decree, and the unemployment problem had become immense. This critical situation was exploited by Adolf Hitler, the leader of the National-Socialist party, who began to rule Germany in 1933. He believed fanatically in the supremacy of the so-called German race, and in his right to assert that supremacy by any means moral or immoral. The rule of the Nazis was the final triumph of atheistic materialism, and was opposed only by those parts of the German nation that had still preserved their faith in Christian and Humanist ideals or were speculating on a new system of values that seemed to be developing in Russia. This opposition was strong, but it was powerless to prevent the systematic attack upon German culture that was undertaken by Hitler's minions after 1933. By brutal police measures, by insidious administrative and financial regulations, by propaganda and mental coercion German culture was defiled and distorted.

The Dissociative and Surrealistic Style

Religious and racial minorities were persecuted; in the end they were simply murdered. The German nation was shocked into an outwardly imposing integration, and all its resources were marshalled to achieve the final aim of revising the Versailles Treaty and enlarging the German geographical and economic base.

Hitler's policies culminated in the Second World War (1939–1945) which ended with the utter defeat of Germany and the bankruptcy of Nazi materialism. This was not merely the result of an accidental political constellation, but the logical consequence of the basic immorality of National-Socialist principles. They necessarily met with the religious and moral forces inside Germany and were defeated by those outside.

At the end of the Second World War traditional Christianity and traditional Humanism remained as the only foundations upon which German culture could be reconstructed. Yet a merely conservative reaction was out of the question, although it appeared as the easiest way out of an unprecedented chaos. For meanwhile new forces had been set in motion in Europe and in the rest of the world, which made a return to the *status quo ante* just as impossible as a simple preservation of the *status quo*.

After 1945 one of the results of the technological revolution reached its final stage. The acceleration of travel and the spread of radio communication systems was reducing global distances to a minimum. Great oceans were becoming mere lakes, and distant continents were becoming next-door neighbors. Parochial thinking about political and cultural questions increasingly became outmoded and dangerous, especially since mankind appeared to be divided into two great armed camps scheming to destroy each other in suicidal global combat. The atomic methods for such destruction were invented together with the means of their fast delivery over distances which but fifty years ago had appeared to be absolutely safe.

If such a gloomy end of culture could be avoided, it was possible only by a complete re-examination of national and individual cultures against the new global background. Western and Christian culture appeared local, when one reflected on its absence in the Middle East, in India, or in China, and the occidental claim to global leadership appeared questionable. At the same time, the nations of the Orient and of the Islamic World were feeling the impact of the new situation, and were revising their traditional cultural tenets and their economic and political systems. Asiatic and Arabic unrest led to a weakening, if not a partial dissolution, of the old British Empire and the French colonial empire.

The Crisis of Individualism

The United States voluntarily renounced its domination over the Philippines, and the Netherlands could not prevent the establishment of an independent Indonesia. In Europe, Germany at the end of the Second World War completely lost its eastern provinces with their rich cultural tradition, and suffered the trenchant division of the rest into a Russian satellite state, the so-called German Democratic Republic, and a Western democratic state, the German Federal Republic. Even this Western democratic state could no longer continue national policies in the customary manner, but in 1957 made the far-reaching decision to combine its industrial and commercial resources with those of other European powers; January 1st, 1958, marked the beginning of the disappearance of continental economic boundaries, which in time might lead to a disappearance also of political boundaries. Farsighted statesmen in all European countries began to realize that only by a generous measure of integration could the old continent continue to exert its influence. Its position of international leadership had become a thing of the past and had been transferred to two new global powers, the United States and Russia. The United States was developing from an unrestricted liberal position into a more bureaucratic state; Russia, under the guise of communism, was ruthlessly forging the sinews of a new industrial empire that in course of time might also lead to a certain measure of democracy; but of course the path toward that goal was destined to be devious and rocky, and might prove too long to offer any immediate hope to mankind. Gloomy prophecies of mankind's impending suicide became journalistic currency.

The generations of German writers and artists experiencing all these revolutionary changes could hardly avoid a growing feeling of insecurity, which in many cases ended in frustration and nihilism, while in other cases it brought about an unrealistic escape into past modes of thinking or an intransigent clinging to the threatened tradition. The basic anxiety and insecurity of the writers and artists impelled all of them to search for new syntheses answering the pressing needs of the changing times. But such syntheses were hard to come by and could mostly assume but a tentative and private character. Contradictions and dilemmas abounded, and even poets devoted to the upholding of valuable tradition were beset by doubts and by problems. As a consequence a new, unified style could not be found, and a superficial review of twentieth-century literature might interpret it as a mere continuation of the individualistic literature of the nineteenth. But the poets of the new age no longer revelled in their individual differences. They wanted to be part

[283

of a movement of servants of a greater whole. They were experiencing individuation as a curse and were trying to submerge their identities in the stream of class, society, nation, or mankind. They were individualists against their will, and their cherished syntheses were conceived as means to overcome individualism and pragmatism. The stylistic tendency common to the many individual attempts can therefore be found only in the desire to disassociate oneself from the reigning individualistic culture and to transcend pragmatism by the subordination of persons and objects to higher potentialities. It is these tendencies which we are designating by referring to the new style as dissociative and surrealistic.

Within this general designation a few typical solutions of the cultural crisis have been attempted in preference to others and will here be illustrated by representative samples. One trend has led to the dissociative adaptation of the German cultural tradition, another to its reduction to a biological basis. A third trend can be discerned in the attempt of art and poetry to retreat to their own spheres and thus partake in the technological world of artifacts. Though this has often produced socially meaningless experiments, it might conceivably open up ways to technological man's forgotten soul and thus create a new stylistic integration.

The following chapters will review each one of these trends in chronological order, although they are basically co-existent. We will not attempt to prophesy to which trend belongs the future, neither will we try to judge whether together they point to a downfall of German culture or to its hopeful revival.

The Third Humanism

THE new sense of crisis found its first expression in the philosophic writings of Friedrich Nietzsche (1844–1900). As the son of a Saxon clergyman he grew up in the Christian and Humanist tradition of German culture. At an early age he became professor of classical philology at the University of Basel, but soon gave up this post to become a freelance philosopher. He early criticized the shallow meliorism and growing liberalism of his century, and found support for such views in the writings of Arthur Schopenhauer and the music-dramas of Richard Wagner. But he also criticized the Christian system of morality and broke with Wagner when the latter in the text of his *Parsifal* revived the Christian idea of charity. In 1883–1885 appeared *Also sprach Zarathustra* ("Thus Spoke Zarathustra"), which in highly poetic language proclaimed the new moral attitude visualized by Nietzsche. In more theoretical form his views were expressed in books such as *Jenseits von Gut und Böse* ("Beyond Good and Evil," 1886), *Zur Genealogie der Moral* ("The Genealogy of Morals," 1886) and *Götzendämmerung* ("The Twilight of Idols," 1888). During a sojourn in Italy in 1889, Nietzsche suffered a mental breakdown that made him insane for the rest of his life; he died in Naumburg in 1900. On the basis of Nietzsche's notebooks his sister constructed his final work *Der Wille zur Macht* ("The Will to Power"). This work never got beyond the planning stage; Nietzsche's sister by her construction made Nietzsche into a more systematic and conclusive philosopher than he had actually been.

One can, of course, single out dominant trends in Nietzsche's thought, but every honest critic admits that he failed to solve the basic contradictions besetting the culture of his time. He was emotionally tied to romantic individualism and aristocratic Humanism, which he saw threatened by the new liberalism and positivism. At the same time he was deeply affected by Darwin's conception of a biological evolution and by Taine's positivist interpretation of history. He heaped scorn upon metaphysical dreams, and bluntly pronounced God "dead." He also denounced Christian morals and declared them to be the hypocritical inventions of the biologically weak. The synthesis of these conflicting trends Nietzsche sought in a vitalist approach to philosophy that combined the romantic abhorrence of the commonplace with the new biological impulses. Vitalism had its German antecedents in the thought of Master Eckhart, of Herder, and of others, but in Nietzsche's works took a trend toward the biological. Life became the supreme value, not in the shallow, unsophisticated manner of the materialists, but a life of intoxicating strength and exuberance to which prose hymns could be written in the manner of *Also sprach Zarathustra*. Life was a mysterious, irrational energy that was feared by the staid burghers and the pale scholars, but was unscrupulously embraced by the *Übermensch*, the "superman." All moral and religious, though not aesthetic, values were subordinate to it, and Nietzsche never tired of underscoring the mysteriously integrated character of life, and expressed it by startling metaphors and obiter dicta. He raved against the conventional dichotomy between body and soul, against the claims of objectivity asserted by abstract thinkers, against the pedantic urge to systematize, against hypo-critical pretensions of every kind. And he did this in an exquisite aph-oristic style, which borrowed from Biblical imagery and from Goethe's poetry, from Luther's straightforwardness and from Heine's and Scho-penhauer's malice. Nietzsche's brilliant prose seduced even contempo-raries who were immune to the tendency of his ideas. Fascinated readers were comparing *Also sprach Zarathustra* to the Christian Bible and to Goethe's *Faust*.

The cathartic effect of Nietzsche's ideas was enormous. Many later poets and philosophers merely spelled them out in detail or used them as ammunition for their own systems of thought. His ear-catching apho-risms became slogans and were used as excuses for various styles of living and thinking, for vigorous Christian evangelism and romantic irration-alism or aestheticism no less than for ruthless immoralism and a life of debauchery and eccentricity. Nietzsche's startling flashes of psychological intuition became the basis of modern psychoanalysis; his criticism of conventional morality led to less rigid interpretations of Christian eth-ics; his views on classical antiquity and Renaissance heroes necessitated philosophical and historical reappraisals; his aesthetic judgments spurred critics and literary historians to new discoveries and re-evaluations.

Nietzsche's most important contribution to modern cultural life was the sense of crisis to which he first gave prominent expression. And there were independent contemporaries who shared his apprehensions and wrote similar warnings. The solitary Swiss poet Carl Spitteler in 1880 began his series of verse epics, which in mythical images portrayed the feeling that the time was ripe for a new era of history, and which upheld a heroic ideal in a period of general leveling. Another Swiss contemporary, the Basel historian Jacob Burckhardt, warned already in 1889 against the extreme simplifiers ushering in the coming century, which later indeed proved to be one of mass culture and mass media. These and other critics of the liberal *Zeitgeist* seemed to confirm the attitude expressed by Nietzsche, and aided the young generation around 1900 in steering a course which he had initiated. This course led first to a restatement of traditional German Humanism that had long been de-manded by the changed cultural climate. The restatement took the form of the so-called "Third" Humanism (with the Humanism of the Refor-mation period counting as first and the Humanism of the Goethe period as second). Among its chief representatives were the poets Stefan George and Hugo von Hofmannsthal, the dramatists Paul Ernst and

286]

The Third Humanism

Gerhart Hauptmann, and the novelist Thomas Mann. In the cases of Thomas Mann and Gerhart Hauptmann the catastrophic developments begun with the First World War led to changes in their literary aims, and we will therefore review their later works in a subsequent chapter.

Of all these writers it was perhaps Thomas Mann (1875–1955) who gained the widest recognition among his contemporaries. Coming from a wealthy merchant's family in the old Hanseatic town of Lübeck, he spent important formative years at Munich and became imbued with the *avant-garde* ideas of the day. Almost overnight he acquired fame with his novel *Buddenbrooks* (1901), which at first glance appeared to be the nostalgic record of a culture hopelessly doomed; the subtitle described the theme as the "Decay of a Family." With an acute sense for significant detail and for a happy turn of phrase, Mann here records his own family's turning from respectable realism and a sense of social obligation to a touchy, anemic sentimentality and a withdrawal into romantic isolation. Yet it becomes clear that the change has its compensations. For while the vital instincts become more and more uncertain, the finer artistic sensibilities increase, and the last Buddenbrook is a real musician. Culture turns out to be a problem, and a synthesis between biological sufficiency and artistic eminence appears hardly possible.

Thomas Mann's attitude toward the inherited middle-class culture might be characterized as ambivalent. It was nurtured by romanticists such as Storm and Wagner; by impressionists such as the German Fontane, the Dane Jens Peter Jacobsen, and the masters of the French and Russian novel; by critical philosophers such as Schopenhauer and Nietzsche. And all of these predecessors influenced Mann's style. From Wagner he learned the technique of the leitmotif that holds the multicolored fabric together. From Flaubert and Fontane he learned the deft employment of adjectival nuances and qualifying concessive clauses. From Nietzsche he learned the art of disturbing inquisitiveness that does not obediently accept artistic and poetic claims, but confronts them experimentally with healthy biological self-sufficiency. Yet in spite of all these often-conflicting antecedents, Mann's special artistic achievement was his own. He successfully fused all the elements of his story into representative and unforgettable pictures, and he marshalled his many qualifying adjectives and clauses with rare and often uncanny syntactical ability.

In a number of short stories Mann varied his early theme of the contrast between bourgeois and artistic modes of existence; *Tristan* (1903) and *Tonio Kröger* (1903) are outstanding examples. About 1910 a change becomes noticeable. *Der Tod in Venedig* ("Death in Venice," 1911) not so much upholds the neurotic and abnormal artist as it shows his frustration and dissolution. Mann's second novel *Königliche Hoheit* ("Royal Highness," 1909) ends on a note of ironic affirmation of social duty and bourgeois morality. During the First World War Mann published *Betrachtungen eines Unpolitischen* ("Reflections of a Nonpolitical Observer"), in which he tried to defend the traditional values of German culture. It was an expository forerunner to his third novel *Der Zauberberg* ("The Magic Mountain," 1924). Here Mann at last found a positive solution to the problem of German culture. His hero, Hans Castorp, visits a sanatorium for tuberculosis patients on a Swiss mountain peak which becomes his "magic mountain" of detachment from healthy normal life. Hans Castorp, one might say, is flirting with death, but death in the end becomes a revelation for him. He listens to all the European debates between liberals and totalitarians, between sceptics and believers, between Eastern and Western ways of life. Mann's panorama of European prewar culture is astonishingly rich and exhaustive, but it is also somber and questioning; the disease of his patients is symbolical. In the end Hans Castorp is able to take a stand. It is a typically German stand, the stand of creative mediation between the conflicting forces. When the First World War breaks out, Hans Castorp chooses sides and shares the fate of his contemporaries as a voluntary soldier. This is by no means a relapse into barbarism and a renunciation of culture, but rather an acceptance of life in its elevating yet tragic aspects. Mann no longer despairs; his hero's devotion to the urgent tasks of the day can be seen as a reaffirmation of the decision taken by Goethe's Wilhelm Meister a century before.

Still, it is a modern reaffirmation, ironical and conditional, and Mann's style has become highly complex. Time here is not treated with naturalistic simplicity but with microscopic scrutiny or telescopic condensation. Space has become strangely transparent and suggestive. And the characters are rarely one-dimensional. Again, the many details are closely interwoven by leitmotifs and suggestive irony, by ambivalent adjectives and contrapuntal themes. Mann has avoided all the easy simplifications and has emphasized the precarious and controversial aspects of the cultural situation. His experimental affirmation of daily life permitted him to go along with the rapidly changing trends of German culture. Mann hopefully accepted postwar German democracy and became its leading representative. But when in 1933 the democratic development was curtailed and the Humanist and Christian tradition was denied by the National Socialists, Mann found himself out of touch with the new masters of German destiny and did not return to Germany from a European lecture tour. His later works were written under a different star.

While Thomas Mann's narrative affirmation of Humanist values was critical and ironical, the attitude of the two leading poets of the Third Humanism appears more positive. Yet they too did not merely continue a tradition; they were fully conscious of the precarious cultural situation. Neither the Rhenish poet Stefan George nor the Austrian poet Hugo von Hofmannsthal can be understood without an awareness of their indebtedness to Nietzsche, to French symbolists such as Baudelaire and Mallarmé, to English Pre-Raphaelites such as Rossetti and Swinburne.

Stefan George (1868–1933) began with impressionistic and neo-romantic experiments, but soon developed a poetic character of his own. While Thomas Mann found in Nietzsche's philosophy a confirmation of his own ironic attitude toward life, George was quite serious. He no longer wanted to achieve an impressionist counterpart of reality, but in strong rhythms to proclaim the covenant of a new culture. Select individuals were to renew the German nation. *Der Stern des Bundes* ("The Star of the Covenant," 1914) was the title of one of George's mature poetic collections, and his last volume was named *Das neue Reich* ("The Kingdom to Come," 1928). George's vision began to assume shape during his lifetime. A number of his followers and disciples formed a loosely knit group as the nucleus of a renewed nation. Distinguished literary historians such as Friedrich Gundolf and Ernst Bertram, philosophers such as Ludwig Klages, poets such as Hugo von Hofmannsthal, Max Dauthendey, and Karl Wolfskehl were either permanently or temporarily associated with this group.

Perhaps Stefan George's vision can be best understood against his Rhenish background, which combined a Roman and a Catholic inheritance. Though he very early rejected the Church of his youth, he always lived in its atmosphere; Dante was his lodestar, and ultimately George created a kind of secularized Catholicism. In *Das Jahr der Seele* ("The Year of the Soul," 1897) he approached life in a mood of delicate sadness, in *Der Teppich des Lebens* ("The Tapestry of Life," 1900) he did it in a more festival mood tinged with somber regret. Yet he nowhere abandoned himself to joyous exuberance. His *Neue Reich* is permeated with monkish and ascetic devotion to transcendental values. George is

[289

up in arms against mundane distractions and against woman as the arch-representative of the devil and the flesh. In her stead he set up the idol of a pure youth (Maximin) as the center of his new religion. George essentially cherished the ideals of medieval knighthood. He denounced democracy and vulgarity in the same breath. In his "realm" there were only masters and disciples, and the disciples devoted their lives to their chosen leaders. Everybody, including the leaders, had his particular task, the leaders to administer and extend the great European spiritual tradition which George always implied when he spoke of Germany. He adumbrated it in his *Bücher der Hirten- und Preisgedichte, der Sagen und Sänge und der hängenden Gärten* ("The Books of Eclogues and Eulogies, of Legends and Lays, and of the Hanging Gardens," 1895). Here "Eclogues and Eulogies" stood for classical antiquity, "Legends and Lays" for the Christian Middle Ages, and "Hanging Gardens" for romantic excursions into the Orient. When George spoke of German culture, he thought of it in Humanistic terms. He was no glorifier of the German nation as it actually existed. In the midst of the First World War, in 1917, he severely chastised the Germans in the long poem *Der Krieg* ("The War"), and interpreted the military events of the time as a manifestation of soulless machinery and cultural disease. George's ideals could be reached only gradually by diligent discipline and devotion. When the National Socialists came to power and claimed the aged poet as their own, he saw no reason to give up his reservations. He died on a vacation trip to Switzerland, where he was buried. Had George lived until the Second World War, he would have applauded the participation of some of his disciples in the assassination plot in 1944 against Hitler.

One of their friends, Albrecht Haushofer, before his execution wrote the *Moabiter Sonette* ("Moabite Prison Sonnets") in the Georgean style. This style can be described as an austere German approach to a new classicism. Even the printed form of George's poems was calculated to frighten off the superficial reader. Capitals are avoided; the poet uses his own special punctuation and spelling; his letters have a peculiar form, more Greek than German. George gives new vitality to commonplace ideas by his choice of unhackneyed, full-sounding words, his exemplary purity of rhyme and rhythm, and by the disciplined brevity of many poems.

From a formal point of view his poems have often reached perfection, and George's pure diction and sensitive rhythm set an example. His attempt at a wider cultural reformation was taken seriously only by an esoteric group. But a number of his individual ideas have continued to inspire German youth. The important revaluation of Hölderlin and Jean Paul was initiated by Stefan George; his translations of foreign poetry set a new German standard of excellence. His selections from Dante represent the closest German approximation to the poetic perfection of that great Florentine.

For a short while the Austrian poet Hugo von Hofmannsthal (1874–1939) also moved in George's orbit. But he soon drifted away and began to enliven the old traditions in his own way. During his lifetime, only a few poets and artistic friends realized his greatness, among them Rudolf Alexander Schröder, Richard Strauss, and Stefan Zweig. A more general conception of Hofmannsthal's singularity is emerging only now.

Yet even in Hofmannsthal's own period it was impossible to escape the sweet magic of his early lyrics, which he wrote as a Viennese youth hardly out of the Gymnasium. Poems such as *Psyche* and *Vorfrühling* ("Early Spring"), *Terzinen über die Vergänglichkeit* ("Terza Rima on Mutability") or *Manche freilich . . .* ("Some, however . . .") are unforgettable. Here the German poetic tradition was alive in a highly sensitive poet aiming at clear yet beautiful form. He was generally misunderstood as decadent and imitative. The lyric dialogue *Der Tor und der Tod* ("Death and the Fool") was classified as derivative from Goethe's *Faust*. Yet such judgments overlooked Hofmannsthal's seriousness, which never denied its affinity to the past tradition but revived it independently. Far from being an impressionist aesthete, Hofmannsthal fought an unending battle with the modern subjectivity and irresponsibility that affected him. There came a time when the sensitive young man forswore lyrical expression, and evoked the help of less egocentric forms against the threatening nihilistic chaos.

The mature Hofmannsthal sought to preserve the continuity of a great culture by reviving its past inheritance and encouraging its living energies. His play *Jedermann* (1911) picked up the theme of the old morality play, *Everyman*, and confronted the modern heir of civilization's rich material treasures with the metaphysical challenge of death. Hofmannsthal also treated marriage problems in dramas that emphasized loyalty to the partner and to the children. And he took a positive view of the state, not a militaristic state, but a state with a cultural mission. Hofmannsthal was an Austrian patriot like Grillparzer, even though he knew that the old Danube monarchy was probably doomed. He had the courage to be different and the courage to be critical. As an editor he selected works from European literature with a wide catholicity, but always with a view to lasting religious and formal values; his anthologies such as *Deutsches Lesebuch* ("German Reader") and *Wert und Ehre deutscher Sprache* ("Value and Glory of the German Language") will outlast most others. While he was never afraid of using expressions from great predecessors, he never merely imitated or repeated them. The later Hofmannsthal found his main inspiration in Calderón, and he wrote *Das Salzburger grosse Welttheater* ("The Great Salzburg Play of the World," 1921) in the same Christian spirit, as a symbolic theatrical expression of the deepest problems of life.

Hofmannsthal's best-known plays are the libretti he provided for the composer Richard Strauss, *Der Rosenkavalier* ("The Rose-Bearer"), *Ariadne auf Naxos* ("Ariadne on Naxos"), and finally *Die Frau ohne Schatten* ("The Woman Without a Shadow"). The theme of the last-mentioned opera Hofmannsthal treated again in narrative form in 1919; the result was one of the most delightful modern fairy tales and also one of the most profound, dealing as it did with the problems of conjugal love and the sacredness of unborn children. Hofmannsthal worked on this fairy tale for seven years, just as he worked on his tragedy *Der Turm* ("The Tower," 1925) for almost ten years. Here he tried to give dramatic form to the most burning problem of his time: the breakthrough of chaotic, demoniac forces in a social order that was no longer true to its own spirit. His last public attempt to oppose cultural chaos was his establishment, with the famous stage manager Max Reinhardt, of the Salzburg Festival. This was intended as a new German center for plays expressing timeless values; and to this day the companies appearing there perform operas by Mozart and present Richard Strauss's settings of Hofmannsthal's libretti, and stage Hofmannsthal's own *Jedermann* and *Das Salzburger grosse Welttheater*.

Compared with Hofmannsthal's valiant, warmhearted and able espousal of the old Austrian universality, the clever poems of his younger Viennese contemporary Josef Weinheber must be rejected as anemic experiments in a sterile classicism and nationalistic idiom.

Hofmannsthal's dramatic efforts were paralleled by other Humanist dramatists. The best known among them was Paul Ernst, while Gerhart Hauptmann's non-naturalistic plays were rarely seen in their true context. Paul Ernst (1866–1933) grew up in the Central German bourgeois tradition, but was early influenced by Darwin and Marx. He was likewise impressed by Nietzsche's penetrating criticism of traditional bourgeois attitudes, and by other poets and thinkers whose works were readily available in this age of inexpensive books and public libraries. The mature Paul Ernst bluntly attested to the collapse of bourgeois idealism in his book *Der Zusammenbruch des bürgerlichen Idealismus* (1919) and then attempted to arrive at a restatement of the time-honored Humanist values, which past idealism had represented but imperfectly. In original and searching essays Ernst examined the literature of many ages and continents, and endeavored to lay the groundwork of a new poetics; perhaps the essays collected in *Der Weg zur Form* ("The Way to Poetic Form," 1906) show the essayist at his best. In sum total all Ernst's theories aimed at a socially responsible poetry, of which he gave numerous interesting examples. His dramas experimented with a severe type of German classicism, which unfortunately were too labored to convince contemporaries. His lyrical and epic experiments were even more curious. He was best in his short stories with their unsentimental language and their clearly outlined characters and situations.

Even a cursory survey cannot hide from the reader the multiplicity of outlook characteristic of the twentieth century. Although the poets mentioned in this chapter agreed in the general direction of their literary efforts, they still differed in so many detailed ways that each of them could be treated as an individual arriving at a private philosophy. Ultimately even the traditionalists contributed to the dissociative character of twentieth-century literature, which manifested itself in a bewildering productivity. Seen from an economic aspect it was the age of feverish literary competition and of mass publications clogging the market. As a result, critics found it hard to recognize exceptional merit, and the individual poet had an uneasy time between the pressure of publishers and his own ambition to adhere strictly to a high standard.

In the work of Gerhart Hauptmann this dangerous literary situation is typified. His early works had given him literary fame, and in 1912 he was awarded the Nobel Prize for literature. Quite naturally he became the darling of impresarios and editors, and he often succumbed to the temptation to publish unfinished and unpolished works. As a consequence the significance of his later development was overlooked by many critics. Yet the mature Hauptmann underwent a decisive personal struggle between Christian and pagan attitudes—a conflict which was both directly and indirectly prompted by Nietzsche.

The novel *Der Narr in Christo Emanuel Quint* ("The Fool in Christ, Emanuel Quint," 1910) was focused on a simple-minded Silesian carpenter's imitation of Christ. Here was revealed Hauptmann's awareness of the social implication of the Christian message and his antipathy toward its theological representatives. The masterful story *Der Ketzer von Soana* ("The Heretic of Soana," 1918) rejected Christian prudery and asceticism in favor of an open acknowledgment of man's natural sexual impulses. The story was the first significant result of Hauptmann's trip to Greece in 1907, which had brought him into the desired personal contact with classical antiquity. Its impetus was augmented by assiduous studies of classical literature in modern, scholarly translations. They deepened in him the Nietzschean conception of a Greece continuously acknowledging the demoniac elemental forces that in the last analysis even the Olympic gods could not control. The Greek drama presented man in the grip of an inexorable fate even stronger than the gods.

As early as 1913 Hauptmann's festival masque in commemoration of the anniversary of the Wars of Liberation (*Festspiel in deutschen Reimen*) showed him under the influence of the *mimus*, a popular dramatic form of late antiquity. But in that play as well as in *Der Ketzer von Soana*, a harmonic fusion of spiritual and demoniac forces still appeared possible. The *Festspiel* ended with a pageant led by Athena, the goddess of all the arts of peace and hopeful search for knowledge. (It was this very ending that so provoked German nationalists and militarists that they engineered the discontinuance of the performances.)

A year later the dream was shattered by the outbreak of the First World War, and a year after the publication of *Der Ketzer von Soana* the chaotic anarchy of defeat and revolution, of social and economic disintegration was harassing Germany. Hauptmann's uncertain optimism disappeared, and the poet started on his final road to an uncompromisingly tragic view of life. It led him close to the surrealistic style of younger contemporaries, and will therefore be discussed later.

The Quest of Despair

B Y about 1910 a new generation had grown up, and began to take stock of the existing culture. It found itself faced by a culture that had lost direction and was threatened by disaster; for although the war did not actually break out till 1914, it was looming on the horizon, and many of the younger writers felt it approaching. They believed that bourgeois values had broken down; they could not see the possibility of a romantic recourse to the past, nor could they put faith in a return to nature. They therefore entered on a desperate quest for new values that could replace the worn-out values. To this quest they gave many different names, of which the most generally accepted was expressionism.

This term was chosen in avowed opposition to the older impressionism. Actually impressionism signified the rapid disintegration of established values; for it substituted individual sensations for the organic whole of human experience. Where general and transcendent values appeared at all, they appeared unintentionally. In its last phase impressionism developed into imagism, i.e., the attempt to present visual or auditory images without any symbolic or philosophic implications.

Expressionism simply went farther in the same direction. It finally destroyed the world of object-centered sensations, and substituted for it the irrational and willful emotions of the artistic ego. This ego could express itself in fragmentary sensory perceptions, if such was its intention; but it always used them freely and without any consideration for their objective character or connection. The artist or poet could distort his perceptions or reduce them to their elements; he could join images from various times and fields of experience through the dream associations of the subconscious mind or the arbitrary techniques of montage and collage; he could finally avoid any direct references to concrete experience and merely offer a suggestive interplay of pure lines, shapes, and colors. The new painters discarded all laws of perspective and coloration; the new sculptors substituted grotesque or freely invented shapes for concrete shapes; the new music indulged in atonalities and disharmonies. Thus a completely new style sprang up all over Europe under many revolutionary slogans, and invaded every field of artistic creation. Among its early representatives in the fine arts were the Norwegian Munch, the Frenchman Gauguin, the Spaniard Picasso, the Dutchman Van Gogh, and the Germans Kokoschka, Lehmbruck, Barlach, Klee, and Franz Marc; its musical *avant-garde* was led by the Germans Schönberg and Hindemith. To the young generation the new style meant the only honest and direct expression of its experience of modern life as disrupted and disjointed, as meaningless and futile, with hope to be found only in a world completely different.

In literature the new experience led to an abrupt break with established stylistic conventions. Lyric poetry became a series of loosely associated outcries, of vaporizing dreams and irrational dream figures, of strange and irregular rhythms and rhymes, of neologisms and choppy sentences, of omitted articles and avoided grammatical subjects. Narrative literature employed exaggerated characters and artificially contrived plots, or it substituted dream coherence and stream of consciousness for realistic relationship and logical consistency. Dramatic literature employed types and caricatures, and chose exotic or abstract localities; it sought to fire its audiences with moral indignation and visions of a better future. Within these stylistic changes a multiplicity of individual attitudes and poses was assumed. Not every representative of the new generation went the whole way from abysmal despair to delirious hope. A few cynics were satisfied with mere destruction. Others bogged down in experiments. The majority of the young people yearned for a better society, a deeper morality, a new or renewed religion, for international peace and for social justice. Occasionally poets deserted visionary writing for political propaganda, and deviated into ideological pamphlets of a democratic, socialistic, or communistic nature. Still, the best poets of expressionism were just as sincere in their attempts to build a new world as the best representatives of Storm and Stress.

The new poetry first appeared around 1910, a few years before the First World War, which began the irretrievable destruction of the past. One of the earliest expressionists was Alfred Mombert, who in Whitmanlike verses conjured up cosmic forces. Another one was Georg Heym, who created grandiose pagan visions of an urban civilization, and presaged the destruction of the metropolitan centers by fire and explosion. Still another was Georg Trakl (1887–1914), whose note was more delicate. He proclaimed brotherly sympathy with other human beings equally condemned to suffering, a feeling which was now replacing the former proud individualism:

Unter Dornenbogen	*Under arches of thorns,*
O mein Bruder klimmen wir	*O my brother, we blind*
Blinde Zeiger gen	*Clock-hands are climbing*
Mitternacht.	*Toward midnight.*

The peaceful evening meal could unite man with his brothers who needed rest from desolate wanderings. Trakl also found a new style for his visions, a style that avoided the harsh realities and used symbolic colors and rhythms:

Sonne, herbstlich dünn und zag,
Und das Obst fällt von den Bäumen.

The Quest of Despair

Stille wohnt in blauen Räumen
Einen langen Nachmittag.

Sterbeklänge von Metall;
Und ein weisses Tier bricht nieder.
Brauner Mädchen rauhe Lieder
Sind verweht im Blätterfall.

*

Sun autumnal, shy and sparse,
And the fruits fall from the trees.
Stillness dwells in azure spaces
A long, weary afternoon.

Deadly sounds of metal,
And a white animal breaks.
Rough songs of brown girls
Are blown away with the falling leaves.

Trakl's expression of the sadness of this transient generation was perhaps the most haunting.

The most popular of the early expressionists was the Prague writer Franz Werfel (1890–1945). In 1914 he gave passionate poetic expression to his new program of human sympathy in the volume *Wir sind!* "We are" here was meant in contrast to the subjectivist "I am"; the poet wanted to bridge the gaps between nations, generations, classes, between man and his fellow creatures. Yet the poetic expression of his creed was seldom original; Werfel at his musical best achieved a German counterpart to the emotional lyricism of Walt Whitman. He was hardly better in the field of the drama, where he produced conventional theatrical effects, although he partly adopted the technical innovations of Strindberg. The meaning of the symbolical events seldom came out clearly. And he disappointed in his novels (e.g., *Das Lied von Bernadette*, "The Song of Bernadette," 1941), which bordered on the average and the sentimental, and sometimes became best sellers.

Of the numerous other poets of the expressionist era most have been already forgotten, and only one has in recent years exercised an influence on young German writers, the West Prussian Gottfried Benn (1886–1956). Though he was born in a Protestant parsonage, he turned early to a Nietzschean nihilism. Benn studied medicine and became a specialist in dermatology and venereal diseases. As such he adopted the disillusioned jargon of medical research and coldly exhibited the disgusting, ugly facts behind the smiling exterior masks of life. All his youthful poems (*Morgue*, 1912; *Schutt*, "Rubbish," 1924) were devoted to the pitiless unmasking of man. They described the stench of the cancer ward, the cynical dissections in the anatomical laboratories, the putrefaction of decaying corpses, and the growth of vermin in the body cavities of drowned suicides. Man had no reason to be proud of his individuality, he was a scab on a festering wound or a pus-filled pimple of the universe. The later Benn sought a way out of this radical nihilism and will therefore be discussed in other connections.

One can be rightly astonished that a time veering sharply away from subjectivism was still producing so many lyricists. The older Hugo von Hofmannsthal abandoned lyrical expression after 1900, and turned to media not demanding a rendering of immediate experience. The Vienna editor Karl Kraus (1874–1936), who belonged to the same generation, cultivated the essay almost to exclusion. In his satirical magazine *Die Fackel* ("The Torch") he unceasingly exposed pseudo-values in all fields of life, and ruthlessly analyzed the style of his literary opponents; from 1911 he was the magazine's sole contributor.

Beside him must be named other older prose writers who early sought a way out of the modern cultural schism. Kraus's fight against cultural hypocrisy and his championship of stylistic lucidity was paralleled by the novelistic prose of Thomas Mann's older brother, Heinrich Mann. The objects of the older Mann's satirical dissection were upholders of the *status quo*, which they put through its paces in the manner of automata. These inwardly depraved or desiccated representatives of the Wilhelmian era were mannequins and caricatures peopling the grotesque world of novels such as *Professor Unrat* (1905, translated as "The Blue Angel"), *Der Untertan* ("The Patrioteer," written in 1914, published in 1918), *Die Armen* ("The Poor," 1912), *Der Kopf* ("The Intellectual," 1925). The limpid prose style of these often acid portrayals was influenced by French models. In the beginning Heinrich Mann was an aggressive liberal; later on he believed in the ideals of Russian communism.

In a different manner the crisis of modern culture was attacked by the Silesian Hermann Stehr (1864–1940). He was long misunderstood as a naturalist, as he mostly dealt with farmers and artisans, with beggars and cripples of his home region, whose attitude toward life was determined by elemental forces of inheritance and environment. Yet for Stehr these forces were strangely transcendent. His characters obeyed inner voices, the sense of which could not be spelled out articulately; the voices could be soothingly divine or destructively demoniac. Stehr's characters had a hard time understanding themselves as humans and achieving a mastery over the nonhuman forces of the universe. Stehr's powerful novel *Der Heiligenhof* ("Saint's Farm," 1917) posed a problem quite similar to the one exhibited in Gerhart Hauptmann's novel *Der Narr in Christo.* Uncertainly wavering between Christian and pagan religion, the hero finds peace of some sort in elemental mysticism. The later Stehr discovered the wisdom of restraint, which led him to a significant combination of emotional humility and rational lucidity. Equally far from hysterical frenzy and ordinary prudence, Stehr found a way to devote himself to the immediate tasks of everyday existence. It was basically the old way of practical mysticism recommended by Tauler. Stehr's last work, *Die Familie Mächler,* a trilogy of novels (1929–1944), probed into German social and political development since 1848, and advocated a workaday ethos of sober devotion to cultural service. The poet's religious orientation and uncompromising morality did not fit into the Nazi ideology of the time and was bypassed by the propagandists. And the translucent style of his last novels disturbed Stehr's original audience, that had read him for his early excesses in baroque metaphor and involution.

While in 1900 Stehr and Heinrich Mann were mature men, Franz Kafka was still an adolescent. But it was left to him to discover the dissociative style that best fitted the new experience. Kafka was born of Jewish parents at Prague in 1883, and spent almost his whole life in this romantic city in which East and West so strangely intermingled in the form of the German, Czech, and Jewish cultures. He achieved a doctorate in laws, and later served as secretary in the workingmen's compensation office. He early contracted tuberculosis, and died in a small Austrian sanitarium in 1924. He was but forty-one years old at the time of his death. However, Schiller had not become much older.

Kafka left comparatively few works, some of them in an incomplete state. Still fewer satisfied the exacting stylistic demands that he imposed on himself. But these few expressed in a significant way the anxiety which was spreading in 1910, and which he felt in an especially poignant way. It was an anxiety comprising more than personal and social fears, for it was fundamentally religious. Man's helplessness and insufficiency in face of his fate is the theme of Kafka's story *Der Prozess* ("The Trial"). The hero of the novel, Josef K., remains anonymous. One morning he is suddenly arrested and accused of a crime, the nature of which is not explained. He is put before a mysterious court, which finally condemns him to death and has him executed. Josef K. does not understand his fate, but must accept his trial and follow the orders of the court in the most conscientious manner. Similarly helpless is the hero in *Das Schloss* ("The Castle"). He tries to gain access to the lord of a mysterious castle which somehow symbolizes security. Again and again he seeks to settle in the village belonging to this castle; he wants nothing better than to become a recognized citizen of the village community, to find a home there. But again and again he is thwarted in his attempt; every apparent success is only partial, and no so-called approach lessens the distance. Between the supplicant and the lord of the castle there lies a whole hierarchical complex of chief administrators and administrative deputies, of castle secretaries and village secretaries, of occasional servants, special messengers, and the like. The ultimate reality seems to elude K.'s grasp, and only when he gives up his passionate quest for it does he find peace—the peace of the mystic before the ineffable. It would be rash to describe this peace in terms of the Christian or Jewish faith, although it is visualized as a religious feeling of belonging. At least Kafka has convincingly described modern man's isolation.

In *Der Prozess* and *Das Schloss* Kafka used bureaucracy as a symbol for the automatism of modern life. This was not his only device for shattering the smugness of the naïve realism of his contemporaries. In the story *Die Verwandlung* ("The Metamorphosis") a man experiences his worthlessness by being turned into a disgusting insect. In still another, man's ridiculous vanity is reflected in an ape who has been trained to imitate a gentleman. Some of these symbols were employed by the German romanticists, by Jean Paul, or by other earlier writers, but Kafka used them in a unique way. To be sure, he often had the transcendental essence manifest its powers in rather ridiculous fashion, yet he needed this grim humor to put us at a distance from ourselves and to put the true world at a distance from the world of actuality. The prose in which his inner experience was set down was lucid and strictly artistic; Kafka disdained to write his own commentary. One may sometimes feel exasperation at being let down by him, but his avoidance of easy solutions is one more proof that his quest was genuine and was leading to more than nihilism.

At the time of his death, the theme of man's anxiety had been developed in many other narratives. Kafka's friend Max Brod, in his novel *Tycho Brahes Weg zu Gott* ("The Redemption of Tycho Brahe," 1916), portrayed the sixteenth-century astronomer arriving at acquies-

The Quest of Despair

cence to the will of God. Gustav Meyrink, another writer from Prague, in *Der Golem* (1915) and *Das grüne Gesicht* ("The Green Countenance," 1916), created a strange surrealist world in which nothing had common shape or color. The popular novelist Jakob Wassermann wrote many stories about voluntary and involuntary exiles from bourgeois society; *Das Gänsemännchen* ("The Goose Man," 1915) and *Christian Wahnschaffe* ("The World's Illusion," 1919) are perhaps most worthy of mention. Yet in all their sincerity Wassermann's novels showed too many stylistic mannerisms and employed too conventional language. They have hardly outlasted their author.

Of greater substance were the novels of Alfred Döblin (1878–1957). In *Die drei Sprünge des Wanglun* ("The Three Leaps of Wanglun," 1915) he visualized a fusion of Eastern and Western mysticism as the answer to modern man's predicament. In *Berge, Meere und Giganten* ("Mountains, Oceans, and Giants," 1924) he pursued European anxiety into a future technical Utopia, and employed a radically different time scheme to rouse the reader from his complacency. The style was of conscious fullness and redundancy, and served to remind contemporaries that man was not the sum total of the universe. Still more novel was the style of *Berlin Alexanderplatz* (1929), which used subconscious association and montage as principles of arrangement. It succeeded in giving a memorable picture of Berlin social conditions before the Hitler era; the author had become intimately acquainted with them as a neurologist residing in Berlin's eastern sector. In 1933 emigration was forced upon Döblin, but the poet was unable to grow roots in foreign soil and immediately after the Second World War returned to Germany. He was now a Catholic convert and took a leading part in the rebuilding of German culture. His last novel *Hamlet oder die lange Nacht nimmt ein Ende* ("Hamlet, or The End of the Night," 1956) gave cautious expression to his hope for a new Europe.

Experiments comparable to Döblin's were also initiated by the Austrian Hermann Broch (1886–1951), the author of the trilogy *Die Schlafwandler* ("The Sleepwalkers," 1931–1932). Broch felt that the novel with a unified technique no longer was an appropriate vehicle, and thus attempted to employ various styles side by side. His narrative *Die Schuldlosen* ("The Innocent," 1950) contained parts written in poetry, in naturalistic technique, in symbolist and in cubist style, and thus tried to picture the kaleidoscopic uncertainty of the German scene of the twenties and the incoherence of its individuals. In *Der Tod des Vergil* ("The Death of Vergil," 1945) Broch chose montage technique to create a vast canvas of a dying culture. His own end came in New Haven, where emigration had cast him.

Another personal style of dissociative character was developed by Robert Musil in his novel *Der Mann ohne Eigenschaften* ("The Man Without Qualities"). Musil was a mechanical engineer who after Hitler's occupation of Austria in 1938 settled in Switzerland, where he lived in isolation until his death in 1942. The first part of his novel appeared in 1931; like Thomas Wolfe's life story, the remainder was never completed. Musil was deeply dissatisfied with the modern bourgeoisie floating on the surface, and fervently longed for an orientation to lasting values. His own basic conflict between the intellect and the emotions he found hard to overcome, and thus he veered toward a mystic withdrawal from the world and a mystic contemplativeness of an Eastern tinge. But the poet never became quite articulate, and the manuscript he left behind was a jumble of drafts both old and new, of partly realized and partly rejected solutions and conclusions. They became documents of another unfinished bout with modern frustration.

It was to be expected that the new generation would find in the drama an excellent vehicle for exhibiting its many contradictions and ambiguities. The older plays of Frank Wedekind (1864–1918) were first in demonstrating the meaningless materialism of modern life in grotesque scenes enacted by robots and puppets talking at each other, but not with each other; they were preferably circus people and dislocated underworld figures. Wedekind also tried to propagandize a new, frankly hedonistic morality, which was neither clear nor convincing. His most ambitious plays were *Erdgeist* ("Earth Spirit," 1897) and its sequel *Die Büchse der Pandora* ("Pandora's Box," 1903). His plays found numerous performances after 1910 and became a model for young dramatists. Additional inspiration came from the Swedish playwright August Strindberg who used the same serial form and the same exaggerated, grotesque characters. Strindberg's plays often took place in unreal dream landscapes, and frequently employed inarticulate shouts and gestures. The stage settings for his plays were the first veering away from an attempted realistic illusion.

Of the German expressionist dramatists, Carl Sternheim early used Wedekind's technique. His comedies satirized the automatisms of the bourgeois world and, even more than Wedekind, distorted its language. Greater originality could be found in Georg Kaiser (1878–1945), who tried to evolve the idea of a new type of man in his fight against the impersonal brutality of the time. Yet Kaiser did not want to return to an old-fashioned individualism; he repeatedly protested that his individual personality was unimportant. Kaiser approached his dramatic writings in an unsentimental way, as intellectual games (*Denkspiele*), but the usual outcome of his expression of the modern situation was a human catastrophe crying for a religious solution. Thus in *Von Morgens bis Mitternachts* ("From Morn till Midnight," 1916) Kaiser portrayed the hectic last hours of a fraudulent cashier. In *Die Koralle* ("The Coral," 1916), *Gas I* (1918) and *Gas II* (1920) he depicted a technological civilization that had outrun human emotional resources, and forecast man's possible self-destruction by his own industrial inventions. In the last analysis Kaiser's numerous plays did not offer any new or unconventional solution for the problems he persuasively posed. In his final years in exile Kaiser wrote blank-verse dramas on Greek themes, conveying an idealistic message in the manner of Schiller.

Kaiser undoubtedly had poetic gifts. Other expressionist contemporaries of his wrote mere propaganda plays against the older generation or for the new man. Even such a promising writer as Fritz von Unruh (born in 1885) finally bogged down in a private mythology of sterile hate and abstract pacifism.

More space must be devoted to the dramatic experiments of Bertolt Brecht (1898–1956), which he himself called *Versuche*. His lifelong rebellion against bourgeois complacency led him into the Communist party and into emigration. Throughout these political activities he was a rather naïve and childlike dreamer, whose eyes were opened to the realities of the communist world only at the very end. His poetry was uneven and often unnecessarily brutal, yet it asked uncomfortable questions and evoked powerful scenes. Brecht's dramas were documentary, employing interpolated announcements and songs, self-elucidations from the actors, and other methods for breaking down illusion. He called this *episches Theater* ("epic theater") and aimed at a *Verfremdungseffekt* ("alienation effect"). The familiar was used in strange connections in order to startle the audience; individual characters were hollowed out into masks and marionettes. One of his early plays, *Trommeln in der Nacht* ("Drums in the Night," 1922), used this technique to uncover the realities of a decadent society for a returning prisoner of war. In later *Lehrstücke* ("Didactic Pieces") such as *Furcht und Elend des Dritten Reiches* ("The Private Life of the Master Race," 1945) Brecht was frankly propagandist. He could, however, achieve lasting dramatic effects, e.g., in *Der gute Mensch von Sezuan* ("The Good Woman of Szechwan," 1940), in the *Dreigroschenoper* ("Threepenny Opera," 1928), a modern adaptation of John Gay's *Beggar's Opera*, and in *Mutter Courage* ("Mother Courage," 1941), a visionary play about the gruesome, unheroic realities of war, in which the main figure was taken from one of Grimmelshausen's seventeenth-century novels and gave a voice to the human masses. Brecht's vigorous, prosaic language betrayed the coarseness of its time, but it often had its own primitive poetic lilt. It was the poetry of a sincere empathy with suffering mankind, which often transcended the assumed pose of the propagandist.

No such direct political message could be found in the dramas of the North German Ernst Barlach (1870–1938), who with stubborn persistency set out to create a new poetic mythology. Barlach has acquired just fame as a most original sculptor in wood and stone, a creator of heavy, earthbound figures who are moved by the wind of eternity and have outgrown themselves. It added to the lasting shame of Nazi art policies that Barlach's truly great art was banned from the museums as *entartete Kunst* ("decadent art") and threatened with destruction. Barlach wrote lyrical dramas as well as novels. An example of his dramatic poetry is offered by *Der tote Tag* ("The Dead Day," 1912). Here we move in a purely surrealist atmosphere, in a world of dream figures rather than ordinary individuals. Their opponents and helpers are kobolds and demons resembling those of popular superstition. These plays have a nightmarish quality, and testify impressively to Barlach's struggle against the moral depravity of man. But as with so many of his gifted contemporaries, Barlach's mythology too is of an entirely private character. It has not replaced existing mythologies and has not opened a new chapter in German literature.

The Recourse to the Elemental

THE literary ways out of the bewildering anxiety of modern man were many, but there was one path that was taken with increasing frequency by those to whom traditional Christianity or traditional Humanism no longer appealed. This was an entirely romantic way

The Recourse to the Elemental

back into a nature idealized in the manner of Rousseau. Popular liter-ature at the beginning of the twentieth century continued the roman-tic regionalism of the nineteenth, and was avidly read by the same bourgeoisie whose real life was one of fierce competition for wealth, power, and prestige, of the strict supervision of disciplined employees, of sumptuously loaded tables and of well-stocked wine cellars. At the turn of the century, bourgeois youth discovered the insincerity of their parents and revolted against it in the so-called Youth Movement. Yet like their elders these young pathfinders and *Wandervögel* ("Birds of the Road") wanted to hold on to the old cultural ideals. They denied the crass materialism and the stuffy class-consciousness of the older generation; in romantic longing they returned to nature, to spiritual and aesthetic values, to a harmless and unprejudiced attitude toward other classes and other professions. It was a repetition of the parental romanticism, and a sincere one. The Youth Movement bypassed the real problems of the age, although in its time it appeared to hold a promise of cultural rejuvenation.

In the literary field the Youth Movement was paralleled by the so-called *Heimatkunst* ("Regional Art"). The naturalists had devoted their attention to the metropolitan slums, to the artisans impoverished by machine competition, to the neurotic journalists and urban intellec-tuals anticipating a different future. Now the naturalist literature was denounced as decadent "Hot House and Asphalt" literature and was replaced by *Wege nach Weimar* ("Roads to Weimar"). Country and village life again became the favorite subject matter, and only technique and style were borrowed from naturalism and impressionism. Most of the *Heimatkunst* authors could be written off as imitators of Keller and Storm, of Ludwig and Raabe. Such a second-rate writer was Adolf Bartels, who later became a literary historian; systematically developing his pronounced anti-Semitic prejudices, he did much to prepare the spiritual climate for National Socialism.

A more gifted writer was Hermann Löns, who became popular through delightful stories on animal life and on hunters of the North German heathlands. He also wrote novels, of which *Der Werwolf* (1910) treated the peasants' participation in the Thirty Years' War; it strangely presaged the coming cataclysm of the First World War, and also anticipated the glorification of brute force later preached by the Nazis. A less one-sided point of view could be found in the Rhenish stories of Wilhelm Schäfer, which excelled in a vivid though some-times affected style. They reinterpreted German history and pointed to the inscrutable acts of a wise Providence, to the strong effects of

[305

moral example and moral decision. Equally excellent is the style of Hans Franck (born 1879), the author of novels, plays, and of story collections such as *Der Regenbogen* ("The Rainbow," 1927). Although he is without doubt a traditional writer, Franck's concern with pure form would also permit his inclusion as a Humanist.

A very gifted regionalist was the Swabian Emil Strauss, who began with novels on the impact of modern culture upon a well-integrated farm and small-town culture. *Der Engelwirt* ("Angel Tavern," 1901) sympathetically depicted the fate of a Swabian emigrant in Brazil. *Freund Hein* ("Death the Comforter," 1902) deftly delineated the tragedy of a schoolboy who could not measure up to the demands of modern school life. All of Strauss's early works excelled in a style of singular lucidity, and his story *Der Schleier* ("The Bridal Veil," 1920) must be counted among the masterpieces of the German *Novelle*. This style also reached perfection in the historical novel *Der Nackte Mann* ("The Naked Man," 1912), which described the struggle of the Lutheran town of Pforzheim against its Calvinist margrave, with the forces of nature coming out on the victorious side. In the Nazi decade Strauss published the panoramic novel *Das Riesenspielzeug* ("The Toy of the Giants," 1934), which was not unaffected by the political prejudices then current. But on the whole it succeeded in a comprehensive delineation of Swabian life before the First World War and in a sympathetic, humanitarian expression of faith in the regenerative powers of the soil.

The example of Schäfer, of Franck, and of Strauss demonstrates that regional tendencies often found expression through historical fiction, to which the German public eagerly responded. Some of the historical novelists were devout Catholics like Enrica von Handel-Mazzetti, who chose historical themes taken from Austrian history. For the most part she depicted the distressing denominational tensions of German life, and tried to solve them in a spirit of Christian forgiveness and tolerance.

Much of this German culture is regional, and it is therefore not always easy to decide whether an author should be grouped with the representatives of the Third Humanism or with the writers allying themselves with the forces of soil and climate, national history, and the continuity of the generations. A critical decision is especially difficult in the field of poetry, where a preoccupation with classical form often hides a mystic belief in the powers of blood and tradition. Such a belief constituted the central faith permeating the ballads of Börries von Münchhausen, Agnes Miegel, and Lulu von Strauss und Torney, which impressively revived the old, strict forms of German balladry. Yet these poets were no blind reactionaries. The two women among them fought for woman's emancipation from asocial spinsterhood, and for her just share in cultural and economic life. And the Baron Börries von Münchhausen often expressed real social feeling, and wrote ballads about the healthy vigor of the peasants rebelling against arrogant and tyrannical aristocrats.

Heimatkunst also left its mark on the German stage. A good example is the Tyrolean dramatist Karl Schönherr, who turned to village problems produced by the conflict between man's primitive instincts and the moral tendencies of social life. In bold, linear strokes he drew his *Weibsteufel* ("The She-Devil," 1915), an untamed hoyden trying to satisfy her sensual appetite. In *Glaube und Heimat* ("Faith and Fireside," 1910) he depicted peasants tied to the soil they had worked and trying to hold on to it in the face of religious persecution.

Thus a few *Heimatkunst* authors broke free from the romantic sentimentalism that carried the movement as a whole. After Darwin's visualization of the struggle for existence and Marx's conception of the class war, after Nietzsche's glorification of the blond beast and Freud's uncovering of our subconscious incestuous and murderous instincts, a romantic idealization of nature began to look suspicious, and a different brand of regionalism appeared to be called for. It came into its own at the end of the First World War and was partly prompted by the war's shattering experience. Writers who had taken part in the war, and had in one way or the other survived it, came home with a renewed awareness of man's brutality and of the cold, technical character of modern civilization. Many soldiers had become cynics, and the spread of this cynicism explained the success of Erich Maria Remarque's novel *Im Westen nichts Neues* ("All Quiet on the Western Front," 1929), an otherwise poorly written piece of work. A return to the simple faith of the fathers was attempted by others, and led to a wave of patriotic and denominational fiction which despite its sincerity was mostly second-rate. The best representatives of the war generation were groping for a new faith, and felt that it had to begin with a reappraisal of man's biological inheritance as a part of his total understanding of himself. This road led either to a new biological mysticism or to a new religiosity that often professed to be Christian, but was actually a pagan pantheism employing Christian language. Both attitudes were also offered as an answer to the quest of the expressionists, which in the eyes of many contemporaries had yielded no tangible results.

The new biological mysticism was the more radical of the solutions

The Dissociative and Surrealistic Style

offered, and was forced upon wider public attention through the propagandist efforts of the National Socialists. The writers riding this wave were less naïve and less romantic, and openly avowed a modern scientific positivism based on a biological view of life. Their attitude had been heralded by a whole century of scientific research, and could have passed as one of the conclusions still open to modern man. Yet unfortunately many of the new writers did not listen to true science, but to a popularized and vulgarized pseudo-science. The official Nazi ideology prescribed in Alfred Rosenberg's *Mythus des 20. Jahrhunderts* ("The Myth of the Twentieth Century," 1930) can only be characterized as half-baked, if not paranoiac. International spiritual crosscurrents were overlooked or repudiated. Physical heredity and geographical surroundings, *Blut und Boden* ("blood and soil"), sufficed to explain man. Of the constituent elements of German culture, the Nazi propagandists and journalists acknowledged only the primitive Germanic element, and even that in a highly arbitrary interpretation. Incorrectly, all Teutons were described as pure Nordics, blond and blue-eyed, a myth conveniently derived from Nietzsche's aphorisms, and the Jewish citizens of German culture were branded as parasites and dangerous genetic influences; in actual life the Nazis boycotted and ostracized them, deprived them of their rights, herded them into ghettos and concentration camps, and finally gassed and burned them in a ruthless plan of liquidation. But many modern writers of so-called "Nordic" parentage also were rejected as *entartet* (degenerate) and barred from writing. This new paganism was the very opposite of classical Humanism or Christian otherworldliness; all of Nietzsche's invocations against the Christian religion were gleefully repeated and broadcast.

The most gifted among the neopagan writers was the novelist Erwin Guido Kolbenheyer (born in 1878), who grew up amidst the national rivalries disrupting the old Austro-Hungarian Empire and therefore developed an aggressive nationalistic complex. He finally found confirmation in an uncompromising biological philosophy, which he expounded in a lengthy treatise. He also propagandized it in stage plays such as *Heroische Leidenschaften* ("Heroic Passions," 1928), *Das Gesetz in Dir* ("The Law Within," 1931), or *Die Brücke* ("The Bridge," 1929), which occasionally excelled in individual characterizations but suffered from a surfeit of abstruse philosophy. More popular were Kolbenheyer's novels, three of which were devoted to the early Renaissance scientist Paracelsus, namely *Die Kindheit des Paracelsus* ("Paracelsus' Childhood," 1917), *Das Gestirn des Paracelsus* ("Paracelsus' Star of Destiny," 1921), and *Das dritte Reich des Paracelsus* ("The Third Reich of Paracelsus," 1925). Here Kolbenheyer, by means of a tour de force, tried to revive the antiquated German dialect of sixteenth-century Switzerland and to interpret Paracelsus as the unsullied Germanic antipode to a Martin Luther tainted by Christianity. These once best-selling novels have now become a curiosity.

Another example of a gifted storyteller misguided by an arrogant nationalistic philosophy was Hans Grimm (born in 1875), whose novel *Volk ohne Raum* ("A Nation without Space," 1925) provided National Socialism with one of its catch phrases. Grimm's deep-seated German resentment was kindled by his personal experiences in the former German colonies and his contacts with English nationals. Grimm angrily repudiated Christian humility as a regrettable weakness of the *deutsche Michel* ("German Mike," a symbol for political insipidity).

The many minor fictioneers of National Socialism have now been forgotten along with its lyrical and dramatic propagandists. But it would be wrong to assume that a biologically oriented writing always led to an alliance with the totalitarian political forces. Some writers of stature such as Ina Seidel and Hans Carossa remained aloof from the political carnival; others, like Ernst Wiechert, openly clashed with the regime.

Ina Seidel (born in 1885) has become the most prominent woman writer recognizing man's determination by his biological inheritance. Writing not from theory but from personal experience, she delineated man's double indebtedness to his past in her historical novel, *Das Labyrinth* (1922). He was determined by male aggressiveness and rationality as well as female emotionality and sensitivity, and found it hard to steer a safe middle course of his own. Another historical novel by Ina Seidel was *Das Wunschkind* ("The Wish Child," 1930), which gave powerful expression to woman's biological urge to bear children; the novel gained an understandable popularity in an age when the consequences of the First World War deprived so many German women of the possibility of following their natural instincts. Ina Seidel was married to a Protestant clergyman, her cousin Heinrich Seidel, who was no mean writer himself, and she was deeply rooted in the German cultural tradition; her husband's father had been a likable nineteenth-century humorist. Her interest in the inherited religion was therefore sincere and natural. But the Christian religion with her assumed a rather unorthodox character. In her warmhearted poems Ina Seidel attributed a soul to plants and animals as well as to men, and her God has revealed Himself not only to Christians:

[309

The Dissociative and Surrealistic Style

Ewige Bramahnen ruf ich,
Und mit meinem Hauch
Alle deine Völker schuf ich—
Die Chinesen auch.

*

Eternal Brahmans I am calling.
I have with My breath
Created all your nations—
Including the Chinese.

In a most recent novel, *Das unverwesliche Erbe* ("The Everlasting Inheritance," 1954), Ina Seidel has probed into the problem of mixed marriages and has reviewed the Catholic point of view with an insight rare among Protestant writers. She was able to do this because in the last analysis her problem was not denominational at all. She probed into the part played by inherited attitudes and local surroundings in seemingly spiritual decisions, and so this novel was another attempt at arriving at a restatement of religion from a scientific determinism. Its style was rather careless.

The East Prussian Ernst Wiechert (1887–1950) also sought religion through a union with nature. The seriousness of his quest brought him three and a half months' imprisonment in a Nazi concentration camp, and constant Gestapo supervision afterwards. Wiechert was no political activist, yet he fearlessly kept his belief in the redeeming power of elemental love and he spoke out (until silenced) for mercy, justice, and purity of heart. In the few years of publication that remained to him after 1945 he testified to the fact that a simple, religious spirit had not died out in Germany, and spoke out for many who had likewise affirmed their Protestant faith in the face of the pagan opposition. Unfortunately there was little new or original in Wiechert's symbols, which matched the sincerity of his beliefs, and his message sounded conventional and unconvincing to German youth. As Wiechert's best stories one may mention: *Die Magd des Jürgen Doscocil* ("The Girl and the Ferryman," 1932), *Die Majorin* ("The Baroness," 1934), *Hirtennovelle* ("The Herdsman's Tale," 1935), *Die Mutter* ("The Mother," 1950). He was less felicitous in his symbolic plays and in his rather conventional lyric poetry.

The German Catholic Church of course stood in unconditional opposition to the Nazi regime. Truly Catholic writing could never subscribe to a frankly pagan point of view. Yet the Catholic Church has always been chary of intellectualism, and has usually adopted a tolerant attitude toward local and traditional customs. In addition some of its forms, e.g., the faith of St. Francis, have had the superficial (though not the actual) look of pantheism. It is therefore not astonishing that a sizable contingent of the new regionalists has been Catholic. Hermann Stehr, who was mentioned in the previous section, came of a Catholic family, and Enrica von Handel-Mazzetti and Karl Schönherr have also already been mentioned. Neither Stehr nor Schönherr, however, wholly agreed with the dogma of the Church.

A special form of regional literature was represented by the auto-biographical books of the sensitive Bavarian physician Hans Carossa (1878–1956). In an unhurried style and in translucent images he unrolled the cultural landscape of his youth and laid bare its spiritual fibers. He was able to make real moral decisions even in war (*Rumänisches Tagebuch*, "Rumanian Diary," 1924), and in the searching story *Der Arzt Gion* ("Doctor Gion," 1933) he described the heroism of an unwed mother who for the sake of her unborn baby was willing to face death in childbed. Carossa was also a lyric poet who could radiantly restate a Goethean reverence for life. The rise of National Socialism was deeply abhorrent to him.

Among Austrian regionalists Joseph Roth (1894–1939) takes a similar place to that of Hans Carossa. In 1933 Roth emigrated, and six years later died in a Paris hospital for the poor. He was a brave soldier of the First World War, and in his later novels glorified the patriarchal universality of the old Danube monarchy, for which he had fought, in novels like *Radetzkymarsch* ("Radetzky March," 1933) or *Die Kapuzinergruft* ("The Capuchin Tombs," 1938). Roth's heroes often appear as Austrian Don Quixotes who in an unheroic period represent a timeless ideal of natural growth, independently acquired virtue and conscious morality. The best form for this ideal may well be legendary or parabolic, and Roth has handled it expertly in *Die Flucht ohne Ende* ("The Endless Flight"), *Hiob* ("Job"), and *Die Legende vom Heiligen Trinker* ("The Legend of the Holy Drunkard").

The second wave of regionalist literature also reached the German stage. During the Nazi regime the plays of Kolbenheyer and of *Heimatkunst* authors were revived, and numerous young dramatists tried to preach the racial and historical doctrines of Hitlerism through open-air performances in garden theaters and market places as well as through professional plays in the legitimate theater. Later, these talents were as quickly forgotten as they were catapulted into fame. The only region-alist dramatist of stature had to flee the German Reich, to which he returned after the Second World War and has proved just as successful as before. This dramatist is Carl Zuckmayer (born in 1896). Zuck-mayer's fame dates from his earthy comedy *Der fröhliche Weinberg* ("The Merry Vineyard," 1925), an expression of his faith in the healing powers of elemental life. He clung to it even in the dark years of the Hitler terror, during which he wrote the exhilarating story *Der Seelen-bräu* ("The Jovial Priest," 1945). It certainly was not a naïve faith, for Zuckmayer early attacked the artificial discipline of German militarism, which threatened to stifle the elemental harmony of natural life. *Der Hauptmann von Köpenick* ("The Captain of Koepenick," 1931) was a bitter dramatic satire on militarism, and expressed the writer's un-compromising pacifism. As a consequence he had to emigrate to America, where he continued his dramatic and narrative efforts. He portrayed the inner corruption of National Socialism in the widely acclaimed play *Des Teufels General* ("The Devil's General," 1946). After his return to Germany, Zuckmayer, in *Der Gesang in Feuerofen* ("The Hymn in the Fiery Furnace," 1950), treated a theme from the French Resistance movement in poignant scenes. And in his recent drama *Das kalte Licht* ("The Cold Light," 1955) he tackled moral problems of the atomic age by a recourse to the story of the atomic spy Klaus Fuchs. Among present-day German dramatists Zuckmayer is perhaps the most popular. Part of his fame undoubtedly derives from the fact that he has utilized the dramatic form created by young Gerhart Hauptmann; he was even chosen to complete one of the Silesian's poetic drafts.

In the last analysis, all the regional literature was an attempt to overcome the breakdown of middle-class values through a recourse to the elemental basis of German culture. This attempt, however, seldom led to the creation of new forms of expression, and must therefore be interpreted as a "holding action." The more radical young writers also tried to overcome the cultural gap by the creation of new forms, and therefore turned away from mere regionalism.

The Struggle for Continuity

W HEN in 1945 the literary censorship of the Nazis ended, the
old problems once more went begging for a solution. The enforced rule of a biological ideology had failed, and the field was again
open to different answers to the threatening cultural nihilism. These
answers could be aesthetic, political, or religious, and were already indicated in the writings of some of the early expressionists. They were
further developed by the opponents of the Nazi regime and by those
of the many refugees from that regime whose writing had survived the
shock of emigration.

The earliest aesthetic answer to the modern dilemma was given by the
Austrian poet Rainer Maria Rilke. He was born in Prague in 1875 and
did not belong to the expressionist generation proper; his fellow countryman, Kafka, was eight years younger. Yet Rilke's delicate physique
made him particularly sensitive to the currents of the time, and like
many of the expressionists he grew up in a family situation with which
he could not identify himself. Thus he early experienced the lonely
anxiety of the moderns; his fate he once described as no personal fate
at all (*Mein Schicksal ist kein Schicksal zu haben*). He early withdrew
from the political and social events of his time, and concentrated on
listening only to his inner voice. He first expressed himself in the style
of conventional romanticism, but soon rejected it as too subjective.
Then he became acquainted with the impressionist style of the Danish
poet Jens Peter Jacobsen, which came close to imagism. Rilke learned
from him to renounce his singularity. He sought further confirmation
on a trip to Russia in 1899–1900, where he went to submerge himself
in endless landscape and a brotherly human community. The result
was *Das Stundenbuch* ("The Book of Hours," 1899–1903), in which
Rilke conjured up the monkish spirit of the Eastern and Western
Churches, and laid down in haunting verses his longing for present-day
transcendental confirmation; however, he arrived at no lasting security,
and did not achieve a form to his satisfaction.

During the next few years Rilke earnestly sought to perfect his style.
Since he did not want to relapse into his early romantic sentimentality
and musicality, he turned to the fine arts and became secretary to the

The Dissociative and Surrealistic Style

French sculptor Rodin. From him Rilke learned to avoid the expression of fleeting moods in favor of a rendering of the lasting substance of things. Poems were no longer emotions, they resulted from lifelong experiences and were to be compressed into self-contained images. The successful image represented the poet's conquest of the dichotomy between his self and the objective world. Imagism seemed the answer to loneliness. Much later Rilke would become the translator of Maurice de Guérin, Gide, and Valéry.

In Rilke's *Neue Gedichte* ("New Poems," 1903–1908) was displayed the poet's ripe mastery of the objective form, his ability to find the fitting word and the effortless rhyme. But at the same time the imagism of these lyrics was rarely pure and strict, and was mostly translucent. A poor blind man could become the center of the cosmos; an imprisoned panther in the zoological garden a symbol for the chilly loneliness of modern solipsism. Rilke's poetry achieved a melodious balance between Russian diffuseness and Latin statuesqueness, and his form could be described as "open" imagism. The firmly grasped object dissolves in front of our eyes; in contrast to C. F. Meyer's satisfaction with the plastic present, Rilke opens it up to the ever-flowing streams of a vague spirituality.

Rilke confessed to his quest for "belonging" in *Die Aufzeichnungen des Malte Laurids Brigge* ("The Notebook of Malte Laurids Brigge," 1904–1910); but unlike his hero the poet did not break down in the effort. After a long wait came the personal certainty expressed in *Duineser Elegien* ("Duino Elegies") and *Sonette an Orpheus* ("Sonnets to Orpheus"). Both were completed in Muzot Castle in Switzerland in 1922. Four years later the solitary poet died.

The *Duineser Elegien* were started at Duino Castle in Dalmatia in 1912. Their writing was interrupted by the First World War, which to a poet of Rilke's delicate sensitivity revealed poignantly the desolation of modern culture. He saw the necessity of finally deserting a style that had previously attempted to find satisfaction in the retinal image. These elegies desperately try to conquer reality and to approach the transcendental. They begin with a moving lament for man's lonely insufficiency, which the poet seeks to overcome by communicating with his angels. But neither the exuberance of love, nor heroic sacrifice, nor immersion in workaday life solace the poet, and he finally resigns himself to the existence into which he has been hurled. He will always be the spectator of a play of which the ultimate meaning is to him unknown:

314]

The Struggle for Continuity

Zuschauer, immer, überall,
Dem allen zugewandt und nie hinaus.

*

Spectator everywhere and always,
Open to all these things, and never within.

The poet's task is conceived of as expressing what he sees and feels,
and hymning the world to the hypostasized angel, the mystique of
poetry finding its meaning in its interpretation of the world in aesthetic
visions overcoming man's isolation:

Erde! . . .
Was, wenn Verwandlung nicht, ist dein drängender Auftrag?

*

Earth! . . .
If not transformation, what else is your urgent commission?

The vers libre of the Elegies becomes ever more dithyrambic. The
desperation of loneliness yields to jubilation over the multiplicity of existence, and the language therefore can become ambivalent and full of
mutually dissolving contrasts.

Praise itself was expressed in the *Sonette an Orpheus*. In these shorter
poems, Rilke communicated a deeply religious feeling of continuously
transmuted reality. Life is continually changed by ever-present death,
but both together constitute existence. Affirming everything in life is
tantamount to affirming everything in death. This is not at all Christian
transcendence, although Rilke has not entirely given up hope of a
"lifting of the curtain" of actuality. His attitude is nearly, yet not quite,
agnostic. Instead of the Christian God one is reminded of Dionysos
or Shiva in Rilke's continuous paean of praise. It encompasses existence
as a whole with its flowers and springs, its breathing and dancing, but
also its continuous passing and dying, its inconstancy and its change.
Rilke's images are no longer self-contained, and his rhythms are multifarious; the individual verses of his unconventional sonnets are closely
interwoven by enjambement, repetition, alliteration, and assonance. He
presents no chiseled sonnets in the conventional sense, but uses an
easy, almost casual rhyme that never burdens the poems' thought; Rilke
prefers everyday words for his rhymes, and uses them as convenient
accents and rivets rather than startling drum beats.

On the whole Rilke's path beyond modern anxiety might be described as neopagan aestheticism. He has succeeded in fusing impressionism with a somewhat romantic spirituality. He has also succeeded in imbuing a Western workaday ethos with Eastern mysticism. But his borrowing of Christian images has confused the issue; as a metaphysical system Rilke's thought is of dubious validity and does not bear logical scrutiny; he is less lucid than Hölderlin, by whose form he was influenced and to whom he has been compared. Some of Rilke's verses are little more than harsh rhetoric, fulsome bombast, or thinly disguised prose. Lastly, he too was a seeker rather than an achiever, a modern poet waiting for God, yet not seeing Him; by his own confession he was praising the world not to God, but to his angel.

A similar flight into pagan aestheticism and Pandean mysticism was undertaken by Wilhelm Lehmann (born in 1882), the author of *Entzückter Staub* ("Enchanted Dust," 1946) and *Der grüne Gott* ("The Verdant God," 1948). To him the historic life that fluctuates in the city is essentially without meaning, while nature in her noon hour holds the essence of life. Man can approach it only by denuding himself of his ego and then experiencing the omnipresence of pagan myth. Lehmann's style can be described as a dithyrambic prose.

Radically different was the aesthetic solution proferred by the mature Gottfried Benn. He expanded his early clinical nihilism into a universal nihilism. All past ideas without exception for him were agonies, all human history was wholly devoid of meaning. Modern historical, psychological, and physical science had finally destroyed the myth of an anthropocentric universe and presaged an end of the *hominine* age:

> *Verlorenes Ich, zersprengt von Stratosphären,*
> *Opfer des Ion—: Gamma-Strahlen-Lamm—,*
> *Teilchen und Feld—: Unendlichkeitschimären*
> *Auf deinem grauen Stein von Notre-Dame.*
> *Die Tage gehn dir ohne Nacht und Morgen,*
> *Die Welt als Flucht.*
> *Bedrohend das Unendliche verborgen—*
> *Die Jahre halten ohne Schnee und Frucht*

*

> *Ego quite lost, by stratospheres exploded,*
> *The ion's victim: lamb of gamma rays—*
> *Part, also field, by chimeras of infinity goaded,*
> *On your gray parapet of Notre-Dame.*

The Struggle for Continuity

The days without nighttime and morn are sliding,
The years bereft of fruit and of the snow's white,
The dangerous infinity in hiding—
The world as flight.

Man might long romantically to revert to the shapeless state of the amoeba; "even the head of a dragonfly or the wing of a sea gull would be too far advanced and subject to too much suffering." But since that longing could not be fulfilled, man had to be satisfied with the expression of his disillusionment. Benn wanted to shape his poems into self-contained artifacts and thus sought an essentially aesthetic solution. He hunted for an "absolute" form, i.e., not logically construed prose (cf. *Gehirne*, "Cerebrums," 1916), that sometimes came close to incoherence. He fought to find an "absolute" verse of skillfully manipulated words. In his best verse Benn expressed in German the same fascination with chaotic evil that haunted the poems of Baudelaire. In his disparagement of reality he sometimes came close to the noncommittal imagism of Mallarmé.

However, Mallarmé at heart was a Platonist, and one must not forget that through the ages nihilism has often been the starting point for conclusions quite different from Benn's. From a nihilistic basis great thinkers such as Tertullian or Pascal arrived finally at a religious faith. Among the early lyricists of expressionism the same path was trodden by Christian Morgenstern, who pointed out the emptiness of imagism and "absolute" poetry, and unfortunately became famous only as a literary clown. His satirical verses (*Galgenlieder*, "Gallows Songs," 1905; *Palmström*, 1910, etc.) were originally conceived as a take-off on solipsistic imagism and subjectivist eccentricity. But unintentionally this nonsense poetry portrayed a haunting world of ghostlike artifacts and robotlike persons—e.g., *Der Schaukelstuhl auf der verlassenen Terrasse* ("The Rocking-Chair on the Deserted Terrace"):

> "*Ich bin ein einsamer Schaukelstuhl*
> *Und wackel im Winde, im Winde.*
> *Auf der Terrasse, da ist es kuhl,*
> *Und ich wackel im Winde, im Winde.*
>   *Und ich wackel und nackel den ganzen Tag,*
> *Und es nackelt und rackelt die Linde.*
> *Wer weiss, was sonst wohl noch wackeln mag*
> *Im Winde, im Winde, im Winde!*"

*

The Dissociative and Surrealistic Style

"I am a lonely rocking-chair
And in the wind I am rocking.
Cool is the draft of the terrace air,
And in the wind I am rocking.
* I am rocking and knocking the whole day long,*
And the lime branches also are knocking.
Who knows what else may be joining the song
Of rocking and ducking and knocking!"

In spite of its grotesqueness such poetry was an adequate expression for an age that was listening to the disembodied voices of the phonograph and the radio, and was viewing the mute shadow world of the first films. The later talkies and television created a fuller illusion—which nevertheless remained an illusion. And the daily papers frequently became so saturated with sensationalism and commercialism, with denominational and political propaganda, that they too replaced reality by a world of phantoms and hallucinations. Modern man's life is based to a great extent on secondhand experience, and his immediate contact with the objects of his thinking has become rather tenuous. Morgenstern pointed this out in his humorous manner, and his fame was therefore well deserved. But few of his readers guessed the underlying seriousness which drove him to seek solace in Rudolf Steiner's Anthroposophy, a peculiar substitute religion derived from Christian as well as Hindu concepts.

Of the dramatists, Gerhart Hauptmann in his old age also arrived at a religious conception. He had always delineated the loneliness of the modern individual, yet at the beginning of the First World War he had envisioned a possible solution to the problem through the healing powers of elemental nature. However, that belief was shattered through the ravages of the war and its aftermath. When finally Hitler's storm-troopers unleashed all the primitive forces of destruction, Hauptmann gave up the last of his optimism. Although the new regime dared not silence him completely, it treated him with suspicion and occasional malice. Hauptmann might have emigrated, but he felt too old to start anew, and thus he remained in Germany and continued writing under a cloud.

Long before the second war the poet portrayed his weariness of Western civilization. In one of his last realistic plays he sketched the moral decay of the German bourgeoisie by an adaptation of the *Lear* theme; it bore the revealing title *Vor Sonnenuntergang* ("Before Sundown," 1932). Hauptmann's other plays published in the twenties and thirties presented an increasing number of themes of horrible cruelty, of shameless incest, of beastly murder preceded by rape. Criminals and harlots could be found in his later narratives. Only in appearance was the story *Das Meerwunder* ("The Sea Monster," 1934) innocuous. It used the romantic symbol of a mermaid married to a sailor to describe man's insoluble existential plight. He is a prey of the elements, yet lacks their innocence; the mermaid of the story shudderingly cries out: *Ich will kein Mensch sein* ("I do not want to be human"). Man always betrays the moral principles which alone make life bearable.

The Sea Monster is set in the same surrealistic world as the fantastic play *Und Pippa tanzt* ("And Pippa Dances," 1906). Surrealism increased in Hauptmann's works and reached astonishing strength in the tragedy *Die schwarze Maske* ("The Black Mask," 1929) and the epic hallucinations of *Der grosse Traum* ("The Grand Dream," 1942). Finally, however, Hauptmann realized that the tragic theme of man's failure required a more universal and more stylized representation. Deeply suffering from the fearful Second World War, the aged poet consummated his long and fitful career by his supreme achievement, *Die Atridentetralogie* ("The Tetralogy of the Atrids," 1941–1948). It treated the same theme that Goethe had treated in his *Iphigenie auf Tauris*, but in a new spirit. Where the Weimar poet was imbued with confidence in man's ability to master the elemental forces, Hauptmann saw man's struggle for the good as a tragic series of defeats. The curse leveled upon the house of Atreus again and again rears its ugly head. Iphigenia's sacrifice at the hands of her father Agamemnon is indeed prevented by the gods; yet other divine powers take her to Tauris, where she is not such a peaceful influence as in Goethe's play, for in obedience to black Hecate, Queen of Hell, she commits human sacrifice. When she is rescued by Orestes and returns to the holy precincts of Delphi, she is unable to resume a normal human existence, and throws herself into the abyss in voluntary expiation for her crimes. But her crimes have been ordained by divine powers, and the dichotomy in the human breast in the last analysis reflects a conflict among the gods.

This outcome should not be described as purely nihilistic, for Hauptmann's nihilism is a cathartic nihilism. The Delphic priests to whom Iphigenia's suicide is reported stand overawed in the presence of transcendental powers, and admonish the audience to revere what they cannot fully understand. Man's struggle for good is to go on, even though to human eyes it may appear futile.

The Dissociative and Surrealistic Style

Hauptmann's last plays revive the Humanist as well as Christian belief in the sacredness of individual existence, and combine it with the modern awareness of the cruel elemental forces preventing its realization. They express this view in rich blank verse developing clear action unfolding against a Greek background fully in keeping with modern scholarship. These plays can be realistic and eerily mystic at the same time, for the ancient Greeks believed in magic powers; they were not enlightened Europeans of the eighteenth century. It reveals Hauptmann's conservatism that he did not yield entirely to surrealism, but subsumed it as but another element of his style.

The same can be said of two great novelists who were forced by the events of the time to revise their previous positions. The older of them was Thomas Mann. When in 1933 he left Germany and emigrated first to Switzerland and later to California, his hopes for a Humanist and democratic Germany had become exceedingly dim. Political action seemed to him of more immediate importance than his literary work alone; Mann shed his conservatism and threw himself into the fray. To be sure, he was not always a wise statesman and should be judged primarily on the strength of his poetic work. But that poetic work too now visualized a political solution to the modern problem. Man as a social developer is the central theme of the great novelistic tetralogy *Joseph und seine Brüder* ("Joseph and His Brothers," 1933–1942). Here Mann revives the immortal stories of the Old Testament by a judicious use of modern Egyptological research. Yet interesting though these stories be by themselves, Mann has also turned them into symbols of man's everlasting struggles. When Joseph resists the wiles of the Egyptian woman, he also resists the irrational forces of night and death; and when he becomes the provider for a people suffering the whim of an untamed river, Joseph also triumphs over a religion that has deified it. Joseph becomes the right hand of Akhenaten, the Pharaoh who sought to replace the people's reverence for the strength of wild black steers by the worship of light and beauty. Joseph in all his sober rationalism is not unmindful of chthonic forces; but he conquers them, and they lend power and depth to his benevolent serenity. In the end he becomes an object of adoration to the Egyptians; he achieves reconciliation with his brothers; and he gives shelter and refuge to the budding nation they represent.

Mann's ideal in *Joseph* approached the all-embracing human ideal of German classicism. It is surely no accident that his style has become clear and restrained. His images are strong and compelling, the words simple and direct, the syntactical structure light and lucid. The Joseph story as a whole in its strong integration is perhaps Mann's greatest achievement, although the turbulent age prevented most contemporaries from coming to grips with his vision. Of his German readers, many could follow him only when he interpreted German and European cultural values in the form of essays. Here he revived the art of expository prose writing and continued the great tradition of Lessing and Goethe, of Schopenhauer and Nietzsche.

During and after the *Joseph* period Mann wrote other stories and novels, but they are either minor works or seem to be lacking in ultimate artistic perfection. It is an unanswered question whether *Doktor Faustus* (1947) will survive the controversies it has engendered. Mann wrote this novel at the end of the Second World War, when the destructive forces of racism and primitivism were gaining the upper hand over German culture. In the life of the composer Adrian Leverkühn he traced the demonic side of German culture, yet not as a cool critic but as one on intimate terms with it. Leverkühn's life significantly reminds one of Nietzsche's and of Hugo Wolf's, and it expresses all Mann's youthful infatuation with the elemental and irrational forces of music. The recent epoch of German culture is seen as a league with the Devil whom Adrian must conjure up for the sake of his self-expression. Self-sufficient aestheticism leads to barbarism and finally evolves into an agony of hopeless despair. If there is any redeeming feature in the dark tapestry, it is the deep humility and pity with which Adrian's friend Serenus Zeitblom sets down the chronicle of his hero's life; he voices a hope against hope.

Doktor Faustus is perhaps too personal in its approach to rank with *Der Zauberberg*, with which it shares its theme. The disease of technological civilization has spread throughout Europe, and *Doktor Faustus* suffers from a certain German myopia. The turbulent war currents precluded a poetic detachment. Almost too many personal experiences and literary reminiscenes have contributed to the web of this novel, with the romantic and the Russian strands predominating. In a highly original fashion the Faust legend has been fused with Dostoevski's immortal theme of Ivan and the Devil in *The Brothers Karamazov*. The political discussions and the delineations of musical theory make unusual demands on the reader's attention, but they belong to the main theme, just as the pedagogic and economic discussions belong to Goethe's *Wanderjahre*. At the highest point of the novel Mann's style has approached the expressionist style of despairing groans and exultant cries. And the use of the Devil figure as such is indication enough that Mann's style has now veered in the direction of surrealistic transcendence. In stories like *Der Erwählte* ("The Holy Sinner," 1951) and *Die vertauschten Köpfe* ("The Transposed Heads," 1940) Mann had gone even farther in the same direction.

Among the other works written during Mann's later years one might single out *Mario und der Zauberer* ("Mario and the Magician," 1929), a *novella* about Italian Fascism, *Lotte in Weimar* ("The Beloved Returns," 1939), a biographical novel about Goethe, and *Bekenntnisse des Hochstaplers Felix Krull* ("Confessions of Felix Krull, Confidence Man"), an unfinished romance of roguery. The novelist remained active until the last as a writer of startling stories and masterly essays and lectures; the fine lecture on Schiller was delivered shortly before Mann's death in 1955.

While Mann overcame modern nihilism by political activity, the other great prose writer of the period achieved a new religious solution. Hermann Hesse was born in Swabia in 1877, and in his early romantic stories followed the pattern of Storm and Keller. Yet he was a romantic rebel rather than a romantic escapist. His was a family of Protestant missionaries, and young Hesse was deeply aware of the contrast between the spirit of Christianity and the prevailing morality. He rebelled against the conventional, authoritarian school, and for a while tried his hand at watchmaking and at selling books. Finally he took to writing, and generally portrayed wanderers and adventurers who were looking for new ways of life. Such ways had become needful not only because of the breakdown of Christian morality, but also because a global consciousness had followed the modern expansion of world trade and world travel. In his parental home Hesse met Hindus and Hindu missonaries, he became acquainted with oriental languages and engrossed in oriental literatures; as a young man he himself took a trip to India. Additional inspiration came from Nietzsche, whose writings encouraged Hesse to find his own individual solution. Hesse rejected European materialism and power politics, and became a confirmed pacifist. The outbreak of the First World War substantiated his worst presentiments, and found him in Switzerland as a German exile who simply refused to join the chauvinistic chorus of the time. The establishment of Hitler's Third Reich and the Second World War confirmed Hesse's stand.

Even before the end of the First World War the poet published the story *Demian* (1917), his first venture in a symbolic style and his avowed break with conventional morality and religion. A few years later the uncompromising individualist Emil Sinclair, the hero of *Demian*, had become a dangerous, criminal adventurer whom Hesse described as a *Steppenwolf*, a "prairie wolf," in the story of that title (1927). Yet the romanticist Hesse also knew that the individual is deeply rooted in his soil, both in a physical as well as a spiritual sense, and that any rebellion is fruitless so long as it merely destroys outmoded customs and institutions, and does not end in the establishment of new values. To his friend Emil Sinclair, Demian held up the mother image, the archetypal symbol of the ever-creative forces of life; the savage face of the *Steppenwolf* was but one of the faces of the lawless individualist Harry Haller (a mask for Hermann Hesse whose names start with the same initials). Thus the poet was impelled to seek a way out of self-centered individualism, and to find some catalyst for the conflicting forces of life. The hero of *Siddhartha* (1922) achieves some kind of equilibrium between a life of activity and a life of Buddhistic contemplation. In *Narziss und Goldmund* ("Death and the Lover," 1930) Hesse presented parallel biographies of a contemplative spiritualist and a widely active and creative Don Juan; yet in the end both heroes discover their mutual need for each other. The contemplative Narziss cannot do without the man of action, and the roving Goldmund needs spiritual guidance. Again, in the surrealistic tale *Die Morgenlandfahrt* ("The Journey to the East," 1932), the spiritualist is saved from ivory-tower seclusion by the lay brother who merely loves and serves.

The very titles of Hesse's later stories suggest that they have little in common with the Swabian regionalism and impressionism of his early narratives. Some of them take place in medieval surroundings or in an Indian locale, but of an almost imaginary character; it was no accident that Hesse wrote numerous delightful fairy tales and enjoyed plays of fancy in words as well as colors. *Demian* and more decidedly *Der Steppenwolf* and *Die Morgenlandfahrt* so twisted and dislocated reality that it became transcendent and, in the ordinary sense, unreal. Surrealism is therefore the proper word for the style of these stories, and it is also the word for the style of Hesse's crowning achievement, the novel *Das Glasperlenspiel* ("Magister Ludi," 1943). In all these stories the plots are incidental to the development of the lyrical and musical theme of the individual's finding its new path out of present-day chaos; the characterizations become complex and dissociative to bring out the richness and depth of the spiritual landscape; and ordinary everyday life is transmuted into symbolic density or is fused with symbols unpredictably crisscrossing it.

Das Glasperlenspiel might be described as Hesse's final answer to the problems of human civilization in its combination of both Eastern and Western ways of life. The hero, to whom the continuation of human culture is entrusted, bears the symbolic name of *Knecht*, servant. The story takes place in a distant but not entirely remote European future. Knecht grows up to become the director of an educational hierarchy of a monkish and ascetic character. The educators are given to contemplation in the Asiatic tradition and live separated from the rest of the world, yet at the same time are actively responsible for the upholding and developing of the cultural tradition in the sense of occidental Christianity.

The same fusion of occidental and oriental elements is symbolized by the *Glasperlenspiel* (literally "game with glass pearls"), an intellectual and likewise artistic exercise which finds and establishes contrapuntal contacts between all the values produced by different ages and different human cultures. In this way a place is found for the rich possibilities of modern individual expression; at the same time some common denominator of a religious nature is found in the public festive display of the *Glasperlenspiel*. The danger of such spiritual exercises is of course that the players lose themselves in mere playfulness and forget that the function of their game is the recognition of the all-pervading spirit of God. The practical and material side of life is represented by Knecht's friend Plinio Designori, a businessman, and by a Franciscan friar who is a historian and at the same time a resourceful diplomat of the Catholic Church. Knecht initially overcomes their opposition and criticism by accepting them also as constituent parts of the world. Yet he continues in doubt and finally renounces the rarefied air of an esoteric community in order to engage himself once more in the more practical side of life. Aesthetic contemplation becomes one-sided idolatry if it does not find the way to practical application. Knecht resigns from his post as "Magister Ludi" and dedicates himself to the education of Designori's son, a single charge both difficult and promising. In supreme dedication to his task Knecht sacrifices his life. But the sacrifice will make his pupil change, and will thus transmit Knecht's message to future generations.

Here Hesse has given poetic form to a new religious awareness that combines true humility with a dedication to the human individual. It is no longer the traditional religion of the Christian churches, nor the traditional aloofness of ordinary Buddhism. It is a new human religion, and supersedes any one-sided approach. Hesse stands at the threshold of a new chapter of German literature, one that again will be European in the same sense in which the German literature of the Middle Ages was such a chapter. The lover of European literature will not find it hard to discover certain similarities between Hesse's writings and those of his contemporaries André Gide and Romain Rolland. He can also point to the fact that like Thomas Mann and Gerhart Hauptmann, Hesse has found the European recognition of a Nobel Prize in literature, the same recognition that was awarded to Gide and Rolland.

The Heirs of the Tradition

THE writers treated in the last section lived and wrote in solitude as far as most of their German contemporaries were concerned. The later works of both Rilke and Hauptmann never became popular, and the later novels of Thomas Mann and Hermann Hesse were kept from the German public by ruthless Nazi censorship, which allowed only the representatives of blood-and-soil literature to function without molestation.

The Fascist tyranny resulted in a total disintegration of national life. The German inhabitants of the eastern provinces, e.g., Prussia and Silesia, were expelled from their homelands, and their independent regional literature ceased. In central Germany there arose under Russian sponsorship the so-called "German Democratic Republic" which decreed a literature of "Socialist Realism." This term is a misnomer because the literature of the German satellite state does not represent reality at all, but reality as wishfully seen through the eyes of the Communist party. It distorts the truth in an artificial attempt at political optimism. Its representatives cannot even be compared to the older workingmen poets, who after 1910 began to create independent poetry out of the depth of their proletarian existence; Gerrit Engelke, Heinrich Lersch, and Max Barthel were the most prominent of them. The so-called proletarian writers of the new "German Democratic Republic" are not allowed such spontaneity. They must not write about individuals, but about types; not about private experiences, but about political and technical programs. The heroes of communist dramas and stories are workers of the steel mills and agricultural combines, of the transportation and health services, and they always behave according to the latest slogans of the party. The lyrical pieces are better called propaganda songs spurring the people on to more work in the interest of the anonymous communist state. There is little room for artistic initiative, and the lifeless monotony of this so-called "socialist" literature is rarely relieved by a genuine enthusiasm. It is revealing that not one of the "grand old men" of German communism has produced a major work under the new regime. Arnold Zweig as well as Anna Seghers (*Das siebte Kreuz,* "The Seventh Cross," 1941) and Johannes R. Becher (1891–1958) wrote their best pieces before the foundation of the German Democratic Republic, and Bert Brecht finally was criticized by the party critics. The German communist literature of today is merely another artificial substitute for a genuine solution of the problems of modern living.

If the German youth of Mecklenburg, Thuringia, and Saxony could write without political interference, it probably would voice feelings similar to the German youth of the Rhineland or Swabia. For all the young Germans of today grew up in a decade of disasters, in a barbarous, catch-as-catch-can world. Brutal and sly terror and resistance, total war and total defeat, flight and dispossession molded the face of the generation that emerged in 1945. Even after the war they were not offered the hope of a brave new world, but rather a questionable survival in a Western culture doubtful of its own values and its ability to defend them, a technological world of "goods" that waited to be consumed. The disintegration of traditional concepts through nuclear physics, psychoanalysis, and unbiased historical research progressed at an alarming pace, and philosophy in the form of "existentialism" all but gave up metaphysical speculation. No wonder that after the collapse of the Hitler regime many of these young people turned to nihilism and once more took up the battle cries of the expressionist movement which alone appeared sincere enough to face the issue. Gottfried Benn enjoyed an unexpected popularity after the war. Kafka's stories were discovered anew, and usually understood only in their negative aspects. Disillusioned American realists such as Wolfe and Hemingway were translated, and the German theater devoted itself to the fashionable nihilism of the French playwright, Sartre.

Of the new lyric poets, some wrote in the fashion of Benn or Trakl, others in that of Lehmann. Among the new narratives, echoes of Kafka could often be heard. Hermann Kasack in *Die Stadt jenseits des Stromes* ("The City Beyond the River," 1947) described a visionary journey through the kingdom of the dead, i.e., Western civilization. In the

The Heirs of the Tradition

dramatic field the postwar anarchy was expressed by the dramas of the Swiss author Friedrich Dürrenmatt (*Der Blinde*, "The Blind Man," 1948; *Der Besuch der alten Dame*, "The Visit," 1956) and by the last play of Wolfgang Borchert (1921–1947), which was entitled *Draussen vor der Tür* ("The Man Outside," 1947); in this, a German soldier was pictured returning from a meaningless war to a meaningless peace. Borchert also wrote prose sketches exhibiting this same attitude in harsh language deliberately shocking in its directness. A cynical matter-of-factness, often coupled with apathy, came to characterize large segments of German youth. It found most direct expression in the new, functional architecture which had already been created in the twenties by the teachers of the Dessau *Bauhaus* (School of the Building Arts).

Still, nihilism was not the only possible answer and was seldom found satisfactory, as it left no way open for active living. As much as one might reject the existing world of cold technical efficiency and unabashed bourgeois comfort, one still felt the need of replacing it with something more positive. The eminent lyricist Ludwig Friedrich Barthel (*In die Weite*, "Widening Perspectives," 1957) found consolation in the awareness of an everlasting creation surrounding and overshadowing our small human lives:

> *Die Sterne werden sein und die Ruhe der Nacht wird sein.*
> *Wir aber werden nicht mehr sein.*
>
> *

> *The stars will be, and the quiet of night will be.*
> *We, though, no longer will be.*

The novelist Erhart Kästner (*Zeltbuch von Tumilad*, "Tent Book from Tumilad," 1950) gained new insight into lasting values as a British prisoner of war in the midst of the desolate Libyan desert. And in the stories of the Catholic writer Heinrich Böll (born at Cologne in 1917) the necessity for a new faith was strongly emphasized. Böll started as a representative of "matter-of-factness," with pointed descriptions of meaningless existence, as can be seen in unsentimental stories such as *Der Zug war pünktlich* ("The Train Was on Time," 1949) or *Und sagte kein einziges Wort* ("Acquainted with the Night," 1953). Böll tells of soldiers pushed by military chess players all over Europe, of veterans abused by callous bureaucrats, of unemployed workers tottering on the brink of physical and spiritual starvation. But his longer stories always lead his characters to a new transcendent faith and moral insight.

[327

The Dissociative and Surrealistic Style

At the same time, Böll's critical depiction of ecclesiastic bureaucracy and dry clerical ritualism attests to the honesty of his attitude. One is not always convinced of the same honesty with the recent converts to Catholicism, who sometimes protest too loudly and construct their stories too artfully. Still, critics like Reinhold Schneider (1903–1958) and novelists such as Gertrud von Le Fort, Elisabeth Langgässer (1899–1950; *Das unauslöschliche Siegel*, "The Ineradicable Brand," 1946), Bernt von Heiseler (*Apollonia*, 1940), and Werner Bergengruen are worthy of respectful attention.

On the Protestant side the fundamentalists are in the minority. Among them can be counted the aged Bremen poet Rudolf Alexander Schröder (born in 1878), who grew up in the poetic climate of Stefan George; since 1930 he has tried to recapture in pure hymn form the spiritual essence of Lutheran Christianity. Of younger authors Willy Kramp (born in 1902; *Die Prophezeiung*, "The Prophecy," 1950) and Albrecht Goes (*Unruhige Nacht*, "Unquiet Night," 1950; *Das Brandopfer*, "The Burnt Offering," 1955) have dealt with ethical and political questions of war and post-wartime. Many fundamentalists have been deeply influenced by the writings of the Danish existentialist Sören Kierkegaard (1813–1855).

Other Protestant authors have replaced fundamentalism by a new mysticism. One of the leading liberal theologists has raised the battle cry of a "Christianity without mythology" (*Entmythologisierung des Christentums*), and even the venerable missionary Albert Schweitzer has found little use for fundamentalist positions. One Protestant sect has introduced Greek Orthodox rituals; another, the so-called *Christengemeinschaft* ("Christian Community"), has taken over ideas from Rudolf Steiner's curious Anthroposophy, which was already embraced by Christian Morgenstern. All this attests to the same dissatisfaction with the prevailing institutions of Christian faith and the same search for a new mysticism that was creatively expressed in the works of Hermann Hesse. Echoes of Hesse's technique can be found in the stories of Ernst Kreuder (born in 1903). Here people are removed from reality and transplanted into a fantastic realm of transcendental truth where they have to revise their attitude and rethink their decisions.

A closer reference to German reality is found in the essays and poems of Rudolf Hagelstange (born in 1912), although he could by no means be described as a simple realist. His *Ballade vom verschütteten Leben* ("Ballad of Buried Life," 1952) has perhaps given lasting poetic expression to the war experience of his generation. Their youthful exuberance soon turned into bitter frustration and guilt-consciousness, until it ended in the agony of despair and the earnest desire for expiation. The poem is written in a meter which freely follows all the changes of mood and yet displays an astonishing sense of formal discipline. It treats of the fantastic story of a group of soldiers who as a result of a bombardment are imprisoned in a subterranean supply dump and thus survive the war. The stored cans of meat and bottles of wine gradually become loathsome material impediments, and the soldiers learn to search their conscience and to face truth and eternity. When long after the war Polish workingmen clean up the rubble and free the imprisoned Germans, only one of them is able to step out alive, and he is forever removed from the naïve pragmatism of the first years of war. Yet he will not indulge in oriental contemplation, but will live what remains of his life in a new awareness of the essential.

Hagelstange's as well as Hesse's path to the transcendental was the time-honored path of withdrawal from the world into the depth of the human soul, although in the end active life was resumed and revalued in the light of new revelation. Rilke's path to the transcendental was that of self-projection into the world, the path of the pantheistic mystic, and this led to an immanent mysticism. This path was also followed by one of the most outspoken representatives of postwar literature, the prose writer Ernst Jünger (born in 1895). Jünger first acquired fame through his pitiless war novels *In Stahlgewittern* ("Storm of Steel," 1920) and *Das Wäldchen 125* ("Copse 125," 1925). They were among the best novels engendered by the First World War, although the most popular was Erich Maria Remarque's novel of disillusionment, *Im Westen nichts Neues* ("All Quiet on the Western Front," 1929). Jünger was a German nationalist; he emphasized not merely the negative aspects of war. An unsentimental ideal of modern man developed, one that could cope with the cold technical destructiveness of the age. This modern man had a clear, wordless social consciousness. Jünger championed the technocratic world of the modern workingman in his book *Der Arbeiter* (1932). But soon thereafter he saw his ideals perverted by National Socialism. This forced him to think them through once more, and finally to revise all his evaluations. In the novel *Auf den Marmorklippen* ("On the Marble Cliffs," 1939) Jünger gave early expression to his reorientation before the outbreak of the Second World War. During the war itself he definitely broke with the regime by circulating a typewritten pamphlet in favor of capitulation, later published as *Der Friede* ("The Peace," 1948). Since then Jünger has written books of essays

[329

and reminiscences (e.g., *Strahlungen,* "Radiations," 1949), in which he fights for intellectual and moral self-preservation, and tries to recapture the virtue of a common European cultural inheritance. He also wrote a novel *Heliopolis* (1949) that was laden with ideas. Yet Jünger must be described as a gifted essayist rather than a teller of stories. He has succeeded neither in establishing a convincing connection with the past nor in formulating a new, integrated ideal. His younger brother Friedrich Georg Jünger has distinguished himself mainly in the lyrical field.

At the time of writing, the future of German literature, as indeed of the whole Western culture, still hangs in the balance. It is easy to succumb to the prophets of an all-pervading gloom, but they need not necessarily be right. After all, the present crisis was brought about by man's search for truth beyond illusion and for justice in interhuman relations. Must we then assume that this noble search is to end in complete failure? Would it not be possible to look at the present age as an age of absorption of the old temporary and partial truths and attitudes into a wider universal and more meaningful pattern? In German literature this absorption is foreshadowed in the final works of Gerhart Hauptmann and Hermann Hesse, to mention but two outstanding examples. By their broadening of German regional and parochial attitudes they have helped the development of a truly European and human consciousness, and have joined hands with similar writers of other Western nations. If Western culture is to survive at all, it will survive in some such form as that envisioned by them. The emergence of a necessary new European consciousness may be no more exclusive a task for literature as a whole than for its German branch, but it can safely be assumed that it will not proceed *without* literature.

Select Bibliography
of Translations

T HE following list of translations is suggested as a first introduction to German literature for readers not familiar with
the language. Preference is given to recently published
books; many of the older ones are now available as paper-
backs. A complete list of translations published up to 1935 can be found
in B. Q. Morgan's *Critical Bibliography of German Literature in English
Translation, 1481–1927, with Supplement Embracing the Years 1928–
1935*, 2nd ed. (Palo Alto, Cal. 1938). A generous selection of translations published up to 1948 is contained in Werner P. Friedrich's
Outline-History of German Literature (New York, 1948).

ABBREVIATIONS: ANON. = anonymous, BIL. = bilingual, ED. =
edition *or* edited by, INTROD. = introduction by, SEL. = selections *or*
selected by, TR. = translation *or* translated by, UNCSGLL = University
of North Carolina Studies in the Germanic Languages and Literatures.

To 1500

BRANT, SEBASTIAN. *The Ship of Fools*, TR. E. H. Zeydel. (Records of
Civilisation, No. 36.) New York, 1944.

[331

Select Bibliography of Translations

ECKHART, MEISTER: *Meister Eckhart Speaks: A Collection of the Teachings of the Famous German Mystic*, ED. O. Karrer, TR. E. Strakosch. New York, 1957.

EKKEHARD. *Waltharius*, TR. (into German) Victor von Scheffel in his *Ekkehard, A Tale of the Tenth Century*, TR. H. Easson. (Everyman's Library.) London, New York, 1940.

Eulenspiegel, Till: Master Tyll Owlglass, His Marvellous Adventures and Rare Conceits, TR. K. R. H. Mackenzie. (Broadway Translations.) London, New York, 1923.

GOTTFRIED VON STRASSBURG. *Tristan and Isolde*, TR. E. H. Zeydel. Princeton, 1948. (SEL.)

Gudrun, TR. (into prose) M. Armour. (Everyman's Library.) London, New York, 1932.

HARTMANN VON AUE. *Der arme Heinrich*, TR. C. H. Bell in *Peasant Life in Old German Epics*. (Records of Civilisation, No. 13.) New York, 1931.

——. *Gregorius*, TR. E. H. Zeydel and B. Q. Morgan. (UNCSGLL, No. 14.) Chapel Hill, N. C., 1955.

JOHANNES VON SAAZ. *Death and the Plowman* or *The Bohemian Plowman*, TR. E. N. Kirrmann. (UNCSGLL, No. 22.) Chapel Hill, N.C., 1958.

Minnesong, TR. M. F. Richey in *Essays on the Mediaeval German Love Lyric with Translations in English Verse*. Oxford, 1943.

NEIDHART VON REUENTAL: A. T. Hatto and R. J. Taylor, TR. *17 Summer and Winter Songs Set to Their Original Melodies with Translations and a Musical and Metrical Canon*. Manchester, New York, 1958.

Nibelungenlied, TR. G. H. Needler. New York, 1904.

Passion Play of Oberammergau, TR. M. J. Moses. New York, 1934.

Redentin Easter Play, TR. A. E. Zucker. (Records of Civilisation, No. 32.) New York, 1941.

ROSWITHA VON GANDERSHEIM. *The Plays*, TR. C. St. John. London, 1923.

Ruodlieb, TR. E. H. Zeydel. (UNCSGLL, No. 23.) Chapel Hill, N. C., 1958. (BIL.)

WALTHER VON DER VOGELWEIDE. *Poems*, TR. E. H. Zeydel and B. Q. Morgan. Ithaca, N. Y., 1952. (BIL.)

WERNHER THE GARDENER. *Meier Helmbrecht*, TR. C. H. Bell in *Peasant Life in Old German Epics*. (Records of Civilisation, No. 13.) New York, 1931.

WITTENWEILER, HEINRICH. *The Ring*, TR. G. F. Jones (UNCSGLL, No. 18.) Chapel Hill, N. C., 1956.

Select Bibliography of Translations

WOLFRAM VON ESCHENBACH. *Parzival*, TR. E. H. Zeydel and B. Q. Morgan. (UNCSGLL, No. 5.) Chapel Hill, N. C., 1951.

Sixteenth and Seventeenth Centuries

BÖHME, JAKOB. *Six Theosophic Points and Other Writings*, TR. J. R. Earle. New York, 1920.

ERASMUS VON ROTTERDAM. *The Praise of Folly*, TR. H. H. Hudson. Princeton, 1941.

Faust: The History of the Damnable Life and Deserved Death of Doctor John Faustus, 1592, ED. W. Rose. (Broadway Translations.) London, New York, 1925.

GRIMMELSHAUSEN, HANS JAKOB CHRISTOFFEL VON. *The Adventurous Simplicissimus*, TR. A. T. S. Goodrick. INTROD. W. Rose. (Broadway Translations.) London, New York, 1924.

GRYPHIUS, ANDREAS. SEL. TR. G. Schoolfield in *German Quarterly*, XXIII (1950), 251; XXIV (1951), 22; XXV (1925), 110.

LUTHER, MARTIN: SEL. in *Harvard Classics*, ED. C. W. Eliot. (New York, 1909–1914), Vol. XXXVI. Also: B. L. Woolf. TR. *Reformation Writings of Luther*. 2 VOLS. London, 1956.

SACHS, HANS. *Three Shrove-tide Comedies*, TR. B. Q. Morgan. Stanford University, Cal., 1937.

SCHEFFLER, JOHANN ("ANGELUS SILESIUS"). *The Cherubinic Wanderer*, TR. W. R. Trask. INTROD. C. von Faber du Faur. New York, 1953.

Eighteenth and Early Nineteenth Century

(BENNETT, E. N., TR. and ED.) *German Short Stories*. (The World's Classics, No. 415.) London, 1934.

(BENTLEY, ERIC, ED.) *The Classic Theatre*. Vol. II: *Five German Plays*. (Anchor Books. No. 155b.) Garden City, N. Y., 1959.

(CARLYLE, THOMAS, TR.) *German Romance: Specimens of Its Chief Authors; with Biographical and Critical Notices*. 4 VOLS. Edinburgh, London, 1827.

CHAMISSO, ADALBERT VON. *The Wonderful History of Peter Schlemihl*, TR. T. Bolton. New York, 1923.

EICHENDORFF, JOSEPH VON. *Memoirs of a Good-for-Nothing*, TR. B. Q. Morgan. (College Translations.) New York, 1955.

(FLORES, ANGEL, ED.) *An Anthology of German Poetry from Hölderlin to Rilke*. (Anchor Books, No. A 197.) Garden City, N. Y., 1960. (BIL.)

Select Bibliography of Translations

(FLORES, ANGEL, ED.) *Nineteenth Century German Tales.* (Anchor Books, No. A 184.) Garden City, N. Y., 1959.

(FRANCKE, KUNO, and WILLIAM GUILD HOWARD, EDS.) *The German Classics of the Nineteenth and Twentieth Centuries.* 20 VOLS. New York, 1913–1914.

GOETHE, JOHANN WOLFGANG. *Faust, Parts I and II,* TR. G. M. Priest, New York, 1932; TR. (abridged) L. Macneice, New York, 1951; TR. (*Part I,* prose) B. Q. Morgan. (The Library of Liberal Arts, No. 33.) New York, 1954.

——: *Goethe the Lyrist,* TR. E. H. Zeydel. (UNCSGLL, No. 16.) Chapel Hill, N. C., 1955. (BIL.)

——. *Great Writings,* ED. and INTROD. Stephen Spender. (Mentor Books, No. MT 235.) New York, 1958.

——. *Iphigenia in Tauris,* TR. B. Q. Morgan. Stanford, Cal., 1954.

——. *Poems,* TR. E. H. Zeydel. (UNCSGLL, No. 20.) Chapel Hill, N. C., 1957. (BIL.)

——. *The Sorrows of Young Werther,* TR. R. D. Boylton; *The New Melusina,* TR. J. S. Untermeyer; *Novelle,* TR. V. Lange; INTROD. V. Lange. (Rhinehart Editions, No. 13.) New York, Toronto, 1949.

——. *The Sufferings of Young Werther,* TR. B. Q. Morgan. (College Translations.) New York, 1957.

——. *Torquato Tasso,* TR. B. Kimpel and T. C. D. Eaves. (University of Arkansas Editions, No. 1.) Fayetteville, Ark., 1956.

GRIMM, JAKOB LUDWIG KARL. *Fairy Tales,* TR. M. Hunt and J. Stern. COMPLETE ED. New York, 1944.

Harvard Classics, ED. C. W. Eliot. New York, 1909–1914. VOLS. 17, 19, 26, 32.

HÖLDERLIN, FRIEDRICH. *Selected Poems,* TR. J. B. Leishman. London, 1944, 2nd. ed. 1954. (BIL.)

KLEIST, HEINRICH VON. *The Prince of Homburg,* TR. C. E. Passage. (The Library of Liberal Arts, No. 60.) New York, 1956.

(LANGE, VICTOR, ED.) *Great German Short Novels and Stories.* (The Modern Library, No. 108.) New York, 1952.

LESSING, GOTTHOLD EPHRAIM. *Laocoon, Nathan the Wise, and Minna von Barnhelm,* TR. W. A. Steel. (Everyman's Library, No. 843.) London, New York, 1930.

——. *Laocoon,* TR. E. Frothingham. New York, 1957.

——. *Nathan the Wise,* TR. B. Q. Morgan. New York, 1955.

LICHTENBERG, GEORG CHRISTOPH: *The Lichtenberg Reader,* SEL. and TR. F. Mautner and H. Hatfield. Boston, Mass., 1959.

Select Bibliography of Translations

LONGFELLOW, HENRY WADSWORTH. *The Poets and Poetry of Europe.* Philadelphia, 1845.

(MÜNSTERBERG, MARGARET, TR. and ED.) *A Harvest of German Verse.* New York, 1916.

NOVALIS. *Hymns to the Night,* TR. M. Cotterell. INTROD. A. Closs. London, 1948. (BIL.)

(PICK, ROBERT, ED.) *German Stories and Tales.* (The Pocket Library, No. 32.) New York, 1954.

PIERCE, FREDERICK ERASTUS, and CARL SCHREIBER. *Fiction and Fantasy of German Romance. Selections from the German Romantic Authors, 1790–1830.* New York, 1927.

(ROTHENSTEINER, JOHN E., TR. and ED.) *A German Garden of the Heart.* St. Louis, Mo., 1934.

Schiller, Friedrich. An Anthology of Our Time, ED. F. Ungar. New York, 1960.

Schiller, Friedrich. *Don Carlos, Infante of Spain,* TR. C. E. Passage. New York, 1959.

———. *Love and Intrigue,* TR. G. Reinhardt. (Barron's Educational Series.) Great Neck, N. Y., 1953.

———. *The Maiden of Orleans,* TR. J. T. Krumpelmann. (UNCSGLL, No. 24.) Chapel Hill, N. C., 1959.

———. *Wallenstein,* TR. C. E. Passage. New York, 1958.

SCHLEIERMACHER, FRIEDRICH. *On Religion: Speeches to Its Cultured Despisers,* TR. J. Oman. New York, 1955.

WIELAND, CHRISTOPH MARTIN. *Oberon,* TR. John Quincy Adams. INTROD. A. B. Faust. New York, 1940.

Nineteenth Century

(BENNETT, E. N., TR. and ED.) (See above.)

(BENTLEY, ERIC, ED.) *The Modern Theatre.* 5 VOLS. (Anchor Books, Nos. 48a–e.) Garden City, N. Y., 1955–1957.

BUSCH, WILHELM. *Max and Moritz, or the Adventures of Two Naughty Boys,* TR. C. Morley. New York, 1932. (NEW ILLUSTRATIONS by "Jay" [Jeanette Warmuth].)

(FLORES, ANGEL, ED.) *Nineteenth Century German Tales.* (Anchor Books, No. 184.) Garden City, N. Y., 1959.

(FRANCKE, KUNO.) (See above.)

GRILLPARZER, FRANZ. *The Golden Fleece: The Guest-Friend, The Argonauts* (1942); *Medea* (1941), TR. A. Burkhard. Yarmouth Port, Mass.

Select Bibliography of Translations

GRILLPARZER, FRANZ. *The Jewess of Toledo, Esther,* TR. A. Burkhard. Yarmouth Port, Mass., 1953.

———. *King Ottocar, His Rise and Fall,* TR. H. H. Stevens. Yarmouth Port, Mass., 1938.

———. *Libussa,* TR. H. H. Stevens. Yarmouth Port, Mass., 1941.

———. *Sappho,* TR. A. Burkhard. Yarmouth Port, Mass., 1953.

———. *Thou Shalt Not Lie,* TR. H. H. Stevens. Yarmouth Port, Mass., 1939.

HEBBEL, FRIEDRICH. *Herod and Mariamne,* TR. P. H. Curts. (UNCSGLL, No. 3.) Chapel Hill, N. C., 1950.

HEINE, HEINRICH. *Germany, a Winter's Tale,* TR. H. Salinger. INTROD. H. Kesten. New York, 1944.

———. *The Poetry* (TR. L. Untermeyer, A. Kramer, *et al.*) *and Prose,* TR. and ED. F. Ewen. New York, 1948.

KELLER, GOTTFRIED. *The Fat of the Cat (Spiegel, das Kätzchen) and Other Stories,* FREELY ADAPTED BY L. Untermeyer. New York, 1925.

———. *The People of Seldwyla, and Seven Legends,* TR. M. D. Hottinger. London, New York, 1931.

———. *A Village Romeo and Juliet,* TR. P. B. Thomas and B. Q. Morgan. New York, 1955.

(LANGE, VICTOR, ED.) (See above.)

LONGFELLOW, HENRY WADSWORTH. (See above.)

MEYER, CONRAD FERDINAND. *The Saint,* TR. E. F. Hauch. New York, 1930.

MÖRIKE, EDUARD. *Mozart on the Way to Prague,* TR. W. and C. A. Phillips. New York, 1947.

(MÜNSTERBERG, MARGARET, TR. and ED.) (See above.)

(PICK, ROBERT, ED.) (See above.)

(ROTHENSTEINER, JOHN E., TR. and ED.) (See above.)

STIFTER, ADALBERT. *Rock Crystal: A Christmas Tale,* TR. E. Mayer and M. Moore. New York, 1945.

STORM, THEODOR. *Aquis Submersus,* TR. J. Millar. Glasgow, 1910.

———. *Eekenhof,* TR. J. Millar. Glasgow, 1908.

———. *A Festival at Haderslevhus,* TR. J. Millar. Glasgow, 1909.

———. *Immensee,* TR. G. P. Upton. Chicago, 1907.

———. *Renate,* TR. J. Millar. Glasgow, 1909.

WAGNER, RICHARD. *Complete Operas,* TR. E. Newman *et al.* Leipzig, 1914.

Select Bibliography of Translations

Recent and Contemporary Literature

BENN, GOTTFRIED. SEL. and TR. E. Lohner and C. Corman in *New Mexico Quarterly* (Summer, 1952), 178–86; *Origin*, VII (1952), 144–47, 151–74; *Quarterly Review of Literature*, VII, 290–97.

(BENTLEY, ERIC, ED.) *The Modern Theatre.* (See above.)

BÖLL, HEINRICH. *Acquainted with the Night* (*Und sagte kein einziges Wort*), TR. Robert Graves. New York, 1954.

——. *The Train Was On Time*, TR. Robert Graves. New York, 1956.

BORCHERT, WOLFGANG. *The Man Outside*, TR. D. Porter. Norfolk, Conn., 1952.

BROCH, HERMANN. *The Sleepwalkers*, TR. W. and E. Muir. Boston, 1932.

——. *The Death of Virgil*, TR. J. S. Untermeyer. New York, 1945.

BROD, MAX. *Redemption of Tycho Brahe*, TR. F. W. Crosse. New York, 1928.

CAROSSA, HANS. *Boyhood and Youth*, TR. A. N. Scott. New York, 1932.

——. *A Childhood*, TR. A. N. Scott. New York, 1932.

——. *Doctor Gion*, TR. A. N. Scott. New York, 1933.

——. *Roumanian Diary*, TR. A. N. Scott. New York, 1930.

(DEUTSCH, BABETTE, and AVRAM YARMOLINSKI, TR. and ED.) *Contemporary German Poetry.* London, New York, 1923.

DICKINSON, T. H. *Chief Contemporary Dramatists.* Boston, 1915, 1921, 1930.

DÖBLIN, ALFRED. *Alexanderplatz, Berlin*, TR. E. Jolas. New York, 1931.

(FRANCKE, KUNO.) (See above.)

GEORGE, STEFAN. *Works*, TR. O. Marx and E. Morwitz. (UNCSGLL, No. 2.) Chapel Hill, N. C., 1949.

GOES, ALBRECHT. *Unquiet Night*, TR. C. Fitzgibbon. Boston, 1951.

HANDEL-MAZETTI, ENRICA VON. *Jesse and Maria*, TR. G. N. Shuster. New York, 1931.

HAUPTMANN, GERHART. *The Dramatic Works*, ED. L. Lewisohn. 9 VOLS. New York, 1912–1929.

——. *The Fool in Christ*, TR. T. Seltzer. New York, 1926.

——. *The Heretic of Soana*, TR. B. Q. Morgan. INTROD. H. von Hofe. New York, 1958.

HESSE, HERMANN. *Death and the Lover* (*Narziss und Goldmund*), TR. G. Dunlop. New York, 1932.

——. *Magister Ludi* (*Das Glasperlenspiel*), TR. M. Savill. London, New York, 1949.

Select Bibliography of Translations

HESSE, HERMANN. *Siddhartha*, TR. H. Rosner. New York, 1951.

———. *Steppenwolf*, TR. B. Creighton. New York, 1929.

HOFMANNSTHAL, HUGO VON. *The Fool and Death*, TR. H. E. Mierow. INTROD. H. W. Hewett-Thayer. (Colorado College Publications, Studies Series, No. 5.) Colorado Springs, 1930.

———. *Lyrical Poems*, TR. and INTROD. C. W. Stork. New Haven, 1918.

———. *The Play of Everyman*, TR. G. Sterling and R. Ordynski. San Francisco, 1917.

———. *Selected Prose*, TR. M. Hottinger and J. and T. Stern. INTROD. H. Broch. (Bollingen Series, No. 33.) New York, 1952.

JÜNGER, ERNST. *On the Marble Cliffs*, TR. S. Hood. Norfolk, Conn., 1947.

———. *The Storm of Steel*, TR. B. Creighton. INTROD. R. H. Mottram. London, Garden City, N. Y., 1929.

KAFKA, FRANZ. *The Castle*, TR. E. and W. Muir. London, 1930.

———. *The Metamorphosis*, TR. A. L. Lloyd. London, 1937. New York, 1946.

KAISER, GEORG. *Gas*, TR. H. G. Scheffauer. Boston, 1924.

(LANGE, VICTOR, ED.) (See above.)

MANN, HEINRICH. *Blue Angel* (*Professor Unrat*), TR. ANON. New York, 1932.

———. *The Patrioteer* (*Der Untertan*), TR. E. Boyd. New York, 1921.

(MANN, KLAUS, and HERMANN KESTEN, EDS.) *Heart of Europe, An Anthology of Creative Writing in Europe, 1920–1940*, INTROD. D. C. Fisher. New York, 1943.

MANN, THOMAS. *Buddenbrooks*, TR. H. T. Lowe-Porter. New York, 1924.

———. *Confessions of Felix Krull, Confidence Man: The Early Years*, TR. D. Lindley. New York, 1955.

———. *Doctor Faustus*, TR. H. T. Lowe-Porter. New York, 1948.

———. *Joseph and His Brothers*, TR. H. T. Lowe-Porter. 4 VOLS. New York, 1934–1944.

———. *The Magic Mountain*, TR. H. T. Lowe-Porter. New York, 1927.

———. *Stories of Three Decades*, TR. H. T. Lowe-Porter. New York, 1936.

MORGENSTERN, CHRISTIAN. *Das Mondschaf; The Moon Sheep*, TR. A. E. W. Eitzen. Wiesbaden, 1953. (BIL.)

(MÜNSTERBERG, MARGARET, TR. and ED.) (See above.)

NIETZSCHE, FRIEDRICH: Walter Kaufmann, ED. *The Portable Nietzsche*. New York, 1954.

(PICK, ROBERT, ED.) (See above.)

Select Bibliography of Translations

REMARQUE, ERICH MARIA. *All Quiet on the Western Front,* TR. A. W. Wheen. Boston, London, 1929.

RILKE, RAINER MARIA. *Selected Poems,* TR. C. F. MacIntyre. Berkeley and Los Angeles, 1958. (BIL.)

——. *Poems, 1906–1926,* TR. and ED. J. B. Leishman. London, Norfolk, Conn., 1957.

——. *Poems from the Book of Hours,* TR. B. Deutsch. Norfolk, Conn., 1941.

ROTH, JOSEPH. *Job,* TR. D. Thompson. New York, 1931.

——. *Radetzky March,* TR. G. Dunlop. New York, 1933.

(ROTHENSTEINER, JOHN E. TR. and ED.) (See above.)

SCHNITZLER, ARTHUR. *Reigen, Anatol, Living Hours, The Green Cockatoo,* TR. M. Mannes and G. J. Colbron. New York, 1933.

——. *Viennese Novelettes,* TR. W. A. Drake *et al.* New York, 1931.

SEGHERS, ANNA. *The Seventh Cross,* TR. J. A. Galston. Boston, 1942.

TRAKL, GEORG. SEL. and TR. D. Luke in *German Life and Letters,* IV, 4 (July, 1951).

VIEBIG, CLARA. *Daughters of Hecuba,* TR. A. Barwell. London, 1922.

WASSERMANN, JAKOB. *The World's Illusion (Christian Wahnschaffe),* TR. L. Lewisohn. New York, 1920.

WEDEKIND, FRANK. *Tragedies of Sex,* TR. S. A. Eliot. New York, 1923.

WERFEL, FRANZ. *Jacobowsky and the Colonel,* TR. S. N. Behrman. New York, 1944.

——. *Poems,* TR. E. A. Snow. Princeton, N. J., 1945. (BIL.)

——. *The Song of Bernadette,* TR. L. Lewisohn. New York, 1942.

——. *Verdi,* TR. H. Jessiman. New York, 1925.

WIECHERT, ERNST. *The Baroness (Die Majorin),* TR. P. and T. Blewitt. New York, 1936.

——. *The Forest of the Dead,* TR. U. Stechow. New York, 1947.

——. *The Girl and the Ferryman (Die Magd des Jürgen Doskocil),* TR. E. Wilkins and E. Kaiser. New York, 1947.

ZUCKMAYER, CARL. *The Captain of Köpenick,* TR. D. Portman. London, 1932.

ZWEIG, ARNOLD. *The Case of Sergeant Grischa,* TR. E. Sutton. New York, 1928.

Index

IN order to be useful, the following index has been kept within manageable proportions. Of topics such as Christianity or German literature, which are discussed throughout the book, only such references are given which provide the reader with definitions, descriptions of important historical developments, etc.

The titles of anonymous works are listed in their original forms. Other titles are excluded. Noblemen living before 1500 are listed under their first names (cf. Wolfram von Eschenbach), later ones under their family names (cf. Ebner-Eschenbach, Marie von).

Index

Index

Buff, Charlotte, 175
Burckhardt, Jacob, 286
Bürger, Gottfried August, 27, 166
Burgtheater, 247
Burkhard, Arthur, 241
Busch, Wilhelm, 269 f.
Byron, Lord, 186, 241, 261

Caesar, 9
Calderón de la Barca, 112, 113, 292
Calvin, John, 98, 106
Calvinism, 106, 222. *See also* Reformed Church.
Carlyle, Thomas, 181, 186, 187, 191, 209
Carmina Burana, 27
Carmina Cantabrigiensia, 14
Caroline Michaelis. *See* Schlegel, Caroline.
Carolingians, 9, 13
Carossa, Hans, 309, 311
Catechism, 101, 106
Catholicism, 35, 84, 95, 96, 97, 99, 103, 104 ff., 114, 121, 128, 258, 268, 289, 310 f.
Celtis, Conrad, 85, 87, 88
Celts, 24, 38, 45
Cervantes Saavedra, Miguel de, 112, 213, 223, 226
Chamisso, Adalbert von, 229
Chanson de Roland, 21, 48
Chapbooks, 93 f., 109, 126
Charlemagne, 9, 11, 14, 64, 183
Charles I of England, 122
Charles IV, 82, 100
Charles V, 97
China, 150, 185, 227, 282
Chivalry, Age of, 25, 28
Chrestien de Troyes, 41, 42
Christ. *See* Jesus.
Christengemeinschaft, 328
Christianity, 7, 9 ff., 18, 22, 61, 74, 76, 77, 96, 116, 126, 282, 328. *See also* Counter-Reformation, Pietism, Reformation.
Christmas, 17, 22
Cicero, 84, 115
Cid, the, 48
Classical antiquity. *See* Antiquity.
Classicism, 138, 143, 147, 157, 168 ff., 206, 209, 210, 233, 290, 293
Claudius, Matthias, 167 f., 264
Clovis, 11

Cluniac literature, 18, 19
Cohen, Clara. *See* Viebig, Clara.
Coleridge, Samuel, 191
Cologne, 20, 60, 61, 85, 327
Columbanus, 11
Comic strips, 270
Communism, 273, 281, 283, 298, 303, 325
Congregationalists, 134
Consensus Omnium, 158, 159
Constantine, 21
Contemporary literature, 283, 295, 304
Copernicus, Nicolaus, 85, 88
Copyright, 236
Corneille, Pierre, 112, 147
Correggio, Antonio, 112
Corvey, 11
Council of Constance, 82, 96
Council of Trent, 104
Counter-Reformation, 105, 114, 116, 119
Crusades, 19, 23, 31, 58
Cusanus, Nicolaus, 80
Customs Union, 235
Czechoslovakia, 1, 235. *See also* Bohemia.

Dante Alighieri, 78, 174, 185, 190, 213, 289, 291
Danube Monarchy. *See* Austria.
Darwin, Charles, 280, 285, 292, 307
Dauthendey, Max, 277, 289
Declaration of Independence, 156
Dedekind, Friedrich, 107
Defoe, Daniel, 140
Dehmel, Richard, 277 f.
Deism, 133
Democracy, 61, 156, 235, 261, 281, 283, 288, 290
Descartes, René, 132, 158
Destouches, Philippe, 148
Dessau, 327
Deutsche Gesellschaften, 138
Dickens, Charles, 262, 265, 270
Didactic style of the Reformation, 81 ff.
Diderot, Denis, 145, 148
Dietmar von Aist, 29
Dietrich von Bern. *See* Theodoric.
Dietrichs Flucht, 55
Dionysius of Syracuse, 152
Dionysus, 315
Diotima, 201, 203
Dissociative Style of the Twentieth Century, 279 ff.

Index

Index

[345

Index

Index

Index

Index

Index

Index

St. Gallen, 11, 14, 15, 17, 54
St. Peter's Cathedral, 112
Salzburg, 292
Sancta Clara, Abraham a, 127
Sand, George, 268
Sängerkrieg auf der Wartburg, 37
Sanskrit, 224
Sappho, 238
Sartre, Jean-Paul, 326
Saxon emperors, 18
Saxon language, 100
Saxons, 11
Saxony, 326
Scandinavia, 2, 49
Schäfer, Wilhelm, 305
Scheffel, Joseph Victor von, 268
Scheffler, Johannes, 119, 120 f.
Schelling, Friedrich Wilhelm Joseph von, 172, 201, 214
Scherenberg, Christian Friedrich, 247
Schildbürgerbuch, 107 f.
Schiller, Friedrich, 36, 127, 145, 146, 152, 157, 163, 164 f., 168, 169, 170, 171, 172, 187 f., 190 ff., 200, 202 f., 206, 208, 213, 220, 247, 249, 269, 299, 303, 322
Schimmelmann, Count, 195
Schlegel, August Wilhelm, 213 f., 224, 226
Schlegel, Caroline, 214
Schlegel, Dorothea, 214
Schlegel, Friedrich, 213 f., 221, 223
Schleiermacher, Friedrich, 211
Schnabel, Johann Gottfried, 140
Schneider, Reinhold, 328
Schnitzler, Arthur, 276
Schönberg, Arnold, 295
Schönherr, Karl, 307, 311
School dramas, 116
Schopenhauer, Arthur, 172, 234, 253, 270, 285, 286, 287, 321
Schröder, Rudolf Alexander, 291, 328
Schubart, Christian Friedrich, 166 f.
Schubert, Franz, 229, 245
Schumann, Robert, 245
Schumann, Valentin, 107
Schütz, Heinrich, 123
Schwärmer und Täufer, 98. *See also* Anabaptists.
Schweitzer, Albert, 328
"*Schweizer, die*," 139
Schwenckfeld, Kaspar, 103
Scots, 198

Scott, Sir Walter, 166, 186
Scudéry, Madeleine de, 112
Sealsfield, Charles, 261 f.
Seghers, Anna, 326
Seidel, Heinrich, 309
Seidel, Ina, 309 f.
Seneca, 84, 88, 115
Seuse, Heinrich, 79
Seven Years' War, 144
Seyfrid, Lied vom Hürnen, 64
Shaftesbury, Anthony Ashley Cooper, Earl of, 133, 169
Shakespeare, William, 112, 116, 146, 147, 148, 149, 153, 160, 161, 162, 163, 174, 183, 189, 190, 192, 197, 213, 224, 226, 264
Shrovetide plays, 75, 92, 103, 107
Sickingen, Franz von, 97
Siemens, Friedrich, 234
Siemens, Werner (von), 234
Silesia, 1, 119, 325
Silesian Wars, 131
Slavic, 2, 6, 160
Socialist Realism, 325
Socrates, 158
Sophocles, 170, 254
Spain, 28, 105, 112, 114, 128, 136, 238
Spanish Succession War, 131
Spee, Friedrich von, 121
Spener, Philipp Jacob, 134
Spielhagen, Friedrich, 269
Spieszsches Faustbuch, 108
Spinoza, Baruch, 119, 132, 177
Spitteler, Carl, 286
Sprüche, 27, 34
Stadion, Count, 151
Staël, Madame de, 186
Stainhöwel, Heinrich, 83
Stehr, Hermann, 298 f., 311
Stein, Baron vom und zum, 226
Stein, Charlotte von, 178, 179, 201
Steiner, Rudolf, 328
Stephenson, George, 155
Sterne, Lawrence, 207, 270
Steven, Henry H., 241
Stifter, Adalbert, 255, 256 ff.
Stoicism, 118, 122
Storm, Theodor, 271, 287, 305
Storm and Stress literature, 135, 143, 157, 158, 161 ff., 176, 179, 201, 208, 209, 225, 234, 296
Stoss, Veit, 83
Strachwitz, Moritz Count von, 247

[351

Index

Index

31423